Conflict, Demand and Economic Development

This book presents a comprehensive overview of three key areas: heterodox macroeconomics, development economics and classical political economy. It offers an alternative macroeconomic framework to analyse policies with an emphasis on issues of equity and justice.

With contributions by leading economists from across the world, it examines the growth and distribution of income; trade and finance in developing countries; classical political economy and Marxist theory; dualism in the US economy; economic crisis; and agrarian economy in poor countries. It explores themes such as the effect of an exogenous shock to wage share; Harrodian instability and Steindlian solutions; economics and politics of social democracy; the role of power in the macroeconomy; economic development through the promotion of domestic value chains; and reflections on primitive accumulation. Going beyond the neo-classical tradition, the volume opens up a new vista of economics by discussing unexplored questions. It provides a refreshing treatment of time-tested ideas as well as discussions of recent developments and current research.

A major intervention in heterodox macroeconomics and a tribute to macroeconomist Amit Bhaduri, this book will be useful to scholars and researchers of economics, political economy, development studies, sociology, political science, public administration, economic theory, economic history, economic geography and critical studies, as well as professionals, economists and policymakers.

Deepankar Basu is Associate Professor in the Department of Economics at the University of Massachusetts, Amherst, USA.

Debarshi Das is Associate Professor in the Department of Humanities and Social Sciences at the Indian Institute of Technology Guwahati, India.

Conflict, Demand and Economic Development: Essays in Honour of Amit Bhaduri demonstrates, without question, that rigorous, important and profoundly insightful economic research is alive and well outside of the narrow, and often misleading confines of 'mainstream' economics. The essays published here by outstanding economists working in the traditions of Marx, Keynes, Kalecki, Robinson, and Prebisch address central economic and political issues of our day, including structural unemployment, worsening inequality within and between countries, technological change, and rural economic development. These essays are of great interest and are a fitting tribute to Amit Bhaduri, who made seminal contributions to help keep alive these dynamic and crucial research traditions.

Gerald Epstein, *Professor of Economics and Co-Director, Political Economy Research Institute (PERI), University of Massachusetts Amherst, USA*

Professor Amit Bhaduri has been one of the truly outstanding economists of our time, whose commitment to changing the world has led to his refusal to be pigeonholed into any narrow specialization. He has made seminal contributions in areas as diverse as macroeconomics, capital theory, economic history and semi-feudal agriculture. The essays in this volume reflecting the diversity of his own interests are a fitting tribute to his renaissance personality.

Prabhat Patnaik, *Professor Emeritus, Centre for Economic Studies and Planning, Jawaharlal Nehru University, Delhi, India*

Conflict, Demand and Economic Development

Essays in Honour of Amit Bhaduri

Edited by Deepankar Basu and Debarshi Das

Routledge
Taylor & Francis Group
LONDON AND NEW YORK

First published 2021
by Routledge
2 Park Square, Milton Park, Abingdon, Oxon OX14 4RN

and by Routledge
52 Vanderbilt Avenue, New York, NY 10017

Routledge is an imprint of the Taylor & Francis Group, an informa business

British Library Cataloguing-in-Publication Data
A catalogue record for this book is available from the British Library

Library of Congress Cataloging-in-Publication Data
A catalog record for this book has been requested

ISBN: 978-0-367-41064-3 (hbk)
ISBN: 978-0-367-81450-2 (ebk)

Typeset in Sabon
by Apex CoVantage, LLC

Contents

Figures

Tables

Contributors

Rohit Azad teaches at the Centre for Economic Studies and Planning, Jawaharlal Nehru University, Delhi, India. He is the author of *It's Not Over: Structural Drivers of the Global Economic Crisis* (2013) and has co-edited *A Quantum Leap in the Wrong Direction* (2019). His areas of interest are macroeconomics, growth and development, climate change, political economy, monetary theory and policy. He has twice been a Fulbright scholar at University of Massachusetts, Amherst, and the New School of Social Research, New York respectively.

Deepankar Basu is Associate Professor in the Department of Economics at the University of Massachusetts, Amherst. His research interests are in the areas of classical political economy and development economics. His work has been published in *Cambridge Journal of Economics*, *Economics Letters*, *Demography*, *Journal of Development Studies*, *Oxford Bulletin of Economics and Statistics*, *Metroeconomica*, *Review of Radical Political Economics* and *World Development*, among other journals. He is Associate Editor of *Review of Social Economy.*

Prasenjit Bose is an independent economist, specialising in political economy, macroeconomics, banking and finance. He served as the Senior Research Associate in the ICSSR Sponsored Project 'Financial Globalisation and India: Internal and External Dimensions' (2014–16). Bose holds a doctorate in economics from the Centre for Economic Studies and Planning, Jawaharlal Nehru University, India.

Debarshi Das teaches economics at the Humanities and Social Sciences Department, IIT Guwahati, India. His research interests include development economics, macroeconomics and political economy, and he likes teaching game theory (basic). Articles authored and co-authored by him have appeared in *Cambridge Journal of Economics*, *Journal of Development Studies*, *Metroeconomica* and *Economic and Political Weekly* among others.

Amitava Krishna Dutt is Professor of Economics and Political Science, University of Notre Dame, IN, USA, and Distinguished Professor, FLACSO,

Ecuador. He is the author of several books, including *Growth, Distribution and Uneven Development* (1990) and *Pathways to Economic Development* (2014), and of many papers published in edited volumes and journals, including *American Economic Review*, *Cambridge Journal of Economics*, *Journal of Post Keynesian Economics* and *World Development*. He is a co-editor of *Review of Social Economy* and *Metroeconomica*.

Leila Gautham is a PhD candidate at the Department of Economics, University of Massachusetts, Amherst, USA. Her research focuses on inequality, development and gender. She has studied the expansion of care work and the growth of US wage inequality, and issues of gender inequality and unpaid care in India. She was previously at the Centre for Economic Studies and Planning at Jawaharlal Nehru University, India.

Subrata Guha has been associated for more than three decades with the Centre for Economic Studies and Planning, the economics department co-founded by Amit Bhaduri at Jawaharlal Nehru University, New Delhi, India, initially as a student and researcher and later as a member of the faculty. While his research publications have been mostly in the area of neoclassical growth and distribution, he also enjoys teaching heterodox growth theory and supervising doctoral students working on heterodox themes.

Eckhard Hein is Professor of Economics at the Berlin School of Economics and Law (HWR) and a co-director of the Institute for International Political Economy (IPE) at the HWR, Germany. He is a member of the coordinating committee of the Forum for Macroeconomics and Macroeconomic Policies (FMM), a managing co-editor of the *European Journal of Economics and Economic Policies: Intervention* and a research associate at the Levy Economics Institute and at the Centre d'Économie de l'Université Paris-Nord (CEPN).

P. Sai-wing Ho is Professor in Economics, University of Denver, Colorado, USA. His research chiefly concerns the trade and investment aspects of globalisation. It clarifies the intellectual roots of the globalisation sceptics through re-examining the works of the classical economists, so-called protectionists and many early generation development economists. These inform his critique of the major agreements reached in multilateral trade negotiations and help critically assess the push toward joining global value chains as a means to achieving national development.

Heinz D. Kurz is Professor Emeritus of Economics at the University of Graz, Austria, and Fellow of the Graz Schumpeter Centre. His main fields of research are economic theory and the history of economic analysis. He is author (with Neri Salvadori) of *Theory of Production, A Long-Period Analysis* (1995) and of *Economic Thought: A Brief History* (2016).

Ivan Mendieta-Muñoz is Assistant Professor in the Department of Economics at the University of Utah in Salt Lake City, USA. He holds a PhD in economics from the University of Kent (Canterbury, UK). Before joining the University of Utah in 2016, he taught at SOAS University of London, University of Kent and UNAM. His research fields are macroeconomics and financial economics; time series econometrics and statistical methods; and economic development in Latin America. His work has appeared in academic outlets such as *Competition and Change*, *Economics Bulletin*, *International Review of Applied Economics*, *Journal of Post Keynesian Economics*, *Macroeconomic Dynamics*, *Metroeconomica*, *Monthly Review* and *Review of Radical Political Economics*.

Tracy Mott is Professor Emeritus from the Department of Economics at the University of Denver, USA. He received his PhD in economics from Stanford University in 1982. His work is in the areas of macroeconomics and monetary economics and on the ideas of Michał Kalecki and John Maynard Keynes. His book *Kalecki's Principle of Increasing Risk and Keynesian Economics* was published by Routledge in 2010.

Petri Piiroinen received his MSc degree in mathematics from Stockholm University, Sweden, in 1998 and his PhD in theoretical and applied mechanics from the Royal Institute of Technology (KTH), Stockholm, in 2002. Between 2007 and 2020 he was a lecturer in applied mathematics at the National University of Ireland Galway (NUI Galway) and from 2020 he is an associate professor in nonlinear mechanics at Chalmers University of Technology in Gothenburg, Sweden. Dr Piiroinen's main research areas are nonsmooth dynamical systems, with an emphasis on numerical methods, and mathematical modelling of systems describing mechanical motions, population dynamics and macroeconomic effects.

Codrina Rada is Associate Professor in the Department of Economics at the University of Utah, USA. She received her PhD in economics from the New School for Social Research in 2007. Her current research gravitates around issues of economic growth and income distribution, with a specific interest in the effects of structural change and global economic integration on macroeconomic dynamics. Her previous research has explored the economics of pensions and ageing, and structural transformation in emerging economies. Her work has appeared in academic outlets such as *Cambridge Journal of Economics*, *Agricultural Economics*, Columbia University Press, *Journal of Policy Modeling*, *Journal of Population Ageing*, *Metroeconomica*, *Structural Change and Economic Dynamics* and *Development and Change*.

Srinivas Raghavendra is Lecturer of Economics in J.E. Cairnes School of Business and Economics at the National University of Ireland, Galway. His current research is focused on a number of themes in the areas of macroeconomics, finance and political economy. His work is published in some of the leading peer-reviewed international journals including *Review of Keynesian Economics*, *Metroeconomica*, *Journal of Economics*, *Feminist*

Economics, *Panoeconomicus*, *Review of Development and Change*, *PLoS ONE*, *European Physics Journal B* and *International Journal of Bifurcation and Chaos*, among others.

Rune Skarstein is Emeritus Associate Professor of Economics at the Norwegian University of Science and Technology (NTNU), Norway. His main research interest is macroeconomics, development economics and economic problems related to climate change. As researcher/lecturer he has spent long periods in Tanzania and visited Argentina and Mexico.

Peter Skott is Professor of Economics at the University of Massachusetts, Amherst (USA) and affiliated with Aalborg University (Denmark). He works primarily on macroeconomic dynamics. Recent research includes the analysis of different post-Keynesian approaches to economic growth, the distributional implications of power-biased technological change, and problems of secular stagnation and the use of fiscal policy in mature and dual economies.

Servaas Storm is Senior Lecturer at Delft University of Technology, Netherlands. He works on macroeconomics, technological progress, income distribution and economic growth, finance, development and structural change and climate change. His work has appeared in *Cambridge Journal of Economics*, *Development and Change*, *Eastern Economic Review*, *Industrial Relations*, *International Review of Applied Economics*, *International Journal of Political Economy*, *Journal of Post Keynesian Economics*, *Journal of Development Economics* and *Structural Change and Economic Dynamics*. His latest book, co-authored by C.W.M. Naastepad, is *Macroeconomics beyond the NAIRU* (2012). Storm is one of the editors of *Development and Change*.

Ramaa Vasudevan is Professor in the Department of Economics, Colorado State University, USA. She has published in the fields of political economy of money and finance, the workings and evolution of international financial systems, and open economy macroeconomics and has authored *Things Fall Apart: From the Crash of 2008 to the Great Slump*. She is on the Editorial Board of *Catalyst* and is Associate Editor of *Review of Political Economy*.

Rudi von Arnim is Associate Professor of Economics at the University of Utah, USA. He completed a PhD from the New School for Social Research in 2008. His research focuses on macroeconomics, specifically the linkages between growth, the business cycle and the distribution of income, economic development and model assessment of international trade agreements. He is a senior research associate at Austrian Foundation for Development Research (ÖFSE), and has worked with and consulted for G24, UNDP, UNCTAD, and ILO's Institute for International Studies (IILS).

Foreword

Amit Bhaduri: the activist as economic theorist

This book celebrates Amit Bhaduri's career in the traditional scholarly form of a *festschrift* of papers addressing various aspects of Bhaduri's own work and interests. It is a fitting tribute to the wide scope and powerful influence of Bhaduri's work.

It is also important, as the editors' Introduction explains, to remember that Bhaduri's scientific and scholarly work is an integral part of his life as a political activist. Bhaduri himself has insisted on this point in his writing, teaching and speaking throughout his career. Bhaduri is an outstanding example of the ongoing tradition of economists whose activism and social criticism have motivated deep and influential scholarly work.[1] Reflecting on the mutual influence of activism on theory and theory on activism in Bhaduri's career gives us an insight into the complex intertwining of politics and scholarly investigation in the long history of political economy.

Activism in Bhaduri's case starts with his concern for the suffering of the urban and particularly rural poor in the India of his birth and upbringing. This concern is reflected in his numerous publications on the historical roots and reproduction of agrarian poverty. It is striking, however, to note that alongside this work firmly situated in detailed empirical study of Indian agriculture, Bhaduri was consistently carrying on another branch of work on much more abstract problems. For example, Bhaduri's first publication concerned the concept of the marginal productivity of capital, and he later worked on the question of price- and quantity-traverses. I conclude from this that Bhaduri had a lively and instinctive understanding of the close relation of abstract theoretical investigation to practical day-to-day issues of political economy. A recognition of this connection, and the successful pursuit of both levels of investigation, is rare in the history of political economy, and the mark of a master.

We might also ask what impact theoretical investigations had on Bhaduri's activism. In this dimension, too, Bhaduri stands out as a thinker who insistently pursues the recognition of the abstract in the concrete, another talent that is rare and to be treasured. The transformation of Indian agriculture and the Indian economy in the last sixty years are examples of traverses in prices and quantities: Bhaduri's underlying method shines through the diversity of his scholarly work. In these respects, Bhaduri carried on and developed the intellectual and political program of his mentor, Joan Robinson, and became an outstanding representative and heir of her thought and activism.

The many strands of Bhaduri's intellectual life converge in his seminal papers on distribution and economic growth co-authored with Stephen Marglin. The major themes of class, employment, income, and economic welfare come together in this work with a remarkable degree of elegance and simplicity of theoretical tools. These papers are influential because of the important message they convey about the ongoing centrality of class relations to modern capitalist society, and equally because they convey that message in a framework simple and general enough to be adopted and developed by other researchers. In the context of an era of stale and scholastic mainstream macroeconomics, these papers are a beacon of good sense and acute analytical thinking.

It is not easy to follow in the footsteps of figures like Robinson and Bhaduri, but I urge younger scholars whose activism combines with the theoretical drive to see the abstract in the concrete to emulate them.

Duncan K. Foley
Leo Model Professor of Economics, New School for
Social Research and External Professor,
Santa Fe Institute, USA

Note

1 I remember attending a luncheon at MIT celebrating Simon Kuznets's award of the Swedish Bank Prize in Economic Sciences in Memory of Alfred Nobel, at which Kuznets was asked how he got interested in economics. "I wanted to understand the Jewish question better", he replied, then went on to explain that Russian treatment of its Jewish population was in his mind representative of the host of unresolved social and economic problems in the Russian empire Kuznets grew up in.

1 Introduction

Deepankar Basu and Debarshi Das

We have both had the good fortune to be students of Amit Bhaduri. As students in the mid-1990s in the Centre for Economic Studies and Planning (CESP), Jawaharlal Nehru University, New Delhi, India, we took courses on macroeconomics and nonlinear dynamical systems with him. As we worked on our own research projects during and after our PhDs, we gradually came to appreciate the enormous contribution Amit has made, through his teaching and research, to the development of contemporary heterodox economics. This *festschrift* is a celebration of his varied contributions as a heterodox economist and as a critical, progressive voice. In this introductory chapter, we first present a short biographical sketch of Amit and then discuss the contents of the other chapters comprising this volume. We end with a brief discussion of some issues at the frontier of contemporary heterodox economics research.

Amit Bhaduri: a biographical note

Born in 1940, Amit Bhaduri's formative years were spent in the newly independent country of India. The left movement which was surging through Bengal in the 1940s and 1950s left a lasting impression on him. He nearly got thrown out of his high school in Calcutta for taking part in street protests against a tram fare hike. Unlike middle-class Indians who took up safe careers in medicine or engineering, Amit did not veer towards the natural sciences. The *zeitgeist* of the era pulled him towards economics. He had the first taste of the subject during his college years at Presidency College (later Presidency University) in Calcutta (later renamed as Kolkata).

He obtained his bachelor's degree in economics from Calcutta (1960), and then Cambridge (1963). The unstructured teaching at Cambridge first baffled him, but later he learned to enjoy the style. After a brief one-year stint at MIT – the macroeconomic wave lengths did not match – he returned to Cambridge to finish his PhD, rather quickly, in 1967. The dissertation was on the time structure of capital related to capital theory, which, at that time, was a rage on both sides of the pond. Amit's first published paper came out in 1966 – a full year before he completed his PhD (Bhaduri, 1966).

During this time – that is, the late 1960s and early 1970s – his academic preoccupations centred around capital theory. It was also during this time that he was introduced by Joan Robinson to Michał Kalecki's seminal contributions. This was to leave a profound impact on his research. In his own words, "I saw immediately the connection between Marx, Keynes and Kalecki." In 1968 he would publish his second paper, on project evaluation, which was influenced by a paper of Kalecki and Rakowski published four years earlier (Bhaduri, 1968).

But this was to change soon. Another vista of his contributions would open up, urged by the social upheavals of the time. Soon after his PhD *viva voce*, he returned to India. Short stints at the Agro-economic Research Centre, Delhi (a non-teaching job), Delhi School of Economics (a teaching job), and Sri Lanka (as advisor to the first Left Front government) followed. During his stay in Sri Lanka, Amit was involved in constructing an input–output model, incorporating a multipurpose irrigation dam. The shifting times did not let his curious soul stay at one place. The turbulent condition in India, and practically all over the world, including Vietnam, soon dragged him out of Sri Lanka. He resigned from his post in Sri Lanka and returned to India, without a job but with a burning desire to understand its villages. His dissatisfaction also had to do with the inability of conventional left parties to respond adequately to the profound changes taking place in society.

Like other parts of the country, rural India was also going through a period of turmoil. In 1967, petty peasants and sharecroppers in the northern fringe area of Naxalbari, West Bengal, India, rose in revolt against local landholders. Although radical workers of the Communist Party of India (Marxist), or CPI(M), had been working in the area, the party did not approve of the radicalism. The state government of West Bengal was being run by a coalition in which the CPI(M) was a major ally. The peasants of Naxalbari briefly took over the land they cultivated, from landlords, and chased away police forces. In the infamous retaliatory crackdown, the state police shot dead a number of sharecroppers, including women. The Naxalbari revolt split the party two years later. The movement sparked by the Naxalbari revolt spread through large swathes of the Indian countryside.

"In those days my interest in politics was far greater than in economics", Amit recollects. Not surprisingly, he landed in West Bengal, from Sri Lanka, in 1971. For months, he roamed the villages of Bengal taking sporadic notes. What he saw and heard would go on to influence much of his later work. These include, in published form, "A Study in Agricultural Backwardness under Semi-Feudalism" (1973), "On the Formation of Usurious Interest Rates in Backward Agriculture" (1977), "Class Relations and the Pattern of Accumulation in an Agrarian Economy" (1981) and *Economic Structure of Backward Agriculture* (1983a, a book).

This is an impressive body of work. The initial puzzle that animated it was this: neither capitalist nor feudal production relations could be clearly discerned in the villages Amit had travelled through. Moreover, it appeared that the momentum of transition from feudalism to capitalism was missing. To be sure, the putative transition is a long-run phenomenon and can be scarcely discerned within a brief time frame. Nonetheless, bereft of any logic of accumulation, even the long-run transformation seemed untenable. Amit's task was to understand this absence of accumulation. His groundbreaking paper of 1973 did precisely that. The logic is compelling in its simplicity. Landlords earn interest income on consumption loans advanced to sharecroppers, who have leased in land from the same landlords and pay them rent. Since interest income is important, the landlord would not have any incentive to invest in land. Thus, agrarian accumulation gets botched.

The idea that credit and land markets in the rural economy could be linked and that this yields unusual outcomes was not novel. The literature on 'interlocking' in the Indian economic lore dealt with it. Krishna Bharadwaj, among others, contributed to the chiselling of this idea. However, Amit's contribution in this respect was salient mainly for two reasons. First, the paper formalised the argument of interlocking in a precise and clear way. It was told with an admirable degree of economy and clarity. This simplicity of exposition has been Amit's forte. Second, it touched the political nerve of the time. That nerve was the stagnancy of productive forces and the fettering of productive forces by production relations. It was suggested that the tension of this dialectic led to political upheavals in the countryside. The established left parties were not responding adequately to this fluid situation. The significance of the 1973 paper, and the related work that followed, was felt both in terms of formal economics and contemporary politics.

The paper left a deep impact on both mainstream development economics as well as the political economy literature in India. Many papers on sharecropping followed in response to Amit's 1973 paper. Criticisms came its way too, including, for example, the claim that the equilibrium outcome was not dynamically stable – although Amit himself had delineated the conditions under which the stagnancy envisaged in the paper could disappear. The debate on the 'Mode of Production' in Indian agriculture, which predated the 1973 paper, was also enriched by its insights. The 'semi-feudalism thesis', which Amit proposed, had many backers. However, as Alice Thorner concluded, it was eventually the 'gradual development of capitalism' thesis which prevailed when the debate wound up in the late 1970s.

In "On the Formation of Usurious Interest Rates in Backward Agriculture" (1977), Amit made another notable contribution to the understanding of rural economy: what determines the rate of interest charged by moneylenders in the rural credit markets? Amit also worked in the field of economic history in "The Evolution of Land Relations in Eastern India under British Rule" (1976). The paper was an attempt to understand the zamindari system of land tenancy, which was instituted in eastern India during British rule. It seemed to lack all momentum, and was contrary to what the British Raj had planned when they crafted the tenurial system of zamindari.

The early 1970s brought two other major changes in his life. He married an old friend, who was in the Indian Foreign Service. To be with her, Amit sojourned to Vienna, where he worked briefly for the United Nations Industrial Development Organization (UNIDO). But in 1972 he left his job at UNIDO, returned to India and joined as a fellow in the newly started – by his former colleague from Delhi School of Economics, Professor K. N. Raj – Centre for Development Studies in Kerala. Soon he shifted to the Centre for Economic Studies and Planning (CESP) in the recently founded Jawaharlal Nehru University (JNU) at New Delhi. The Centre started teaching a master's course in economics as he joined with a handful of colleagues – he was a founding faculty member. As Amit describes, "my unambiguous acceptance of an academic career began then". This appointment, with an intermission, lasted till he retired in 2001. He was conferred the position of emeritus professor in the same department. In January 2020, he resigned from the position of emeritus professor in protest against the throttling of dissent by the JNU administration.

After getting recruited to teach macroeconomics at JNU, he had to acquaint himself with different strands of the literature. This engagement resulted in a rich body of work, including "On the Analogy between Quantity- and Price-Traverse" (1975), "Accumulation and Exploitation: An Analysis in the Tradition of Marx, Sraffa and Kalecki" (1980) co-authored with Joan Robinson, "Multimarket Classification of Unemployment: A Sceptical Note" (1983b) and "The Rise of Monetarism as a Social Doctrine" (1985) with Joseph Steindl. A number of agriculture-related interventions also saw the light of day. These include the book *Economic Structure of Backward Agriculture* (1983a) as well the articles "Cropsharing as a Labour Process, Size of Farm and Supervision Cost" (1983c), and "Persistence and Polarisation: A Study in the Dynamics of Agrarian Contradiction" (1986) co-authored with Hussain Zillur Rahman and Ann-Lisbet Arn.

In 1982, Amit resigned from JNU and travelled to Mexico with his wife who was posted there. He taught at El Collegio de Mexico and later at Stanford University. During this time his already-growing interest in macroeconomics found a notable outlet. In 1986 he published a textbook on macroeconomics, entitled *Macroeconomics: the Dynamics of Commodity Production* (1986). The book was a marked departure from the usual treatment of the subject one finds in college- or university-level textbooks. The connections and differences between monetarist, Keynesian and Kaleckian macroeconomics are explained with the simplicity in which Amit excels. Karl Marx's contributions, in particular how his ideas of money and profit affected latter-day thinking, were noted. Rather than a drab, mechanical rendering of the subject, the book was a celebration of various schools of thought. One would be hard-pressed to find the word 'capitalism' in a standard book of macroeconomics. And here is Amit, in the very Introduction: "Most of the material covered here grew out of my attempts to teach a useful course on the macroeconomics of capitalism in various universities in India, Europe and Mexico." The book was translated into Spanish and several other European languages. It became a bestseller in Latin America. It was well received in Europe as well. But not so much in the USA and UK, where neoliberal ideas were ruling academia by then.

After less than a year's stint at Stanford, Amit returned to Central Europe, via Mexico, in 1986. He taught for three years in Europe (1986–1989), first at the University of Linz in Austria, and then at the University of Vienna. Two more papers on macroeconomics came out during this period. The first was on chaotic macroeconomic dynamics, "The Complex Dynamics of the Simple Ricardian System" (1987) with Donald J. Harris. The other was on the prospects of getting trapped by external debt, "Dependent and Self-reliant Growth with Foreign Borrowing" (1987). During this period a few of his co-authored works were published in Spanish-language academic journals as well.

Amit's collaborative work with Stephen Marglin at WIDER (World Institute of Development Economic Research, Helsinki) on characterizing the postwar 'golden age of capitalism' was first conceived during this period. It finally led to the paper "Unemployment and the Real Wage: the Economic Basis for Contesting Political Ideologies" (1990), and this must be mentioned at some length. This is one of the most influential papers in the field of heterodox macroeconomics published in the last several decades. How does the tilt of wage-profit distribution affect output and employment in a capitalist economy? The paper sought to answer this question in a static Keynesian framework. There is no clear answer, it turned out. It all depends on parametric values, but this ambiguity is not necessarily a bad thing. The paper provided an overarching framework in which underconsumptionist ideas (wage-led output growth) and non-underconsumptionist ideas (profit-led output growth) could be accommodated as sub-cases. The analysis highlighted links between contesting political ideologies and macroeconomic theory within the Keynesian framework.

A plethora of academic research in the neo-Kaleckian and Keynesian tradition, both theoretical and empirical, has been spawned in the wake of Bhaduri and Marglin (1990). Later, in 2008, Amit would follow it up in "On the Dynamics of Profit-led and Wage-led Growth" (2008), and "Wage- and Profit-led Regimes under Modern Finance: An Exploration" (2017) with Srinivas Raghavendra.

In the late 1980s Amit was mostly in Europe, teaching and touring Eastern Europe to deliver invited lectures. He returned to Calcutta, with the idea of starting a cooperative among rural, small handloom workers, with his own savings. To make ends meet, he took up the job of Professor of Economics at the Indian Institute of Management, Calcutta. The cooperative experiment was not doing particularly badly, but he lost interest in running a cooperative full time. He went back to Germany where his wife was posted, and where the Berlin Wall was about to fall. During this period, he taught at the University of Bremen, the Norwegian University of Science and Technology, University of Bologna and was also a fellow for a year at the Institute of Advanced Studies in Berlin. The mid-1990s brought him back to JNU, New Delhi, once more at the invitation of the then vice-chancellor. He continued as Professor of Economics at CESP, JNU, till he took premature retirement in 2001.

The 1990s was also the time when quite a few of his books were published. *Unconventional Economics Essays* (1993) and *On the Border of Economic Theory and History* (2000) were collections of his previously published academic articles. As the Eastern Bloc disintegrated in the early 1990s, the political economy of India underwent a major shift as well. In 1991 the newly appointed central government, which was in a minority position in the national parliament, adopted a comprehensive set of measures to open up sections of the economy to global and domestic capital. This "liberalisation" drive would be the subject of critical inquiry in a small book co-authored by Amit and his colleague at JNU, Deepak Nayyar, *An Intelligent Person's Guide of Liberalization* (1996).

This book, we can say with the benefit of hindsight, was the beginning of the fourth batch of Amit's less technical, and more popular, contributions. His work would focus increasingly on the profound and often deleterious impact the entry of big, corporate capital makes on the lives of the people in a developing country. The books *Development with Dignity: A Case of Full Employment* (2005), *The Face You Were Afraid to See: Essays on the Indian Economy* (2009) and *Malignant Growth* (2016) fall in this line of work which derived sustenance not so much from books as from his participation in many popular movements. However, he continued to publish on the related academic literature of inter-sectoral interaction models of development, as evidenced in, "Effective Demand and the Terms of Trade in a Dual Economy: A Kaldorian Perspective" (2003) with Rune Skarstein, and more recently, "A Study in Development by Dispossession" (2018). Needless to say, he contributed many articles on completely different themes during this period as well, e.g., "Nationalism and Economic Policy in the Era of Globalization" (2002), "Endogenous Economic Growth: A New Approach" (2006) and "A Model of Interaction between the Virtual and the Real Economy" (2006) with Kazimierz Laski and Martin Riese.

The papers and books mentioned here by no means exhaust the entire list of contributions Amit Bhaduri has made over the last fifty years in many areas of economics. Even as we speak, his agile mind must be pondering over new ideas and thinking how to render them elegantly for us. To recognise and honour the contributions of Amit Bhaduri, we organised a conference in the Department of Economics at the University of Massachusetts, Amherst, on 22–23 March 2019. Most of the fifteen chapters that make up this *festschrift* were presented in that conference. We now turn to introducing them.

Conflict, demand and economic development: essays in honour of Amit Bhaduri

Faith in the efficiency of the unfettered market mechanism was severely eroded, at least outside the discipline of mainstream economics, during and after the financial and economic crisis of 2008. Simultaneously, interest in non-neoclassical traditions of economics has been on the rise. Students of economics at several universities across the world have been demanding to learn a version of economics that is rooted in their day-to-day experience, experience that indicates that markets may do a bad job in curbing income and wealth inequality, or reducing unemployment, or ensuring stable growth, or bringing about structural transformation of underdeveloped economies. New pedagogical material, such as *The Economy*, an undergraduate economics textbook, are being produced to meet this growing demand.

Over a stellar career spanning several decades, Amit Bhaduri has made a signal contribution in understanding the economy from such alternative, non-neoclassical viewpoints. His work has grappled with questions of aggregate demand, failure of market mechanisms, dynamics of class, persistence of exploitation and the interaction of technological stagnation and underdevelopment, themes that are often ignored in mainstream economics. The chapters in this book are located within a broad heterodox tradition of economics that has been enriched by Amit's work. They seek to understand society and economy from points of view that do not conform to strictures of the neoclassical tradition.

This book contains fifteen chapters, in addition to this Introduction, and is divided thematically into three parts – each dealing with an area of heterodox economics where Amit has made significant contributions. The first part deals with post-Keynesian macroeconomics, the second part engages with classical political economy and the third part contains contributions in development economics.

Post-Keynesian macroeconomics: growth and distribution

Over the years, Amit Bhaduri's work has dealt with various aspects of power – power of landlords over sharecroppers, power of capitalists over workers, power of pro-market ideas. In the chapter "Power, Income Inequality and Economic Growth", **Amitava Krishna Dutt** skilfully weaves elements of power into a post-Keynesian macroeconomic model. After offering an overview of the various ways in which power has been conceptualised in the social sciences, Dutt develops an innovative macroeconomic model of growth and distribution that incorporates power – operating between capitalists and workers – into its functioning and highlights its sources and consequences. Power, conceived relationally, impacts the ability of the two classes to push for outcomes in their interest in two distinct struggles captured in Dutt's model: the struggle over the distribution of national income, and the struggle over the direction of government policy related to expenditure and taxation. Dutt shows that the two-way causal relationship between inequality and power can be the source of macroeconomic instability.

From instability arising from the operation of power, we move to dynamic instability of the Harrodian variety. In the chapter, "Harrodian Instability in Kaleckian Models and Steindlian Solutions: An Elementary Discussion", **Eckhard Hein** offers a novel perspective on ongoing debates about dynamic instability in post-Keynesian macroeconomics. Roy Harrod's seminal contributions from the late 1930s have highlighted the possibility of dynamic instability of economic growth in capitalist economies – coming about because of possible divergence of actual from warranted rates of growth (which is the rate of growth needed to realise the desired rate of utilisation of productive capacities). Modern Kaleckian macroeconomics has dealt with this problem by conceptualising the warranted rate as endogenous – which adjusts to the actual rate in the long run – because the rate of capacity utilisation is endogenous. Responding to critiques of this Kaleckian resolution of Harrodian instability, Hein fleshes out two arguments put forward by Josef Steindl. The warranted rate can be partially endogenous because: (a) the capital-output ratio can itself become endogenous through capital scrapping by firms; and (b) the aggregate saving rate can be endogenous through adjustment in government balances. Because such mechanisms exist, Hein concludes, contemporary heterodox economists should not be overly concerned about dynamic instability of the Harrodian variety.

In the chapter "Conflict as Closure: A Kaleckian Model of Growth and Distribution under Financialization", **Srinivas Raghavendra and Petri T. Piiroinen** take the debate between Kaleckian and Harrodian strands of heterodox macroeconomics one step further. The key novelty of this chapter is to introduce an important feature of contemporary capitalism into macroeconomic models: the dominance of shareholders in corporate governance. They demonstrate that conflict between shareholders and managers over the profit rate can generate long-run variation in the rate of capacity utilisation. Not only does the capacity utilisation rate vary in the short run – as would emerge from fluctuations of demand – but it also varies in a plausible range of values in the long run – an issue that had been touched upon by Hein in the previous chapter. In effect, therefore, Raghavendra and Piiroinen offer a modelling strategy that differs from both the Kaleckian – where the actual capacity utilisation rate feeds onto and changes the desired capacity utilisation rate – and the Harrodian – where a desired capacity utilisation rate is taken as given. By offering an alternative to the two dominant strands of contemporary heterodox macroeconomics, this chapter has the potential to generate interesting new conversation on the vexed question of the long-run behaviour of the capacity utilisation rate.

While the question of long-run behaviour of the capacity utilisation rate has been a matter of debate and discussion in contemporary heterodox macroeconomics, there has been little appreciation, if any, of the limitations of demand-led frameworks for analysing policy issues in developing economies. This is especially surprising when we recall that Kalecki's writings on development economics had explicitly argued that problems of aggregate demand are not the crucial problems faced by developing economies (Kalecki, 1960). The chapter by **Peter Skott** entitled "Aggregate Demand Policy in Mature and Dual Economies", is a much-needed corrective. Skott argues that while aggregate demand matters in both the short and long run, it is important to distinguish between mature and dual economies. In mature economies, i.e. advanced capitalist economies, lack of adequate aggregate demand can be a structural problem – giving rise to tendencies towards secular stagnation – and full employment growth might require sustained fiscal stimulus. But in a dual economy, i.e. an underdeveloped economy with significant reserves of underemployed labour, the key problem is one of structural transformation, i.e. transferring labour from low- to high-productivity work, not of inadequate aggregate demand.

When thinking of long-run growth of capitalist economies, questions of technological change become salient. While the initial literature on neoclassical growth theory conceptualised technological change as exogenous, pioneering contributions by Paul Romer and Robert Lucas in the late 1980s kicked off the endogenous growth literature in mainstream macroeconomics. Bhaduri (2006) offered a different type of endogenous growth model, one that weds the demand-led framework of Keynes and Kalecki to insights on competition and technical change from Marx. The chapter "Competition, Technological Change and Demand-led Growth" by **Subrata Guha** extends Bhaduri (2006). Abstracting from class struggle between capitalists and workers (and its impact on labour-saving technical change), using exogenous income shares between classes à la Kalecki, but endogenising the degree of intra-class competition between capitalists, Guha shows that growth can still be demand-led – even though it also depends on the relative strengths of the two-way causal impact of competition on technical change. In contrast to Bhaduri (2006), Guha's analysis highlights that in models of demand-constrained output, the long-run steady state growth rate of output and productivity that is consistent with steady rates of unemployment are determined by saving/investment behaviour, rather than by competition and technical change.

Perhaps it is not too far-fetched to assert that the political manifestation/programme of post-Keynesian economics is social democracy, especially its Northern European, postwar variety – a radical version of which can be traced all the way back to Keynes (Crotty, 2019). But there is an inherent dilemma within social democracy: in the short run, it has to shore the very institutions that it wishes to undermine in the long run (Bhaduri, 1993). In the chapter "The Economics and Politics of Social Democracy: An Update", **Servaas Storm** extends Bhaduri's (1993) insightful analysis of the question to understand the failure of New Labour in Europe, and to think of strategies for renewal after the financial crisis of 2007–08. After providing a historically informed analysis of the limitations of the New Labour experiment, Storm contends that a resurgence of social democracy must build on at least four ideas: (a) an outright rejection of the mainstream new consensus macroeconomics (NCM), (b) an equally forthright rejection of the putative trade-off between growth and equality, (c) an open acceptance of public discussion, instead of the fabled market mechanism, to solve difficult issues of public policy, and (d) reigning in the power of finance. An interesting alternative that Storm does not discuss is revolutionary socialism – which is not prisoner to the dilemma that plagues social democracy, because it keeps the long-term goal of transcending capitalism at the centre of its political vision, unlike social democracy which forsakes it for short-term gains (Wolff, 2020).

The last chapter in this section, "What Is the Impact of an Exogenous Shock to the Wage Share? VAR Results for the US Economy, 1973–2018", by **Deepankar Basu and Leila Gautham**, presents econometric analysis of an issue that has been hotly debated in contemporary heterodox macroeconomics: wage-led versus profit-led growth. The seminal contribution in Bhaduri and Marglin (1990) established that capitalist economies can be either wage-led or profit-led in terms of both demand and growth. In the former case, a shift of income in favour of wages will lead to higher demand and growth; in the latter case, the opposite will hold. Bhaduri and Marglin (1990) demonstrated that there is no *a priori* reason to believe that capitalist economies are either wage-led or profit-led; the determination – for particular economies – will need to be empirically verified. While a large literature has investigated the empirical question, the results have often suffered from lack of careful attention to questions of identification. Since changes in wage share can be impacted by changes in demand and economic growth, ascertaining the impact of a change in the former on demand (capacity utilisation rate) and growth (rate of growth of real GDP) is a non-trivial econometric problem. Basu and Gautham draw on a methodology developed by Christiano, Eichenbaum and Evans (2005) to investigate the effect of an exogenous change in the wage share on demand and growth. Using data for the US economy between 1973 and 2018, they find evidence in favour of profit-led demand and growth.

Classical political economy: conflict and exploitation

Amit Bhaduri's initial work – during and immediately after his PhD – was on classical themes related to the Cambridge capital controversy, which drew insight and inspiration from the work of Piero Sraffa. The chapter "'Superhuman Efforts" and the Theory of Value and Distribution: Sraffa on Pareto" by **Heinz D. Kurz** is in this vein and discusses an interesting question in the history of economic thought: the relationship between Sraffa and Pareto. Drawing on unpublished notes and manuscripts left by Sraffa, Kurz – the general editor of Sraffa's works and correspondence – argues that Sraffa benefited from his critical engagement with Pareto. Pareto's critique of the "literary economists" offered Sraffa an opportunity to develop his own system of equations about value and distribution. Thus, while it might be futile to search for the origins of Sraffa's equation system, it is nonetheless useful to know of Sraffa's engagement with Pareto and the role it played in Sraffa's development as a classical economist.

There is a popular misconception in heterodox economics that issues of aggregate demand are not seriously dealt with in classical-Marxian political economy. One only need to study the debate between Rosa Luxemburg and Tugan-Baranovsky to disabuse oneself of this misconception. In the chapter "Rosa Luxemburg, Mikhail Tugan-Baranovsky and the Current State of Economic Crisis", **Tracy Mott and P. Sai-wing Ho** revisit this debate and draw some interesting conclusions about the current economic crisis. Luxemburg had conceptualised a capitalist economy as forever short of adequate, internally generated aggregate demand; hence the need for export markets. Tugan-Baranovsky's critique of Luxemburg pointed to the role of investment expenditure as a possible source of demand, which, if of the right magnitude, could solve the problem of aggregate demand. Kalecki's review of the Luxemburg-Tugan-Baranovsky debate highlighted the shortcomings of both positions – though he was more sympathetic to Luxemburg's than to Tugan-Baranovsky's argument. While postwar Keynesian demand management through fiscal policy has been thought of as a robust way to solve the problems Luxemburg and Tugan-Baranovsky grappled with, Kalecki's political business cycle theory points to the limitations of such demand management strategies as well. Drawing on Kalecki's work, Mott and Ho argue for a radically different macroeconomic strategy for stabilising a capitalist economy: public control over the aggregate profit margin.

While public control of profit margins might be a way to stabilise an advanced capitalist economy, economic development in the periphery – erstwhile colonies and semi-colonies – requires a rather different type of public intervention. In the chapter "Some Reflections on 'Primitive Accumulation'", **Rune Skarstein** engages with Amit Bhaduri's recent writings on the process of development in India. The end of the Cold War has seen the consolidation of an aggressive, virulent form of capitalism – built on privatisation of public assets, globalisation of production and finance and significant weakening of the welfare state. In developing countries, this neoliberal form of capitalism has used the state to get hold of resources like land, minerals, water, for a song. This resource grab has meant dispossession of large sections of the most vulnerable segments of the population in these countries (like India). Skarstein uses Marx's concept of 'primitive accumulation of capital' to understand this resource grab-led development, and given its brutality and inequality-inducing outcomes, argues for an alternative, more humane and just form of development: democratic socialism.

Economic development in the periphery has to address the agrarian question – because of the preponderance, still, of the agricultural sector in the aggregate economy, especially in terms of employment. In the chapter entitled "A Model of the Marxist Rent Theory", **Debarshi Das** fleshes out important pieces of the theory of ground-rent developed by Marx in Volume III of *Capital* and uses it to discuss conditions of stagnation in Indian agriculture. In this chapter, Das offers a careful reading of Marx's theory of ground-rent but, more importantly, formalises key ideas of Marx into a coherent and precise theory. Following Marx, Das shows that the total ground-rent on any plot of land can be decomposed into three components: differential rent of the first variety (*DRI*), differential rent of the second variety (*DRII*) and absolute rent. *DRI* arises from differences in quality of plots of land; *DRII* arises due to multiple units of capital invested on the same plot; and the source of absolute rent is the lower-than-average organic composition of capital in agriculture. After developing the theory, Das uses it to offer insights about the continued stagnation in Indian agriculture.

Development economics: duality and underdevelopment

Amit Bhaduri has made many important contributions to the study of underdevelopment, especially its agrarian aspects. Building on Bhaduri (1985), the chapter "Rural Poor or Peasant-Proletarians: Agrarian Change and Labour Markets in Eastern United Provinces in the Colonial Period" by **Ramaa Vasudevan** discusses different modalities of labour migration in two contiguous districts of Eastern UP. While the focus in Bhaduri (1985), which had also studied UP, was on the land market, Vasudevan shifts the emphasis to the labour market. The chapter traces the historical evolution of regimes of labour in Gorakhpur and Basti – both districts in Eastern UP – and shows how differences in the pattern of migration impacted on class formation at the source of migration. Gorakhpur saw migration primarily to industrial centres, which facilitated the emergence of a class of peasant-proletarians. On the other hand, Basti witnessed indentured and other types of contract migration, which prevented any dynamic effects from spilling over into rural areas. In both cases, of course, peasants kept their attachment to land intact, foreshadowing the precarious, informal labour of contemporary times.

The next chapter discusses the dynamics of dualism, paradoxically it would seem, in the context of the US economy. In the chapter, "Rising Inequality and Dualism in the US Economy: Evidence and Potential Explanations", **Ivan Mendieta-Muñoz, Codrina Rada and Rudi von Arnim** discuss two important features of the postwar US economy: shift in the trend of the labour share of income and rise of structural dualism. Using a Divisia index decomposition methodology for fourteen component sectors of the US economy, the chapter identifies the manufacturing sector as playing a dominant role both in the Golden Age (1948–1979) and in the Neoliberal Era (1979–2017). Even as its share in employment declined in the first period, growth of real compensation moves in lock-step with the growth of labour productivity; in the second period, on the other hand, real compensation lagged far behind the growth of labour productivity. Structural dualism manifests in the shift of labour towards stagnant sectors with low productivity, a trend the authors identify as a "reverse Lewis" shift, where stagnant sectors function as labour sinks, and labour in the dynamic sectors experience slow real wage growth. The chapter ends with some ideas about the role of aggregate demand in facilitating structural transformation.

The next two chapters discuss concrete issues of policy within the context of contemporary debates about economic growth and development. In the chapter entitled "India's Growth Story: A Model of 'Riskless Capitalism'?", **Rohit Azad and Prasenjit Bose** focus on India's growth experience with the initiation of the neoliberal economic reforms in the early 1990s. Both supporters and critics of the economic reforms in India agree that it has had a salutary effect on growth – the difference among the viewpoints rest on the socio-economic aspects of growth, whether it increased inequality, and whether it improved broader measures of well-being. In this chapter, Azad and Bose take a different route and look more closely at the two episodes of growth acceleration in the post-reforms period, 2003–2007 and 2009–2010. After establishing the crucial role of credit expansion – through the banking sector but also supported by external debt finance – in sustaining the two booms, the authors use a Kaleckian macroeconomic model to explain the trajectory of growth. The analysis of the chapter highlights the instability of the growth trajectory where small shocks can pull the economy either into a low growth path (stagnation) or increase pressure on the domestic public banking sector's balance sheets.

In the final chapter entitled "Supporting Domestic Development through Coordinating the Promotion of Domestic Value Chains", **P. Sai-wing Ho** engages the recent literature on global value chains. Ho sees a return and reaffirmation of neoliberal economic thinking in the current emphasis on global value chains as a tool for economic development – which ultimately facilitate liberalisation of trade and investment. Countries need not concern themselves with industrial policies to promote development, an important strand of contemporary thinking argues. All they need to do is encourage their firms to find a foothold within some global value chain. Rapid productivity growth, followed by income growth and aggregate economic growth, will follow, so the argument goes. This chapter highlights the deficiencies of such strategies for economic growth. Building on dynamic insights from Adam Smith and Albert Hirschman, the chapter argues for an alternative strategy where generation of domestic demand takes precedence over the search for export markets. In this alternative strategy that the chapter proposes, a reoriented value chain structure that focuses on the domestic market – rather than the global economy – can be a valuable for fostering stable economic growth and robust employment.

In lieu of a conclusion

Amit Bhaduri is a leading heterodox economist of the postwar generation. The chapters in this volume reflect on, engage with and try to extend his pioneering contributions in some of the sub-fields of heterodox economics that he has worked on. It is heartening to note that the heterodox tradition in economics in general and the three particular sub-fields emphasised in this volume have seen a lot of interesting work over the past few decades – work that has been inspired by and extends the ideas and insights of Amit Bhaduri.

For the benefit of readers who want to engage with this emerging literature, we would like to briefly discuss some recent work in the three sub-fields that has been the focus of this volume: post-Keynesian macroeconomics, classical political economy and heterodox development economics. It is not our intention to present a comprehensive survey of this large and growing body of research in heterodox economics. In fact, that is not even possible within the confines of this introductory note. Hence, what we discuss here is necessarily an idiosyncratic take, driven by our own interests and expertise and limited by considerations of space, on an emerging body of research in heterodox economics.

Recent research in post-Keynesian macroeconomics has seen some very interesting debates. Here we would like to mention some issues/sub-areas that have seen significant work. The first issue that has been the focus of intense research and discussion is the question of whether capitalist economies are best characterised as wage-led or profit-led, both in terms of aggregate demand and economic growth. If an economy is wage-led in terms of demand and growth, then an exogenous shift in the distribution of income in favour of wage income will boost demand and growth; if the economy is profit-led, an exogenous shift of income towards wage earners will have the opposite effect – it will reduce demand and growth. This issue had entered heterodox macroeconomic discussions with the seminal contributions of Amit Bhaduri and Steve Marglin in the late 1980s. It has spawned a large, and possibly growing body of literature, but disagreement among scholars persists – please see Oyvat, Öztunali and Elgin (2020) for a review of the literature.

The second issue that has seen a lot of interesting work relates to the conceptualisation of capacity utilisation in the long run. Ranged on one side of the debate are scholars of neo-Kaleckian persuasion who argue that capacity utilisation is variable even in the long run; hence, they argue, there is no justification for the concept of a 'normal' or 'desired' rate of capacity utilisation. On the other side of this debate are scholars who, using a variety of arguments, believe that capitalist economies return to a 'normal' rate of capacity utilisation in the long run. The debate on this issue remains unresolved, and the interested reader can turn to Nikiforos (2012), Volume 63, Issue 1 of *Metroeconomica* (a special issue on Kaleckian growth theory), chapter 12 in Foley, Michl and Tavani (2019) and chapter 6 in Blecker and Setterfield (2019) for a flavour of the contributions.

The third sub-area that has seen interesting contributions lies at the intersection of finance, inequality and corporate governance. The evolution of capitalist economies since the early 1980s has been marked by growing financialisation, dominance of shareholder corporate governance and a rising inequality in the distribution of income and wealth. Heterodox macroeconomists have been attentive to these developments and had started incorporating them in their models even before things came to a head with the financial crisis of 2008. Two interesting and related directions in which heterodox macroeconomic models have developed in response to these developments are: (a) incorporating a third class, over and above capitalist and workers, in macroeconomic models; and (b) incorporating financial dynamics within macroeconomic models. Incorporating a third class (or group of income earners) has allowed heterodox macroeconomics to go beyond the functional distribution of income and to study the macroeconomic effects of inequality of income between workers, capitalists and supervisors/managers. Incorporating financial dynamics has often gone hand in hand with paying close attention to the corporate structure and to explicitly take account of equity and debt financing of corporate investment. This is an active area of research, and the interested reader can turn to chapter 7 in Blecker and Setterfield (2019) and chapter 15 in Foley, Michl and Tavani (2019) for an introduction to ongoing work.

While the three sub-areas have seen both theoretical and empirical work, it would be useful to discuss the latter separately. This is because heterodox macroeconomics in general and post-Keynesian macroeconomics in particular has seen a lot of interesting and important empirical work over the past few decades – some of them falling outside the three sub-areas. As we have already mentioned, an active area of research has been the analysis of wage-led and profit-led regimes of demand and growth. On this topic, much of the work has been empirical (see, for instance, Barbosa-Filho and Taylor, 2006). The chapter in this volume by Deepankar Basu and Leila Gautham provides a survey of the discussion. Disagreement remains about whether most capitalist economies are wage-led or profit-led in terms of demand and growth. Oyvat, Öztunali and Elgin (2020) report that in their sample of 41 countries, 21 are wage-led and the rest profit-led. They also analyse the impact of wage inequality, trade openness and higher household debt on the probability of economies being wage-led or profit-led.

A second area of interesting empirical research has been related to important features of the neoliberal era: financialisation and the increasing dominance of shareholder orientation of firms. The key questions analysed by this literature are the following: How does one measure and quantify financialisation? What is the impact of financialisation and shareholder dominance on the real economy, especially its impact on capital accumulation? Orhangazi (2008) was an early contribution in this area and was significantly extended by Davis (2018). The general finding in this literature is that financialisation and the increasing shareholder orientation have negative impacts on real investment, a finding that is in line with the seminal qualitative research on these issues by William Lazonick (see, for instance, Lazonick, 2014). The interested reader might turn to Davis (2017) for a survey of the empirical literature on financialisation and capital accumulation.

A third sub-area that has seen some interesting empirical work relates to cyclical growth. While mainstream economics has developed an elaborate framework to explain cyclical fluctuations in aggregate economic activity as a result of the accumulation of stochastic shocks, the heterodox tradition has a long tradition of understanding cyclical fluctuations as being generated endogenously by the economic system. One prominent model that captures this intuition is the Goodwin model. In this model, first formulated in the late 1960s by Richard Goodwin, the wage share and the employment rate interact non-linearly in a predator-prey type of dynamical system to generate, under certain parameter restrictions, a perpetual cyclical path for both the wage share and the employment rate. Building on and extending earlier contributions, Grasselli and Maheshwari (2018) test and find evidence in support of a modified Goodwin-type model in a sample of 10 advanced capitalist economies for the period 1960–2010.

The state of debate in classical political economy can be discerned from two recent contributions: Hahnel (2017) and Cogliano et al. (2018). The fault lines in this area remain the same as those established in the 1970s with the contribution of Steedman (1977). The Sraffian tradition argues against the labour theory of value – on the grounds that it is redundant, and even misleading, to the study of capitalism. Hahnel (2017) is a re-statement of that position. In addition to the standard Sraffian argument, it also offers an engagement with the question of environmental degradation from a Sraffian standpoint. Cogliano et al. (2018) presents a sophisticated rebuttal of many Sraffian claims from a Marxian standpoint. Building on seminal contributions of Peter Flaschel (1983), Cogliano et al. (2018) develop a labour theory of value that is free from many of the problems associated with its standard interpretation. Such a labour theory of value, the authors show, can deal consistently with joint production and fixed capital – something which the standard interpretation is not capable of doing.

Classical political economy has also seen some interesting empirical work in recent decades (for a brief survey, see Basu, 2017). The first area in classical political economy that has seen substantial empirical work relates to the debate between Marxian and Sraffian economists about the labour theory of value. While many Marxian economists accept the Sraffian analysis of prices of production, they claim that the deviation of relative prices (of production) from relative labour values are small in actual capitalist economies. The reason for this is that the interconnectedness of different industries reduces the magnitude of deviation between relative prices and relative values – which would have otherwise been large, given the variation in the organic composition of capital across industries. Hence, claim Marxist economists, one should turn to empirical analysis to choose between Sraffian and Marxian analysis. The survey in Basu (2017) reports that most empirical analysis finds the deviation between relative prices and values to be small – even though there are some methodological problems in the existing studies.

The second area that has seen much empirical work in the classical political economy tradition relates to profitability analysis. The motivation for much of this work relates to the central role of the profit rate in capitalist dynamics, especially insofar as it governs the crisis tendencies of capitalist economies. Starting with the seminal contribution of Weisskopf (1979), a large literature in Marxist economics has carried out decomposition analyses of the profit rate – both from a short-run and a medium-run perspective – to identify crisis tendencies and their underlying drivers for different countries and periods (for references, see Basu, 2017). An important limitation of this strand of Marxist literature is that it cannot address questions of causality. Because it is based on a decomposition of the profit rate, such analyses can at most identify important components that drive movements in the rate of profit – it can neither analyse the causes of movements in the rate of profit nor can it test the causal impact of the profit rate on capital accumulation.

The third area in classical political economy that has seen some recent empirical work is the sub-area of classical-Marxian growth theory. Pioneering work by Duncan Foley and Tom Michl (1999) highlighted an important difference between neoclassical and classical-Marxian growth theory. While the former posits the equality of the real wage rate and the marginal product of labour, the latter allows them to be different. A recent literature has tested these alternative hypotheses about the relationship between the real wage rate and the marginal product of labour (Michl, 2009; Basu, 2010; Campbell and Tavani, 2019). This literature shows that there is overwhelming support against the neoclassical view of income distribution.

While there has been interesting and important work in growth theory from the classical-Marxian and post-Keynesian perspectives, they suffer from a serious shortcoming. Just like the neoclassical and endogenous growth models of mainstream economics, most of the classical-Marxian and post-Keynesian growth models are for a one-sector capitalist economy. Perhaps because of this reason, both classical-Marxian and post-Keynesian growth theory has seen very little work that attempts to answer two key questions of economic development: (a) Why are some countries so much poorer than others? (b) Why do some countries manage to grow so much faster than others over long periods of time? The first question is about explaining the variation in per capita (or per worker) income *levels* across countries; and the second question is about explaining the variation in long-run *growth rates* across countries.[1] While much work has been done to address these questions in the neoclassical and endogenous growth frameworks, the answers provided by them remain unconvincing (for a discussion, see chapter 8 in Ros, 2013). Heterodox growth theories – both classical-Marxian and post-Keynesian – have an opportunity to make a significant contribution to our understanding of the world if they can provide plausible and convincing answers to these fundamental questions of economic growth,

While heterodox growth theories of the classical-Marxian or post-Keynesian varieties have not yet made much headway in explaining cross-country variations in either the levels of growth rate of per capita income, another strand of heterodox economics – which we will call heterodox development economics – has made significant progress in this direction. Interesting and important work in heterodox development economics has been brought back into discussion by Ros (2000) and Ros (2013). Heterodox development economics departs from the neoclassical tradition in two significant ways. First, while neoclassical (and endogenous) growth theory study questions of economic growth in a one-sector mature capitalist economy (just like classical-Marxian and post-Keynesian growth theory), heterodox development economics moves away from this perspective with the recognition that developing economies comprise of at least two distinct sectors: a modern, capitalist sector and a non-capitalist, traditional sector. While the initial theorists in the classical development economics tradition visualised the modern-traditional division as being coterminous with the industry-agriculture (and urban-rural) division, the traditional sector can be expanded to include an informal sector (located both in urban and rural areas).

The second way in which heterodox development economics departs from neoclassical orthodoxy is by recognising that aggregate demand can have long-run growth implications (in this respect, it is close to post-Keynesian growth theory). While incorporating the role of aggregate demand, heterodox development economics recognises key ways in which context is important. In a mature economy, aggregate demand deficiencies can be addressed with fiscal and monetary policies. On the other hand, aggregate demand problems show up as various types of structural constraints in a developing economy, like wage goods constraint, foreign exchange constraint, etc. Hence these aggregate demand problems cannot be addressed with the tools of fiscal and monetary policy alone. They can be addressed effectively only through policies that facilitate structural transformation (Ros, 2013; and the chapter in this volume by Peter Skott).

We hope that chapters of this book will inspire readers to join efforts at strengthening heterodox economics and contribute towards making the world a more just, equitable and humane place – concerns that have animated Amit's work over the decades.

Note

1 There is one strand of post-Keynesian macroeconomics that has much more to offer on these two questions. These are the export-led cumulative causation (ELCC) approach and the balance of payments constrained growth (BPCG) approach (for details, see chapters 8, 9 and 10 in Blecker and Setterfield, 2019). The ELCC approach ignores balance of payments constraints, which might be relevant for many developing economies. The BPCG approach suffers from both theoretical and empirical problems (for details, see Blecker, 2016). In our opinion, this strand is certainly best positioned within the heterodox tradition to tackle questions of income level and income growth variations across countries. Unfortunately, we do not have the space to review this strand of literature in greater detail in this introductory note.

References

Amit Bhaduri's work

Bhaduri, A. 1966. The concept of the marginal productivity of capital and the Wicksell effect. *Oxford Economic Papers* 18(3): 284–288.
Bhaduri, A. 1968. An aspect of project selection: Durability vs construction-period. *Oxford Economic Papers* 78(310): 344–348.
Bhaduri, A. 1973. A study in agricultural backwardness under semi-feudalism. *The Economic Journal* 83(329): 120–137.
Bhaduri, A. 1975. On the analogy between quantity- and price-traverse. *Oxford Economic Papers* 27(3): 455–461.
Bhaduri, A. 1976. The evolution of land relations in Eastern India under British rule. *The Indian Economic and Social History Review* 83(329): 120–137.
Bhaduri, A. 1977. On the formation of usurious interest rates in backward agriculture. *Cambridge Journal of Economics* 1(4): 120–137.
Bhaduri, A. 1981. Class relations and the pattern of accumulation in an agrarian economy. *Cambridge Journal of Economics* 5(1): 33–46.
Bhaduri, A. 1983a. *Economic structure of backward agriculture*. London & New York: Academic Press.
Bhaduri, A. 1983b. Multimarket classification of unemployment: A sceptical note. *Cambridge Journal of Economics* 7(3/4): 235–241.
Bhaduri, A. 1983c. Cropsharing as a labour process, size of farm and supervision cost. *The Journal of Peasant Studies* 10(2/3): 88–93.
Bhaduri, A. 1985. Class relations and commercialization in Indian agriculture: A study in the post-independence agrarian reforms of Uttar Pradesh. In K. N. Raj, N. Bhattacharya, S. Guha and S. Padhi (Eds.), *Essays in commercialization of agriculture in India* (pp. 306–318). Bombay: Oxford University Press.
Bhaduri, A. 1986. *Macroeconomics: The dynamics of commodity production*. London: Macmillan Education Limited.
Bhaduri, A. 1987. Dependent and self-reliant growth with foreign borrowing. *Cambridge Journal of Economics* 11(3): 269–273.
Bhaduri, A. 1993. *Unconventional economics essays*. New Delhi: Oxford University Press.
Bhaduri, A. 2000. *On the border of economic theory and history*. New Delhi: Oxford University Press.
Bhaduri, A. 2002. Nationalism and economic policy in the era of globalization. In D. Nayyar (Ed.), *Governing globalization: Issues and institutions* (pp. 19–50). Oxford: Oxford University Press.
Bhaduri, A. 2005. *Development with dignity: A case of full employment*. New Delhi: National Book Trust.
Bhaduri, A. 2006. Endogenous economic growth: A new approach. *Cambridge Journal of Economics* 30(1): 69–83.
Bhaduri, A. 2008. On the dynamics of profit-led and wage-led growth. *Cambridge Journal of Economics* 32(1): 147–160.
Bhaduri, A. 2009. *The face you were afraid to see: Essays on the Indian economy*. New Delhi: Penguin India.
Bhaduri, A. 2016. *Malignant growth*. New Delhi: Aakar Books.
Bhaduri, A. 2018. A study in development by dispossession. *Cambridge Journal of Economics* 42(1): 19–31.

Bhaduri, A. and D. J. Harris. 1987. The complex dynamics of the simple Ricardian system. *The Quarterly Journal of Economics* 102(4): 893–902.

Bhaduri, A., K. Laski, and M. Riese. 2006. A model of interaction between the virtual and the real economy. *Metroeconomica* 57(3): 412–427.

Bhaduri, A. and S. Marglin. 1990. Unemployment and the real wage: The economic basis for contesting political ideologies. *Cambridge Journal of Economics* 14(4): 375–393.

Bhaduri, A. and D. Nayyar. 1996. *An intelligent person's guide of liberalization*. New Delhi: Penguin India.

Bhaduri, A. and S. Raghavendra. 2017. Wage- and profit-led regimes under modern finance: An exploration. *Review of Keynesian Economics* 5(3): 426–438.

Bhaduri, A., H. Z. Rahman, and A. Lisbet. 1986. Persistence and polarisation: A study in the dynamics of agrarian contradiction. *The Journal of Peasant Studies* 13(3): 82–89.

Bhaduri A. and J. Robinson 1980. Class relations and the pattern of accumulation in an agrarian economy. *Cambridge Journal of Economics* 4(2): 103–115.

Bhaduri, A. and J. Steindl. 1985. The rise of monetarism as a social doctrine. In P. Arestis and T. Skouras (Eds.), *Post Keynesian economic theory* (pp. 56–78). Sussex, UK: Wheatsheaf Books.

Bhaduri, A. and R. Skarstein. 2003. Effective demand and the terms of trade in a dual economy: A Kaldorian perspective. *Cambridge Journal of Economics* 27(4): 583–595.

General references

Barbosa-Filho, N. H. and L. Taylor. 2006. Distributive and demand cycles in the US economy: A structuralist Goodwin model. *Metroeconomica* 57(3): 389–411.

Basu, D. 2010. Marx-biased technical change and the neoclassical view of income distribution. *Metroeconomica* 61(4): 593–620.

Basu, D. 2017. Quantitative empirical research in Marxist political economy: A selective review. *Journal of Economic Surveys* 31(5): 1359–1386.

Blecker, R. A. 2016. *The debate over "Thirlwall's law": Balance-of-payments growth reconsidered*. Available here (http://fs2.american.edu/blecker/www/research/Blecker-BPCG-debate-revised0816.pdf). Accessed March 16, 2020.

Blecker, R. A. and M. Setterfield. 2019. *Heterodox macroeconomics: Models of demand, distribution and growth*. Cheltenham, UK: Edward Elgar Publishing.

Campbell, T. and D. Tavani. 2019. Marx-biased technical change and income distribution: A panel data analysis. *Metroeconomica* 70(4): 655–687.

Christiano, L. J., M. Eichenbaum, and C. L. Evans. 2005. Nominal rigidities and the dynamic effects of a shock to monetary policy. *Journal of Political Economy* 113(1): 1–45.

Cogliano, J. F., P. Flaschel, R. Franke, N. Frolich, and R. Veneziani. 2018. *Value, competition, and exploitation: Marx's legacy revisited*. Cheltenham, UK: Edward Elgar Publishing.

Crotty, J. 2019. *Keynes against capitalism: His case for liberal socialism*. London: Routledge.

Davis, L. 2017. Financialisation and investment: A survey of the empirical literature. *Journal of Economic Surveys* 31(5): 1332–1358.

Davis, L. 2018. Financialisation and the nonfinancial corporation: An investigation of firm-level investment behaviour in the US. *Metroeconomica* 69(1): 270–307.

Flaschel, P. 1983. Actual labour values in a general model of production. *Econometrica* 51(2): 435–454.

Foley, D. K. and T. R. Michl. 1999. *Growth and distribution*. First edition. Cambridge, MA: Harvard University Press.

Foley, D. K., T. R. Michl, and D. Tavani. 2019. *Growth and distribution*. Second edition. Cambridge, MA: Harvard University Press.

Grasselli, M. R. and A. Maheshwari. 2018. Testing a Goodwin model with general accumulation rate. *Metroeconomica* 69: 619–643.

Hahnel, R. 2017. *Radical political economy: Sraffa versus Marx*. New York: Routledge.

Kalecki, M. 1960. Unemployment in underdeveloped countries. In M. Kalecki (Ed.), *Essays on developing economies* (with an introduction by J. Robinson, 1976, pp. 17–19). Hassocks, UK: The Harvester Press.

Lazonick, W. H. 2014. Profits without prosperity. *Harvard Business Review* 92(9): 46–55.

Michl, T. R. 2009. *Capitalists, workers and fiscal policy: A classical model of growth and distribution*. Cambridge, MA: Harvard University Press.

Nikiforos, M. 2012. *On the "utilization controversy": A theoretical and empirical discussion of the Kaleckian model of growth and distribution*. Working paper no. 739, Levy Economics Institute of Bard College.

Orhangazi, O. 2008. Financialisation and capital accumulation in the non-financial corporate sector: A theoretical and empirical investigation of the US economy: 1973–2003. *Cambridge Journal of Economics* 32(6): 863–886.

Oyvat, C., O. Öztunali, and C. Elgin. 2020. Wage-led versus profit-led demand: A comprehensive empirical analysis. *Metroeconomica*. First published March 6, 2020. https://doi.org/10.1111/meca.12284

Ros, J. 2000. *The economics of growth*. Ann Arbor, MI: University of Michigan Press.

Ros, J. 2013. *Rethinking economic development, growth and institutions*. New York: Oxford University Press.

Steedman, I. 1977. *Marx after Sraffa*. London: New Left Books.

Weisskopf, T. E. 1979. Marxian crisis theory and the rate of profit in the postwar US economy. *Cambridge Journal of Economics* 3(4): 341–378.

Wolff, R. D. 2020. *Understanding socialism*. New York: Democracy at Work.

Part I

Post-Keynesian macroeconomics

Growth and distribution

2 Power, income inequality and economic growth

Amitava Krishna Dutt

Professor Amit Bhaduri has made many significant contributions to economics and political economy. I first came across his work in his paper on agricultural stagnation (Bhaduri, 1973), in which he shows that, under conditions of semi-feudalism (because of the perpetual indebtedness of the borrower-tenant), poverty and inequality persist. In this paper, the *jotedar* is both landlord and moneylender, and the *kishan* is both sharecropper and borrower. Consequently, agricultural growth through technological change does not occur because the *jotedar* uses power to prevent the *kishan* from adopting new technology to increase agricultural production even though it increases the rent income for the former, because it may reduce total income due to a diminution of money-lending income (since the latter's income also increases and reduces borrowing needs); even if total *jotedar* income rises, the new technology will be resisted because it "weakens the system of semi-feudalism, where the economic and political power of the landowner is largely based on his being able to keep the *kishan* constantly indebted to him" (Bhaduri, 1973, 135). This paper was a revelation to me as an undergraduate economics student at Presidency College, Calcutta (where Bhaduri had studied), where only neoclassical theory was taught, and where heterodox ideas entered only when the real world was discussed without any explicit theories.

Later, I was exposed to other formal heterodox theories in the MA program in economics at Calcutta University and, more extensively, at the Massachusetts Institute of Technology (where Bhaduri also had studied), studying under Lance Taylor and attending some talks by Stephen Marglin. I then became aware of the weaknesses of neoclassical optimizing models and understood how macroeconomic models could be developed along alternative lines by building on what can be called stylized facts and accounting relations, just as Bhaduri's paper had done for a microeconomic setting.

I have started with this paper because it deals with three themes emphasized in this chapter: power, growth (or its absence) and inequality, themes that have recurred in Bhaduri's writings. To give just a few examples, growth, distribution and inequality are major issues in Bhaduri (1986), especially in chapter 7, which deals with capital accumulation in the long run; and are the central issues of Bhaduri and Marglin (1990), although the analysis is confined to what they call the short period, without the explicit analysis of long-run growth. Bhaduri (2007) analyzes the dynamics of growth and distribution and their interaction with technological change. Growth and accumulation in an agrarian economy are analyzed in a theoretical framework that examines the interaction between productive and unproductive investment and two ruling classes, capitalists and merchants and moneylender in Bhaduri (1981, 1983). Power is a theme that frequently appears in Bhaduri's writings, although I am aware of only one published work with that word (in the sense that is relevant for this chapter) in its title (Bhaduri, 1991). In addition to the examination of power in agriculture, and between capitalists and workers, Bhaduri and Steindl (1983) analyzed the rise on monetarism in terms of a global shift in power from industry to banks. While I was finishing the first draft of this chapter, I came across a lecture delivered by him given in 2017, entitled "How to Think about the Role of Power in the Social Sciences" which briefly reviews some ideas about power in economics and the other social sciences and proposes a generalizable way in which power manifests itself.[1]

The purpose of this chapter is to provide a general discussion of power and develop a simple model of economic growth, income distribution and inequality, and power. The rest of the chapter proceeds as follows. The next section provides very brief comments on notions of power in economics and other social sciences. The third section develops a simple model of growth and distribution, and the fourth analyzes the dynamics of power in terms of that model. The fifth section concludes.

Power

Power is often defined as the ability of some individual or group to make others act in ways that they would not have otherwise done and which is against their perceived interests.[2] Power can also be exercised by shutting off or vetoing options for others,[3] or more broadly by circumscribing issues and setting the agenda of negotiations; since this goes beyond the first definition, it has come to be called the second face of power (Bachrach and Baratz, 1962). Lukes (2005) points to a third face, according to which the preferences and values of people can be influenced by the powerful to their advantage, so that the dominated acquiesce to their domination. Digeser (1992) refers to a fourth face, drawing on Foucault's (1977) writings, in which power can exist because individuals are not biologically predetermined but socially constructed as constellations of values or social norms, and power and its use are reflected in the process by which such values are constructed. This is not just the manipulation of preferences of individuals since it has a social dimension in which knowledge and values are shared and which affect people's behavior even without explicit attempts to manipulate. One can continue down this route to add to things that are influenced by the powerful to affect not just values and norms, but also other forms of institutions, including laws and organizations, as well as other aspects of society (such as technology) that change slowly, or what can collectively be called "structures". Structural power, thus, can be seen as power embodied in the structures of society, within which structures individuals and groups act, and does not require the ability to use or to exercise power. The structures, of course, can change, partly through the use of power but also for other reasons, including those unintended by any person or groups.

Mainstream economics has traditionally had almost nothing to say about power, focusing on models of perfect competition with price taking agents, both in Walrasian general equilibrium and Marshallian partial equilibrium analysis.[4] More recently, mainstream neoclassical economics (by which we mean economics which attempts – as an ideal – to use the optimizing agents as the basis for all explanation) has examined power in several ways: by introducing, price-setting firms with market power under conditions of monopoly, monopolistic competition and oligopoly in the 1930s and even before Walras, in the writings of Cournot; assuming that information is not "perfect" and agreements are not binding, such as in models of asymmetric information and costly monitoring (see Bowles and Gintis, 2008) and transactions costs (see Williamson, 1985); in models of non-cooperative games with strategic interaction between actors and in cooperative games (see Ozanne, 2016); and in theories of collective action, in which narrow interest groups can wield power by overcoming free rider problems (Olson, 1965). Power that exerts its influence by changing people's preferences, and even some aspects of structural power, can also be examined by taking into account actions to change the preferences of others and create hierarchical organizations (see Bartlett, 1989).

However, such approaches can be criticized for producing a narrow notion of power, for a number of reasons. First, they confine attention to *intentional* actions of people and groups and examine – if at all – *unintended* consequences in a world of certainty or risk, but not uncertainty in the Keynes-Knight sense in which the future is simply not known and probabilities cannot be assigned to possible outcomes in any objective way. Second, they do not (and arguably do not lend themselves to) provide an analysis of the complex and multiple sources (and consequences) of power, a direct result of examining power in terms of *specific* market imperfections. Third, they do not adequately deal with the distinction between relational power (that is, power that comes into play in the relation between different people or groups) and *structural* power. Other approaches – such as the classical-Marxian (see Palermo, 2007; Kurz, 2018), institutionalist (see Galbraith, 1976, 1983; Dugger, 1980) and post-Keynesian (Kalecki, 1943; Pressman, 2007) in economics, and some outside economics (for instance, in international relations and global political economy, see Strange, 1988; Guzzini, 1993) – that do not start from the individual optimizing agent but instead examine structures within which individuals and groups interact following norms and rules of thumb in a world of uncertainty without all-encompassing goals such as utility maximization – arguably provide a richer perspective. They do so by examining how structures can confer more power to some, how structures can change due to a variety of reasons, including the intentional and unintentional, intended and unintended, and conscious and unconscious, exercise of power. Moreover, they can examine different spheres and sources of power, such as in production, finance, violence, knowledge and culture, and organizations. Power in these different spheres can have complicated, unintended and interacting effects and cannot be reduced to only the relations between individuals or groups.

Rather than seeking to develop a general and unified conception of power – the possibility of doing so may be left as an open question – I will examine power in a specific context; that is, in terms of an *analytical* framework and a theory based on it, and a specific real-world *question*. The analytical framework, for reasons just discussed, is a structuralist one that draws on heterodox economics and other approaches outside economics, the specific theory represented by a model is an extension of what has been called the post-Keynesian-Kaleckian (PKK) one, and the real-world question is income inequality between workers and capitalists.

A model of growth and inequality

The simple PKK model (see Dutt, 1984; Rowthorn, 1982) examines a closed economy which produces one good, which can be consumed and invested, with two factors of production, labor and capital. There are two classes: workers, who provide labor and receive wage income, and who do not save and hold capital; and capitalists, who receive profits from production after the payment of wages, save a fraction of their income, s, and own and manage firms. Workers are in abundant supply.

The government taxes only profits at the rate of $\tau < 1$, given for now, and spends at a varying level G in real terms balancing its budget, so that

$$G = \tau r K \tag{1}$$

where r is the rate of profit before taxes and K is the stock of physical capital.

Firms set the price of the good as a fixed markup over labor costs (see Kalecki, 1971), so that

$$P = (1+z)Wa_0 \tag{2}$$

where P is the price level, W the given money wage and a_0 the given unit labor requirement, and the markup rate, z, is given by the market power of firms, representing inter-firm competition, and the relative power of capitalist firms and workers, among other factors. Firms maintain excess capital and adjust output according to its demand, and they hire labor according to the needs of production, so that labor employment is

$$L = a_0 Y \tag{3}$$

where Y denotes real output or income. Using equation (2), the rate of profit is given by

$$r = \frac{z}{1+z}u \tag{4}$$

where $u = Y/K$ measures capacity utilization. The share of profits gross of taxes in income, π, is fixed since z is fixed, at

$$\pi = \frac{z}{1+z} \tag{5}$$

Assuming that profit recipients are rich and workers are not, π is a measure of inequality.

Firms make investment plans according to the investment function

$$\frac{I}{K} = g(\pi, u, \tau) \tag{6}$$

where the partial derivatives take the signs $g_\pi > 0$, $g_u > 0$, and $g_\tau < 0$. This is a modification of the investment function of Bhaduri and Marglin (1990) to include the tax rate. It shows that investment plans depend on expected profitability, represented by the expected (net) profit rate, which in turn, because of equations (4) and (5), depends on the actual profit share, the rate of capacity utilization and the tax rate. We adopt this formulation rather than make investment depend on the profit share net of taxes because expectations regarding the gross profit share and taxes may be formed differently, and investment is likely to be affected mainly by taxes on the profits of firms, and not the profits that go to capitalists as a composite class, that can include rentiers.

Total consumption is thus

$$C = wL + (1-s)(1-\tau)rK \tag{7}$$

where $w = \dfrac{W}{P}$ is the real wage.

In the short run, output adjusts to aggregate demand to equalize aggregate demand and output, given K. Short-run equilibrium is obtained when

$$C + I + G = Y \tag{8}$$

Dividing through by K and using equations (1) through (7), we get

$$g(\pi,u,\tau)-s(1-\tau)\pi u=0 \tag{9}$$

which solves for the short-run equilibrium level of u. This equilibrium is stable if and only if $s(1 - \tau)\pi > g_u$, that is, the responsiveness of saving to changes in capacity utilization exceeds that of investment. Substituting this value into equation (6) yields the short-run equilibrium value of the investment-capital ratio which, assuming away the depreciation of capital, is the rate of growth of the stock of capital, $g=\widehat{K}$, with the overhat denoting the rate of growth.

The effects of changes in π and τ, which are given in the short run, are found from equation (9) and shown by

$$\frac{du}{d\pi}=\frac{g_\pi-s(1-\tau)u}{s(1-\tau)\pi-g_u} \tag{10}$$

and

$$\frac{du}{d\tau}=\frac{g_\tau+s\pi u}{s(1-\tau)\pi-g_u}. \tag{11}$$

While the stability condition implies that the denominators in the two derivatives are positive, since the numerators can take either sign, neither expression can be definitively signed. An increase in the profit share reduces capacity utilization if the responsiveness of investment to the profit share, shown by g_π, is small; the expression in equation (10) is thus negative. An increase in the wage share increases capacity utilization by increasing the income share of workers who have a lower propensity to save, so there is wage-led expansion. A large investment response to the profit share, however, may make capacity utilization rise when the profit rate rises, so that expansion is profit led, with the rise in the profit share having a stronger positive effect on investment than the negative consumption effect. A balanced-budget increase in the tax rate and government spending increases capacity utilization if the negative effect of the tax increase on investment, shown by g_τ, is small, by increasing aggregate demand due to an increase in government spending which has a stronger effect than the negative effect on capitalist consumption, which is partly saved and partly taxed. However, a large negative investment effect can reduce capacity utilization.

The effects on the growth rate $g = I/K$, using equation (6), are shown by

$$\frac{dg}{d\pi}=g_\pi+g_u\frac{g_\pi-s(1-\tau)u}{s(1-\tau)\pi-g_u} \tag{12}$$

and

$$\frac{dg}{d\tau} = g_\tau + g_u \frac{g_\tau + s\pi u}{s(1-\tau)\pi - g_u} \tag{13}$$

These expressions also cannot be definitively signed. Even if $\frac{du}{d\pi} < 0$ and $\frac{du}{d\tau} > 0$, since $g_\pi > 0$, $\frac{dg}{d\pi} > 0$ is possible, so that we may have profit-led *growth* (but wage-led *expansion*), and since $g_\tau < 0$, $\frac{dg}{d\tau} < 0$, so that we may have expansionary fiscal policy reducing growth even though fiscal expansion increases capacity utilization. However, with small absolute magnitudes for g_π and g_τ, we will have wage-led growth and expansionary fiscal policy-led growth. If, however, $\frac{du}{d\pi} > 0$ and $\frac{du}{d\tau} < 0$, we must have $\frac{dg}{d\pi} > 0$ and $\frac{dg}{d\tau} < 0$; that is, profit-led growth, and expansionary fiscal policy reducing growth.

The dynamics of power

Apart from a reference to monopoly power in the determination π, we have not invoked the concept of power in the previous section. Power actually enters the model in at least two ways. First, broad *structural* power is possessed by capitalists by virtue of their monopoly over capital ownership in the capitalist mode of production: capitalists do not have to exercise any power over workers to induce them to work against their wishes, since workers must work in order to earn wages and survive.[5] This kind of power places capitalists in a privileged position as long as the economy remains capitalist. Second, *relational* power of capitalists and workers is reflected in the levels of π and τ, which have been held constant so far. These can change over time depending on the relative power of the two classes, what can be called the state of class struggle in the "economic" arena, or economic class struggle over π, and the state of class struggle in the "political" or policy arena over τ, or political class struggle.[6] It is tempting to interpret these two parameters as representing economic and political power but, as we will see later, to do so would be inaccurate.

We assume that capitalists intend to increase their share of profits from production, that is, π, while workers intend to increase their share by reducing π.[7] Capitalists do so because in their struggle against workers, other things constant, it increases their profits, while workers resist the efforts of capitalists, attempting to maintain or increase their wages. We also assume that capitalists intend to reduce the tax rate on their income, τ, while workers want to increase it. It can be argued that capitalists may wish to pay higher taxes because by doing so, they will provide the government more revenues to increase government spending and to increase aggregate demand, thereby possibly increasing their sales and profits. However, as Kalecki (1943) argued, capitalists have many reasons not to like increases in government expenditures, because: they do not appreciate the government having a great role in the economy because it threatens their position, for instance, by blunting their ability to hold the economy hostage by reducing investment due to a capital strike; they do not like the adverse effect on worker discipline when the unemployment is low; government investment may reduce their investment opportunities (for instance, in public utilities); and they hold on to the ethical claim "that 'You shall earn your bread in sweat' – unless you happen to have private means" (Kalecki, 1943, 326).

Although capitalists and workers may have intentions, they may not be able to achieve them. Whether or not, and the extent to which, they will do so depends on what can be called the relational power of capitalists and workers and on what can be called "frictions" in the society. Even if they achieve their intentions to some degree, the outcome may not actually help to serve their interests, since these depend on a variety of factors, either which they do not know about or over which they do not have full control. Thus, it is possible that if they are successful in achieving their intentions, they may end up hurting their interests as they see them. We first consider the determinants of relational power of the two classes, then frictions, and finally turn to actual outcomes, for which we use the model of the previous section.

We assume that the relational power of the two groups depends on their relative income in a broad sense, as well as on other factors, which we denote by Θ. We use a broad measure of inequality to denote relative income,

$$\iota = \frac{Y_c}{Y_w} \tag{14}$$

the ratio of capitalist net income to the income of workers which takes into account wages and has been called their "social wage" where σ is the share of total government expenditure that is devoted to the social wage.[8] We have

$$Y_c = (1-\tau)\pi Y \tag{15}$$

and

$$Y_w = (1-\pi)Y + \sigma G \tag{16}$$

which, using equations (1), (3) and (5), implies

$$\iota = \frac{\pi(1-\tau)}{1-\pi(1-\sigma\tau)} \tag{17}$$

This measure of inequality is seen to depend positively on π, because of the increase in the share of profits out of production income, although this is partly attenuated by the increase in the social wage that results from the higher tax revenue, negatively on τ because of the reduction in the net income of capitalists and the increase in the social wage made possible by the increase in the tax rate, and positively on σ because of the increase in the social wage.

Although ι may seem to be a measure of relative economic power, it can be taken to be an overall measure of relative power based on relative income that captures a variety of sources of power, including violence, income, finance and knowledge, which combines not only aspects of economic power or what can be called political power. While income power is obvious, the other sources of power deserve some comment. A higher relative income allows capitalists to have a stronger influence on the state (with its monopoly of legitimate violence) and on government policies, including fiscal, monetary, financial, labor and monopoly policies, either by changes in the government through elections, or by a change in the ruling party. It is well known that, even in democracies, relative income has a significant effect on electoral outcomes and also affects government policies through lobbying and, possibly, corruption (see, for instance, Bonica et al., 2013, for the case of the United States). A higher relative income of capitalists also provides capitalists with financial power and easier access to finance, which allows them – in Kalecki's (1971) words – to earn what they spend by borrowing whereas workers spend what they earn.[9] Finally, relative income can influence power over knowledge, by influencing, through "philanthropy" and ownership, educational institutions (schools and universities), the media, as well as the nature of technological change, that is the extent to which labor is displaced or disciplined (from which we abstract in this chapter).

Not all the determinants of the relational power of the two classes can be captured by their relative income in our broad sense. This may be shown by examining two sources of power: organizational power, and power that depends on the personal characteristics of leaders. Organizational power refers to how well the two groups are organized and united in their ability to push forward their agenda; stronger organizations imply higher levels of power. While economic resources can be used to make organizations stronger, or to change laws and policies that strengthen them, which in turn depend on their economic resources, other factors may well be at work. Ethnic differences and the way work is organized can affect the organization of workers through labor unions and other political organizations representing workers. The same may be true of firms which may be more or less cohesive, for instance, due to membership in chambers of commerce or trade associations, or because of the ability of some powerful firms to influence other firms.[10] Leadership power depends on the respect and charisma of leaders which affect their ability to unite their classes and the general public in favor of their cause. Although economic resources can help to create and amplify the messages of leaders, some personal qualities cannot be purchased. These are only examples of power that may be independent of relative income. The other sources of power may also be affected by factors other than income; for instance, knowledge power can be affected by the spread of information technology, and power based on violence can depend on the availability of arms, which may affect the power of the two classes differentially. We represent these with the symbol Θ, which represents determinants of the relative power of capitalists that do not depend on ι. It will be held constant in developing the model that follows, although we can examine the effects of exogenous changes in them using our model.

In addition to these determinants of the relative power of the two classes, it is useful to consider what may be called frictions in society, which impose barriers to the use of power of the groups to change π and τ. Clearly, it is not possible for any group to indefinitely increase or reduce the two state variables because they must be fractions bounded by 0 and 1. Moreover, there may be constraints on how much power can be exercised before these limits are reached, due to the existence of social norms. These social norms are expressed in such statements are "the rich should pay their fair share of taxes", and "the rich are getting too high a share of income".[11] They may also be affected by the views of scholars and the influence they have on social norms, if scholars and public intellectuals find extreme levels of π and τ to be problematic.

To capture the effects of ι, Θ, and these frictions, on actual outcomes involving changes in π and τ, we assume that

$$\dot{\pi} = \mu(\iota, \pi, \tau, \Theta) \tag{18}$$

and

$$\dot{\tau} = \lambda(\iota, \tau, \Theta) \tag{19}$$

where overdots denote time derivatives. The partial derivatives of the functions have the signs $\mu_\iota > 0, \mu_\pi < 0, \mu_\tau < 0, \mu_\Theta > 0, \lambda_\iota < 0, \lambda_\tau < 0$, and $\lambda_\Theta < 0$.[12]

The reasons for the signs of the partials with respect to ι and Θ have already been discussed earlier in the general examination of intentions and power, but we may emphasize some of the specific effects for ι. Starting with μ_ι, an increase in ι increases the ability of capitalists to influence government policy that weakens the bite of anti-trust policy, which allows firms to increase their markups, weakens protections for workers as represented by unemployment benefits and weakens the power of labor unions, and directly in wage negotiations by allowing firms to have deeper pockets, and workers to have fewer alternatives to fall back on when industries are more concentrated. All of this contributes to an increase in π at a higher rate. Note, then, that this equation relates to changes in both the spheres of what are usually referred to as politics and economics. The partial λ_ι reflects exclusively government policies and works directly through the ability of capitalists to reduce taxes through their impact on fiscal policy and, in a more general framework, through tighter monetary policy that prevents increases in government spending by monetary expansion. The relative income of the classes can also have these policy effects through their influence on the media and the "views" of experts, including scholars, who are swayed by financial benefits.

The signs of the own direct partials, μ_π and λ_τ, are kept separate from the influences of these variables through ι because we interpret them more as external constraints or "frictions". It will be assumed that these own partial derivatives become strongly negative at high or low values of these variables and quite weakly negative (or even absent) at intermediate levels. In other words, the frictions become stronger the further the system departs from what is considered fair or appropriate. Finally, μ_τ captures the effect of lower taxes increasing efforts at increasing income through rent-seeking efforts to increase incomes of the rich, especially at high levels of income (see, for instance, Stiglitz, 2012; Piketty, 2014).

Using equations (17), (18) and (19), we obtain the system given by equations

$$\dot{\pi} = M(\pi, \tau, \sigma, \Theta) \tag{18}$$

and

$$\dot{\tau} = \Lambda(\pi, \tau, \sigma, \Theta) \tag{19}$$

An increase in π increases ι which increases $\dot{\pi}$ but directly reduces $\dot{\pi}$, an effect that becomes stronger at low and high values of π. Thus, the partial M_π is negative at lower values of π, positive at intermediate values and negative at higher values. At low and high values of π, the negative own effect is stronger and therefore will dominate the effect through ι, while at intermediate levels of π positive effect through ι overwhelms the negative effect. An increase in τ reduces ι, which reduces $\dot{\pi}$, and it reduces $\dot{\pi}$ directly from equation (17), so that the overall effect is to make $M_\tau < 0$. An increase in π increases ι, which reduces $\dot{\tau}$, so that the partial $\Lambda_\pi < 0$. An increase in τ reduces ι which tends to increase $\dot{\tau}$ but directly reduces $\dot{\tau}$, an effect that becomes stronger at low or high values of τ. Thus, the partial Λ_τ can be assumed to be negative at lower values of τ, positive at intermediate values and negative again at lower values and negative at higher values of τ. Regarding the parameters of the system, σ and Θ, since an increase in σ reduces ι, we have $M_\sigma < 0$ and $\Lambda_\sigma > 0$, and since an increase in Θ increases the relative power of capitalists, we have $M_\Theta > 0$ and $\Lambda_\Theta < 0$.

The dynamics can now be shown in phase diagrams. The sign pattern of the partials just discussed implies that we may draw the $\dot{\pi} = 0$ and $\dot{\tau} = 0$ loci as shown in Figure 2.1. Many different configurations of the loci are possible, of which one is shown in the figure, in which there are three long-run equilibria. The lower and higher ones are unstable, but the middle one is saddle-point unstable. Unless we start on the separatrix that goes through the upper equilibrium, eventually the economy moves on a dynamic path along

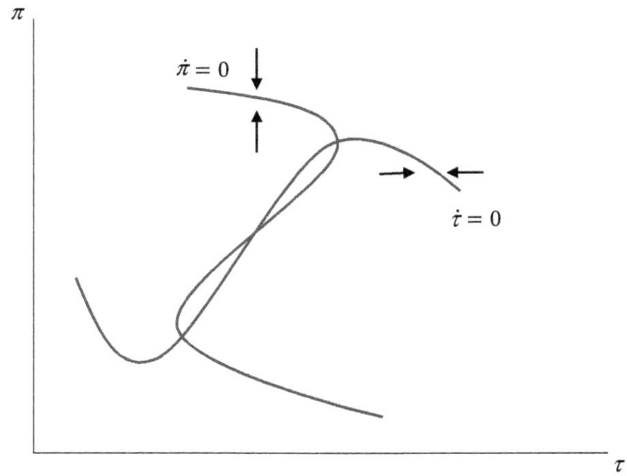

Figure 2.1 The dynamics of power: unstable case

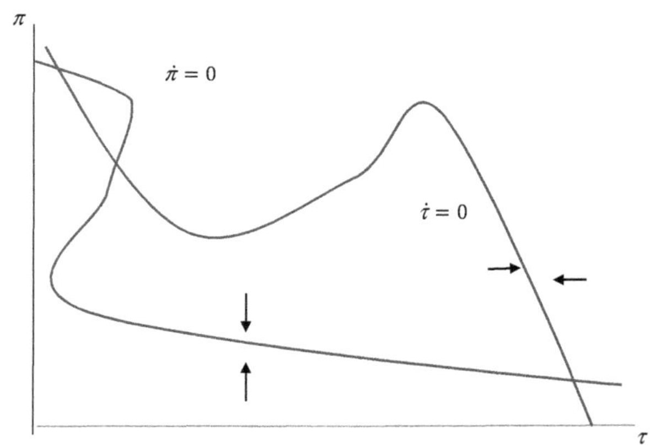

Figure 2.2 The dynamics of power: with stabilizing social norms

which π rises and τ falls, the relative income of capitalists keeps increasing and inequality keeps growing; or π falls and τ rises, the relative income of workers keeps increasing and inequality keeps falling. The system seems to be balanced on a knife-edge, reaching one or both of the limiting values of the state variables.

But this does not present the only possible configuration of the curves. Another one is shown in Figure 2.2, which also has three equilibria. In this case the equilibria at the two extremes – one with high π and low τ, and another with low π and high τ – are stable because of the role of the stabilizing norms, but the intermediate equilibrium is saddle-point unstable.

Although the dynamic system examined here does not show changes in u and g, the changes in the state variables obviously affect them. We could introduce variables directly into equations (18) and (19) to, for instance, show that a higher rate of growth increases employment growth and the wage share and thereby tends to negatively affect $\dot{\pi}$. Rather than complicating the analysis with such a modification, however, we can interpret the effects of these variables as representing crises, which can lead to what can be called regime changes that may affect the shapes and positions of the μ and λ functions (for instance, due to changes in σ and Θ). For instance, as shown in Figure 2.1, although it is possible that along a dynamic path in which π keeps falling and τ keep rising, and we have wage-led growth and fiscal policy expansion-led growth, capacity utilization and the rate of growth of the economy will keep increasing. However, this process is likely to be unsustainable, since taxes rise so much that investment falls, and the profit share falls so much that capacity utilization and investment falls, and a profit-led growth and expansionary fiscal policy-led contractionary situation results. There is a profit-squeeze crisis, which is not in the interests of workers because employment growth is low. In the opposite dynamic path in which inequality rises, stagnation may set in if growth is wage-led and fiscal expansion-led. Even if the economy is profit-led and growth is increased by lower taxes that boost investment, as inequality increases, it is likely to become wage-led, and as excess capacity increases, growth and profits will fall, and there will be stagnation due to insufficient demand and a socio-economic crisis due to a very low tax rate, which is not in the interests of capitalists. Of course, the stabilizing role of social norms may prevent the economy from going to such extremes of crises, as shown in Figure 2.2.

Several features of this model should be stressed. First, it implies that imbalances in power are likely to affect the distribution of income which, in turn, exacerbates the imbalances in power, Thus, if capitalists (workers) are relatively powerful, they are likely to be more successful in increasing their share of a broad measure of income, exacerbating (reducing) inequality and leading to further increases in their power.

Second, which of these cases is more likely to prevail depends on the initial levels of π and τ, and on the positions of the two curves shown in the figures which, in turn, depend on the exogenous determinants, σ, and the catchall parameter, Θ. It may be surmised that capitalists are likely to be relatively more powerful, since their relational power is built on the foundation of the structural power that they possess, given their monopoly of the ownership of capital. This is not to imply that the power of capitalists is uncontested, or even that workers are unable to push society to further their own perceived interests and against the perceived interests of the capitalists. The fact that there are many more low-income workers than high-income capitalists may provide the power of numbers in democracies and even authoritarian regimes if popular support is attractive for leaders. However, the power of numbers is likely to be offset by factors such as financial power, knowledge power obtained through the control of media and education, the problem of organizing workers to effectively influence the state. The relative power of workers or lower-income groups is likely to be high if inequality is high, and it appears that output and growth are wage-led and expansionary fiscal policy is required to boost aggregate demand, social movements and scholars and public intellectuals argue in favor of reducing inequality and charismatic leaders representing the workers are able to provide appropriate leadership.

Third, the instability discussed earlier is not likely to make society necessarily move toward extreme levels of inequality. This is in part because moves towards the extremes can lead to the economic crises due to the lack of aggregate demand (when capitalists push society unintentionally to situations of extreme inequality) or a profit squeeze (when workers push society unintentionally to a situation of low profits and low investment). What is likely to happen as a result of such crises depends on how Θ is affected and how this affects the dynamics of the system. But society can also be stabilized by social norms which keep inequality within limits that prevent such crises. When such norms are weak, reversals can come about due to democratic elections, perhaps influenced by social movements and even through violence or its threat. It is possible that societies can find themselves experiencing oscillations between what is often called the right and the left.

Finally, in terms of the model, power cannot easily be classified as economic or political, but rather invokes political economy – involving the interaction between what can be called economic (as reflected in shares of income from production, captured by π) and political (as reflected in government policies, captured by τ). As noted earlier, this power can come from a variety of sources, that is, control of production, finance, knowledge and organization, as well as violence.

Conclusions

This chapter has sought to characterize power and its sources and consequences using a simple model of distribution and growth. In addition to broad structural power which allows capitalists to be in an advantageous position because of their ownership of capital, relational power is interpreted as the ability of capitalists and workers to affect outcomes in markets and government policies in their perceived interests. This kind of power depends, among other things, on the relative access to economic resources, measured by a simple indicator of income inequality that takes into account not only the income of each class but also the public resources made available to them through government expenditures. Power affects the ability of the two classes to push outcomes in their interests in the two struggles, one over their share in production and the other over government policies, which affects taxes on capitalists and, with a balanced budget, government expenditures. Income distribution, among other things, affects power, and power in turn affects class struggle and inequality. This can lead to instability in the system which can, because of the interaction between inequality, taxes and growth, result in crises, the effects of which were discussed informally. However, the power struggle does not occur in a vacuum, but in the context of social norms regarding the profit share and the size of the government. If such social norms are strong enough, they may be able to contain this kind of instability and keep it within bounds, thereby avoiding crises.

The simple analysis presented in this chapter can be extended in several ways. First, it can be used to formally endogenize the effects of capacity utilization and growth on power and thereby show the interactions of power, inequality and economic growth, more explicitly integrating the models outlined in the previous two sections. Second, it can be used to extend the model to incorporate additional issues such as government debt and deficits, borrowing by firms and workers, financial markets and monetary policy, additional classes including rentiers, professionals, managers and supervisors, and financiers, technical change and international factors (see Dutt, 2017, for instance). The last can involve the effect of income distribution on external competitiveness, the effect of government policies on international capital flows and the international projections of power across national boundaries favoring one group over others. Third, the approach to power examined here – based on structures and the conflict between different groups in different spheres – can be used to examine other issues such as the nature of technical change, electoral outcomes, changes in social norms and gender and ethnic inequality.

While this chapter has adopted a purely theoretical perspective, its relevance for understanding real-world issues and events can be illustrated with a few examples. First, increasing inequality and stagnant aggregate demand in the US and elsewhere can explain the onset of the Great Depression in the 1930s. However, financial issues involving stock market speculation, bank failures and debt deflation could be introduced into the model, in addition to international transmission mechanisms, to capture additional complexities. Second, the high levels of unemployment and low rates of growth paved the way for policies that increased the role of the government in the economy, increasing government spending on infrastructure, regulating the financial system and strengthening the power of labor unions. The economic and financial crises of the times created greater mistrust of the efficacy of free markets in countries such as the US and UK, and World War II also enhanced the role of the government in the economy. Such shifts were also given an impetus by the theories of Keynes and others that focused on policies that increased aggregate demand and reduced inequality. However, in some parts if the world, such as Germany, Italy and Japan, there was a different response, that of fascism and militarism.[13] This illustrates how a crisis with high inequality can lead to a regime change that leads the society to change its course. Third, the profit squeeze of the 1970s and 1980s could also have led to a regime shift that resulted in a rightward ideological shift that then resulted in increases in inequality and tax cuts. This shift interacted with shifts in knowledge power away from Keynesianism and state activism to monetarism in its different guises. However, it is not clear whether the mechanisms examined in the model provide the major explanation, or whether exogenous shocks, for instance, the rise in oil prices, and US military spending were more important for stagflation and in the advent and spread of neoliberalism. Fourth, the rolling back of the state in terms of public spending and rising income inequality in the neoliberal period, with the spread of these ideas around the world, set the stage for a new crisis due to a fall in aggregate demand. However, such a denouement was postponed by growing consumerism fueled by conspicuous consumption and keeping up with the Joneses, and easier access to credit due to financial deregulation responding to the growing power of financiers. However, increasing consumer debt as well as further increases in inequality caused by other aspects of financialization then paved the way to financial and economic crises and the Great Recession. Extending the model to include the financial sector, housing markets and international trade and capital flows can, of course, provide a fuller understanding of this crisis. Limited government expansionary policies were able to contain the crisis, but whether or not this will lead to a stronger role of the state and a concerted effort to reduce economic inequality by strengthening the power of lower income groups, or exacerbate the rise of xenophobia and authoritarianism led by demagogues, is an open question. Fifth, countries with social norms that favor greater equality may be able to avoid pendulum swings and settle at a long-run equilibrium with low levels of inequality and higher levels of government spending. This may provide an explanation of capitalist democracies with low inequality such as Sweden and Denmark. Finally, the model can be used to understand swings between rightist and leftist parties in some Latin American countries, although international factors need to be explicitly taken into account to show how aggregative demand-led booms under leftist governments can lead to balance of payments problems rather than only profit squeezes due to high wage shares, and how powerful countries and global organizations can affect these outcomes.

Acknowledgement

I am grateful to Deepankar Basu, Amit Bhaduri, Gilberto Lima, Wilson Perez, Diego Sanchez-Anochea, Christian Schroeder, Mark Setterfield, Roberto Veneziani, an anonymous referee, and other participants at the conference honoring Amit Bhaduri at the University of Massachusetts at Amherst, MA, March 2019, at the Analytical Political Economy workshop at the University of Massachusetts, and at a faculty seminar at FLACSO-Ecuador.

Notes

1 The lecture was given at the Azim Premji University in Bangalore, India, and is available on YouTube at www.youtube.com/watch?v=bK1zSwOaXmQ, part I.

2 See, for instance, Dahl (1957) in political science and Bardhan (1991) in economics, who have somewhat different definitions.
3 Bhaduri's own definition used in the lecture cited in note 1 is similar to this one.
4 Although power seems to be hiding below the surface, embodied in the enforcer of property rights and contracts and the auctioneer.
5 This Marxian notion of structural power does not disappear even if workers manage to save some portion of their income, if the size of their saving is small and the entry barriers to owning firms are large.
6 It is possible that π and τ change over time according the level of u, for instance, due to changes in labor market and goods market conditions and government policy playing a stabilizing role. But these could be considered to be short-run influences that can be neglected to focus on long-run changes in the dynamics of power which involves structural change, although of a narrower kind than a change in the capitalist structure or mode of production.
7 They may do this by trying to change W and P, dynamics not explicitly examined here.
8 Some of it represents transfers (such as unemployment benefits), while some represents expenditures on goods and services (such as government-financed employment schemes and spending on health services targeted to lower-income groups). Since we are assuming that workers are not taxed, it does not matter whether the total amount includes direct government spending or transfers to workers that are spent on consumption. Capitalists do not benefit from a social wage because they may not make use of government-provided services, or because it is a negligible portion of their resources.
9 Access to credit does not, of course, necessarily imply more power. Workers as debtors, as experience with consumer debt, including mortgage debt, shows in many countries, can increase their precariousness, whereas capitalists can run into such problems during financial crises.
10 This form of power is likely to depend on the degree of industrial concentration, where the latter, in addition to affecting the markup, z, π and hence ι, can also affect Θ.
11 It is irrelevant for our purposes whether there is an "objective" standard of fairness since, in any case, the overall effects of the change in these state variables will depend on the relative power of the two groups, which can affect their ability to shape norms through the use of power.
12 This way of formalizing power has some similarity with Ozanne's (2016) proposal to examine power in terms of a physics metaphor, in which mass × acceleration = force. Mass can be thought of as power, while acceleration depends on perceived interests and the extent to which power is used. A more complete analysis can examine some costs that need to be used to exercise power, which can result in groups trading off the use of power in, say, moving π and moving τ. While Ozanne views power as the ability to *change* an equilibrium, we use it here as the ability to push something in a certain direction, an ability that may be contested, which is captured by relative income, ι, and other factors, Θ, and thus to *determine* an equilibrium, as well as to change it. Frictions, such as social norms, provide external constraints on the exercise of power.
13 There are obvious similarities between these ideas and Polanyi's (1944) discussion of the ebb and flow of free markets and state intervention, in which the retreat of the state causes markets to create social problems which then starts a movement that seeks to regulate markets to reduce these problems. Polanyi analyzed the rise of economic liberalism and the consequent rise of fascism in his times. The analysis here focuses on inequality rather than on the role of the state as such, although the two are obviously related. But it also views markets and the state as being interrelated and sites of struggle in terms of power dynamics.

References

Bachrach, Peter, and Baratz, Morton S. (1962). "Two faces of power", *American Political Science Review*, 56(4), 947–952.

Bardhan, Pranab (1991). "On the concept of power in economics", *Economics and Politics*, 3(3).

Bartlett, Randall (1989). *Economics and power: An inquiry into human relations and markets*, Cambridge, UK: Cambridge University Press.

Bhaduri, Amit (1973). "A study in agricultural backwardness under semi-feudalism", *Economic Journal*, 83(329), 120–137.

Bhaduri, Amit (1981). "Class relations and the pattern of accumulation in an agrarian economy", *Cambridge Journal of Economics*, 5(1), 33–46.

Bhaduri, Amit (1983). *Economic structure of backward agriculture*, New York: Academic Press.

Bhaduri, Amit (1986). *Macroeconomics: The dynamics of commodity production*, Armonk, NY: M E Sharpe.

Bhaduri, Amit (1991). "Economic power and productive efficiency in traditional agriculture", in B. Gustafsson ed., *Power and economic institutions: Reinterpretations in economic history*, Aldershot, UK: Edward Elgar, 53–68.

Bhaduri, Amit (2007). *Growth, distribution and innovations: Understanding their interrelations*, New York and Abingdon, UK: Routledge.

Bhaduri, Amit and Marglin, Stephen (1990). "Unemployment and the real wage: The economic basis for contesting political ideologies", *Cambridge Journal of Economics*, 14, 375–393.

Bhaduri, Amit, and Steindl, Joseph (1983). "The rise of monetarism as a social doctrine", Thames polytechnic: Thames papers in political economy, reprinted in Philip Arestis and Thanos Skouras eds., *Post Keynesian economic theory: A challenge to neoclassical economics*, New York: Sharpe, 1985.

Bonica, Adam, McCarry, Nolan, Poole, Keith, and Rosenthal, Howard (2013). "Why hasn't democracy slowed rising inequality?", *Journal of Economic Perspectives*, 27(3), 103–124.

Bowles, Samuel and Gintis, Herbert (2008). "Power", in Steven Durlauf and Laurence Blume eds., *New Palgrave dictionary of economics*, Basingstoke, UK: Palgrave Macmillan.

Dahl, Robert A. (1957). "The concept of power", *Behavioral Science*, 2(3), 201–215.

Digeser, Peter (1992). "The fourth face of power", *The Journal of Politics*, 54(4), 977–1007.

Dugger, William M. (1980). "Power: An institutional framework of analysis", *Journal of Economic Issues*, 14(4), 897–907.

Dutt, Amitava Krishna (1984). "Stagnation, income distribution and monopoly power", *Cambridge Journal of Economics*, 10(1), 25–40.

Dutt, Amitava Krishna (2017). "Heterodox theories of growth and distribution: A partial view", *Journal of Economic Surveys*, 31(5), 335–351.

Foucault, Michel (1977). *Discipline and punish: The birth of the prison*, Alan Sheridan tr., New York: Random House.

Galbraith, John Kenneth (1976). *The new industrial state*, London: Hamish Hamilton.

Galbraith, John Kenneth (1983). *The anatomy of power*, Boston, MA: Houghton Mifflin.

Guzzini, Stefano (1993). "Structural power: The limits of neorealist power analysis", *International Organization*, 47(3), 443–478.

Kalecki, Michał (1943). "Political aspects of full employment", *The Political Quarterly*, 14(4), 322–330, reprinted in Kalecki (1971).

Kalecki, Michał (1971). *Selected essays on the dynamics of the capitalist economy*, Cambridge, UK: Cambridge University Press.

Kurz, Heinz (2018). "Elements of a science of power: Hobbes, Smith and Ricardo", in Manuela Mosca ed., *Power in economic thought*, Basingstoke, UK: Palgrave Macmillan.

Lukes, Steve (2005). *Power: A radical view*, 2nd edition, Basingstoke, UK: Palgrave Macmillan.

Olson, Mancur (1965). *The logic of collective action*, Cambridge, MA: Harvard University Press.

Ozanne, Adam (2016). *Power in neoclassical economics*, Basingstoke, UK: Palgrave Macmillan.

Palermo, Giulio (2007). "The ontology of economic power in capitalism: Mainstream economics and Marx", *Cambridge Journal of Economics*, 31(4), 539–561.

Piketty, Thomas (2014). *Capital in the 21st century*, Arthur Goldhammer tr., Cambridge, MA: Harvard University at the Belknap Press.

Polanyi, Karl (1944). *The great transformation*, New York: Reinhart.

Pressman, Steven (2007). "Economic power, the state, and post-Keynesian economics", *International Journal of Political Economy*, 35(4), 67–86.

Rowthorn, Robert (1982). "Demand, real wages and growth", *Studi Economici*, 18, 3–54.

Stiglitz, Joseph E. (2012). *The price of inequality: How today's divided society endangers our future*, New York: WW Norton & Company.

Strange, Susan (1988). *States and markets: An introduction to international political economy*, Oxford, UK: Basil Blackwell.

Williamson, Oliver (1985). *The economic institutions of capitalism*, New York: Free Press.

3 Harrodian instability in Kaleckian models and Steindlian solutions

An elementary discussion

Eckhard Hein

The notion of dynamic instability of demand-driven growth put forward by Harrod (1939) has triggered several responses in the history of economic thought. Neoclassical economists like Solow (1956) ignored Harrod's original problem of a potential cumulative deviation of the demand-driven actual growth rate from the warranted rate of growth at which target rates of utilisation of productive capacities are realised. Instead, assuming Say's law to hold, the focus turned towards showing that the warranted rate of growth will adjust towards the natural rate of growth, determined by exogenous labour force growth and technological progress, through capital-labour substitution and a long-run variable capital-output ratio. The first-generation post-Keynesian distribution and growth models by Kaldor (1957, 1961) and Robinson (1956, 1962) shifted the focus back to Harrod's original problem and made the warranted rate of growth adjust towards the actual rate through changes in distribution and thus the average propensity to save; Kaldor (1957, 1961) also endogenised the capital-output ratio via his 'technical progress function'. The second-generation post-Keynesian distribution and growth models, based on the works of Kalecki (1954, 1971) and Steindl (1952), and put forward by Rowthorn (1981), Dutt (1984, 1987), Bhaduri/Marglin (1990) and Kurz (1990), rather considered the rate of capacity utilisation to be endogenous beyond the short run. It was thus assumed, explicitly or implicitly, that the warranted rate of growth is either irrelevant or endogenous in the long run, eliminating the problem of Harrodian instability.

Against this background, the modern debate has focused on the viability of this Kaleckian approach, and several authors have criticised the treatment of the rate of capacity utilisation as an endogenous variable in the medium to long run – and thus the assumption of the irrelevance or the endogeneity of the warranted rate of growth. Duménil/Levy (1999), Shaikh (2009) and Skott (2010, 2012) have proposed models with local Harrodian instability around the normal rate of capacity utilisation which is then globally contained by monetary policy (Duménil/Levy), changes in retention ratios and thus aggregate propensities to save (Shaikh) or by changes in investment behaviour (Shaikh, Skott). The conclusions drawn from these Harrodian and

Marxian critiques has been that the main features of the Kaleckian model, the paradox of thrift and the possibility of a paradox of costs,[1] may hold in the short and the medium run, but not in the long run when the system has been brought back to the normal rate of capacity utilisation. Or, as Duménil/Levy (1999) have famously put it, one can be 'Keynesian in the short term' but has to be 'classical in the long term'.

Hein/Lavoie/van Treeck (2011) reviewed these contributions and did not find the proposed models to be fully convincing. In Hein/Lavoie/van Treeck (2012), they instead considered several Kaleckian justifications for the treatment of the rate of capacity utilisation as an endogenous variable.

First, Chick/Caserta (1997), for example, argued that expectations and behavioural parameters, as well as norms, are changing so frequently that a long-run equilibrium, defined as fully adjusted position at normal or target rates of capacity utilisation, is not very relevant. Instead, they argued that the focus should be on short-run analysis and on medium-run or provisional equilibria, in which the goods market equilibrium rate of capacity utilisation may deviate from firms' target rate without triggering further reactions. The long run is thus nothing else as a succession of medium-run provisional equilibria, an interpretation which is faithful with Kalecki's (1971, p. 165) view that 'the long-run trend is but a slowly changing component of a chain of short-period situations; it has no independent entity', and also with Steindl's (1952, p. 12) remark that '[t]here is no good reason why a state of disequilibrium, with undesired excess capacity, should not persist. For practical purposes, disequilibrium may be permanent.

Second, Dutt (1990, pp. 58–60, 2010) and Lavoie (1992, pp. 327–332, pp. 417–422) have suggested that the notion of a normal or target rate of utilisation should be defined as a range and not as a single value. Under the conditions of fundamental uncertainty, firms may be quite content to run their production capacity at rates of utilisation that are within that acceptable range for the normal or target rate without triggering adjusting reactions of investment. The normal rate of utilisation thus becomes endogenous with respect to the actual rate within that range.

Third, Dallery/van Treeck (2011), building on Lavoie (2002), have argued that firms have multiple goals and targets, the achievement of which may be mutually inconsistent. Therefore, they may have to accept variations in capacity utilisation and hence deviations from their target or normal rate in order to achieve or to come close to achieving other goals; for example, a certain target rate of return imposed by shareholders.

Fourth, Lavoie (1995, 1996) and Cassetti (2006) have argued that firms' assessment of the trend growth of demand and of the normal rate of capacity utilisation becomes endogenous to their past experience and thus to actual growth and actual utilisation.[2] Therefore, in the long-period equilibrium we have an equality of actual and normal rates of utilisation, because the latter adjusts towards the former. Schoder (2012) has recently presented empirical support for this view, and Nikiforos (2013) has provided a microeconomic rationale based on the choice of the cost-minimising number of shifts determining the normal rate of utilisation.

Fifth and finally, if we consider the normal rate of utilisation to be determined by a stable-inflation rate of capacity utilisation targeted by inflation-averse central banks, Hein (2006, 2008, chapter 17) has shown that this rate becomes endogenous to the central bank's interest rate policies reacting upon deviations of the actual rate of utilisation from the stable inflation rate of utilisation. The normal rate of utilisation is thus affected by the actual rate of utilisation, albeit in an indirect and complex way.

Furthermore, recently, several authors have turned towards introducing a Sraffian supermultiplier process into Kaleckian models of distribution and growth.[3] In these models, the autonomous growth rate of a non-capacity creating component of aggregate demand, i.e. autonomous consumption, residential investment, exports or government expenditures, determines long-run growth and, under the conditions that Harrodian instability in the investment function is not too strong, provides for a stable adjustment towards the normal rate of capacity utilisation. In those models, a change in the propensity to save or in the profit share will have no effect on the long-run growth rate but will affect the traverse and thus the long-run growth path. The paradox of saving and the possibility of a paradox of costs from the short run thus disappear with respect to the long-run growth rate, but they remain valid with respect to the long-run growth path.

In the debate around Harrodian instability in Kaleckian models, however, two arguments proposed by Steindl (1979, 1985) in favour of at least partial endogeneity of Harrod's (1939) warranted rate of growth and thus on the containment of Harrodian instability have so far received little attention. The first is related to the endogeneity of the capital-output ratio through endogenous capital scrapping (Steindl 1979) and has been used by Allain/Canry (2008) and Cassetti (2006), for example.[4] The second refers to government budget balances and the related effects on the aggregate propensity to save (Steindl 1979, 1985).

Starting from the reviews by Hein/Lavoie/van Treeck (2011, 2012), in this chapter we will therefore discuss in particular the two Steindlian arguments. For this purpose the model framework proposed by Hein/Lavoie/van Treeck (2011, 2012) will have to be extended in order to allow for endogenous capital scrapping and endogenous overall propensities to save through variations in the government financial balance. Within this framework we will then discuss the Steindlian solutions to Harrodian instability and compare them to the other approaches in the literature mentioned thus far. The next section will present the problem of Harrodian instability in a basic neo-Kaleckian model and will briefly discuss some of the mechanisms proposed by the critics of the Kaleckian model to tame Harrodian instability. The model will then be amended to allow for depreciation of the capital stock, capital scrapping and replacement investment in order to discuss the first Steindlian stabilisation mechanism. We will then introduce government deficit spending into the model and examine Steindl's second potential stabilisation process. The final section will summarise and conclude.

Harrodian instability in a basic neo-Kaleckian/ Steindlian model

Following Hein/Lavoie/van Treeck (2011, 2012),[5] we can, in a nutshell, introduce Harrodian instability into the very basic neo-Kaleckian/Steindlian distribution and growth model for a one-good closed economy without government activity, without technical progress, without depreciation of the capital stock and without overhead labour by including a normal or target rate of capacity utilisation (u_n) into the model:

$$r = h\frac{u}{v} = r_n\frac{u}{u_n} \tag{1}$$

$$\sigma = s_\Pi r = s_\Pi h\frac{u}{v}, \qquad 0 < s_\Pi \leq 1 \tag{2}$$

$$g = \alpha + \beta(u - u_n), \qquad \alpha, \beta > 0 \tag{3}$$

$$g = \sigma \tag{4}$$

$$\frac{\partial \sigma}{\partial u} > \frac{\partial g}{\partial u} \qquad \Rightarrow \qquad s_\Pi \frac{h}{v} > \beta \tag{5}$$

Equation (1) defines the realised profit rate (r), which depends on the realised rate of capacity utilisation (u), on the profit share (h) being determined by markup pricing of firms, and on the capital-potential output ratio (v). The equation can also be rewritten in terms of the normal profit rate (r_n) and the normal rate of capacity utilisation (u_n).

The normal rate can be interpreted as the rate of utilisation which firms expect to prevail or target in the long run when making their decisions to invest and thus to expand the capital stock. The normal rate of utilisation in this sense does not imply that firms expect to operate at the technically given maximum capacity (u_{max}) in Figure 3.1. Nor does it mean that they will necessarily operate at the unit total cost minimum level of capacity utilisation (u_{cmin}) if they have chosen to hold excess capacity in order to deter entry by threatening competitors with price wars, for example. The variables p, mc, uvc, ufc and utc represent price, marginal costs, unit variable costs, unit fixed costs and unit total costs, respectively.

The normal rate as a target rate of utilisation of firms differs from the goods market equilibrium rate of utilisation, which is the rate of utilisation at which output of firms is equal to aggregate demand in the goods market. We assume that firms have expectations about demand in the goods market and that they adjust capacity utilisation towards actual demand within the

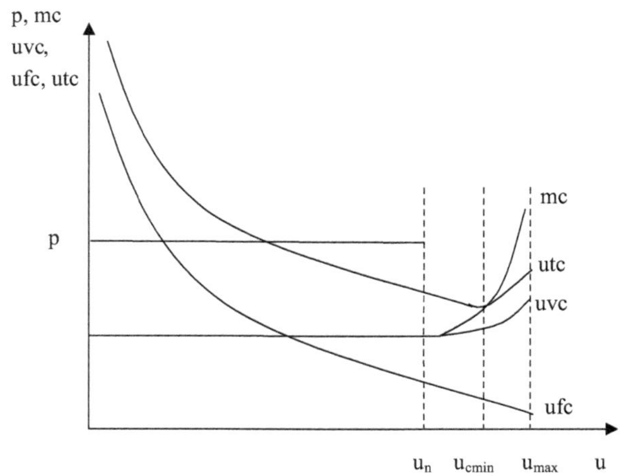

Figure 3.1 Unit costs and normal/target rate of capacity utilisation

period. The short-run goods market equilibrium rate of capacity utilisation is thus the rate at which firms' short-run expectations regarding aggregate demand are met and no further adjustment of output and capacity utilisation for this purpose is required.

The saving function in equation (2) relates saving to the capital stock and is the standard classical function for the saving rate (σ), which assumes away saving out of wages, with a propensity to save out of profits equal to s_{Π}. The propensity to save out of profits may itself be determined by the retention ratio of corporations (s_C) and the propensity to save (s_R) out of rentiers' income (R), consisting of interest and dividend payments of corporations:

$$s_{\Pi} = \frac{S_{\Pi}}{\Pi} = \frac{\Pi - R + s_R R}{\Pi} = s_C + s_R\left(1 - s_C\right) \tag{6}$$

Equation (3) is the investment function, where the rate of capital accumulation (g) depends on a parameter α, which represents 'animal spirits', and on the deviation of actual from normal capacity utilisation. If actual utilisation equals normal utilisation, capital accumulation will be equal to α, which therefore can also be viewed as the expected trend rate of growth of sales and output expected by firms. Whenever the rate of capacity utilisation is above its normal rate, firms will be accumulating capital at a rate that exceeds the assessed trend growth rate of sales; whenever capacity utilisation is below its normal rate, firms will slow down capital accumulation. But unless there is some kind of fluke, the actual and the normal rates of capacity utilisation will differ in this neo-Kaleckian model without any further adjustment. Equation (4) is the goods market equilibrium condition and in equation (5) we find the Keynesian stability condition for the goods market equilibrium, saying that the saving rate has to respond more elastically to a change in capacity utilisation than the rate of capital accumulation.

For the goods market equilibrium of the model, the following utilisation and accumulation rates are obtained from equations (2) – (4):

$$u^* = \frac{\alpha - \beta u_n}{s_\Pi \frac{h}{v} - \beta} \tag{7}$$

$$g^* = \sigma^* = \frac{s_\Pi \frac{h}{v}\left(\alpha - \beta u_n\right)}{s_\Pi \frac{h}{v} - \beta} \tag{8}$$

As condition (5) tells us, Keynesian stability in this model requires that capital accumulation is not too sensitive to changes in the rate of capacity utilisation and the slope of the saving rate function exceeds the slope of the accumulation rate function with respect to capacity utilisation. Keynesian instability would arise when the accumulation rate function is steeper than the saving rate function, and capital accumulation responds more vigorously towards changes in capacity utilisation than the saving rate in the short run.

From this short-run Keynesian instability we can distinguish Harrodian instability as a long-run problem, which arises because of a deviation of the short-run equilibrium rate from the long-run normal rate of utilisation. Harrodian instability can be introduced into our model if we treat the parameter α of the investment function not as a constant but as a rising (decreasing) variable whenever the short-run equilibrium rate of capacity utilisation persistently exceeds (is below) its normal rate, with a dot on the variable denoting the time rate of change:

$$\dot{\alpha} = \upsilon\left(u^* - u_n\right), \ \upsilon > 0 \tag{9}$$

The reason for this is that in equation (3), the parameter α is interpreted as the assessed trend growth rate of sales and output, and thus as the expected secular rate of growth of the economy. When the short-run equilibrium rate of utilisation is consistently higher than the normal rate ($u^* > u_n$), this implies that the growth rate of the economy is consistently above the assessed secular growth rate of sales ($g^* > \alpha$). Thus, as long as entrepreneurs react to this in an adaptive way, they should eventually make a new, higher, assessment of the trend growth rate of sales and output, thus making use of a larger parameter α in the investment function.

Equation (9) may be interpreted as a slow process. Entrepreneurs react with enough inertia to generate short-run Keynesian stability. When rates of utilisation rise above their normal rates (or fall below their normal rates), entrepreneurs take a 'wait and see' attitude, not modifying their parametric behaviour immediately, until they are convinced that the discrepancy is there to stay. If during a certain number of periods the achieved short-run equilibrium rate of utilisation exceeds the normal rate, then the investment function will start shifting up, thus leading to ever-rising rates of capacity utilisation, and hence to an unstable process. This is illustrated in Figure 3.2.

Let us assume that the economy is in an initial equilibrium at the normal rate of utilisation in point A, and now the propensity to save out of profits declines or the profit share is reduced, so that the saving rate function rotates clockwise from σ_0 to σ_1. Since the paradox of thrift and the paradox of costs each hold in the simple neo-Kaleckian model, the economy achieves a higher short-run equilibrium at point B, with a higher rate of capital accumulation and the rate of capacity utilisation exceeding the normal rate of utilisation ($u_1^* > u_n$). If this equilibrium persists, the constant in the investment function will move up from α_0 to α_2 and shift the accumulation function up to g_2, and short-run equilibrium capacity utilisation will hence be moved to point C and to u_2^*, which is even further away from the normal rate. This will then, after some time, shift the constant in the accumulation function up to α_3, pushing the accumulation function to g_3, the new short-run equilibrium to point D, the equilibrium capacity utilisation to u_3^* and so on. Thus, according to the critics, the equilibrium described by the Kaleckian model in point B will not be sustainable; it will shift to C, D and further on and will hence not last in the long run.

In principle, upwards (downwards) Harrodian instability can be contained by forces either rotating the saving function counter-clockwise (clockwise) or forces shifting the investment function down (up), each questioning the validity of the paradoxes of thrift and costs in the long run (Hein 2014, pp. 446–451; Hein/Lavoie/van Treeck 2011, 2012).

The Cambridge price mechanism, initially advocated by Kaldor (1955/56, 1957) and Joan Robinson (1956, 1962), is the main mechanism in the

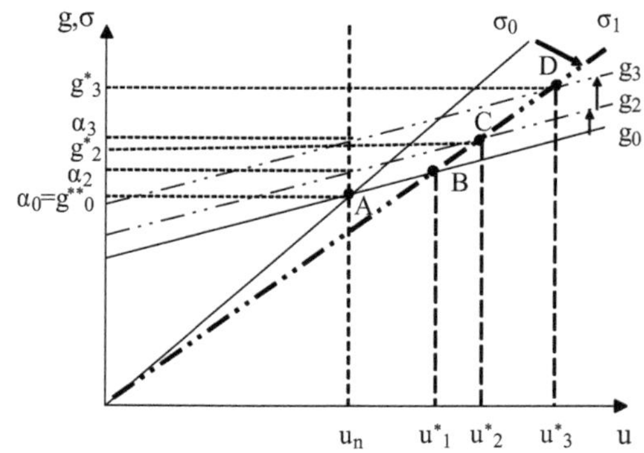

Figure 3.2 Harrodian instability in the basic neo-Kaleckian/Steindlian model

first-generation post-Keynesian Kaldor-Robinson distribution and growth model, which assumes normal or full capacity utilisation in long-run growth equilibrium (Hein 2014, chapter 4.5; Lavoie 2014, chapter 6.1). Whenever aggregate demand growth exceeds supply growth at the normal rate of capacity utilisation, and capacity utilisation tends to exceed the normal rate, increases in the price level and the profit share brings the economy back towards the normal rate of utilisation by means of restraining demand growth. In the present model, the Cambridge price mechanism would thus mean a rotation of the saving rate function in Figure 3.2 such that an intersection with the shifted accumulation rate function at the normal rate of utilisation is re-established. However, the Cambridge price mechanism is not generally convincing as a stabiliser, because lower real wages (or a lower wage share) that are negotiated and accepted by workers and labour unions can hardly be squared with low unemployment rates and more powerful labour unions that are associated with utilisation rates exceeding the normal rate. Rising real wages and higher wage shares enforced by stronger labour unions and thus falling profit shares, as implied by Kalecki (1954, Chapters 1–2, 1971, Chapters 5–6, 14), or a price-wage-price spiral, hence Robinson's (1962, p. 58) 'inflation barrier', are therefore more likely outcomes. Redistribution in favour of the wage share would then bring our model farther away from the normal rate of utilisation.[6] And accelerating inflation cannot be considered a long-run equilibrium condition either.

Accelerating inflation would require the introduction of economic policy responses in order to bring the system back to the normal rate of capacity utilisation. This is the mechanism proposed in the model by Duménil/Lévy (1999). In their model, whenever short-run equilibrium capacity utilisation exceeds (falls short of) the normal rate, inflationary (disinflationary) pressures will be triggered, and monetary authorities will respond with restrictive (expansive) policies to bring the system back to stable inflation at the normal rate of utilisation. In our simple model this would mean that we make the capital accumulation function in equation (3) interest-elastic, so that the adjustment towards the normal rate of capacity utilisation would be achieved by an appropriate shift in the accumulation function in Figure 3.2. However, this adjustment process cannot be taken for granted either, as soon as distribution and cost effects of unexpected inflation and of changes in the monetary policy instrument – the interest rate – are taken into account (Lima/Setterfield 2010). In particular, changes in the interest rate will have an influence both on the actual and on the normal rate of utilisation. The normal rate as understood by Duménil/Lévy – a non-accelerating inflation rate of capacity utilisation (NAICU) – is hence affected by the actual goods market equilibrium rate of utilisation via monetary policy interventions, and the former becomes endogenous to the latter, albeit in an indirect and complex way (Hein 2006; Hein 2008, chapters 16 and 17; Hein/Lavoie/van Treeck 2012).

Apart from economic policies as a stabiliser in the face of Harrodian instability, other models have been suggested in which instability is contained or even prevented by the behaviour of capitalist firms themselves. Shaikh (2009) assumes that firms increase their retention ratio as soon as utilisation exceeds its normal rate, thus leading to an increase in the overall saving rate. It is hence a rotation of the saving rate function in Figure 3.2, which brings back the economic system to the normal rate of utilisation. Harrodian instability is thus contained. However, the economic rationale for such behaviour is far from obvious. For example, Dallery/van Treeck (2011) argue that the retention ratio may be endogenous, but under the current paradigm of shareholder value orientation, managers may not be able to change the retention ratio on the basis of the discrepancy between the actual and the normal rates of capacity utilisation, because the decision to distribute profits is likely to be determined by the shareholders' power and claims on profitability. In an alternative model, Shaikh (2009) assumes that firms reduce their accumulation rate as soon as the actual growth rate of sales exceeds the assessed long-run rate, thus shifting down the accumulation rate function in Figure 3.2. Harrodian instability is hence avoided and utilisation is back at the normal rate. However, this kind of behaviour requires rational expectations on the side of the firms – firms have to know the growth rate of sales when making their investment decisions. But this rate is determined by the actual investment decisions of other firms. There is thus a coordination problem, which is swept away by Shaikh in this model, as also argued by Franke (2015).

In Skott's (2010, 2012) models of a 'mature economy', that is an economy with inelastic labour supply, Harrodian instability is bounded by a Marxian labour market mechanism which generates a limit cycle around the steady growth path determined by labour force growth and the normal rate of utilisation. Capitalists reduce output growth as soon as actual utilisation rates exceed the normal rate, because the rate of unemployment falls and approaches some critically low value, and firms increasingly have problems in recruiting additional labour. Workers and labour unions are strengthened vis-à-vis management, workers' militancy increases, monitoring and surveillance costs rise, and hence the overall business climate deteriorates. This negative effect of increasing employment finally dominates the production decisions of firms, output growth declines, capacity utilisation rates fall, investment falters and, finally, profitability declines. In our simple model, this means again that the capital accumulation function in Figure 3.2 gets shifted downwards whenever utilisation exceeds the normal rate. But also Skott's behavioural assumptions lack plausibility when applied to a capitalist market economy characterised by decentralised production and investment decisions as well as competitive pressures. As already argued, with tight labour markets, either rising real wages and higher wage shares, which would move the actual rate of utilisation further away from the normal rate in our model (and which would be stabilising only in a profit-led regime generated in a post-Kaleckian model), or a destabilising price-wage-price spiral can be expected – or a combination of both.

In the following sections we will look at the properties of the Steindlian stabilisation mechanisms in the face of Harrodian instability, amending our basic model.

Steindlian stabilisation I: endogenous capital scrapping and replacement

The first approach based on Steindl's work focuses on an endogenous capital-potential output ratio ($v = K/Y^p$) instead of an endogenous rate of capacity utilisation ($u = Y/Y^p$) as an adjustment variable in the long run. This can make the output-capital ratio *Y/K* a variable, although the rate of capacity utilisation may be equal to a given and constant normal rate. This approach can be based on Steindl (1979, p. 115), who has argued that

> a high growth rate and high utilisation will tend to retard withdrawal of equipment . . . a low growth rate and utilisation will lead to some premature withdrawal of equipment.

As previously noted, Cassetti (2006) has already made use of such a mechanism, claiming that the rate of capital scrapping is sped up (slowed down) as long as the actual rate of capacity utilisation lies below (above) its normal rate. Similarly, Allain/Canry (2008) argue that low (high) rates of capacity utilisation will lead to more (fewer) bankruptcies, which entail more (less) capital scrapping and hence a reduction (an increase) of the available capacity. As a result, demand will be spread over a reduced (enlarged) available capacity, thus tending to reduce the discrepancy between measured rates of capacity utilisation and their normal value. Also, Schoder (2014) claims that the capital-potential output ratio will rise (fall) when demand is low (high) and the rate of utilisation has a tendency to fall short of (exceed) the normal rate. He also presents some empirical evidence for this argument based on US manufacturing data (1955–2012). However, the mechanism he refers to is related not to capital scrapping as such but rather to counter-cyclical capital-potential output ratios via the (speed of) implementation of technical progress and via the variation of the number of shifts.[7]

Inspired by the approach of Cassetti (2006), we can introduce the notion of endogenous capital scrapping and replacement by extending the saving and investment equations (2) and (3):

$$\sigma = s_{\Pi} h \frac{u}{v} + \delta, \qquad 0 < s_{\Pi} \leq 1, \delta \geq 0 \qquad (10)$$

$$g = \alpha + \beta(u - u_n) + \rho, \qquad \alpha, \beta > 0, \rho \geq 0 \qquad (11)$$

The gross saving function now includes saving out of profits and the depreciation of the capital stock. The gross investment function includes net investment and replacement investment determined by capital scrapping.

The rate of depreciation relative to the gross capital stock in value terms (δ) that is included in the saving function may deviate from the actual rate of physical capital scrapping (ρ), which requires replacement investment, in the accumulation function. As shown by Bhaduri (1972), the replacement rate will usually fall behind the depreciation rate, since the former is a decreasing function of growth whereas the latter is a constant. In a growing economy, $\delta - \rho$ will thus be positive. This means that firms will accumulate non-reinvested depreciations as part of gross profits, which, cet. par., will put downward pressure on aggregate demand. Only in a stationary state will $\delta = \rho$ hold, provided that planned and actual lifetime of a capital good are equal. Apart from this, firms may either decide to drop machinery, etc., prematurely, or they may decide to keep the already-depreciated capital goods operating in the firm. In the former case, the difference $\delta - \rho$ will decline relative to its trend. In the latter, it will rise relative to the trend. The short-run equilibrium derived from equations (4), (10) and (11) now turns into:

$$u^* = \frac{\alpha - \beta u_n + \rho - \delta}{s_\Pi \frac{h}{v} - \beta} \tag{12}$$

$$g^* = \sigma^* = \frac{s_\Pi \frac{h}{v}(\alpha - \beta u_n + \rho) - \beta\delta}{s_\Pi \frac{h}{v} - \beta} \tag{13}$$

The rate of capital scrapping has a positive effect on the short-run equilibrium rates of capacity utilisation and accumulation. An increase of this rate reduces the capital stock, raises the demand for newly produced investment goods, aggregate demand, capacity utilisation and hence accumulation. A reduction in the scrapping and replacement rate increases the capital stock and will reduce utilisation and accumulation. As noted earlier, a fall in the scrapping rate is endogenous to positive growth, but it may also be reinforced by decisions of firms to extend the use of already-depreciated capital goods.

For the short-run equilibrium we obtain the well-known properties of the neo-Kaleckian distribution and growth model. Whereas the scrapping rate has a positive effect on equilibrium capacity utilisation, accumulation and growth, the depreciation rate has a negative effect. Firms' assessment of long-run growth positively affects the equilibrium values. The paradox of saving and the paradox of costs will hold; aggregate demand, capital accumulation and growth are thus wage-led:

$$\frac{\partial u^*}{\partial s_\Pi} = \frac{-\frac{h}{v}(\alpha - \beta u_n + \rho - \delta)}{\left(s_\Pi \frac{h}{v} - \beta\right)^2} = \frac{-\frac{h}{v}u^*}{s_\Pi \frac{h}{v} - \beta} < 0 \tag{12a}$$

$$\frac{\partial g^*}{\partial s_\Pi} = \frac{-\beta \frac{h}{v}(\alpha - \beta u_n + \rho - \delta)}{\left(s_\Pi \frac{h}{v} - \beta\right)^2} = \frac{-\beta \frac{h}{v} u^*}{s_\Pi \frac{h}{v} - \beta} < 0- \tag{13a}$$

$$\frac{\partial u^*}{\partial h} = \frac{-\frac{s_\Pi}{v}(\alpha - \beta u_n + \rho - \delta)}{\left(s_\Pi \frac{h}{v} - \beta\right)^2} = \frac{-\frac{s_\Pi}{v} u^*}{s_\Pi \frac{h}{v} - \beta} < 0 \tag{12b}$$

$$\frac{\partial g^*}{\partial h} = \frac{-\beta \frac{s_\Pi}{v}(\alpha - \beta u_n + \rho - \delta)}{\left(s_\Pi \frac{h}{v} - \beta\right)^2} = \frac{-\beta \frac{s_\Pi}{v} u^*}{s_\Pi \frac{h}{v} - \beta} < 0 \tag{13b}$$

As suggested by Steindl (1979), Allain/Canry (2008) and Cassetti (2006), capital scrapping and replacement will now depend on the dynamics of demand. On the one hand, this means that the scrapping rate will be negatively affected by the rate of capital accumulation, as already noticed by Harrod (1970) and formally shown by Bhaduri (1972). On the other hand, this means that the capital scrapping rate will also depend on the deviation of the short-run goods market equilibrium rate of capacity utilisation from the normal or the firms' target rate of utilisation. Since a higher short-run equilibrium rate of capital accumulation will be associated with a higher rate of capacity utilisation, we make use of a simple dynamic equation in line with Cassetti (2006) and also with Steindl (1979, p. 116), who argues that the change in the difference between the depreciation and the scrapping rate 'acts, however, only as long as the transition to a new equilibrium proceeds':[8]

$$\dot{\rho} = \psi\left(u^* - u_n\right), \ \psi < 0 \tag{14}$$

Higher growth rates and short-run equilibrium rates of utilisation above the normal or target rate will reduce the capital scrapping rate, increase productive capacity, dampen investment demand and hence aggregate demand and thus also capacity utilisation. This may then stabilise the Harrodian instability process described in equation (9). Therefore, in equations (9) and (14) we now have a two-dimensional dynamic system. Plugging in equation (12) for the short-run equilibrium rate of capacity utilisation, we can evaluate the Jacobian Matrix for this system:

$$J = \begin{pmatrix} \frac{\partial \dot{\alpha}}{\partial \alpha} & \frac{\partial \dot{\alpha}}{\partial \rho} \\ \frac{\partial \dot{\rho}}{\partial \alpha} & \frac{\partial \dot{\rho}}{\partial \rho} \end{pmatrix} \tag{15}$$

Local stability of the long-run equilibrium requires a negative trace and a non-negative determinant for the Jacobian matrix of the dynamic system. From equations (9), (12) and (14) we obtain:

$$TrJ = \frac{\upsilon + \psi}{s_{\Pi}\frac{h}{v} - \beta} < 0, \; if: \upsilon + \psi < 0 \qquad (16)$$

$$DetJ = 0 \qquad (17)$$

With a zero determinant and hence one zero eigenvalue, we have a zero root model, and the system displays a continuum of (locally) stable equilibria and thus path dependence, as acknowledged by Cassetti (2006).

Assuming the short-run stability condition (5) to hold, for long-run stability it is thus required that the speed of change in capital scrapping exceeds the Harrodian instability parameter: $-\psi > \upsilon$. Whether the change in the scrapping rate is able to contain Harrodian instability is thus an empirical question; it depends on the relative strengths of each of these forces. Graphically this can be shown as in Figure 3.3.

If we start again in the initial equilibrium in point A, assume a fall in the propensity to save out of profits or a fall in the profit share and thus a clockwise rotation in the saving function from σ_0 to σ_1, the economy will move to a short-run equilibrium in point B. This will then trigger the Harrodian instability process, shifting up the investment function from g_0 to g_2 through a rise in the firms' assessment of the trend rate of growth from α_0 to α_2. This will move the economy towards the new short-run equilibrium in point C. If the change in capital scrapping is supposed to bring the economy back to the normal rate, the scrapping rate will have to fall from ρ_0 to ρ_2, which will reduce gross capital stock growth relative to net capital stock growth. For this to happen, we need $-\dot{\rho} > \dot{\alpha}$ and hence $-\psi > \upsilon$, as derived earlier. In the new long-run equilibrium

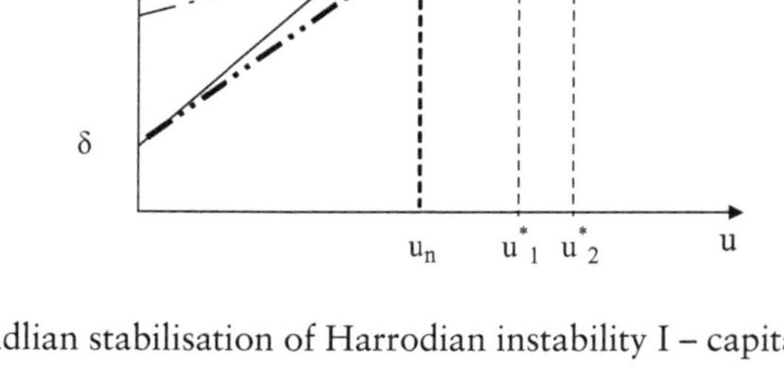

Figure 3.3 Steindlian stabilisation of Harrodian instability I – capital scrapping

at the normal rate of capacity utilisation, we now have a higher net accumulation rate ($\alpha_2 > \alpha_0$) but a lower gross accumulation rate ($\alpha_2 + \rho_2 < \alpha_0 + \rho_0$). The former does not mean an increasing rate of demand for and production of new capital goods but rather an increasing rate of use of existing capital goods due to the reduction in the scrapping rate and hence in the replacement rate. Furthermore, the share of depreciation in gross saving (δ/σ) is higher in the new long-run equilibrium than in the equilibrium from which we have started, because σ is now lower whereas δ has been assumed to be constant.

For the long-run equilibrium rates of capacity utilisation and capital accumulation presented in Figure 3.3, we obtain:

$$u^{**} = u_n \tag{18}$$

$$g^{**} = \alpha_2 + \rho_2 = \alpha_0 + \rho_0 + (\upsilon + \psi)\left(u_1^* - u_n\right) \tag{19}$$

Since both firms' assessment of the long-run growth rate (α) and the rate of capital scrapping (ρ) turn endogenous, the long-run equilibrium rate of capital accumulation at $u^{**} = u_n$ will now depend on the initial values of firms' assessment of long-run growth (α_0) and the initial values of the scrapping rate (ρ_0), as well as on the adjustment triggered by any deviation of the short-run goods market equilibrium rate of capacity utilisation from the normal rate. If the long-run stability condition holds, i.e. $\upsilon + \psi < 0$, a positive deviation of u^* from u_n will force the long-run equilibrium rate of capital accumulation down, while a negative deviation will force it up. A stable long-run equilibrium thus turns to be path dependent.

As is already obvious from Figure 3.3, in the long run the paradox of saving as well as wage-led growth will disappear. A fall in the propensity to save out of profits or in the profit share, each of which may cause the clockwise rotation of the saving function, will lead to a lower accumulation rate in the new long-run equilibrium. Higher accumulation and growth would require a higher propensity to save and/or a higher profit share. Alternatively, also the depreciation rate could rise which would mean an upwards shift in the gross saving function in Figure 3.3. Growth thus turns profit-led in the long run. This can also be shown by plugging equation (12) into equation (19) and deriving the respective partial derivatives:

$$\frac{\partial g^{**}}{\partial s_\Pi} = \frac{-(\upsilon+\psi)\frac{h}{v}(\alpha_0 - \beta u_n + \rho_0 - \delta)}{\left(s_\Pi \frac{h}{v} - \beta\right)^2} = \frac{-(\upsilon+\psi)\frac{h}{v}u_1^*}{s_\Pi \frac{h}{v} - \beta} > 0 \tag{19a}$$

$$\frac{\partial g^{**}}{\partial h} = \frac{-(\upsilon+\psi)\frac{s_\Pi}{v}(\alpha_0 - \beta u_n + \rho_0 - \delta)}{\left(s_\Pi \frac{h}{v} - \beta\right)^2} = \frac{-(\upsilon+\psi)\frac{s_\Pi}{v}u_1^*}{s_\Pi \frac{h}{v} - \beta} > 0 \tag{19b}$$

Table 3.1 Responses of stable short- and long-run equilibria to changes in exogenous variables

	Short-run equilibria		*Long-run equilibria*			
	u^*	g^*	u^{**}	g^{**}	α^{**}	ρ^{**}
α	+	+	0			
ρ	+	+	0			
δ	–	–	0	+	–	+
s_{Π}	–	–	0	+	–	+
h	–	–	0	+	–	+

$$\frac{\partial g^{**}}{\partial \delta} = \frac{-(v+\psi)}{s_{\Pi}\frac{h}{v}-\beta} > 0 \tag{19c}$$

We can finally summarise our findings for the short- and long-run stable equilibria of the capital scrapping model as in Table 3.1.

Steindlian stabilisation II: government financial balances

Let us now look at a second potential mechanism which may dampen or reverse Harrodian instability, the change in government budget balances and the related effects on the aggregate propensity to save. Steindl (1979, p. 113), discussing downward Harrodian instability, amends the stabilising mechanism discussed in the previous section, the increase in the scrapping and replacement rate, by referring to government's financial balances:

> This downward movement may be braked by increased drop-outs of equipment and, if government is introduced into the model, by automatically increasing budget deficits.

Since there is this tendency of the drop-out rate to fall increasingly short of the depreciation rate with positive growth in the long run, he finally relies on government deficits as the only way out in order to prevent persistent utilisation problems and the related downward instability and long-run stagnation problems. Also in Steindl (1985, pp. 161–162), it is argued that the increase in the budget deficit (and in the foreign balance surplus) will soften the downward pressure on aggregate demand triggered by a rigid or even rising profit share in an economy dominated by oligopolies:[9]

> But there is, of course, the budget deficit which as explained above, may contribute a great deal to the accommodation of a low growth rate.

Somewhat paradoxically, the flexibility of the budget facilitates the rigidity of the profit margin.

Including the role of government financial balances into our simple neo-Kaleckian/Steindlian model, we assume for simplicity that there are no taxes and that government expenditures are financed by credit creation, or even more simply by money creation which relieves us from considering government interest payments. The government deficit rate (d), relating government deficits to the capital stock, can therefore be included into the saving function of our model which turns into:

$$\sigma = s_{\Pi} h \frac{u}{v} - d, \quad 0 < s_{\Pi} \leq 1, d \geq 0 \tag{20}$$

From equations (2), (4) and (20) we obtain the short-run equilibrium values for capacity utilisation and capital accumulation:

$$u^{*} = \frac{\alpha - \beta u_n + d}{s_{\Pi} \frac{h}{v} - \beta} \tag{21}$$

$$g^{*} = \sigma^{*} = \frac{s_{\Pi} \frac{h}{v} (\alpha - \beta u_n) + \beta d}{s_{\Pi} \frac{h}{v} - \beta} \tag{22}$$

It will not come as a surprise that the paradox of saving holds in this variant too, as does the paradox of costs and hence wage-led demand and growth:

$$\frac{\partial u^{*}}{\partial s_{\Pi}} = \frac{-\frac{h}{v}(\alpha - \beta u_n + d)}{\left(s_{\Pi} \frac{h}{v} - \beta\right)^2} = \frac{-\frac{h}{v} u^{*}}{s_{\Pi} \frac{h}{v} - \beta} < 0 \tag{21a}$$

$$\frac{\partial g^{*}}{\partial s_{\Pi}} = \frac{-\beta \frac{h}{v}(\alpha - \beta u_n + d)}{\left(s_{\Pi} \frac{h}{v} - \beta\right)^2} = \frac{-\beta \frac{h}{v} u^{*}}{s_{\Pi} \frac{h}{v} - \beta} < 0 \tag{22a}$$

$$\frac{\partial u^{*}}{\partial h} = \frac{-\frac{s_{\Pi}}{v}(\alpha - \beta u_n + d)}{\left(s_{\Pi} \frac{h}{v} - \beta\right)^2} = \frac{-\frac{s_{\Pi}}{v} u^{*}}{s_{\Pi} \frac{h}{v} - \beta} < 0 \tag{21b}$$

$$\frac{\partial g^{*}}{\partial h} = \frac{-\beta \frac{s_{\Pi}}{v}(\alpha - \beta u_n + d)}{\left(s_{\Pi} \frac{h}{v} - \beta\right)^2} = \frac{-\beta \frac{s_{\Pi}}{v} u^{*}}{s_{\Pi} \frac{h}{v} - \beta} < 0 \tag{22b}$$

Automatic stabilisers and discretionary fiscal policies will affect the government deficit rate in a counter-cyclical way:

$$\dot{d} = \gamma\left(u^{*} - u_{n}\right), \ \gamma < 0 \tag{23}$$

Equation (23) can be seen as a dynamic version of the functional finance approach proposed by Lerner (1943), in which government financial balances and thus fiscal policies should stabilise the economy at some target, here given by the normal rate of capacity utilisation, irrespective of the size of the required government deficit and the accumulated stock of government debt.[10]

In equations (9) and (23) we have again a two-dimensional dynamic system for the long run of this model. Plugging in equation (21) for the short-run equilibrium rate of capacity utilisation, we can evaluate the Jacobian matrix for this system:

$$J = \begin{pmatrix} \frac{\partial \dot{\alpha}}{\partial \alpha} & \frac{\partial \dot{\alpha}}{\partial d} \\ \frac{\partial \dot{d}}{\partial \alpha} & \frac{\partial \dot{d}}{\partial d} \end{pmatrix} \tag{24}$$

Local stability of the long-run equilibrium requires a negative trace and a non-negative determinant for the Jacobian matrix of the dynamic system. From equations (9), (21) and (23) we obtain:

$$TrJ = \frac{\upsilon + \gamma}{s_{\Pi}\frac{h}{v} - \beta} < 0, \ if: \upsilon + \gamma < 0 \tag{25}$$

$$DetJ = 0 \tag{26}$$

Assuming the short-run stability condition (5) to hold, for long-run stability it is thus required that the speed of change in the government deficit rate exceeds the Harrodian instability parameter. Long-run stability thus becomes an issue of the responsiveness of fiscal policies. With a zero determinant, we have again a zero root model with a continuum of (locally) stable equilibria and hence path dependence. Graphically, this can be shown as in Figure 3.4.

We start again in the initial equilibrium in point A, assume a fall in the propensity to save out of profits or a fall in the profit share and thus a clockwise rotation in the saving function from σ_0 to σ_1, which will move the economy to a short-run equilibrium in point B. This will then trigger the Harrodian instability process raising firms' assessment of long-run growth from α_0 to α_2, shifting up the investment function from g_0 to g_2 and moving the economy towards the new short-run equilibrium in point C. Counter-cyclical

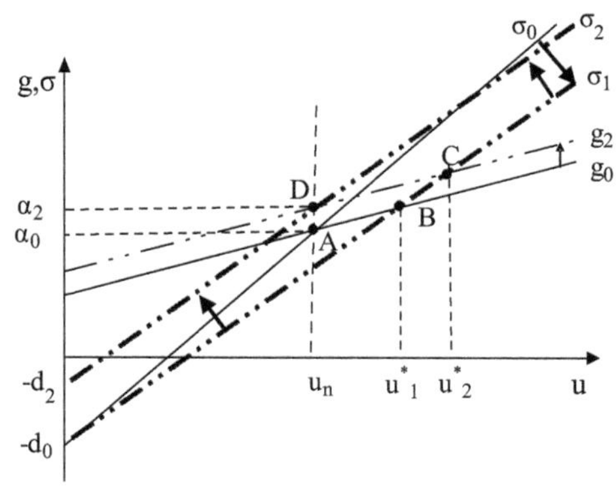

Figure 3.4 Steindlian stabilisation of Harrodian instability II – government financial balances

government expenditures, both automatic and discretionary, will have to reduce the government deficit rate from d_0 to d_2, which shifts the total saving function up from σ_1 to σ_2. If the change in the government deficit rate is sufficiently strong, this will move the economy back to the normal rate of utilisation at point D. For stability, we need $-\dot{d} > \dot{\alpha}$ and hence $-\gamma > \upsilon$. In the new long-run equilibrium at the normal rate of capacity utilisation, we now have a higher accumulation rate ($\alpha_2 > \alpha_0$) due to the interim improvement of firms' assessment of the trend rate of growth, which is more than compensated for by a lower government deficit rate ($d_2 < d_0$), so that we have $d_2 - d_0 > \alpha_2 - \alpha_0$. Therefore, we will now have a higher rate of accumulation and growth, and a higher saving rate due to the endogenous accommodation of the government deficit rate. For the long run equilibrium in Figure 3.4, we thus obtain:

$$u^{**} = u_n \tag{27}$$

$$g^{**} = \alpha_2 = \alpha_0 + \upsilon\left(u_1^* - u_n\right) \tag{28}$$

$$d^{**} = d_2 = d_0 + \gamma\left(u_1^* - u_n\right) \tag{29}$$

In the long run, both firms' assessment of the long-run growth rate (α) and the government deficit rate (d) are now endogenous. The long-run equilibrium rate of capital accumulation at $u^{**} = u_n$ will thus depend on the initial values of firms' assessment of long-run growth (α_0) and on the adjustment triggered by the deviation of the short-run goods market equilibrium rate of capacity utilisation from the normal rate. A positive deviation of u^* from u_n will force the long-run equilibrium rate of capital accumulation up; a negative deviation will force it down. The long-run government deficit rate will over-compensate for this and will move down if u^* exceeds u_n, and will move up when u^* falls short of u_n, and will thus guarantee that the economy will converge towards the long-run equilibrium. The stable long-run equilibrium rates of capital accumulation and the related government deficit rate are thus path dependent.

As is already clear from Figure 3.4, the paradox of saving as well as wage-led growth will now also hold in the stable long-run equilibrium. A fall in the propensity to save out of profits or in the profit share, each of which may cause the clockwise rotation of the saving function, will lead to a higher accumulation rate in the new long-run equilibrium. Higher accumulation and growth require a higher overall saving rate, which is provided by a lower government deficit rate. Growth thus remains wage-led with proper government adjustments, even if the economy operates at a given normal rate of utilisation in the long run. This can also be shown by plugging equation (21) into equations (28) and (29) and deriving the respective partial derivatives:

$$\frac{\partial g^{**}}{\partial s_\Pi} = \frac{-\upsilon\frac{h}{v}(\alpha_0 - \beta u_n + d_0)}{\left(s_\Pi\frac{h}{v} - \beta\right)^2} = \frac{-\upsilon\frac{h}{v}u_1^*}{s_\Pi\frac{h}{v} - \beta} < 0 \tag{28a}$$

$$\frac{\partial g^{**}}{\partial h} = \frac{-\upsilon\frac{s_\Pi}{v}(\alpha_0 - \beta u_n + d_0)}{\left(s_\Pi\frac{h}{v} - \beta\right)^2} = \frac{-\upsilon\frac{s_\Pi}{v}u_1^*}{s_\Pi\frac{h}{v} - \beta} < 0 \tag{28b}$$

$$\frac{\partial d^{**}}{\partial s_\Pi} = \frac{-\gamma\frac{h}{v}(\alpha_0 - \beta u_n + d_0)}{\left(s_\Pi\frac{h}{v} - \beta\right)^2} = \frac{-\gamma\frac{h}{v}u_1^*}{s_\Pi\frac{h}{v} - \beta} > 0 \tag{29a}$$

$$\frac{\partial d^{**}}{\partial h} = \frac{-\gamma\frac{s_\Pi}{v}(\alpha_0 - \beta u_n + d_0)}{\left(s_\Pi\frac{h}{v} - \beta\right)^2} = \frac{-\gamma\frac{s_\Pi}{v}u_1^*}{s_\Pi\frac{h}{v} - \beta} > 0 \tag{29b}$$

Table 3.2 summarises our results for the short- and long-run stable equilibria of the model with government financial balances as a stabiliser of Harrodian instability.

The mechanism providing these long-run results bears some similarities with the recent approaches introducing a Sraffian supermultiplier process into Kaleckian models of distribution and growth, as referred to in the introduction. In those models, the autonomous growth rate of a non-capacity creating component of aggregate demand, i.e. autonomous consumption, residential investment, exports or government expenditures, determines long-run growth and provides for a stable adjustment towards the normal

Table 3.2 Responses of stable short- and long-run equilibria to changes in exogenous variables

	Short-run equilibria		*Long-run equilibria*			
	u^*	g^*	u^{**}	g^{**}	α^{**}	d^{**}
α	+	+	0			
d	+	+	0			
s_Π	–	–	0	–	–	+
h	–	–	0	–	–	+

rate of capacity utilisation, under the condition that Harrodian instability in the investment function is not too strong. However, in those models, a change in the propensity to save or in the profit share will have no effect on the long-run growth rate but will affect only the long-run growth path. The paradox of saving and the paradox of costs from the short run thus disappear with respect to long-run growth. In our model, however, in which government expenditure is not constrained by an expenditure path rule, we have maintained the two paradoxes also with respect to the long-run growth rate.

Conclusions

Starting from the debate on Harrodian instability in Kaleckian distribution and growth models, in this chapter we have focused on two stabilising mechanism to be found in Steindl's work, a variable capital scrapping rate and the variation of government financial balances. Each of these mechanisms may affect Harrod's warranted rate of growth, preserving a given and constant normal or target rate of capacity utilisation. A variable capital scrapping rate has an impact on the capital-potential output ratio; a variable government deficit affects the economy-wide propensity to save. We have integrated each of these mechanisms into the elementary model framework to deal with Harrodian instability in Kaleckian models proposed by Hein/Lavoie/van Treeck (2011, 2012) and have derived the conditions under which these processes will stabilise the economy at a normal rate of capacity utilisation in the long run. We have not examined the joint effects of the two stabilising mechanisms but would assume that they will not contradict each other in the sense that 'two stabilising mechanisms may be jointly destabilising', a possibility Franke (2019b) has recently shown.

Since the long-run dynamic models turn out to be zero root models, with the long-run stability conditions given, the long-run equilibrium rates of capital accumulation and growth turn path dependent. For the capital scrapping model, we have shown that for the path-dependent long-run equilibria the paradoxes of thrift and costs, and hence wage-led growth, although prevailing in the short run, will disappear in the long run. For this model, a higher propensity to save and a higher profit share will each lead to a higher rate of growth in long-run equilibrium; growth thus turns profit-led in the long run. For the model with government financial balances, the paradoxes of saving and costs are maintained in the long-run equilibrium and the economy remains wage led. A lower propensity to save and a lower profit share will each lead to a higher rate of accumulation and growth in the long run, and to a lower government deficit rate.

Whether the long-run stability conditions actually prevail and whether the Steindlian mechanisms are strong enough to prevent global Harrodian instability, stabilising the economy at a given and constant normal rate of utilisation, is an empirical question with regard to the capital scrapping rate and an economic policy question with regard to the government deficit rate. As we have mentioned in the previous section, Steindl (1979) himself argues that the capital scrapping mechanism will need to be amended by the proper adjustment of government financial balances, particularly in the long run of an oligopolistic economy. And, regarding government financial balances, he is quite pessimistic because of the change in the economic policy stance in the mid-to-late 1970s, which he terms 'stagnation policy', i.e. the reluctance to accept the required government deficits to improve capacity utilisation (and employment).[11] The result, however, is not a violent downturn of the economy, which would have to be stabilised by other forces, but rather stagnation as a trend with persistently low rates of capacity utilisation. This is also in line with Steindl's (1952, p. 12) earlier microeconomic conclusion, which we have previously quoted, that '[t]here is no good reason why a state of disequilibrium, with undesired excess capacity, should not persist. For practical purposes, disequilibrium may be permanent'. This is also consistent with viewing a normal or target rate of utilisation rather as a corridor than a fixed and given point. Only if the economy is driven out of the corridor are stabilising processes required, among them the two Steindlian processes, which seem to be more plausible then the other mechanism proposed by Duménil/Levy, Shaikh and Skott, discussed in Hein/Lavoie/van Treeck (2011) and briefly reviewed earlier in this chapter. Furthermore, we should also be aware that in his later work, even Harrod (1948, pp. 89–91; 1959; 1973, pp. 32–37) himself discussed and allowed for the endogeneity of the warranted rate growth within bounds, through changes in the average propensity to save based on distributional effects of variations in demand, through changes in the capital-potential output ratio in the course of the cycle because of autonomous investment, and also through changes in the firms' target rate of utilisation. Furthermore, he has argued with respect to the warranted rate of growth that '[i]t requires a fairly large deviation, . . . to bring the instability principle into play' (Harrod 1973, p. 33). Therefore, both Steindl and Harrod would probably advise current heterodox authors not to become overly obsessed with Harrodian instability, but, of course, to consider it as a serious problem which may arise if economies are driven out of some normal corridor and enter into particularly deep recessions.

Notes

1 The paradox of costs and a unique wage-led demand and growth regime, i.e. a higher profit share having a depressing effect on the equilibrium rates of capacity utilisation, profit, capital accumulation and growth, is a feature of the neo-Kaleckian distribution and growth model for a closed private economy, as initially proposed by Rowthorn (1981) and Dutt (1984, 1987). However, in the open economy version of this model by Blecker (1989) and then in the post-Kaleckian model put forward by Bhaduri/Marglin (1990) and Kurz (1990), we have the possibility of wage-led or profit-led regimes, or some intermediate cases, depending on model parameters. See Blecker (2002), Hein (2014, chapters 6–7) and Lavoie (2014, chapter 6.2 and 6.3) for overviews.

2 For a recent assessment of this mechanism, see the critical contribution by Girardi/Pariboni (2019) and the more supportive modelling in Franke (2020).

3 See, for example, Allain (2015, 2019), Fiebiger (2018), Fiebiger/Lavoie (2019), Lavoie (2016), Nah/Lavoie (2017, 2018, 2019a, 2019b), Palley (2019), Pariboni (2016); for a recent controversy, see Lavoie (2017) and Skott (2017); for a recent survey, see Dutt (2019); for some further critical assessments, see Nikiforos (2018) and Skott (2019).

4 Franke (2019a) has recently proposed another stabilising mechanism via the capital-output ratio making use of Harrod's notion of long-run capital outlays which are not affected by demand dynamics in the goods market. As Franke acknowledges, such a mechanism can be found in the early trade cycle models by Kaldor and Kalecki.

5 See also Hein (2014, chapter 11).

6 See Hein/Stockhammer (2010) for an analysis of a neo-Kaleckian model with conflict inflation. Within a post-Kaleckian model, however, redistribution in favour of wages may dampen aggregate demand and capital accumulation and thus stabilize the economy around the normal rate of capacity utilisation, provided that the economy is in a profit-led regime. See Stockhammer (2004a; 2004b, chapter 2) for a stability analysis of the post-Kaleckian model.

7 For the latter mechanism see also Nikiforos (2013, 2016).

8 According to Steindl (1979), a pro-cyclical change in the profit share through overhead cost digression and counter-cyclicality in the intensity of price competition, and thus a shift (or rotation) in the saving function, contributes to the convergence towards the new equilibrium in a competitive economy. However, in an oligopolistic economy, the profit share remains rather rigid and misses sufficient downward flexibility, in particular, thus blocking this adjustment mechanism. A long-run downwardly flexible utilisation rate replaces the flexible profit share – and contributes to further stagnation. See also Steindl (1985).

9 Upwards instability, however, is limited by capacity constraints: 'Bottlenecks make it impossible for the real investment to increase beyond a certain volume, and via the multiplier the rest of the economy is constrained too. This is the basic reason why the boom usually does not get out of hand' (Steindl 1985, p. 156).

10 For a more extensive analysis of government deficit and debt dynamics in Kaleckian distribution and growth models, see Dutt (2013), Hein (2018a) and You/Dutt (1996), for example.

11 For an application of the Steindlian concept of 'stagnation policy' to the current stagnation tendencies in general and in the Eurozone in particular, see Hein (2016, 2018b).

References

Allain, O. (2015), 'Tackling the instability of growth: a Kaleckian-Harrodian model with an autonomous expenditure component', *Cambridge Journal of Economics*, 39 (5), 1351–1371.

Allain, O. (2019), 'Demographic growth, Harrodian (in)stability and the supermultiplier', *Cambridge Journal of Economics*, 43 (1), 85–106.

Allain, P., Canry, N. (2008), 'Growth, capital scrapping, and the rate of capacity utilisation', paper presented at the 12th conference of the Research Network Macroeconomics and Macroeconomic Policies, October 2008, Berlin.

Bhaduri, A. (1972), 'Unwanted amortisation funds: a mathematical treatment', *The Economic Journal*, 82, 674–677.

Bhaduri, A., Marglin, S. (1990), 'Unemployment and the real wage: the economic basis for contesting political ideologies', *Cambridge Journal of Economics*, 14, 375–393.

Blecker, R.A. (1989), 'International competition, income distribution and economic growth', *Cambridge Journal of Economics*, 13, 395–412.

Blecker, R.A. (2002), 'Distribution, demand and growth in neo-Kaleckian macromodels', in M. Setterfield (ed), *The Economics of Demand-Led Growth*, Cheltenham: Edward Elgar.

Cassetti, M. (2006), 'A note on the long-run behaviour of Kaleckian models', *Review of Political Economy*, 18 (4), 497–508.

Chick, V., Caserta, M. (1997), 'Provisional equilibrium in macroeconomic theory', in P. Arestis, G. Palma and M. Sawyer (eds), *Capital Controversy, Post-Keynesian Economics and the History of Economic Thought: Essays in Honour of Geoff Harcourt*, London: Routledge.

Dallery, T., van Treeck, T. (2011), 'Conflicting claims and equilibrium adjustment processes in a stock-flow consistent macro model', *Review of Political Economy*, 23, 189–211.

Duménil, G., Lévy, D. (1999), 'Being Keynesian in the short term and classical in the long term: the traverse to classical long-term equilibrium', *The Manchester School*, 67, 684–716.

Dutt, A.K. (1984), 'Stagnation, income distribution and monopoly power', *Cambridge Journal of Economics*, 8 (1), 25–40.

Dutt, A.K. (1987), 'Alternative closures again: a comment on "growth, distribution and inflation"', *Cambridge Journal of Economics*, 11 (1), 75–82.

Dutt, A.K. (1990), *Growth, Distribution and Uneven Development*, Cambridge, UK: Cambridge University Press.

Dutt, A.K. (2010), 'Equilibrium, stability and path dependence in Post Keynesian models of economic growth', in A. Birolo, D. Foley, H.D. Kurz and I. Steedman (eds), *Production, Distribution and Trade: Alternative Perspectives*, London: Routledge.

Dutt, A.K. (2013), 'Government spending, aggregate demand, and economic growth', *Review of Keynesian Economics*, 1 (1), 105–119.

Dutt, A.K. (2019), Some observations on models of growth and distribution with autonomous demand growth', *Metroeconomica*, 70 (2), 288–301.

Fiebiger, B. (2018), 'Semi-autonomous household expenditures as the *causa causans* of postwar US business cycles: the stability and instability of Luxemburg-type external markets', *Cambridge Journal of Economics*, 42 (1), 155–175.

Fiebiger, B., Lavoie, M. (2019), 'Trend and business cycles with *external markets*: non-capacity generating semi-autonomous expenditures and effective demand', *Metroeconomica*, 70 (2), 247–262.

Franke, R. (2015), 'An examination of Professor Shaikh's proposal to tame Harrodian instability', *European Journal of Economics and Economic Policies: Intervention*, 12 (1), 7–19.

Franke, R. (2019a), 'Harrod's long-range capital outlay as a stabilizer of Harrodian instability', *Metroeconomica*, 70 (2), 302–312.

Franke, R. (2019b), 'On Harrodian instability: two stabilizing mechanisms may be jointly destabilizing', *Review of Keynesian Economics*, 7 (1), 43–56.

Franke, R. (2020), 'An attempt at a reconciliation of the Sraffian and Kaleckian view on desired utilization', *European Journal of Economics and Economic Policies: Intervention*, 17 (1), 61–77.

Girardi, D., Pariboni, R. (2019), 'Normal utilization as the adjusting variable in Neo-Kaleckian growth models: a critique', *Metroeconomica*, 70 (2), 341–358.

Harrod, R.F. (1939), 'An essay in dynamic theory', *The Economic Journal*, 49, 14–33.

Harrod, R.F. (1948), *Towards a Dynamic Economics*, London: Macmillan.

Harrod, R.F. (1959), 'Domar and dynamic economics', *The Economic Journal*, 69, 451–464.

Harrod, R.F. (1970), 'Replacement, net investment and amortisation funds', *The Economic Journal*, 80 (317), 24–31.

Harrod, R.F. (1973), *Economic Dynamics*, London: Macmillan.

Hein, E. (2006), 'On the (in-)stability and the endogeneity of the "normal" rate of capacity utilisation in a post-Keynesian/Kaleckian "monetary" distribution and growth model', *Indian Development Review*, 4, 129–150.

Hein, E. (2008), *Money, Distribution Conflict and Capital Accumulation: Contributions to 'Monetary Analysis'*, Basingstoke: Palgrave Macmillan.

Hein, E. (2014), *Distribution and Growth after Keynes: A Post-Keynesian Guide*, Cheltenham: Edward Elgar.

Hein, E. (2016), 'Secular stagnation or stagnation policy? Steindl after Summers', *PSL Quarterly Review*, 69 (276), 3–47.

Hein, E. (2018a), Autonomous government expenditure growth, deficits, debt and distribution in a neo-Kaleckian growth model, *Journal of Post Keynesian Economics*, 41 (2), 216–238.

Hein, E. (2018b), 'Stagnation policy in the Eurozone and economic policy alternatives: a Steindlian/neo-Kaleckian perspective', *Wirtschaft und Gesellschaft*, 44 (3), 315–348.

Hein, E., Lavoie, M., van Treeck, T. (2011), 'Some instability puzzles in Kaleckian models of growth and distribution: a critical survey', *Cambridge Journal of Economics*, 35, 587–612.

Hein, E., Lavoie, M., van Treeck, T. (2012), 'Harrodian instability and the "normal rate" of capacity utilisation in Kaleckian models of distribution and growth – a survey', *Metroeconomica*, 63, 139–169.

Hein, E., Stockhammer, E. (2010), 'Macroeconomic policy mix, employment and inflation in a post-Keynesian alternative to the new consensus model', *Review of Political Economy*, 22, 317–354.

Kaldor, N. (1955/56), 'Alternative theories of distribution', *Review of Economic Studies*, 23, 83–100,

Kaldor, N. (1957), 'A model of economic growth', *The Economic Journal*, 67, 591–624.

Kaldor, N. (1961), 'Capital accumulation and economic growth', in F.A. Lutz and D.C. Hague (eds), *The Theory of Capital,* London: Macmillan.

Kalecki, M. (1954), *Theory of Economic Dynamics*, London: George Allen and Unwin.

Kalecki, M. (1971), *Selected Essays on the Dynamics of the Capitalist Economy, 1933–70*, Cambridge, UK: Cambridge University Press.

Kurz, H.D. (1990), 'Technical change, growth and distribution: a steady-state approach to "unsteady" growth', in H.D. Kurz (ed), *Capital, Distribution and Effective Demand*, Cambridge, UK: Polity Press.

Lavoie, M. (1992), *Foundations of Post Keynesian Economic Analysis*, Aldershot, Brookfield: Edward Elgar.

Lavoie, M. (1995), 'The Kaleckian model of growth and distribution and its neo-Ricardian and neo-Marxian critiques', *Cambridge Journal of Economics*, 19, 789–818.

Lavoie, M. (1996), 'Traverse, hysteresis and normal rates of capacity utilization in Kaleckian models of growth and distribution', *Review of Radical Political Economics*, 28 (4), 113–147.

Lavoie, M. (2002), 'The Kaleckian growth model with target return pricing and conflict inflation', in M. Setterfield (ed), *The Economics of Demand-led Growth*, Cheltenham: Edward Elgar.

Lavoie, M. (2014), *Post-Keynesian Economics: New Foundations*, Cheltenham: Edward Elgar.

Lavoie, M. (2016), 'Convergence towards the normal rate of capacity utilization in neo-Kaleckian models: the role of non-capacity creating autonomous expenditures', *Metroeconomica*, 67 (1), 172–201.

Lavoie, M. (2017), 'Prototypes, reality, and the growth rate of autonomous consumption expenditures: a rejoinder', *Metroeconomica*, 68 (1), 194–199.

Lerner, A.P. (1943), 'Functional finance and the federal debt', *Social Research*, 10 (1), 38–51.

Lima, G.T., Setterfield, M. (2010), 'Pricing behaviour and the cost-push channel of monetary policy', *Review of Political Economy*, 22, 19–40.

Nah, W.J., Lavoie, M. (2017), 'Long-run convergence in a neo-Kaleckian open-economy model with autonomous export growth', *Journal of Post Keynesian Economics*, 40 (2), 223–238.

Nah, W.J., Lavoie, M. (2018), 'Overhead labour costs in a neo-Kaleckian growth model with autonomous expenditures', IPE Working Papers 111/2018, Berlin School of Economics and Law, Institute for International Political Economy (IPE).

Nah, W.J., Lavoie, M. (2019a), 'Convergence in a neo-Kaleckian model with endogenous technical progress and autonomous demand growth', *Review of Keynesian Economics*, 7 (3), 275–291.

Nah, W.J., Lavoie, M. (2019b), 'The role of autonomous demand growth in a neo-Kaleckian conflicting-claims framework', *Structural Change and Economic Dynamics*, 51, 427–444.

Nikiforos, M. (2013), 'The (normal) rate of capacity utilization at the firm level', *Metroeconomica*, 64, 513–538.

Nikiforos, M. (2016), 'On the utilisation controversy: a theoretical and empirical discussion of the Kaleckian model of growth and distribution', *Cambridge Journal of Economics*, 40 (2), 437–467.

Nikiforos, M. (2018), 'Some comments on the Sraffian supermultiplier approach to growth and distribution', *Journal of Post Keynesian Economics*, 41 (1), 659–674.
Palley, T. (2019), The economics of the super-multiplier: a comprehensive treatment with labor markets', *Metroeconomica*, 70 (2), 325–340.
Pariboni, R. (2016), 'Household consumer debt, endogenous money and growth: a supermultiplier-based analysis', *PSL Quarterly Review*, 69 (278), 211–233.
Robinson, J. (1956), *The Accumulation of Capital*, London: Macmillan.
Robinson, J. (1962), *Essays in the Theory of Economic Growth*, London: Macmillan.
Rowthorn, R.E. (1981), 'Demand, real wages and economic growth', *Thames Papers in Political Economy*, Autumn, 1–39.
Schoder, C. (2012), 'Hysteresis in the Kaleckian growth model: a Bayesian analysis for the US manufacturing sector from 1984 to 2007', *Metroeconomica*, 63, 542–568.
Schoder, C. (2014), 'Effective demand, exogenous normal utilization and endogenous capacity in the long run: evidence from cointegrated vector autoregression analysis for the USA', *Metroeconomica*, 65, 298–320.
Shaikh, A. (2009), 'Economic policy in a growth context: a classical synthesis of Keynes and Harrod', *Metroeconomica*, 60, 455–494.
Skott, P. (2010), 'Growth, instability and cycles: Harrodian and Kaleckian models of accumulation and income distribution', in M. Setterfield (ed), *Handbook of Alternative Theories of Economic Growth*, Cheltenham: Edward Elgar.
Skott, P. (2012), 'Theoretical and empirical shortcomings of the Kaleckian investment function', *Metroeconomica*, 63, 109–138.
Skott, P. (2017), 'Autonomous demand and the Harrodian criticism of Kaleckian models', *Metroeconomica*, 68 (1), 185–193.
Skott, P. (2019), Autonomous demand, Harrodian instability and the supply side', *Metroeconomica*, 70 (2), 233–246.
Solow, R.M. (1956), 'A contribution to the theory of economic growth', *Quarterly Journal of Economics*, 70, 65–94.
Steindl, J. (1952), *Maturity and Stagnation in American Capitalism*, Oxford: Blackwell, 2nd edition, New York, London: Monghly Review Press, 1976.
Steindl, J. (1979), 'Stagnation theory and stagnation policy', *Cambridge Journal of Economics*, 3, 1–14, reprinted in J. Steindl, *Economic Papers, 1941–88*, Basingstoke: Macmillan, 1990 (page numbers in the text refer to the reprint).
Steindl, J. (1985), 'Distribution and growth', *Political Economy. Studies in the Surplus Approach*, 1, 53–68, reprinted in J. Steindl, *Economic Papers, 1941–88*, Basingstoke: Macmillan, 1990 (page numbers in the text refer to the reprint).
Stockhammer, E. (2004a), 'Is there an equilibrium rate of unemployment in the long run?', *Review of Political Economy*, 16, 59–77.
Stockhammer, E. (2004b), *The Rise of Unemployment in Europe: A Keynesian Approach*, Cheltenham: Edward Elgar.
You, J.-I., Dutt, A.K. (1996), 'Government debt, income distribution and growth', *Cambridge Journal of Economics*, 20 (3), 335–351.

4 Conflict as closure

A Kaleckian model of growth and distribution under financialization

Srinivas Raghavendra and Petri T. Piiroinen

The principle of effective demand underpins the post-Keynesian theories of growth and distribution whereby the rate of profit is determined by growth, particularly those based on Michał Kalecki (1971) and Josef Steindl (1952). In contrast to the classical models, in these models the independence of capital accumulation of firms from saving at the macroeconomic level is related to the determination of income distribution by the power struggle between capital and labour via the firm-level profit markup. In this tradition, models by Bhaduri and Marglin (1990), and independently by Kurz (1990), provided a framework to study the impact of distribution on growth in terms of "two ways to expand" depending on the relative response of capital accumulation to profitability and demand/capacity utilization. One of the central results in these models was to show that the redistribution of income towards wages can indeed lead to growth under the condition that capital accumulation responds more strongly to capacity utilization than profitability. In terms of the heterodox growth literature, these two perspectives emerge from the Kaleckian and the classical traditions.

The class of post-Keynesian models, inspired by the Kaleckian tradition, assume endogenous variation in capacity utilization and essentially show its impact on aggregate demand in the long run. However, the variability of capacity utilization in the long run is severely criticized by authors from the classical (Marxian) tradition because it is anchored to a fixed "normal" rate of utilization on which firms base their accumulation decisions (for example, Auerbach & Skott, 1988). These authors use the Harrodian instability mechanism to argue that the deviation of actual utilization from the normal rate of utilization will create instability.

In contrast, post-Keynesian authors claim that the *normal* rate of utilization itself is influenced by the actual rate of utilization (Lavoie, 1995, 2010; Dutt, 1997; Commendatore, 2006; Hein, 2012), thus arguing for "hysteresis" in the normal rate of capacity utilization. Furthermore, the Kaleckian response to the Harrodian instability has been in terms of positing shifts in the capital accumulation function (g^i) through changes in the intercept term (assumed to capture Keynes's notion of "animal spirits"), which is assumed to change with respect to the deviation between the actual and normal rates of utilization (Hein, Lavoie & van Treeck, 2012). The classical (Marxian) authors have rejected the so-called "hysteresis" in the normal rate of utilization claim on the basis that it lacks solid behavioural foundations.

The post-Keynesian authors further justified the presence of the hysteresis effect in the normal rate of utilization based on behavioural micro-foundations. Setterfield (2018) proposed a model based on the satisficing behaviour of firm where they showed long-run variation in the capacity utilization even when firms adhere to a fixed *normal* rate of capacity utilization. The reason is that the satisficing firms will tolerate – within limits – deviation of actual values of variables from their target values. The line of reasoning goes back to Dutt (2010) and Lavoie (1992), and using this behavioural micro-foundation, Setterfield (2018) showed the variation in the capacity utilization rate within a certain range of the fixed normal rate, thereby providing a model that combines the Harrodian-Kaleckian insights, i.e. variability in the capacity utilization rate in the presence of a fixed normal rate.

In this chapter, we attempt a different microeconomic underpinning that is based on conflict, which drives the endogenous adjustment in capacity utilization and offers an economic rationale for the range of values within which the long-run value of the rate of utilization falls. We show how the conflict between the shareholders (owners) and managers of firms in terms of profit rates generates dynamics between growth and distribution that results in a long-run variation in the capacity utilization rate. Interestingly, the dynamics of the model generates oscillations in the rate of capacity utilization in the short to medium term before settling down to its long-run value. Furthermore, the long-run value of the rate of capacity utilization falls within a range of plausible values, and this range is determined by the conflict between shareholders and managers.

Our contribution to the literature is two-fold:

1 The introduction of conflict provides a more realistic microeconomic underpinning to study the impact of distribution on accumulation and long-run utilization. In doing so, we have not taken the approach of the existence of normal utilization rate that is relied upon by the Harrodian authors (Skott 2008; Skott & Ryoo, 2008) and the endogenization of animal spirits in such a way that the actual utilization influences the desired or normal rate of utilization by the Kaleckian authors (Hein, 2012; Lavoie, 2003). In contrast, in our model, the actual utilization endogenously adjusts in such a way to find a resolution to the conflict between the shareholders and managers. However, this does not mean that the variables in the system have reached "fully adjusted positions" because conflict is never fully solved. Although we have not endogenized conflict in this model, we show here that for various values of a conflict parameter, we have a different level of equilibrium rate of utilization, i.e. there thus exists a range of long-run equilibrium

rates of utilization onto which the utilization settles, and the range is defined by the conflict between shareholders and managers.

2 Second, we believe much of the discussion in the literature stems from the fact that these models try to capture the complex dynamics between growth and distribution through linear models, which at best captures very short-term behaviour. In this chapter, we aim to take a step forward in terms of proposing a dynamic model that exploits the non-linearities (through natural feedback mechanisms) of the long-term behaviour, which is lacking in the existing literature. To develop our model, we use the basic Kaleckian growth model developed by Hein et al. (2011, 2012) and the micro theory of firm developed by Lavoie (2002) and further extended to include the conflict claims by Dallery and Van Treeck (2011).

Accumulation decision of firms under financialization

We start from the post-Keynesian theory of the firm, originally presented by Wood (1975) and formalized and developed by Lavoie (1992). It was further developed by Dallery (2009) in the context of financialization. One of the essential differences between these articulations is the role of shareholders in the firm. For instance, Lavoie (1992, p. 107) neglects the role of shareholders to influence the strategic orientation of firms and assumes that shareholders play a passive role in the "Galbraithian and Post-Keynesian firm". Whereas Dallery (2009) picks up the argument from the seminal works of Berle and Means (1933) to articulate firms as places of conflict between mangers and shareholders, particularly in the context of financialization. Drawing from the post-Keynesian literature, Hein (2012) identifies that shareholder power over managers is one of the channels through which financialization impacts on accumulation and growth of firms:

> Both the objectives and the constraints of firms as a whole may be affected by increasing financialization. On the one hand, rising shareholder power dominates management's and workers' preference for (long-run) growth of the firm over shareholders' preference for (short-term) profitability. On the other hand, increasing dividend payments, share buybacks and so forth restrict the availability of finance for firms' real investment projects. Distribution of income is affected by changes in power relations between shareholders, managers, and workers, which then feedback on investment and consumption.
>
> (Hein, 2012, p. 476)

Crotty (1990) has shown that the conflation of ownership and control is one of the shortcomings in the theories of Keynes, Tobin and Minsky. He argues for conceptualizing semi-autonomous agents that he believes create a realistic theoretical vision for the study of real and financial sector interaction and one that is moving through historic time in an ever-changing, institutionally contingent relationship, where there is neither one of perfect coordination nor one of complete independence. Crotty (1990) was arguing for conceptualizing varying degrees of semi-autonomy, or varying degrees of conflict between shareholders and managers for the study of real-financial interaction.

The separation between ownership and control has consistently been emphasized not only in the post-Keynesian literature but also the mainstream Agency-theory literature (Panda & Leepsa, 2017). In the latter, studies have identified different types of agency problems depending on whether it is driven by "manager opportunism" or the "misalignment effect" (Type I problem) (Jensen & Meckling, 1976; La Porta, Lopez-de-Silane & Shleifer, 1999; Eklund, Palmberg, & Wiberg, 2013) and it is dominated by the shareholders and known as "owner opportunism" or the "entrenchment effect" (Type II problem) (Demsetz & Lehn, 1985).

Finance frontier and expansion frontier

To see this more formally, we rely on the post-Keynesian theory of firm that is well developed in the literature. The analytical apparatus has two frontiers – the finance frontier and the expansion frontier in the profit rate (r) and accumulation rate (g) space (Lavoie, 1992). Whereas the finance frontier indicates the profit rates required to sustain different growth strategies, the expansion frontier associates each growth strategy with the profit rate that can be optimally be realized.

The finance frontier can be derived from the equality of sources and uses of funds, where we assume that the firm has decided its productive investment based on its retained earnings and external funds. In terms of the derivation of the finance frontier, we use Dallery (2009), with some minor modifications. Starting from the equality of use and source of funds, i.e.

$$I = IF + OF \tag{1}$$

$$I = (\Pi - i_s K_s - i_l K_l) + a(\Pi - i_s K_s - i_l K_l)$$

where IF ($= \Pi - i_s K_s - i_l K_l$) is the internal funds (or retained earnings), which in turn is profits Π minus dividend payments $i_s K_s$ and interest payments $i_l K_l$ to loans, and OF is the outside or external finance which is a multiple (a) of retained earnings, signifying Kalecki's Principle of Increasing Risk.

Further, assume that firms also finance a percentage x of their investment from external sources, say new net share issues (x_s) and new net debt (x_d) each as a ratio of physical investment. Letting i be the interest rate as before, D the existing stock of debt and e_r the retained earnings, we can rewrite the above equality as

$$I = e_r(\Pi - iD) + x_s I + x_d I,$$

$$\Pi = I\left[\frac{1-x_s-x_d}{e_r}\right]+iD.$$

Dividing by K and letting $r=\frac{\Pi}{K}$, $g=\frac{I}{K}$ and $d=\frac{D}{K}$ yield a simple linear formulation of the finance frontier given by

$$r = g\left[\frac{1-x_s-x_d}{e_r}\right]+id$$

or simply

$$r = l_1 g + l_0 \tag{2}$$

where $l_1=\left[\frac{1-x_s-x_d}{e_r}\right]$ and $l_0 = id$.

The expression for the finance frontier in equation (2) can also be expressed terms of profit share (h), since $r=\frac{hu}{v}$, where u is the rate of capacity utilization and v is capital to potential output ratio. Assuming markup pricing, it follows that the finance frontier can be associated with the pricing behaviour of the firm. In that case, the finance frontier yields the minimum *profit margin* necessary to secure investment, which is incorporated into pricing decisions.

The finance frontier (2) is a linear function that relates the minimum rate of profit, r, that is necessary to implement any rate of accumulation, g. The more the firm desires to invest, the higher the profit rate (or profit margin) is necessary to finance its accumulation goal, given the average rate of interest payable on its capital. Similarly, a higher rate of interest requires a higher rate of profit to implement a given rate of accumulation; and a higher the leverage ratio (the ratio of borrowed funds to the retained earnings l_1) requires a higher rate of profit to implement a given rate of accumulation, g. As we will see later in this section, the finance frontier (2), even in this simple characterization, provides a way to capture the power struggle between shareholders and managers through endogenizing the leverage ratio. The area under the finance frontier is not accessible in the long run for firms since companies in this zone could not sustain their rate of growth since external finance would no longer be forthcoming.

The second curve of the theory of the firm is called by the expansion frontier, Lavoie (1992), which provides a schedule of the maximum level of profitability that can be reached for each rate of investment. The expansion frontier is argued to have a concave relation between accumulation and the rate of profit. This is because of the *Penrosian effect*, which argues that when a firm grows, there are positive effects on profitability up to a certain rate of growth, and thereafter negative effects set in due to managerial limitations in handling the speed of expansion, in contrast to the absolute size of the organization.

Putting these together in the (g, r) space, Figure 4.1(a) shows both the finance frontier (FF) and the expansion frontier (EF). The rate of profit, r_{sh}, refers to the shareholders maximizing their preference, and the corresponding accumulation level is given by g_{sh}. Similarly, r_{sm} is the rate of profit corresponding to the accumulation level g_{sm}, which is managers' preferred position as it both satisfies the finance constraint as well as delivers a higher level of accumulation.

The effect of financialization on these frontiers is well theorized in the literature (Lavoie, 1992; Dallery, 2009; Dallery & Van Treeck, 2011; Stockhammer, 2004). In terms of the finance frontier, from our point of view, as shareholders put pressure on managers for a higher rate of profit, managers distribute more dividends, in which case the retained earnings e_r goes down, or they try to preserve the share value in the market by not issuing new net shares (xs falls), or they increase the share value through share buy-backs (xs becomes negative) or increase indebtedness (d) consecutive to debt-financed spending (increase in xd). In the case where the firm increases its dividend payments (or reduces its retained earnings), the finance frontier would rotate counter-clockwise (a positive rotation) via the l_1 term. The shift in the finance frontier is caused by new net borrowing, i.e. via changes in the l_0 term.

In terms of the expansion frontier, facing increasing pressure from shareholders for a higher profit rate, managers can react in three possible ways. This can be seen from the profit-rate decomposition – either by increasing the profit margin, by increasing the utilization rate, through a higher capital coefficient or a combination of the three. However, here we assume the competitive nature of the product market does not allow the managers to change their markup or profit margin. Therefore, in the short run, yielding to shareholders' pressure, achieving a higher profit rate is possible either through higher productivity or wage reductions. In this model, we assume that managers, instead of taking the route of nominal wage reduction which usually

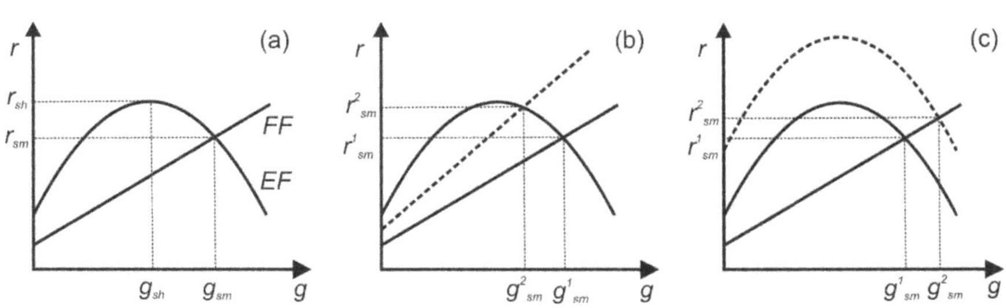

Figure 4.1 (a) The finance and expansion frontiers FF and EF, respectively, of the post-Keynesian firm. (b) A positive rotation of the finance frontier. (c) An upward shift in the expansion frontier.

evokes sharper negative response from workers, would heed to shareholders' pressure through a more intense use of productive capacity. This would imply that managers accept to operate above the rate of capacity utilization that corresponds to their accumulation target, if it allows them to reach a better profit rate. Thus, in the context of conflict, managers face a trade-off between shareholders' profit-rate target and their own utilization target, and in terms of the expansion frontier, the increase in the rate of utilization shifts the frontier upwards. Consequently, the firm will be exposed to an increased risk of default in case of an unexpected rise in demand.[1] The effect on financialization on these two frontiers by way of shifts in these curves are shown in Figures 4.1(b) and (c).

The model

The aim here is to show how conflict between shareholders and managers results in the endogenous emergence of a long-run equilibrium rate of utilization for the firm. Our approach does not invoke any "normal" rate of utilization, nor does the actual utilization rate change the normal rate of utilization. We show that the conflict between the owners and the managers results in a range of values for the long-run equilibrium rate of utilization and that range is defined by the conflict.[2] We show that using conflict as a behavioural closure provides a more realistic way to understand the long-run equilibrium value, which is usually assumed to be "fully adjusted position". In such a case the long-run equilibrium values must correspond to situations where all conflicts are resolved and that the economy is in a state of "perfect harmony". However, conflict is a continuing undercurrent in the evolution of capitalism, and its persistence is what makes the system more unequal. Our analytical approach aims to bring out this essential characteristic in the context of long-run growth dynamics. In what follows, we discuss the assumptions and set up the model.

Expansion frontier

Following the discussion in the previous section, we introduce the expansion frontier to represent the expected profitability of a firm's investment possibilities. The expansion frontier gives us the accumulation rate for any given profit rate, and taking the Penrosian effect into account, we can define it as a concave function in the (g, r) space as shown in Figure 4.1. In the context of conflict, as shareholders demand a higher proportion of profits, managers negotiate and accommodate their demands by adjusting the rate of utilization. To reflect this aspect, we propose the following simple expansion frontier that has the required properties

$$EF(g,u) = ug(a - bg) \tag{3}$$

for some positive parameters a and b.

In our characterization, the profit rate is proportional to the rate of utilization as in the Kaleckian growth models, which implies that the expansion frontier will shift for any change in u, i.e. the expansion frontier is defined for a particular utilization rate and any change in the actual utilization, both strategic or forced, will lead to a shift in the expansion frontier. Note that the expansion frontier is updated according to the current utilization rate. The formulation (3) provides a simple way to capture the impact of conflict on the expansion frontier through the actual utilization rate and also allows us to see the emergent behaviour of rate of profit, accumulation rate and long-run equilibrium rate of utilization.

Finance frontier

The finance frontier given in (2) is a linear function that relates the minimum rate of profit, r, that is necessary to implement any rate of accumulation, g. The more the firm desires to invest, it should aim for a higher profit rate (or profit margin) to finance its accumulation goal. In the context of the dominance of shareholders, who demand higher proportion of profits, this has a bearing on the accumulation and utilization goals of managers. We posit a simple linear finance frontier as in (2), but in our formulation the leverage ratio is endogenized, to capture the conflict, and is given by

$$FF(g,u) = l_1(u)g + l_0 \tag{4}$$

for the adaptive parameter $l_1(u)$ and constant l_0.

Conflict dynamics

We model the conflict between the shareholders and managers of a firm in the following way.[3] For ease of exposition, we first describe the conflict using Figure 4.2 before formalizing the argument. In Figure 4.2, point A, the shareholders maximize their profit claim at r_{sh}, which is given at the accumulation rate g_{sh}. The rate of accumulation that satisfies the finance constraint, g_{sm}, and

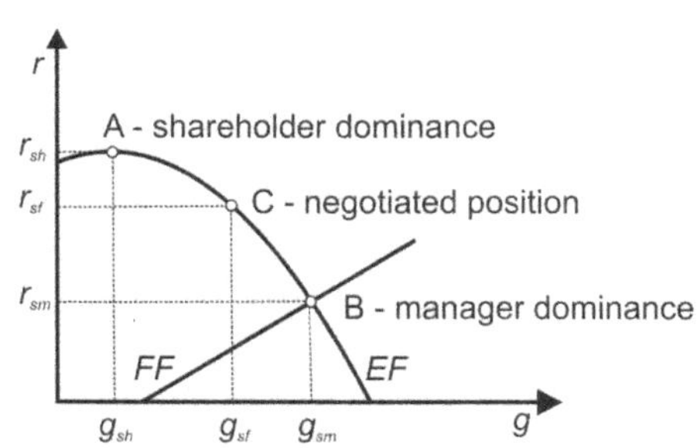

Figure 4.2 The points A (g_{sh},r_{sh}), B (g_{sm},r_{sm}), and C (g_{sf},r_{sf}) of the post-Keynesian firm

the corresponding rate of profit, r_{sm}, is where managers achieve maximum growth (point B) given the expansion and finance frontiers.

We introduce conflict using an exogenously given parameter δ, which lies between 0 and 1, and define

$$r_{sf} = \delta r_{sh} + (1-\delta) r_{sm},\ 0 \le \delta \le 1 \tag{5}$$

where r_{sf} is the negotiated rate of profit between the shareholders and managers. From an economic point of view, the δ parameter decides what proportion of profit rate is divided between shareholders and managers. When $\delta = 1$, shareholders dominate and demand the target rate of profit to be at the maximum permissible rate (r_{sh}). In other words, where $\delta = 1$, the profit rate is at its maximum and the shareholders get max(EF) – FF. When $\delta = 0$, managers prevail, and the negotiated rate of profit coincides with the economically viable rate of accumulation rate given by g_{sm} and the corresponding rate of profit of r_{sm}; in other words, the shareholders get nothing, where EF = FF.

Given the respective power of shareholders and managers, i.e. for a given value of δ the corresponding negotiated rate of profit (r_{sf}) may lie between the two extremes and we define the evolution of actual rate of profit towards r_{sf} as

$$\frac{dr}{dt} = -\rho\left(r - r_{sf}\right), \qquad \rho > 0. \tag{6}$$

For a given δ, if the current rate of profit r is less (greater) than the negotiated target rate of profit r_{sf}, then the firm will aim at increasing (decreasing) the actual or current rate of profit. Simply put, the differential equation (6) drives the profit rate to the target rate, which is not a given number but a relation between the highest (shareholders) and the lowest (managers) profit rates, which in turn are determined by the expansion and finance frontiers.

Once the negotiated rate of profit for a given δ is set, the managers want to maximize the growth or rate of accumulation rate to the largest possible value (g_{sf}), which lies on the expansion frontier (see point C in Figure 4.2). In the (g, r) space, a simple evolution of the rate of accumulation (g) corresponding to (6) can thus be given by

$$\frac{dg}{dt} = -\gamma\left(g - g_{sf}\right), \qquad \gamma > 0. \tag{7}$$

The realization of firm-level conflicting claims on profit rate is subject to the effective demand constraint at the macroeconomic level. We incorporate the demand side, where the actual utilization (u) is driven in a simple way by aggregate demand, so that the dynamics of utilization is given by

$$\frac{du}{dt} = \mu\left(g - g^{s}\right), \qquad \mu > 0, \tag{8}$$

where g is rate of capital accumulation. The function g^s is the saving rate, which is determined by the rate of profit (Hein et al., 2012) and is given by

$$g^s = s_f r + s_z\left(1 - s_f\right)r, \tag{9}$$

where $s_f, s_z \in (0,1)$ are the saving propensities of managers and shareholders, respectively.

Summarizing the discussion in this section, our model is given by the system of three differential equations

$$\begin{aligned} \frac{dr}{dt} &= -\rho\left(r - r_{sf}\right), \quad \rho > 0, \\ \frac{dg}{dt} &= -\gamma\left(g - g_{sf}\right), \quad \gamma > 0, \\ \frac{du}{dt} &= \mu\left(g - g^s\right), \quad \mu > 0, \end{aligned} \tag{10}$$

where ρ, γ and μ are the respective speed of adjustment parameters, and the four functions for the expansion frontier, the finance frontier, the negotiated profit rate given by the parameter δ and the savings rate, which are given by

$$EF(g,u) = ug(a - bg),$$

$$FF(g,u) = l_1(u)g + l_0,$$

$$r_{sf} = \delta r_{sh} + (1-\delta)r_{sm}$$

and

$$g^s = s_f r + s_z\left(1 - s_f\right)r,$$

respectively. The conflict between shareholders and managers, given by the parameter δ, drives the system by triggering a change in the r and g dynamics in (10). Given the target profit (r_{sf}), corresponding to the value of δ, both the rates of profit and capital accumulation gets adjusted by shareholders and managers respectively, which is captured by the $\frac{dr}{dt}$ and $\frac{dg}{dt}$ equations in (10). As managers try to adjust the rate of accumulation corresponding to the target profit rate by changing the actual utilization rate, it triggers a shift in the expansion frontier and consequently changes the slope of the finance frontier. The disequilibrium dynamics play out in the short run and the system settles to a long-run equilibrium rate of utilization when the rate of capital accumulation equals the saving rate. Thus, the long-run equilibrium rate of utilization is a "solution" for a value of δ, after exhibiting short-run fluctuations in the variables g, r and u.

Results and discussion

To investigate equation (10) we can use standard methods for dynamical systems such as linear stability analysis of equilibria and bifurcation analysis (Kuznetsov, 2004). For the purposes of this chapter, we used numerical methods to highlight some long-run implications of power struggle.[4]

The long-run equilibrium

First, the time histories or the evolution of the variables g (capital accumulation), r (rate of profit) and u (rate of capacity utilization) for two different values of the conflict parameter (δ), with the same initial conditions, are shown in Figure 4.3. As can be seen in the figure, there are short-run fluctuations in the rate of profit (r) and in the rate of utilization (u) before settling down to their respective long-run equilibrium values. In this specific case, the rate of capital accumulation monotonically converges to its long-run value. It can also be noted from Figure 4.3 that in this specific case, the higher the value of the conflict parameter ($\delta = 0.9$; see Figures 4.3(b) and 4.3(d)), which signifies the dominance of shareholders vis-à-vis managers, the larger the short-run fluctuations in the rate of profit (r). Also, the rate of utilization (u) and the capital accumulation (g) settles down to lower long-run equilibrium values. Thus, when shareholders' power is dominant over managers, the model results in larger disequilibrium fluctuations with the capital accumulation settling to a lower long-run equilibrium value.

Conflict and the long-run equilibrium

From Figure 4.3, it is clear that the long-run dynamics (equilibrium values) are different as δ varies. To highlight this, in Figure 4.4 we show how the equilibrium values vary as the parameter δ is varied. We see that when δ is small (manager dominated), the equilibrium growth and profit rates are higher than for large δ (shareholder dominated). As the value of the conflict parameter increases, i.e. as shareholders begin to dominate managers, the long-run equilibrium values of the rate of profit (r), capital accumulation (g) and the rate of utilization (u) decline. This is particularly interesting in the case of rate of utilization, where the model yields distinct long-run equilibrium values for each value of the conflict parameter. Thus, the dynamics of the conflict result in a range of values for the long-run equilibrium rate of utilization, and the range is given by the conflict. Even if one argues that the long-run equilibrium rate of utilization is the "normal" rate of utilization, we show, particularly in the context of conflict between shareholders and managers, that the normal rate of utilization is not unique, and it lies within a range defined by conflict.

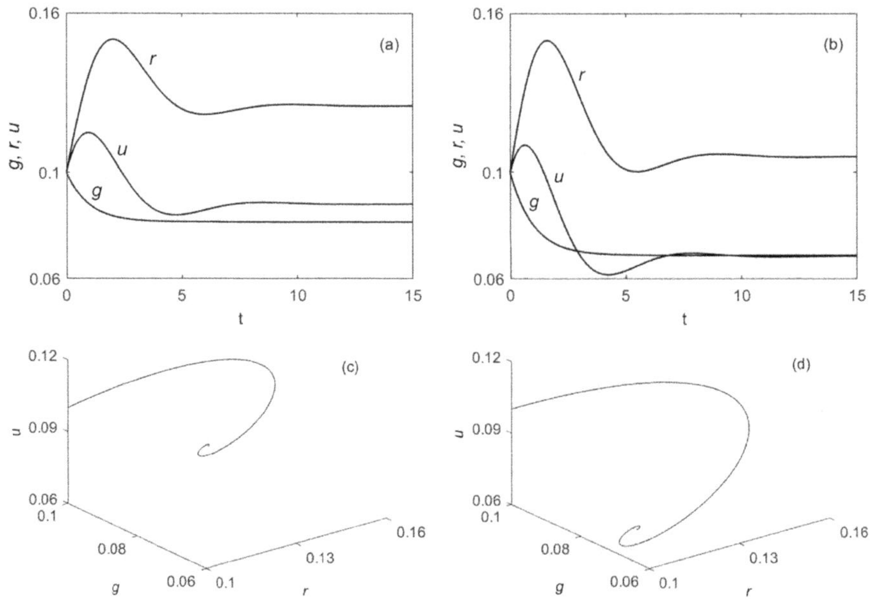

Figure 4.3 Time histories for $g(t)$, $r(t)$ and $u(t)$

Note: In (a) and (c), $\delta = 0.1$, and in (b) and (d), $\delta = 0.9$.

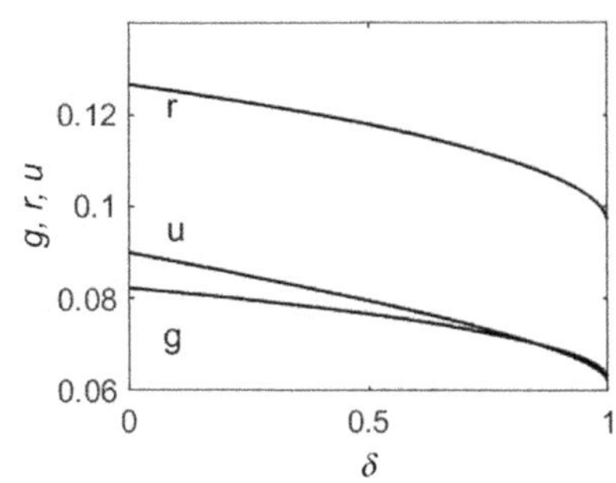

Figure 4.4 Equilibrium values of g, r and u points when varying δ

Paradox of thrift in the long run

The paradox of thrift result holds in the long run. We show this result in Figure 4.5, where the long-run equilibrium values of the rate of profit (r) and rate of utilization (u) decline as the saving propensities of both the managers (firm) and the shareholders, i.e. s_f and s_z respectively, are increased. Thus, our model shows the long-run relevance of effective demand in the case where there is conflict between the shareholders and managers. However, it would

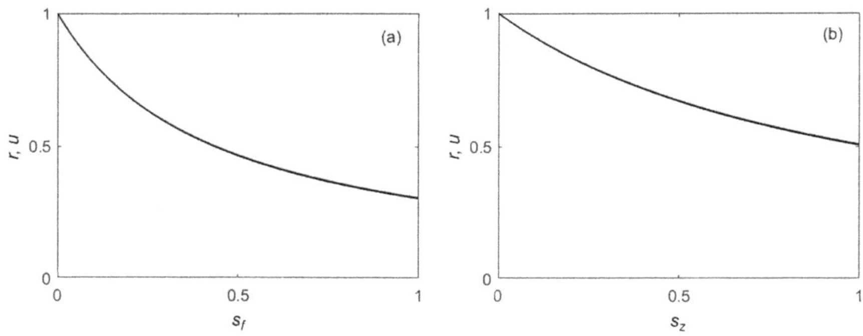

Figure 4.5 Normalized equilibrium values for r and u when varying the savings parameters (a) s_f and (b) s_z

Note: The normalized r and u evolve very similarly with the savings parameters. Both figures highlight the paradox of thrift.

be interesting to see if the results hold when we extend our model to include workers and their conflict with the managers.

Dynamics of power struggle

Finally, our model yields an interesting insight into the dynamics of power struggle between shareholders and managers. We analysed the behaviour of our proposed model in two scenarios. In the first scenario, shareholders are powerful and managers struggle to regain some autonomy, which is the case where the conflict parameter δ is varied from a higher value to a lower value. In the second scenario, we analysed the opposite case, where managers are powerful to start with and shareholders try to regain control of the firm, and this case is represented by varying the conflict parameter δ from a lower value to a higher value. Figure 4.6 shows the results of our analysis in the (g, r) space.

Figure 4.6(a) shows the case when shareholders are dominant and managers try to regain control of the firm. The value of the conflict parameter is varied from $\delta = 0.9$ to $\delta = 0.1$. Since managers are dominant to begin with and shareholders try to regain control, as δ is gradually decreased, the long-run equilibrium values of the rate of profit (r) and capital accumulation (g) increase. This because managers' aim is to grow the firm, the expansion frontier shifts upwards and together, the finance frontier rotates counter-clockwise to make the system move from the long-run equilibrium I to the higher long-run equilibrium value of II. In this case, managers' struggle to wrest power from the shareholders expands the firm.

On the other hand, when mangers are dominant and shareholders try to regain control of the firm, shown in Figure 4.6(b) where the conflict

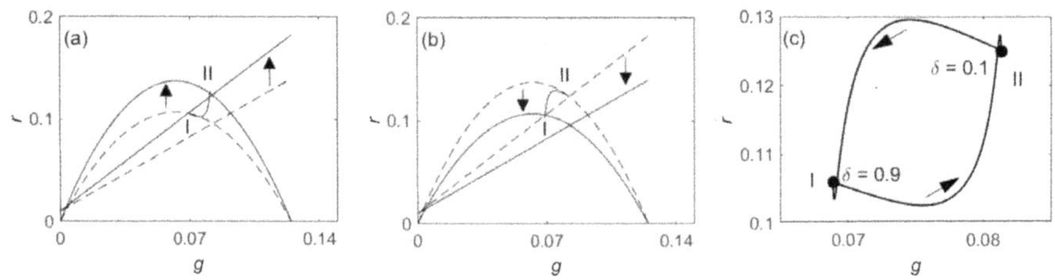

Figure 4.6 Trajectories showing hysteresis when switching δ back and forth between 0.1 and 0.9

parameter is varied from $\delta = 0.1$ to $\delta = 0.9$. In this case, as shareholders try to regain control from managers, i.e. as δ is gradually increased, the long-run equilibrium values of the rate of profit (r) and capital accumulation (g) fall. This is because as shareholders' pressure for higher profits keeps increasing, managers have no other option but to reduce the rate of utilization, which in turn shifts the expansion frontier downwards. Starting from the long-run equilibrium II, the system shrinks to the lower long-run equilibrium value I.

Interestingly, the disequilibrium trajectories when switching the control parameter δ back and forth between 0.1 and 0.9 do not follow the same path, as shown in Figure 4.6(c). The system shows hysteresis as the trajectories take different paths for moving back and forth between the same values of the control parameter. This is interesting from an economic point of view, as our model shows the distinct disequilibrium dynamics in terms of the growth paths arising from the conflict between managers and shareholders. In other words, our results show the implications of the struggle between short-term profitability objectives pursued by shareholders versus the long-term growth objectives pursued by the managers on the growth path of the firm.

Conclusions

Post-Keynesian models of growth and distribution inspired by the Kaleckian tradition assume the endogenous variation in capacity utilization to essentially show the impact on aggregate demand in the long run. However, the variability of capacity utilization in the long run is severely criticised by authors from the classical (Marxian) tradition based on the Harrodian instability principle because of the existence of the so-called fixed "normal" rate of utilization and argue that any deviation of actual utilization from the normal rate will create instability. But post-Keynesian authors argue that the normal rate of capacity utilization itself is influenced by the actual rate of utilization and use Keynes's notion of "animal spirits" to capture the deviation between the actual and normal rates of utilization. The classical (Marxian) authors have rejected the so-called "hysteresis" argument on the basis that it lacks behavioural foundations. Recently, post-Keynesians attempted to address the micro foundations shortcoming by proposing the "satisficing" principle for the firm, where firms will tolerate, within limits, any deviation of actual values of variables from their "normal", or "target" values, which in turn allowed long-run variation in the capacity utilization even when firms adhere to a fixed normal rate of capacity utilization. However, there is no general principle by which one can discern what would the tolerance range in terms of the deviation of the actual rate of utilization from the normal rate of utilization.

In this chapter, we proposed a different microeconomic underpinning that is based on conflict. This drives the endogenous adjustment in capacity utilization and offers an economic rationale for the range of values within which the long run values of the rate of utilization falls. We show how the conflict between the shareholders (owners) and managers of firms in terms of profit rates generates oscillations in the rate of capacity utilization in the short term before settling down to its long-run equilibrium value. Furthermore, the long-run equilibrium value of the rate of capacity utilization falls within a range of plausible values, and this range is determined by the conflict between shareholders and managers.

We also used a different approach in that we neither invoked the notion of "normal" rate of utilization used by the classical (Marxian) authors nor endogenized "animal spirits" in such a way that the actual utilization influences the desired or normal rate of utilization by the post-Keynesian authors. In our model, the actual rate of utilization endogenously adjusts and settles down to its long-run equilibrium value before exhibiting short-run oscillations. Although we have not endogenized conflict, we showed that for various values of the conflict parameter, our model yields different levels of equilibrium rate of utilization, i.e. there thus exists a range of long-run equilibrium rates of utilization. We also believe that our approach takes a step forward in terms of proposing a dynamic model with nonlinear feedback to generate long-term behaviour of the variables in question. We believe much of the discussion in this literature uses linear models, which at best capture short-term behaviour and do not allow to exploit the nonlinearities and nonlinear feedback between various variables. We believe our model provides a step in this direction.

The model developed here yields some interesting insights for the study of long-run growth and distribution. First, the disequilibrium dynamics of model generates short-run fluctuations, in terms of oscillations, before settling to a long-run equilibrium values for rate of profit, and the rate of capacity utilization. Second, the long-run equilibrium values are not unique, and there exists a range defined by the conflict parameter. Given a particular value of the conflict parameter, where a higher value of δ signifies shareholders' dominance and a lower value signifies managers' dominance, the dynamics of our model shows how the long-run equilibrium is reached. In a sense, there exists a long-run equilibrium rate of utilization which can be seen as a "solution" for each value of δ. Therefore, there exists a range of "solutions", and the range is defined by the range of the conflict parameter, and for each value of the conflict parameter, the system finds a temporary resolution by settling to a particular long-run equilibrium value of utilization. From the perspective of our model, the notion that the long-run equilibrium value is a unique "normal" rate of utilization does not hold, since even if one thinks that is the case, our results show that conflict generates a range of values for the "normal" rate of utilization.

Furthermore, we see that when δ is small (manager dominated) the long run equilibrium growth and profit rates are higher than for large δ (shareholder dominated). This is an interesting result particularly in the context of the dynamics of power struggle between managers and shareholders. In the case where shareholders are dominant and managers try to regain some autonomy, the case where the conflict parameter δ is varied from a higher value ($\delta = 0.9$) to a lower value ($\delta = 0.1$), the dynamics of this power struggle result in the higher level of equilibrium rate of profit and capital accumulation (Figure 4.6(a)). On the other hand, when managers are dominant and shareholders try to regain control, the case where the conflict parameter δ is varied from a lower value ($\delta = 0.1$) to a higher value ($\delta = 0.9$), the dynamics of power struggle result in a lower level of equilibrium rate of profit and capital accumulation (Figure 4.6(b)). The disequilibrium trajectories when switching the control parameter δ back and forth between 0.1 and 0.9 do not follow the same path, as shown in Figure 4.6(c), and the system exhibits hysteresis as the trajectories take different paths for moving back and forth between the same values of the control parameter. The distinct disequilibrium dynamics in terms of the growth paths arising from the conflict between managers and shareholders is interesting from an economic point of view as it points to the relative fragility of the short-term profitability motives pursed by firms under pressure from the shareholders.

Our results also reveal the existence of paradox of thrift in the long run (Figures 4.5(a) and 4.5(b)), which signifies the relevance of effective demand in the long run. This result must be taken with a caveat that it is sensitive to the functional form of the expansion frontier. Unlike in the post-Keynesian models with linear investment function, we do not assume any explicit functional form for capital accumulation (g), and hence this result is sensitive to the form and shifts of the expansion frontier and the finance frontier. The other result of paradox of costs seem to hold, which can be intuitively seen from the lower long-run equilibrium values of rate of profit, rate of utilization and capital accumulation for a high conflict parameter value (Figure 4.4). This result needs further verification in a full model where pricing policy of the firm is included in the analysis.

Nonetheless, even within the limited scope of investigation, our results highlight emergent properties due to the feedback mechanisms within the system and without resorting to any stochastic shocks or other artefacts. We believe that our model provides a more realistic behavioural micro foundation in terms of conflict and implications to long-run equilibrium growth. On the methodological front, the dynamical systems approach provides us with a way to understand complex dynamics using simple feedbacks as well as to characterize the emergent long-term dynamics without the need for assumptions such as "normal" rate of utilization. While our model needs further extension, we believe it offers a starting point to build simple feedback models and to study the long-run dynamics of capital accumulation and distribution.

Notes

1 This is referred to as "risk transfer" in the literature (Dallery, 2009), as managers try to balance the *real* security based on their growth objective and the profitability demands stemming from shareholders, the risk of accommodating latter groups' demand exposes the firm to the risk of satisfying market demand at a higher level of utilization – transfer of financial risk into a real risk.
2 One could also argue that the long-run equilibrium value of utilization is the "normal" rate of utilization. However, we show that this need not be unique and that there exists a range of value defined by the conflict.
3 This formulation is similar to that of Dallery and Van Treeck (2011), except that ours is in dynamic form.
4 Note that all simulations and numerical analyses are conducted using MATLAB (2018).

References

Auerbach, P., & Skott, P. (1988). Concentration, competition and distribution: A critique of theories of monopoly capital. *International Review of Applied Economics*, *2*(1), 42–61.

Berle, A., & Means, G. (1933). *The modern corporation and private property*. New York: Macmillan.

Bhaduri, A., & Marglin, S. (1990). Unemployment and the real wage: The economic basis for contesting political ideologies. *Cambridge Journal of Economics*, *14*(4), 375–393.

Commendatore, P. (2006). *Are Kaleckian models relevant for the long run?* Classical, Neoclassical and Keynesian Views on Growth and Distribution, 288.

Crotty, J. R. (1990). Owner–manager conflict and financial theories of investment instability: A critical assessment of Keynes, Tobin, and Minsky. *Journal of Post Keynesian Economics*, *12*(4), 519–542.

Dallery, T. (2009). Post-Keynesian theories of the firm under financialization. *Review of Radical Political Economics*, *41*(4), 492–515.

Dallery, T., & Van Treeck, T. (2011). Conflicting claims and equilibrium adjustment processes in a stock-flow consistent macroeconomic model. *Review of Political Economy*, *23*(2), 189–211.

Demsetz, H., & Lehn, K. (1985). The structure of corporate ownership: Causes and consequences. *Journal of Political Economy*, *93*(6), 1155–1177.

Dutt, A. K. (1997). Dependence and hysteresis in post Keynesian models. *Markets, Unemployment, and Economic Policy*, 2, 238.

Dutt, A. K. (2010). The role of aggregate demand in classical-Marxian models of economic growth. *Cambridge Journal of Economics*, *35*(2), 357–382.
Eklund, J., Palmberg, J., & Wiberg, D. (2013). Inherited corporate control and returns on investment. *Small Business Economics*, *41*, 419–431.
Hein, E., Lavoie, M., & van Treeck, T. (2011). Some instability puzzles in Kaleckian models of growth and distribution: A critical survey. *Cambridge Journal of Economics*, *35*(3), 587–612.
Hein, E., Lavoie, M., & van Treeck, T. (2012). Harrodian instability and the "normal rate" of capacity utilization in Kaleckian models of distribution and growth: A survey. *Metroeconomica*, *63*(1), 139–169.
Jensen, M., & Meckling, W. (1976). Theory of the firm: Managerial behaviour, agency costs and ownership structure. *Journal of Financial Economics*, *3*, 305–360.
Kalecki, M. (1971). *Selected essays on the dynamics of the capitalist economy 1933–1970*. Cambridge: Cambridge University Press.
Kurz, H. D. (1990). *Capital, distribution and effective demand: Studies in the "classical" approach to economic theory*. Cambridge, UK: Polity Press.
Kuznetsov, Y. (2004). *Elements of bifurcation theory*. New York: Springer-Verlag.
La Porta, R., Lopez-de-Silane, F., & Shleifer, A. (1999). Corporate ownership around the world. *Journal of Finance*, *54*, 471–517.
Lavoie, M. (1992). *Foundations of post-Keynesian economic analysis*. Aldershot, UK: Edward Elgar.
Lavoie, M. (1995). The Kaleckian model of growth and distribution and its neo-Ricardian and neo-Marxian critiques. *Cambridge Journal of Economics*, *19*(6), 789–818.
Lavoie, M. (2002). The Kaleckian growth model with target return pricing and conflict inflation. Edited by M. Setterfield, *The economics of demand-led growth* (Chapter 10, pp. 172–188). Cheltenham, UK: Edward Elgar.
Lavoie, M. (2003). Kaleckian effective demand and Sraffian normal prices: Towards a reconciliation. *Review of Political Economy*, *15*(1), 53–74.
Lavoie, M. (2010). Surveying short-run and long-run stability issues with the Kaleckian model of growth. In *Handbook of alternative theories of economic growth* (pp. 132–156). Cheltenham, UK, and Northampton, MA: Edward Elgar.
MATLAB. (2018). *9.4.0.813654 (R2018a)*. Natick, MA: The MathWorks Inc.
Panda, B., & Leepsa, N. M. (2017). Agency theory: Review of theory and evidence on problems and perspectives. *Indian Journal of Corporate Governance*, *10*(1), 74–95.
Setterfield, M. (2018). Long-run variation in capacity utilization in the presence of a fixed normal rate. *Cambridge Journal of Economics*, *43*(2), 443–463.
Skott, P. (2008). *Theoretical and empirical shortcomings of the Kaleckian investment function. Working Paper 2008–11*. Amherst: Department of Economics, University of Massachusetts.
Skott, P., & Ryoo, S. (2008). Macroeconomic implications of financialization. *Cambridge Journal of Economics*, *32*(6), 827–862.
Steindl, J. (1952). *Maturity and stagnation in American capitalism*. Oxford, UK: Basil Blackwell.
Stockhammer, E. (2004). Financialisation and the slowdown of accumulation. *Cambridge Journal of Economics*, *28*(5), 719–741.
Wood, A. (1975). *A theory of profits*. Cambridge: Cambridge University Press.

5 Aggregate demand policy in mature and dual economies

Peter Skott

The possibility of 'secular stagnation' in the US and other advanced economies gained renewed attention during the 'great recession'. Emerging economies have also experienced problems recently. Many Latin American countries have seen a reversal of fortunes, and China may face the prospect of slower economic growth. The analysis of these long-run growth issues must, I shall argue, consider the supply side as well as aggregate demand. Supply and demand factors interact, and policy recommendations that make sense for advanced economies may cause great harm if applied to emerging economies.

Aggregate demand policy is important, both in the short and the long run. There is a basic distinction, however, between labour-constrained mature economies and capital-constrained dual economies. Mature economies may suffer from a structural aggregate problem (secular stagnation): full employment growth may be impossible in the absence of sustained fiscal stimulus. Dual economies with high levels of open or hidden unemployment, by contrast, do not face long-run structural aggregate demand problems. They require public investment in key areas, including education and infrastructure, but the key problems concern the composition of demand and the need to expand the modern sector. These economies face structural transformation problems.

The next section of this chapter outlines a simple one-sector framework for analysing steady growth. This is followed by a discussion of the application of the framework to mature economies. The challenges and policy priorities in dual economies are then analysed, followed by a few concluding remarks.

Goods market equilibrium and the warranted growth rate

In line with most post-Keynesian growth models, I assume a Leontief production function

$$Y = \min\{\sigma K, \lambda L\}$$

The fixed coefficients may be the *ex-post* reflection of a choice of technique.

A particular capital intensity may be desirable from a welfare perspective. The maximisation of consumption per efficiency unit of labour in a Solow model with perfect competition, for instance, requires that the capital intensity be consistent with the 'golden rule': the rate of return on capital (the marginal product of capital) must be equal to the rate of growth. The golden rule and the assumptions behind the Solow model may not be appealing, but the existence of a policy target for capital intensity does not depend on a neoclassical production function with smooth substitution. The set of available techniques can be specified more generally, and the existence of a choice of technique is consistent with the insights from the Cambridge capital controversy, including reswitching and capital reversing. Indeed, the choice-of-technique argument is in line with Sraffa's (1960, p. 33) suggestion that the rate of profits "can well be determined from outside the system of production, in particular by the level of the money rate of interest". Thus, I shall take the policy-determined real rate of interest and the Leontief coefficients as given, an approach that is also consistent with Lerner's principle of functional finance (cf. endnote 7 in this chapter).

My concern in this chapter is with long-run growth and, disregarding short-run lags, I take consumption to be a linearly homogeneous function of disposable income and wealth.[1] With this assumption, the goods market equilibrium condition for a closed economy can be written as

$$Y = C(Y - T, W) + I + G \tag{1}$$

Y, C, I and G denote output, consumption, investment and government spending on goods and services. T is taxes net of transfers, where transfers include interest payments on the public debt; W is private sector wealth.

Dividing through by Y, we have

$$\begin{aligned} 1 &= \frac{C(Y^D, W)}{Y} + \frac{I}{K}\frac{K}{Y} + \frac{G}{Y} \\ &= f(t, w) + (g+\delta)\frac{K}{Y} + \gamma; \qquad f_t < 0, f_w > 0 \end{aligned} \tag{2}$$

where g, δ, γ, t and ω denote the growth rate, the rate of depreciation, the share of government spending in output (G/Y), the share of taxes net of transfers (T/Y), and the ratio of private wealth to income (W/Y). For simplicity, I take private wealth to be the sum of fixed capital and government debt; that is,[2]

$$\omega = \frac{K + B}{Y}$$

By assumption the choice of technique – the technically determined maximum output-capital ratio σ – is given. The actual output capital ratio is determined by the choice of technique and the utilisation rate of capital, u.

I shall assume that in steady growth the utilisation rate will be at the desired level, $u = u^d$. This desired level will be determined by structural characteristics and may change as the result of changes in, for instance, the degree of product market competition or the volatility of firm-level demand. For present purposes, however, there is no harm in taking the desired rate of utilisation as constant.[3] With these assumptions, the capital-output ratio in steady growth is given as $K = Y = (\sigma u^d)^{-1} = \nu$, and equation (2) describes a trade-off between the rate of accumulation g and the share of private plus public consumption in income $(f(t, \omega) + \gamma)$.

The trade-off corresponds to the well-known consumption-growth frontier in classical economics. But the interpretation of the trade-off is Harrodian: equation (2) defines a warranted rate of growth, g. This warranted growth rate need not be equal to the natural growth rate (the growth rate of the labour supply in efficiency units, taking into account labour-saving technical change). The warranted growth path, second, is likely to be unstable: the economy does not automatically converge to the warranted path.

The implications of the general framework in this section depends on the supply side, and I consider two stylised cases: mature economies and dual economies.

Mature economies

The capital stock is large relative to the labour supply in a mature economy, and long-run economic growth is constrained by the growth rate of the labour supply in efficiency units.

To avoid misunderstanding, it should be stressed, first, that a mature economy need not have 'full employment'. An economy is mature if fast growth rates of aggregate demand would create labour constraints within a relatively short period. The USA, Japan and most Western European countries are mature in this sense: Chinese-style growth rates of 10 percent a year would lead to overheating and labour shortages within a few years. Thus, an economy with 5, 10 or 15 percent unemployment can be mature, even taking into account discouraged workers and the limitations of the official unemployment rate as a measure of labour market conditions in these economies. In some economies, however, the official unemployment rate is meaningless as an indicator of labour constraints on economic growth. An example is India, whose official unemployment rate stands at less than 4 percent. This official rate is pretty meaningless; the expansion of the modern sector in India is not held back by labour constraints.

The notion of maturity, second, does not require an exogenous growth rate of the labour supply in efficiency units. The natural growth rate may respond to labour shortages, both because of induced technical change as firms search for labour-saving innovations and because in open economies high employment rates may soften the attitudes of policymakers and the electorate towards immigration. This endogeneity of the natural rate is compatible with maturity. Long-run labour constraints are relevant – even with an endogenous natural growth rate – as long as the natural rate has an upper limit and does not adjust fully to any possible increase in the growth rate of aggregate demand.[4]

Extensions of the model that include endogeneity of the natural rate do not change the qualitative argument, but to simplify the exposition, I shall take the natural growth rate n – the growth rate that is required to maintain a constant, target rate of employment – as given. For convenience, the target rate of employment will be referred to simply as 'full employment'.

Now consider the equilibrium condition for the goods market in a mature economy. With a constant capital-output ratio, $K/Y = v$, the accumulation rate g must be equal to the growth rate of output. Thus, full-employment growth requires that $g = n$, and the share of public and private consumption must take a particular value:

$$\frac{C+G}{Y} = f(t,w) + \gamma = 1 - (n+\delta)\nu \tag{3}$$

The size of the public sector – the share of government consumption in income (γ) is contentious: people differ widely in their views on the role of government and the appropriate share of government spending in GDP. Arguably, however, the exigencies of demand management should not be decisive in the determination of the levels of spending on government programs. I therefore take γ as exogenous.[5]

Taking γ as given, equation (3) – the condition for full-employment growth – must be satisfied through adjustments in private consumption. The ratio of private sector wealth to potential output (ω) is predetermined in the short run and, having pinned down n, δ, ν and γ, there is only one free variable, the share of taxes in income. Thus, equation (3) determines a full-employment trajectory for the tax rate t. Government debt and household wealth ($\omega = \nu + b$) change endogenously over time, and the tax rate associated with full-employment growth therefore will be time-varying too.

Intuitively, consumption – private or public – must fill the gap between full-employment output and investment. This gap can be large when low natural rates of growth limit the need for additional capital capacity: if the private saving rate is high and the government runs a balanced budget, the warranted growth rate may exceed the natural growth rate. When this happens, the economy faces structural aggregate demand problems or, using Hansen's (1939) terminology, secular stagnation.[6]

Secular stagnation calls for fiscal policy along the lines suggested by Lerner's principle of functional finance.[7] Private saving rates that are excessive in relation to the natural growth rate can be countered by a reduction in taxes and an increase in the government deficit (which raises consumption and reduces the aggregate saving rate). Analogously, private saving rates that are too low relative to the natural growth rate call for contractionary policies (which raise the aggregate saving rate).

The use of fiscal policy to counteract long-run aggregate demand problems raise questions of 'debt sustainability'. Countless exercises have addressed the sustainability question by looking at the implications of exogenously specified paths of primary deficits and aggregate output (e.g. Chalk 2000). Exercises of this kind represent a peculiar approach to policy. If it is taken for granted *a priori* that output will follow some exogenous trajectory of 'potential output', then by assumption there is no need for fiscal policy. And if one abandons the exogenous output trajectory, why would anyone want to maintain a constant ratio of primary deficits to GDP? Arbitrary policies rarely bring great results. If fiscal policy is used sensibly in accordance with the principles of functional finance, primary deficits will not be independent of movements in private sector demand. On the contrary, fiscal policy must be adjusted to keep aggregate demand growing at a rate that is consistent with full employment and price stability. The sustainability analysis should consider sensible policies of this kind.

Continuous adjustments of the tax rate t to satisfy equation (3) generate dynamic trajectories for government debt and private wealth. Taxes T are net of transfers, and transfers are defined in equation (1) to include interest payments on the public debt. Thus, at each moment the change in government debt is given by

$$\dot{B} = G - T = (\gamma - t)Y$$

or

$$\dot{b} = \gamma - t - nb \tag{4}$$

where $b = B/Y$ is the debt-GDP ratio, and the tax rate t is determined by equation (3). The tax rate depends on the wealth ratio ω, and we have $\omega = \nu + b$. Substituting the solution for the tax rate into equation (4), we get a one-dimensional differential equation to determine the dynamics of the debt ratio b.

The precise implications for public debt depend on the specification of consumption behaviour. The qualitative properties are quite robust, however:[8]

- A fiscal policy based on functional finance produces strong stabilising effects on the debt-income ratio. As debt increases, households' wealth and interest income both increase. Consequently, private consumption demand will tend to rise, fiscal policy needs to be tightened, and the debt ratio ceases to grow. These stabilizing feedback effects produce a stable stationary solution for the debt ratio, $b \rightarrow b^* < \infty$.

  This result addresses the long-run sustainability question: low growth rates of potential output necessitate expansionary policy if secular stagnation is to be avoided. But the debt ratio need not explode.

- High natural rates of growth are associated with low long-run values of the debt ratio b^*, and the causal link unambiguously runs from growth to debt.

  This result has obvious implications for the interpretation of negative correlations between debt ratios and the rate of growth. The influential study by Reinhart and Rogoff (2010) contained elementary spreadsheet errors, but a negative correlation can still be found in the data (albeit in a much milder form) after correction of these errors. Correlation, however, is not causation, and the result shows that we should expect a causal effect from low growth to high debt: in the model, the high debt unambiguously represents an effect, not a cause of low growth.[9] A less expansionary policy would not raise the rate of economic growth but lead to secular stagnation.

- The long-run debt ratio b^* depends on the structure of taxation. Taxing low-income households with a high marginal consumption rate produces a high debt ratio; taxing high-income households with a low marginal consumption rate produces a low debt ratio.

  This result has implications, *inter alia*, for the recent Trump tax reform in the US. Other aspects of the reform – including its direct implications for inequality – may be much more significant, but the reform implies as well that the long-run debt ratio will increase as the relative tax burden shifts from the rich towards low- and middle-income households. The short-run increase in deficits and public debt following the tax cuts will not be reversed in the long run, if full employment is to be maintained.

- Paradoxically, high levels of government consumption produce low debt ratios in the long run.

  This result has implications for austerity policies which aim to reduce public debt by cutting government consumption. These policies can have – and have had – devastating short- and medium-run economic and social consequences, and the political fallout has included the rise of right-wing nationalism. The analysis shows that in the long run, the policies will also fail on their own terms in economies with a structural demand problem: a return to full employment will require an increase in the debt ratio if the share of government consumption in income has been reduced.

Clearly fiscal policy does not always follow a pure functional finance prescription – European austerity policy after the financial crisis is an obvious example. But real-world policies often amount to a kind of 'impure functional finance'. It is no coincidence that Japanese public debt rose rapidly from the early 1990s or that the US implemented a fiscal stimulus package in 2009. The analysis of 'pure functional finance' therefore has real-world relevance. It is of descriptive interest because of automatic fiscal stabilisers and because policymakers facing high unemployment will be pulled towards expansionary discretionary policies. It is of prescriptive interest because it shows that fears of 'debt unsustainability' are unfounded, but that the debt implications depend on the structure of taxation.

There are complications and caveats. Economies, first, that do not issue debt in their own currency cannot control the interest rate on public debt and may be forced to default, a possibility that severely limits their policy space. Even if debt is being issued in a sovereign currency, second, the conduct of fiscal policy in open economies must consider the balance of payments and the real exchange rate as well as unemployment and inflation. High debt levels, finally, can have negative side effects with respect to the effectiveness of monetary policy and the intra-generational distribution of income.

But functional finance starts from the right premise: fiscal and monetary policies should be judged on their implications for outcomes that we care about. Moreover, fiscal policy can be crucial in addressing structural aggregate demand problems: in the absence of a sustained fiscal stimulus, a mature economy may experience a structural aggregate demand problem or secular stagnation. The achievement of full employment growth may require low taxes (high disposable income) and/or high public debt (high ratios of household wealth to income) in order for consumption to fill the gap between full-employment output and the sum of investment and government consumption.

Dual economies

Dating back to Lewis (1954), stylised versions of dual economies have distinguished between two sectors, a modern/formal sector and a traditional/informal sector. As a first approximation, the supply of labour to the modern sector is perfectly elastic. The capital stock in the modern sector – rather than the labour supply – represents the binding supply-side constraint in the modern sector, and this difference fundamentally alters the policy problem.

It is the low natural rate of growth that generates a structural aggregate demand problem in mature economies. This problem does not arise in dual economies. There are no labour constraints, and it should be a top priority to expand the modern sector and create high-productivity jobs for the underemployed workers in the informal sector – the faster the accumulation rate, the better, and fast accumulation boosts aggregate demand.

The absence of labour constraints does not imply that there are no supply-side constraints on the expansion of the modern sector. Utilisation rates in the modern sector vary significantly in the short run, and stabilisation policy can be essential in economies with any kind of Harrodian instability.[10] Upward instability will be curbed eventually by capacity ceilings but can cause serious damage in the form of inflation and/or balance of payments crises if the instability remains unchecked until these limits kick in; downward instability meets no similar capacity floors, and stabilisation policy may be necessary to prevent crises and long-term stagnation. But stabilisation is distinct from permanent fiscal stimulus.

Assuming successful stabilisation, the capital-output ratio fluctuates around levels associated with the desired rate of utilisation, and the economy faces a consumption-investment trade-off.[11] A one-sector model can be used to formalise this argument if it is assumed that the modern sector can draw on an infinitely elastic labour supply from the traditional sector, but that otherwise each of the two sectors is entirely self-contained.[12] With this assumption, the equilibrium condition (2) still holds for the modern sector. The difference compared to the mature economy lies in the absence of labour constraints; there is no natural rate of growth for the modern sector in a dual economy.

Re-writing equation (2), we have

$$g = \left[1 - \frac{C}{Y} - \frac{G}{Y}\right] \Big/ \nu - \delta = \left[1 - f(t, \omega) - \gamma\right] / \nu - \delta \tag{5}$$

From equation (5) it follows that consumption must be squeezed to allow high accumulation. This squeeze on consumption can be achieved by increasing taxes. Successful development therefore will typically be associated with low government deficits and low public debt: the higher is the growth rate g, the lower must be the share of private consumption $f(t, \omega)$, and the higher, therefore, the required share of taxes in income and/or the lower the debt ratio b and the ratio of private sector wealth to income ω.

Several comments may be in order. It is important to emphasise, first, that squeezing consumption need not imply a reduction in the living standards of the poor. Not all profits are invested, and many dual economies have rich elites. In principle, the resources for investment could come from policies that curb luxury consumption; in practice the political and economic power of the elites present obstacles to policies along these lines. It should be noted also that large parts of 'consumption' are mislabelled and should be considered investment. An obvious example is the misleading classification of public spending on education as public consumption. Spending on healthcare, food and housing for low-income families also contain significant elements of investment: a healthier and better educated workforce can raise labour productivity and profitability in the modern sector and improve the prospects for future growth. Thus, prioritising investment does not imply squeezing everything that is classified as consumption in the national accounts.

Second, it is clearly not enough to create space for private sector investment by cutting down consumption. Many essential investment projects will not be carried out by the private sector. Public investment in infrastructure, education and health is crucial for successful development; it complements and crowds in private investment. In this context it should be noted as well that not all modern-sector activities are equally conducive to long-term economic growth and that industrial policy can play a decisive role in promoting structural transformation (e.g. Chang 2008).

Third, because of the importance of public investment, it may be useful to distinguish explicitly between government consumption and government investment. Let γ denote the share of government *consumption* in income and let μ be the fraction of total investment that is undertaken by government, $I^G = \mu I$. If the growth rate g and the capital-output ratio ν are given independently of the share of government investment in total investment, it is now readily seen that a rise in the share of government investment increases the government deficit. The required tax share t, which is determined by equation (5), will be independent of μ. By contrast, μ affects the share of total government spending which is given by $\gamma + \mu(g + \delta)$. Consequently, the importance of public investment introduces a caveat with respect to the inverse relation between public deficits and successful development. The deficits are increasing in μ, and to the extent that successful development – fast growth of the modern sector – is associated with active government intervention and a large share of government investment in total investment, the implications for government deficits become ambiguous.

Equation (5) and the formal analysis in this chapter, fourth, has focused on long-term growth, largely ignoring critical and difficult issues of stabilisation. Macroeconomic instability deters long-term private investment, and aggregate demand policy should aim to secure a stable macroeconomic environment with appropriate levels and growth rates of demand for the output of the modern sector. Recessions should be countered by expansionary measures, but, equally important, overheating of the economy should be avoided. The use of monetary policy to target inflation poses particular dangers in this respect. To the extent that the use of interest rates to control inflation is successful, it may owe its success in large part to the effects on the real exchange rate. Exchange rate appreciation can put a damper on inflation, but overvalued exchange rates and balance of payments crises can also do great damage. Large fluctuations in real exchange rates, more generally, impede the long-run development of a modern tradable sector.[13]

As an illustration, consider the Brazilian experience since the early 2000s. The Brazilian economy benefited from the commodities boom which saw broad indices of commodity prices treble between 2002 and 2008 and then, following a blip immediately after the financial crisis, return to and fluctuate around the 2008 level until 2014.

The commodities boom relaxed the balance of payments constraint, and Brazilian GDP grew relatively fast at about 4 percent between 2003 and 2011. The growth was driven in large part by consumption which increased at an average rate of about 5 percent. Private consumption was boosted by an impressive reduction in inequality; the Gini coefficient fell from about 58 percent in 2002 to 52 percent in 2014. The real minimum wage increased by more than 5 percent a year between 2000 and 2014, and social transfers expanded significantly, partly as a result of the indexation of many programs to the minimum wage (Summa and Serrano 2018). Policy intervention also contributed to a relaxation of credit constraints. Household debt increased from 10 percent of GDP in 2003 to more than 25 percent by 2012; car sales more than trebled between 2002 and 2012; GDP from construction almost doubled between 2002 and 2012; and the ratio of employment in nontradables over tradables sector rose from about 1.15 in 2002 to more than 1.6 in 2015 (Garber et al. 2018).

Inflation was kept in check by an appreciation of the Real. Inflation, which had peaked at over 17 percent in 2003, declined rapidly between 2003 and 2007, as the exchange rate moved from 3.8 Reais to one US dollar in 2003 to 1.6 Reais to the dollar in 2008. From 2007, however, inflation started increasing again, rising from about 3 percent in 2007 to about 10 percent in 2014. The current account had moved into surplus in 2003 – partly reflecting the rise in commodity prices and the benefits of a real depreciation of the Real between 2000 and 2003 – but the surplus was short-lived. The current account soon deteriorated; it moved into deficit in 2007, and the deficit widened in the following years.

By 2014 Brazil was already moving towards a recession when commodity prices dropped precipitously. A deep recession followed, and ascendant right-wing movements are busily working to reverse the gains in income distribution.

This rough outline raises several questions. The large reductions of inequality were real achievements. But the distributional progress would have become more sustainable, and the economy would have been in a better state when commodity prices collapsed, if some of the windfall gains from the commodity boom had been used to expand the formal sector. The relaxation of the balance of payments constraint could have allowed faster accumulation as well as some increase in consumption, without running up deficits on the current account. This did not happen. The share of investment in GDP increased modestly from a trough of about 18.5 percent of GDP in 2002–2005 to about 21 percent in 2006–2008, but residential investment made up an increasing proportion of total investment (and the overall investment share stayed below its levels in the mid-1990s and far below the levels in the 1970s). The profit share started to fall from 2004 (Martins and Rugitsky 2018).

Putting it differently, the analysis points to some unpleasant Marxian arithmetic. In order to achieve significant, sustainable gains for the poor as well as an increase in accumulation, it may be necessary to confront entrenched interest and cut luxury consumption. The commodities boom gave Brazilian policymakers extra degrees of freedom, but their failure to confront the hard choices sacrificed accumulation and real progress in the structural transformation of the Brazilian economy in favour of short-term transfers. This left Brazil – and the left-wing movements in Brazil – in a bad place when the commodities boom came to an end.

Conclusion

The general theme of this paper can be put succinctly: the supply side matters.[14] It is important to make this fairly obvious point in part because the supply side has not always received the attention it deserves in the post-Keynesian literature.[15]

A recognition of the supply side has more than purely academic interest. Aggregate demand policies that work well in one economy may be disastrous in economies with a different supply side. The distinction between stylised mature and dual economies illustrates this general point.

A permanent stimulus may be needed in mature Harrodian economies with a low natural rate of growth. The warranted growth rate must be brought into equality with the natural rate, and the fiscal stimulus is helpful precisely because it retards the warranted rate. In dual economies, by contrast, a retardation of the warranted growth rate is the opposite of what one wants. Policy, instead, should aim at stabilizing the actual growth rate at a high warranted rate.

If the expansion of the capital stock relies on private investment, incentives must be created for firms in the modern sector to carry out the investment. Adequate demand for the formal-sector output becomes critical, and the management of aggregate demand becomes an essential prerequisite of fast growth. But capital constraints complicate the picture. It is not enough to create incentives for investment; the resources for investment must be available too.

In a capital-constrained economy, a sustained increase in the rate of accumulation requires reductions in the shares of private or public consumption (or an increase in net imports). Simply boosting aggregate demand is not a viable development strategy. Dual economies face a two-fold challenge. They must create incentives for the expansion of the modern/dynamic/high-productivity sector and ensure that the resources for expansion will be available.

Notes

1 The specification has empirical support; e.g. Hendry and Muellbauer (2018).

2 In a corporate economy, household wealth takes the form of financial assets, including equity and corporate bonds, rather than direct ownership of fixed capital. The analysis is extended in this direction by Ryoo and Skott (2013).

3 This Harrodian assumption differs from Kaleckian specifications. Amit Bhaduri's work with Steve Marglin has been foundational for the Kaleckian literature on growth and distribution (Bhaduri and Marglin 1990; Marglin and Bhaduri 1990). I have found Bhaduri's contributions on this and other issues to be consistently inspiring and thought provoking, even if at times I have taken different positions.

4 Maturity in this sense excludes specifications like the one in Dutt (2006). Dutt assumes that the *growth rate of the growth rate* of labor productivity depends on the employment rate. This assumption implies that productivity growth becomes perfectly elastic in the long run; there is no upper bound on productivity growth and no long-run supply constraints from the labour market. Dutt's specification

suggests that the US or the European economies can achieve long-run growth rates of 5, 10 or 20 percent annually without encountering labour constraints.

5 This argument does not rule out changes in the timing of government spending to counteract recessions or serious overheating of the economy. Uncertainty, lack of information and lags of all kinds complicate stabilisation policy. The lags and inflexibilities may be particularly severe for fiscal policy, at least in the US; many European economies with parliamentary systems have greater flexibility.

6 Recently, Summers (2013, 2015) has generated widespread interest in the possibility of secular stagnation; Krugman (1998) raised similar issues for Japan. Outside the mainstream, structural aggregate demand problems have been discussed by, among others, Godley (1999), Wray (2000), Skott (2001), Palley (2002) and Nakatani and Skott (2007).

7 The principle of functional finance

> prescribes, first, the adjustment of total spending (by everybody in the economy, including the government) in order to eliminate both unemployment and inflation . . . second, the adjustment of public holdings of money and of government bonds, by government borrowing or debt repayment, in order to achieve the rate of interest which results in the most desirable level of investment; and, third, the printing, hoarding or destruction of money as needed for carrying out the first two parts of the program.
>
> (Lerner 1943, p. 41)

The setting of interest rates to achieve a "desirable level of investment" in the short run translates into choosing a desirable capital-output ratio in the long run. By assumption, fiscal policy is designed to keep output at the level associated with full employment, and $I/Y = (I/K)\ (K/Y) - (n + \delta)\ (K/Y)$. Thus, choosing the investment-output ratio corresponds to choosing the capital-output ratio in the long run.

8 Ryoo and Skott (2013) consider a stock-flow consistent Keynesian model; Skott and Ryoo (2014) analyse a standard OLG models, and Skott and Ryoo (2017) a modified 'Keynesian OLG model'; Skott (2016a, 2016b) discuss the main findings in greater detail. An earlier paper by Schlicht (2006) derived some of the results using a traditional Keynesian model.

9 A number of studies, including Ash et al. (2017), find evidence that slow growth tends to precede the rise in debt. It is difficult, however, to establish causal links between debt and growth from purely empirical methods. Theory is needed to help sort out long-run causation.

10 Ryoo and Skott (2017) analyse the stabilisation of a Harrodian economy using fiscal and monetary policy; see also Franke (2018).

11 The expansion of the modern sector requires high accumulation rates, and high accumulation rates are associated with high shares of investment in income. The investment share has approached 50 percent in China, and the positive correlation between growth and the investment share is well established (e.g. Girardi and Pariboni 2018).

12 See Skott (2020) for two- and three-sector extensions of the analysis.

13 The argument has affinities with development theory, both new and old; e.g. Razmi et al. (2012), Ros (2013), Bresser-Pereira et al. (2015), Damill et al. (2016), Martins and Skott (2020) analyze inflation targeting and its effects in developing economies.

14 The chapter has not addressed the most challenging supply-side constraint. Climate change – and environmental problems more generally – pose existential threats to all economies. A recognition of these threats, however, does not obviate the need to analyse the ways in which other supply-side constraints affect different economies. These differences exist independently of the environmental

challenges, and an understanding of the differences will be important in designing policies to meet the challenges.

15 Some prominent contributions appear to see the absence of supply-side constraints as a defining characteristic of the Kaleckian strand of post-Keynesian economics. Lavoie (2014) outlines "four crucial aspects" of the Kaleckian approach, one of them being that "the rate of utilisation is assumed to be generally below unity, and labour is assumed not to be a constraint" (p. 360). In a similar vein, Hein (2014) describes the Kaleckian approach as treating "the rate of capacity utilisation as an adjusting variable, not only on the short run, but also in the medium and long run" (p. 243) and suggests that "the labour supply cannot generally be seen as a constraint to growth" (p. 181).

References

Ash, M., Basu, D. and Dube, A. (2017) "Public Debt and Growth: An Assessment of Key Findings on Causality and Thresholds". *UMass Department of Economics WP 2017-10.*

Bhaduri, A. and Marglin, S. (1990) "Unemployment and the Real Wage: The Economic Basis of Contesting Political Ideologies". *Cambridge Journal of Economics*, 14(4), pp. 375–393.

Bresser-Pereira, L.C., Oreiro, J.L. and Marconi, N. (2015) *Developmental Macroeconomics*. Abingdon: Routledge.

Chalk, N.A. (2000) "The Sustainability of Bond-Financed Deficits: And Overlapping Generations Approach". *Journal of Monetary Economics*, 45, pp. 293–328.

Chang, H. (2008) *Bad Samaritans: The Myth of Free Trade and the Secret History of Capitalism*. New York: Bloomsbury Press.

Damill, M., Rapetti, M. and Rozenwurcell, G. (eds.) (2016) *Macroeconomics and Development: Roberto Frenkel and the Economics of Latin America*. New York: Columbia University Press.

Dutt, A.K. (2006) "Aggregate Demand, Aggregate Supply and Economic Growth". *International Review of Applied Economics*, 20(3), pp. 319–336.

Franke, R. (2018) "Can Monetary Policy Tame Harrodian Instability?". *Metroeconomica*, 69(3), pp. 593–618.

Garber, G., Mian, A., Ponticelli, J. and Sufi, A. (2018) "Household Debt and Recession in Brazil". *NBER WP 25170.*

Girardi, D. and Pariboni, R. (2018) "Autonomous Demand and the Investment Share". *UMass Amherst Economics Working Paper 201818.*

Godley, W. (1999) "Seven Unsustainable Processes". *Strategic Analysis*, January, Levy Economics Institute. Downloaded from www.levyinstitute.org/publications/seven-unsustainable-processes

Hansen, A. (1939) "Economic Progress and Declining Population Growth". *American Economic Review*, 29(1), pp. 1–15.

Hein, E. (2014) *Distribution and Growth After Keynes*. Cheltenham, UK: Elgar.

Hendry, D.F. and Muellbauer, J.N.J. (2018) "The Future of Macroeconomics: Macro Theory and Models at the Bank of England". *Oxford Review of Economic Policy*, 34(1–2), pp. 287–328.

Krugman, P. (1998) "It's Baaack: Japan's Slump and the Return of the Liquidity Trap". *Brookings Papers on Economic Activity*, 29(2), pp. 137–206.

Lavoie. M. (2014) *Post-Keynesian Economics*. Cheltenham, UK: Elgar.

Lerner, A.P. (1943) "Functional Finance and the Federal Debt". *Social Research*, 10(1), pp. 38–51.

Lewis, W.A. (1954) "Economic Development with Unlimited Supplies of Labour". *The Manchester School*, 22(2), pp. 139–191.

Marglin, S. and Bhaduri, A. (1990) "Profit squeeze and Keynesian theory". In S. Marglin and J. Schor (eds.), *The Golden Age of Capitalism: Reinterpreting the Postwar Experience*. Oxford: Clarendon, pp. 153–186.

Martins, G.K. and Rugitsky, F. (2018) "The Commodities Boom and the Profit Squeeze: Output and Profit Cycles in Brazil (1996–2016)". *FEAUSP Working Paper 2018–9*.

Martins, G.K. and Skott, P. (2020) "Sources of inflation and the effects of balanced budgets and inflation targeting in developing economies". *UMass Economics Working Papers 2020–08*.

Nakatani, T. and Skott, P. (2007) "Japanese Growth and Stagnation: A Keynesian Perspective". *Structural Change and Economic Dynamics*, 18(3), pp. 306–332.

Palley, T. (2002) "Economic Contradictions Coming Home to Roost? Does the U.S. Economy Face a Long-Term Aggregate Demand Generation Problem?". *Journal of Post Keynesian Economics*, 25(1), pp. 9–32.

Razmi, A., Rapetti, M. and Skott, P. (2012) "The Real Exchange Rate and Economic Development". *Structural Change and Economic Dynamics*, 23, pp. 151–169.

Reinhart, C.M. and Rogoff, K.S. (2010) "Growth in a Time of Debt". *American Economic Review Papers and Proceedings*, 100(May), pp. 573–578.

Ros, J. (2013) *Rethinking Economic Development, Growth and Institutions*. Oxford: Oxford University Press.

Ryoo, S. and Skott, P. (2013) "Public Debt and Full Employment in a Stock-Flow Consistent Model of a Corporate Economy". *Journal of Post Keynesian Economics*, 35(4), pp. 511–527.

Ryoo, S. and Skott, P. (2017) "Fiscal and Monetary Policy Rules in an Unstable Economy". *Metroeconomica*, 68(3), pp. 500–548.

Schlicht, E. (2006) "Public Debt as Private Wealth: Some Equilibrium Considerations". *Metroeconomica*, 57(4), pp. 494–520.

Skott, P. (2001) "Demand policy in the long run." In P. Arestis, M. Desai and S. Dow (eds.), *Money Macroeconomics and Keynes*. Abingdon, UK: Routledge, pp. 124–139.

Skott, P. (2016a) "Public debt, secular stagnation and functional finance". In M.O. Madsen and F. Olesen (eds.), *Macroeconomics After the Financial Crisis: A Post-Keynesian Perspective*. Abingdon, UK: Routledge.

Skott, P. (2016b) "Aggregate Demand, Functional Finance and Secular Stagnation". *European Journal of Economics and Economic Policies: Intervention*, 13(2), pp. 172–188.

Skott, P. (2020) "Fiscal Policy and Structural Transformation in Developing Economies". *UMass Economics Working Paper, 2020–11*.

Skott, P. and Ryoo, S. (2014) "Public Debt in an OLG Model with Imperfect Competition: Long-Run Effects of Austerity Programs and Changes in the Growth Rate". *BE Press Journal of Macroeconomics*, 14(1), pp. 533–552.

Skott, P. and Ryoo, S. (2017) "Functional Finance and Intergenerational Distribution in a Keynesian OLG Model". *Review of Keynesian Economics*, 5(1), pp. 112–134.

Sraffa, P. (1960) *Production of Commodities by Means of Commodities*. Cambridge, UK: Cambridge University Press.

Summa, R. and Serrano, F. (2018) "Distribution and Conflict Inflation in Brazil Under Inflation Targeting, 1999–2014". *Review of Radical Political Economics*, 50(2), pp. 349–369.

Summers, L.H. (2013) *Presentation at the IMF Fourteenth Annual Research Conference in Honor of Stanley Fischer*. http://larrysummers.com/imf-fourteenth-annual-research-conferencein-honor-of-stanley-fischer/.

Summers, L.H. (2015) "Demand Side Secular Stagnation". *American Economic Review: Papers and Proceedings*, 105(5), pp. 60–65.

Wray, R. (2000) "Can the Expansion Be Sustained? A Minskian View". *Levy Institute Policy Note 2000/5*.

6 Competition, technological change and demand-led growth

Subrata Guha

Introduction: revisiting Bhaduri (2006)

This chapter has been inspired by a paper written by Amit Bhaduri nearly a decade and a half earlier. In contrast to endogenous growth models in the neoclassical tradition, Bhaduri (2006) aimed to develop a 'new approach to endogenous growth' wherein effective demand plays a central role through the determination of aggregate income, and competition between classes (workers and capitalists) and within classes (rival capitalists) influences the evolution of both technology and income distribution. The new approach, therefore, combined the insights of Keynes and Kalecki regarding the role of effective demand with those of classical economists, most notably Marx, and Schumpeter regarding the effects of competition.

Bhaduri (2006) takes the reader through a sequence of growth models, the first two serving as pointers in the development of the final model. In the final model the rate of growth of labour productivity increases or decreases with a rising or falling wage share in the economy. This relates to one thread of Marx's thought relating to technical progress: that it is driven by labour-saving innovations adopted by capitalists to maintain the reserve army of labour. Here technical progress is a result of inter-class competition. On the other hand, the average price level in Bhaduri's model declines continuously due to the introduction and diffusion of a continuous stream of new technologies by firms. The rate of decline depends on the extent to which innovations reduce unit labour requirements and the rate of diffusion of innovations. The rate of diffusion is assumed to be exogenously determined by the degree of intra-class competition between rival capitalists. This incorporates another thread prominent in Marx's thought:[1] that technical progress is driven by the desire of capitalists to gain a competitive advantage over rivals using existing techniques of production by lowering their own unit cost of production, or to protect their competitive position against rivals already operating with newer and more cost-effective techniques.[2]

The definitive contribution of Bhaduri's paper lies in the central role it ascribes to intra-class competition as a source of sustained technical progress and growth in a demand-constrained economy. His assumptions about technical progress imply that in any economy in which the money wage rate and the wage share are constant, the growth rate of output *has* to equal the rate of diffusion of innovations in the economy. Since Bhaduri assumes that the unemployment rate is a stable and decreasing function of the money wage rate, steady state growth with a constant unemployment rate and a constant wage share is possible only if this exogenously specified rate of technological diffusion is equal to a specific value determined by other model parameters (including those related to saving and investment). Absent the possibility of steady state growth, the rate of diffusion has to lie within specified ranges of values determined by other factors for 'stable and positive growth' in the long run.

This centrality of intra-class competition in inducing technical progress and growth is attractive because it relates to a more fundamental question about the relative roles of the two kinds of competition in explaining long-run growth in economies where output is constrained by effective demand. In Marx's explanation of technical progress due to inter-class competition, situations of labour shortage arising out of the depletion of the reserve army of the unemployed induce technical progress in the form of labour-saving innovations. In economies in which output is demand constrained, one cannot expect such situations to be the norm. In fact, asserting that prolonged labour scarcity is the most powerful incentive for labour-saving innovations, Kaldor (1954) makes the related argument that high rates of long-run growth can be a feature only of economies with sustained high rates of employment (and, by implication, no sustained problem of effective demand).[3]

Yet, despite the extraordinary significance of Bhaduri's paper, his assumptions about technical progress make for rather precarious foundations in a model of demand-led growth. In order to appreciate this, note that Bhaduri assumes that prices of firms are determined through a uniform markup factor k over their unit labour (variable) costs, there is a common money wage rate w faced by firms, p and (L/Y) denote respectively the average price level and average labour coefficient (unit labour requirement) of firms in the economy, and p^f and (dL/dY) denote respectively the price and labour coefficient of the firm with the frontier technology. On the assumption that the frontier technology diffuses at a uniform rate and that it takes T periods for the technology to diffuse completely throughout the economy, Bhaduri deduces that the change in the *average price level* in each period is given by $[(p^f - p)/T]$. There is some reason to question this deduction. The direct effect of diffusion of technology is on underlying labour coefficients rather than prices, and the initial conclusion which should follow from the assumption of the uniform rate of diffusion is that the change in the *average labour coefficient* is given by $[\{(dL/dY) - (L/Y)\}/T]$. Bhaduri's assumption about adjustment in the average price level is then valid only if kw remains unchanged over time. This is because $p = kw(L/Y)$ and $p^f = kw(dL/dY)$.

Proceeding in the same manner as Bhaduri but, replacing p and p^f by (L/Y) and (dL/dY) respectively, equation (13) in Bhaduri's paper can be rewritten as

$$\left(\frac{L_{t+1}}{Y_{t+1}}\right)-\left(\frac{L_t}{Y_t}\right)=\Delta\left(\frac{L_t}{Y_t}\right)\cong\frac{d\left(\frac{L}{Y}\right)}{dt}=\lambda\left[\left(\frac{dL}{dY}\right)-\left(\frac{L}{Y}\right)\right], \textit{where}\, \lambda=(1/T)$$

Noting that the rate of growth of labour productivity $g_x = -(Y/L)[d(L/Y)/dt]$, it then follows from the previous equation that

$$g_x = g_y - g_L = \lambda\left[1-\left(\frac{g_L}{g_y}\right)\right]=\lambda\left(\frac{g_x}{g_y}\right)$$

where g_y and g_L denote the rates of growth of output and employment respectively. This equation is, in fact, the counterpart to Bhaduri's equation (14) if we replace the rate of inflation there with the rate of growth of the average labour coefficient (rate of decline of labour productivity). The equation, however, implies that the rate of growth of output g_y is *always* equal to the exogenously given rate of technological diffusion λ, leaving little room for demand-side factors to play a role.

More pertinent to this chapter is the fact that Bhaduri's specification of the rate of technological diffusion as an exogenous constant even in the long run, determined by some given degree of intra-class competition (and a given regime of intellectual property rights), leaves his analysis open to the kind of criticism he levels against Kalecki's assumption that income shares in the long run are determined by some given degree of monopoly. In fact, whether we consider Kalecki's assumption of constant income shares or Bhaduri's assumption of a constant rate of technological diffusion, both abstract from possible feedback effects on the degree of competition that arise in the process of long-run growth and technological change. Hypothesising about such effects is no doubt an ambitious task, but the writings of Marx and Schumpeter, which underpin Bhaduri's discussion of the effect of competition on technological change, also provide valuable insights about the effects of technological change on competition. This chapter is an attempt to incorporate some of these into a model of demand-led growth.

Beginning with the simple hypothesis that the degree of competition in the economy is determined by the number of firms in existence, this chapter considers Marx's discussion of changes in the relative size (capital) of individual firms in the *Capital* to formulate a simple workable hypothesis about changes in the degree of competition which can be incorporated in a demand-led growth model where intra-class competition determines both technical progress and income shares. The hypothesis is formulated in the next section and then incorporated in a growth model.

Following that, we carry out an analysis of the model. We demonstrate that, under certain conditions, a unique and stable steady state exists in which both the growth rate and the degree of competition in the economy are determined and growth is indeed demand-led. The steady state growth rate also depends on how strongly competition affects technical progress and income distribution as well as by how strongly technical progress impacts the degree of competition. The steady state distribution of income, which is determined entirely by the degree of competition, is similarly influenced by the strength of interlinkages between competition and technical progress as well as by conditions relating to thrift and investment. Some concluding comments are presented in the final section.

Since all variables in any equation in this chapter will relate to the same point in time, we will omit time subscripts or arguments for variables to make the presentation less cumbersome. The growth rate of any variable v will be denoted by g_v, and (except for the variables I and Y) the steady state value of any variable v will be denoted by v^*. All constants in the equations are assumed to be positive.

Change in the degree of intra-class competition

Our discussion presupposes an economy where the number of firms in the economy is sufficiently small so that the competitive struggle takes the form of a struggle of rival firms over market shares. In contrast to notions of competition in which firms are viewed as competing on the basis of prices using the same technology, we follow Bhaduri in adopting the classical view of competition in which firms try to lower prices below that of their competitors by adopting innovations which lower unit costs of production. Within these boundaries, we can hypothesise that the measure of the (average) degree of competition in the economy is an increasing function of the number of firms in the economy (say, $Q \geq 1$). We, in fact, adopt the precise assumption that the measure of the degree of competition is given by the logarithm of the number of existing firms ($q = ln\ Q \geq 0$). The *rate of change* in the degree of competition in the economy is then given by the rate of growth in the number of firms (and for convenience, we will treat Q as a continuous variable).

The rate of growth in the number of firms ($\dot{q}$) in the economy depends, of course, on the rate of entry of new firms and the rate of exit of old firms. Volume 1 of the *Capital*[4] has a discussion on this. There Marx considers the factors that promote or prevent an increase in the capital of individual firms relative to the total social capital. The capital of each firm would, in general, increase with the process of accumulation in proportion to the total social capital so that its relative size is maintained. However, as "the number of capitalists grows to a greater or less extent . . . the increase of each functioning capital is thwarted by the formation of new and the sub-division of old capitals." At the same time, this "splitting-up of the total social capital into many individual capitals or the repulsion of its fractions one from another, is counteracted by their attraction." This counteracting force is the process of 'centralisation of capitals' which involves "expropriation of capitalist by capitalist, transformation of many small into few large capitals."

Marx goes on to identify competition and credit as the primary factors driving the process of centralisation. The role of the financial system is no doubt more important in modern economies than it ever was in Marx's lifetime. However, given that we restrict our analysis to a single sector growth model, regrettably we have to abstract from any consideration of how the working of the financial sector affects the degree of competition in the real sector. Instead we focus on the role of competition in determining the rate of exit of firms.

The process of competition between firms is accompanied by the continuous exit of firms because, in Marx's words, the "battle of competition is fought by cheapening of commodities." The greater the rate of innovation induced by competition, the greater the extent to which firms using old techniques of production are placed at a competitive disadvantage. In the ensuing struggle for survival, firms, which are able to undertake in time the investments required to upgrade to newer techniques of production, survive; those which cannot, have to exit. The rate of exit of firms therefore depends on the rate of innovation in the economy, which, in our subsequent analysis, we assume to be adequately represented by the rate of growth of labour productivity.

In looking for determinants of the rate of entry of firms, it seems intuitively obvious that the incentive for entry should depend on the rate of profit in the economy. It is also quite plausible to think that with a higher rate of profit prevailing in the economy, incumbent firms would be equipped with deeper pockets and would be better able to bear the recurring losses from competition and the continuous flow of expenditures needed to upgrade technology. Marx's views as presented in the *Capital* seem to provide some support for this proposition. Small firms, according to Marx, are always at a disadvantage in the process of competition because adoption of new techniques of production require an increase in capital outlay. Therefore, firms which are relatively small in size are also the first to be faced with the prospect of exiting an industry when a more efficient technique of production is introduced. A passage in Volume III notes that

> a fall in the rate of profit . . . hastens the concentration of capital and its centralisation through expropriation of minor capitalists. . . . On the other hand, the rate of self-expansion of the total capital, or the rate of profit, being the goad of capitalist production . . . its fall checks the formation of new independent capitals and thus appears as a threat to the development of the capitalist production process.
>
> (Marx, 1894, p. 171)

We therefore proceed by assuming the simple hypothesis that the rate of growth in the number of firms in the economy is positively related to the rate of profit (r) and is negatively related to the rate of growth of labour productivity (g_x). Assuming a linear relation,

$$\dot{q} = -\beta_0 + \beta_r r - \beta_x g_x \tag{1}$$

Assuming a zero rate of depreciation of capital and denoting by Y, Y^*, z, h and k respectively the level of actual output, the level of full capacity output, the degree of capacity utilisation, the profit share and the ratio of full capacity output to the book value of capital (assumed to be a constant) in the economy, it follows that

$$z = \frac{Y}{Y^*} \text{ and } r = khz \tag{2}$$

(1) and (2) then together imply that

$$\dot{q} = -\beta_0 + k\beta_r hz - \beta_x g_x \tag{3}$$

A growth model with intra-class competition

We begin by specifying the role of intra-class competition in determining technological change and income distribution in the economy.

The relation between competition and technical progress is specified very simply as

$$g_x = \theta q \tag{4}$$

Equation (4) represents the hypothesis that the greater the intensity of intra-class competition, the greater the growth rate of labour productivity in the economy. It also implies that intra-class competition is essential for technological change, so that if there is a single firm in the economy ($q = 0$), there is no technical progress ($g_x = 0$).

We maintain the assumption by Bhaduri that, in setting prices, firms adopt a uniform rate of markup over unit wage costs. This rate of markup determines the profit share h in the economy. According to Kalecki's characterisation h also measures the "degree of monopoly," the primary reason behind changes in h being the "process of concentration in industry" (Kalecki, 1971, p. 49). We will also assume that h depends inversely on the number of firms in the economy.

$$h = \frac{1}{\gamma_0 + \gamma_q q}, \quad \gamma_0 > 1 \tag{5}$$

Output is assumed to be determined by effective demand in the short run. Considering a closed economy and abstracting from government expenditure and taxes, it follows that investment determines saving.

$$I = S \tag{6}$$

Following Kalecki (1971) and Robinson (1962), investment is taken to be exogenously given in the short run so that actual investment expenditure I can differ from desired investment expenditure I^*. Actual investment adjusts to desired investment with a lag, the specific form of adjustment given by

$$\left(\frac{I}{Y^*}\right)^{\bullet} = \alpha\left(\frac{I^*}{Y^*} - \frac{I}{Y^*}\right) \tag{7}$$

where the left-hand side denotes the rate of change in (I/Y^*).

Since we want to focus on the effects of competition working through technical progress rather than the distribution of income, like Bhaduri we choose to abstract from the effect of income distribution on saving and desired investment. The saving function is taken to be

$$S = sY \tag{8}$$

Using the definition of z in (2),

$$\frac{S}{Y^*} = sz \tag{9}$$

The investment function is specified as follows:

$$\frac{I^*}{Y^*} = i_0 + i_z z + i_x g_x \tag{10}$$

The investment function presented here is in tune with Marx's view that investment is predominantly a matter of compulsion rather than choice for firms in the economy. If firms want to protect their market shares, they have to invest continuously in order to upgrade their technologies and to maintain a margin of excess capacity to guard against the risk of not being able to meet unanticipated increases in demand.[5] We assume, in addition, that not only the Keynesian stability condition $s > i_z$ but, the stronger condition

$$s > i_0 + i_z$$

is satisfied. This implies that at full-capacity utilisation, absent any growth in labour productivity, there is excess supply in the economy. The condition is necessary for the existence of a steady state with $z < 1$ in our model.

Analysis of the model

Equations (6) and (8) imply that output is related to investment by the multiplier $1/s$. Therefore,

$$g_Y = g_I \tag{11}$$

From equations (6), (7) and (9),

$$g_I - g_{Y^*} = \frac{\alpha\left(\dfrac{I^*}{Y^*} - sz\right)}{sz} \tag{12}$$

From equation (2), $g_z = g_Y - g_{Y^*}$. Therefore, using equations (11) and (12) and then equation (10), we finally obtain

$$\dot{z} = \frac{\alpha}{s}\left[i_0 + i_x g_x - (s - i_z)z\right]$$

The rate of change in the degree of capacity utilisation is, therefore, decreasing in its own value when the Keynesian stability condition is satisfied but is always increasing in the growth rate of labour productivity because of the increase in investment induced by the latter. From equation (4), it then follows that

$$\dot{z} = \frac{\alpha}{s}\left[i_0 + i_x \theta q - (s - i_z)z\right] \tag{13}$$

Therefore,

$$\dot{z} \lesseqgtr 0 \; according \; as \; z \gtreqless \frac{i_0 + i_x \theta q}{s - i_z} \tag{14}$$

The graph of $\dot{z} = 0$ drawn in the q–z plane (Figure 6.1) is, therefore, a positively sloped straight line AB with a positive intercept. The vertical arrows in

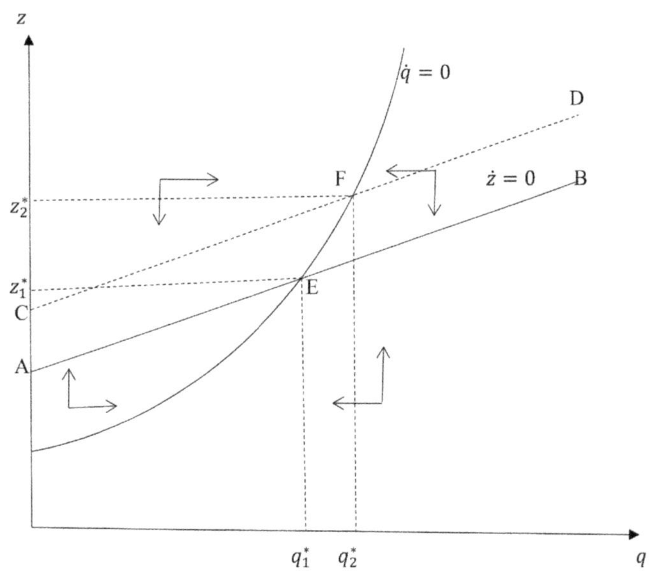

Figure 6.1 Effect of a rise in i_0

Figure 6.1 indicate the direction of change in z (the sign of $\dot{z}$) in the four regions into which the q–z plane is divided by the $\dot{z} = 0$ and $\dot{q} = 0$ curves.

Using equations (3)–(5) we can also express the rate of growth in the number of firms in the economy as a function of q and z.

$$\dot{q} = -\beta_0 + \frac{k\beta_r z}{\gamma_0 + \gamma_q q} - \beta_x \theta q \tag{15}$$

Growth in the number of firms is increasing in z because a higher z signifies (for a constant profit share) a higher profit rate in the economy. The existing number of firms, on the other hand, has a depressing effect on further growth in firm numbers. A larger number of firms leads to greater competition. This signifies not only a lower profit share and (for constant z) a lower profit rate in the economy but, also faster innovation, leading to a higher rate of exit for firms in the economy.

From equation (15), it follows that

$$\dot{q} \lesseqgtr 0 \, according \, as \, z \lesseqgtr \frac{\beta_0\gamma_0 + \left(\beta_0\gamma_q + \beta_x\gamma_0\theta\right)q + \beta_x\gamma_q\theta q^2}{k\beta_r} \tag{16}$$

The graph of the equation $\dot{q} = 0$ in Figure 6.1 is, therefore, a positively sloped curve with a positive intercept. The curve has an increasing slope and tends to become vertical as q approaches ∞. The horizontal arrows in Figure 6.1 signify the direction of change in q (the sign of $\dot{q}$) in the different regions into which the $\dot{z} = 0$ and $\dot{q} = 0$ curves divide the q–z plane.

In order to focus on the case where a unique steady state growth path always exists for the economy, we assume that the intercept of the $\dot{z} = 0$ curve is greater than that of the $\dot{q} = 0$ curve in Figure 6.1, i.e.

$$\frac{i_0}{s - i_z} > \frac{\beta_0\gamma_0}{k\beta_r}$$

The point of intersection E of the straight line AB, the graph of $\dot{z} = 0$, with the nonlinear curve, the graph of $\dot{q} = 0$, then represents a unique steady state (q^*, z^*) if and only if $z^* < 1$. In the Appendix to this chapter, we demonstrate that if

$$\frac{i_x\theta}{s - i_z} < \frac{\beta_0\gamma_q + \beta_x\gamma_0\theta}{k\beta_r}$$

and the difference between i_0 and $\frac{\beta_0\gamma_0}{k\beta_r}\left(s - i_z\right)$ is not too large, $z^* < 1$. We also prove that this steady state is locally stable.

The steady state rate of growth of output $\overset{*}{g_Y}$ can be derived as follows. Note, first, that the ratio of output to the book value of capital has been assumed to be a constant k. Therefore,

$$g_{Y^*} = k\frac{I}{Y^*} = k\frac{S}{Y^*} = ksz \tag{17}$$

Equation (17) then implies that

$$g_Y = g_{Y^*} + g_z = ksz + g_z$$

Since in steady state, $g_z = 0$, the steady state growth rate of output is

$$g_Y^* = ksz^* \tag{18}$$

Two general conclusions can be drawn about steady state values of variables even at this stage. Since (q^*, z^*) is the solution of the equations $\dot{z} = 0$ and $\dot{q} = 0$, it is obvious from equations (14) and (16) that all the parameters in the model have an influence on the steady state values of variables. Further, as shown in Figure 6.1, both the curves for these equations are upward sloping in the q–z plane. Therefore, any change in conditions in the economy which shifts one of the curves but leaves the position of the other unchanged will change the steady state values of q and z in the same direction.

We can illustrate the demand-led nature of growth in the model by considering the simple example of a rise in i_0, the parameter in the investment function representing exogenous influences on investment (the state of 'animal spirits'). Condition (14) implies that this will lead to a parallel upward shift in the $\dot{z} = 0$ line, represented by a movement from AB to CD in Figure 6.1, but leave the curve $\dot{q} = 0$ unchanged. As a result the steady state values of both q and z increase, from q_1^* to q_2^* and z_1^* to z_2^* respectively. A rise in 'animal spirits' therefore also increases the steady state growth rate in the economy (see equation (18)) and lowers the steady state value of the profit share (see equation (5)).

We can also consider whether the demand regime is stagnationist or exhilarationist and whether growth is wage-led or profit-led in the model. Consider the effect of a fall in the parameter γ_0 in equation (5), representing exogenous influences on income distribution, on the values of z^* and g_Y^*. A fall in γ_0 means that for any given degree of competition in the economy, the profit share in the economy is higher. The effect on the steady state values of z and q is captured graphically in Figure 6.2, where the position of the $\dot{q} = 0$ curve shifts downwards from AB to CD and the steady state moves from E to F. Capacity utilisation rises in steady state, showing that the demand regime is unambiguously exhilarationist. Since the steady state growth rate also rises as a result, growth is clearly profit-led in nature. The result is not surprising given that the model abstracts from the direct effects of income distribution on saving and investment.

Figure 6.2 can also be used to discuss the effect of a fall in β_x because this also results in a downward shift of the $\dot{q} = 0$ curve. The value of this parameter captures the destructive effect of technological change on competition, the Marxian process of centralisation of capital. Figure 6.2 reveals that a weaker effect of technological change on competition (say, because upgrading to newer technologies now require smaller capital outlays) will lead to an

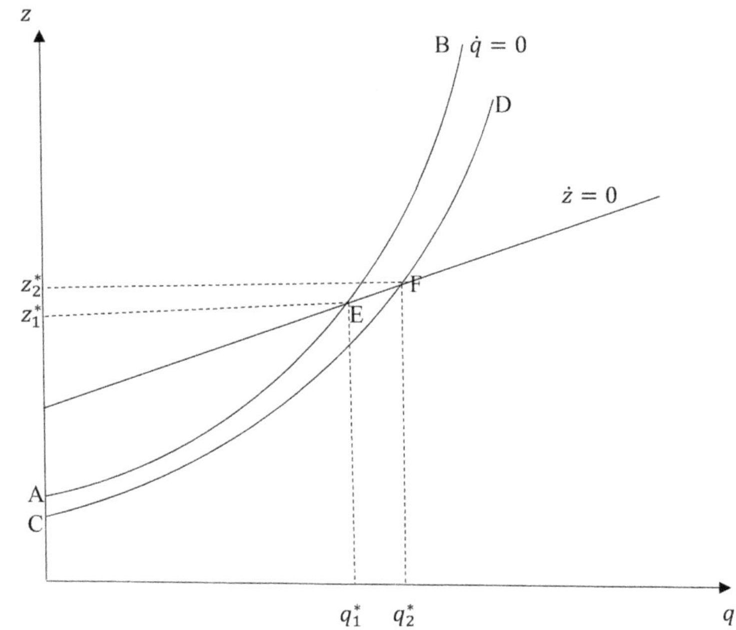

Figure 6.2 Effect of a fall in γ_0 or β_x

increase in the steady state rate of growth. A rise in the rate of technological change inevitably increases its competition-destroying effect, and the latter generates a negative feedback on the rate of technological change itself. The weaker the transmission from technological change to competition, the less the negative feedback, and the stronger the demand-creating effect of faster technological change.

An analysis of the effect of a change in the parameter Θ, which captures the impact of competition on technological change, is more difficult. In this case a graphical analysis is inconclusive because a rise in Θ will shift upwards the $\dot{q} = 0$ curve as well as the $\dot{z} = 0$ line (see conditions (14) and (16)). However, because (q^*, z^*) is, by definition, the solution to the equations $\dot{q} = 0$ and $\dot{z} = 0$, it is possible to deduce that

$$\frac{dz^*}{d\theta} \lesseqgtr 0 \text{ according as } q^* \lesseqgtr \frac{\dfrac{i_x}{s-i_z} - \dfrac{\beta_x \gamma_0}{k\beta_r}}{2\dfrac{\beta_x \gamma_q}{k\beta_r}}$$

This implies that z^* and g_Y^* will always increase with Θ provided $\dfrac{i_x}{s-i_z} < \dfrac{\beta_x \gamma_0}{k\beta_r}$.

Therefore, at least under certain conditions, a stronger effect of competition on technological change leads to an increase in the steady state rate of growth in the model.

We can complete our analysis in this section by noting that the steady state rate of growth of employment is given by

$$g_Y^* - g_x^* = ksz^* - \frac{(s - i_z)z^* - i_0}{i_x} \tag{19}$$

Since the rate of growth of the labour force, n, does not enter into the determination of z^*, there is nothing in this model to ensure that the right-hand side expression will be equal to n. Therefore, if the value of n is exogenously specified, it is only by accident that the unemployment rate can remain stationary along the steady state growth path.

Conclusion

The primary objective of the chapter was to emulate Bhaduri (2006) in building a growth model with demand-constrained output in which the evolution of technology and income distribution was an outcome of processes of competition. The model in the chapter has some broad distinguishing features compared to that of Bhaduri. The role of inter-class competition in inducing technical progress in a demand-constrained economy is disregarded; income shares in the economy are directly specified following the Kaleckian convention; and the degree of intra-class competition is endogenously determined and dependent on the rate of technical progress through the Marxian process of 'centralisation of capital.'

In developing the model, precise functional forms were chosen largely for analytical convenience and specific configurations of parameter values ensuring the existence of unique stable steady states were assumed, eschewing a more general treatment of existence and stability. The model can, therefore, at best be taken as an exploration, following Bhaduri (2006), of how classical ideas about the interplay between competition and technological change can find place in a demand-based growth model. Its implications are therefore to be considered only as indicative of a part of what might emerge from a more general analysis.

The results from our analysis can be summarised as follows. Growth of output in steady state is demand-led but also depends on the strength of the interlinkages between competition and technical progress in the economy. A rise in the inducement to invest, or a fall in the propensity to save, leads to a rise in the wage share in steady state due to an increase in the degree of competition between firms in the economy. Competition increases as the positive effect of higher-capacity utilisation initially increases the profit rate at the existing wage share and induces faster entry and slower exit of firms. Weaker competition-destroying effects of technological change yield unambiguously higher growth rates of output in steady state and, under certain conditions, stronger effects of competition on technical progress also have a positive impact on the steady state growth rate. The unemployment rate, however, can keep on increasing or decreasing in steady state if the growth rate of labour is exogenously determined.

The absence of feedback from changing unemployment rates and the invariance of the saving rate to changes in income distribution indicate the obvious directions in which the broad framework underlying the current model can be extended for a more complete analysis, allowing for a comparison of results with the existing literature on demand-led growth. A wider research agenda could, in addition, include a consideration of alternative views about the interplay of technical progress and competition (Schumpeter comes readily to mind) as well as a more nuanced characterisation of Marx's thoughts on the nature of that interaction. The process of centralisation of capital, for example, can be viewed from Marx's perspective not only as slowing technical progress through its deleterious effect on competition, but also as enabling further technical progress through a continuous increase in the scale of production.

Notes

1 As with many other ideas in economic thought, the basic idea is present in Adam Smith's *The Wealth of Nations*. See citation by Bhaduri (2006, p. 70).
2 On these two 'causes' of technical progress and their relative importance in Marx's explanation for a falling tendency of the rate of profit, see Shaikh (1978).
3 "An economy, which, over longer periods, shows a relatively high rate of growth is almost certain to be one which keeps 'bumping against the full-employment ceiling' fairly regularly, and with reasonable sized bumps. . . . Scarcity of labour . . . directly stimulates population growth . . . But prolonged scarcity of labour is also the most powerful incentive to the invention and introduction of labour-saving devices" (Kaldor, 1954, pp. 67–68).
4 Marx (1887, pp. 440–442).
5 A more complete analysis would also account for the effects of changes in competition working through changes in the distribution of income and, by including the profit share in the investment function, make it more consistent with the standard post-Kaleckian form popularised by Bhaduri and Marglin (1990).

References

Bhaduri, Amit (2006): "Endogenous economic growth: a new approach," *Cambridge Journal of Economics*, 30(1), 69–83.
Bhaduri, Amit and Sephen Marglin (1990): "Unemployment and the real wage: the economic basis for contesting political ideologies," *Cambridge Journal of Economics*, 14(4), 375–393.
Kaldor, Nicholas (1954): "The relation of economic growth and cyclical fluctuations," *Economic Journal*, 64(253), 53–71.
Kalecki, Michał (1971): *Selected Essays on the Dynamics of the Capitalist Economy*, Cambridge: Cambridge University Press.

Marx, Karl (1887): *Capital: A Critique of Political Economy*, Volume I, edited by Friedrich Engels, Moscow: Progress Publishers. Online version at Marx/Engels Internet Archive, www.marxists.org/archive/marx/works/1867-c1/.

Marx, Karl (1894): *Capital: A Critique of Political Economy*, Volume III, edited by Friedrich Engels, New York: International Publishers. Online version at Marx/Engels Internet Archive, www.marxists.org/archive/marx/works/1894-c3/.

Robinson, Joan (1962): *Essays in the Theory of Economic Growth*, London: Macmillan.

Shaikh, Anwar (1978): "Political economy and capitalism: notes on Dobb's theory of crisis," *Cambridge Journal of Economics*, 2(2), 233–251.

Appendix

Sufficient conditions for existence of steady state

From condition (14),

$$z^* = \frac{i_0 + i_x \theta q^*}{s - i_z}$$

From conditions (14) and (16), $q = q^*$ satisfies

$$\frac{\beta_x \gamma_q \theta}{k\beta_r} q^2 + \left(\frac{\beta_0 \gamma_q + \beta_x \gamma_0 \theta}{k\beta_r} - \frac{i_x \theta}{s - i_z} \right) q + \left(\frac{\beta_0 \gamma_0}{k\beta_r} - \frac{i_0}{s - i_z} \right) = 0$$

Since $\left(\frac{\beta_0 \gamma_0}{k\beta_r} - \frac{i_0}{s - i_z} \right) < 0$ and $q^* > 0$, therefore, q^* is equal to

$$\frac{\left(\frac{i_x \theta}{s - i_z} - \frac{\beta_0 \gamma_q + \beta_x \gamma_0 \theta}{k\beta_r} \right) + \sqrt{\left(\frac{\beta_0 \gamma_q + \beta_x \gamma_0 \theta}{k\beta_r} - \frac{i_x \theta}{s - i_z} \right)^2 + 4 \frac{\beta_x \gamma_q \theta}{k\beta_r} \left(\frac{i_0}{s - i_z} - \frac{\beta_0 \gamma_0}{k\beta_r} \right)}}{2 \frac{\beta_x \gamma_q \theta}{k\beta_r}}$$

If $\left(\frac{i_x \theta}{s - i_z} - \frac{\beta_0 \gamma_q + \beta_x \gamma_0 \theta}{k\beta_r} \right) < 0$, then as $i_0 \to \frac{\beta_0 \gamma_0 (s - i_z)}{k\beta_r}$, $q^* \to 0$ and $z^* \to \frac{i_0}{s - i_z} < 1$. That is, for values of i_0 sufficiently close to $\frac{\beta_0 \gamma_0 (s - i_z)}{k\beta_r}$, we have $z^* < 1$ with $q^* > 0$.

Local stability of steady state

From equations (13) and (15), the Jacobian matrix for the system $\dot{q} = 0$, $\dot{z} = 0$, evaluated at the steady state (q^*, z^*) is given by

$$J^* = \begin{pmatrix} -\dfrac{k\beta_r\gamma_q z^*}{\left(\gamma_0+\gamma_q q^*\right)^2} - \beta_x\theta & \dfrac{k\beta_r}{\gamma_0+\gamma_q q^*} \\ \dfrac{\alpha i_x\theta}{s} & -\dfrac{\alpha\left(s-i_z\right)}{s} \end{pmatrix}$$

Therefore, trace $J^* = -\dfrac{k\beta_r\gamma_q z^*}{\left(\gamma_0+\gamma_q q^*\right)^2} - \beta_x\theta - \dfrac{\alpha\left(s-i_z\right)}{s} < 0$. Also, determinant

$$J^* = \frac{\alpha\left(s-i_z\right)}{s}\left[\frac{k\beta_r\gamma_q z^*}{\left(\gamma_0+\gamma_q q^*\right)^2} + \beta_x\theta\right] - \frac{\alpha i_x\theta}{s}\frac{k\beta_r}{\gamma_0+\gamma_q q^*}$$

$$= \frac{\alpha\left(s-i_z\right)}{s}\frac{k\beta_r}{\gamma_0+\gamma_q q^*}\left[\frac{\gamma_q z^*}{\gamma_0+\gamma_q q^*} + \frac{\beta_x\theta\left(\gamma_0+\gamma_q q^*\right)}{k\beta_r} - \frac{i_x\theta}{s-i_z}\right]$$

$$= \frac{\alpha\left(s-i_z\right)}{s}\frac{k\beta_r}{\gamma_0+\gamma_q q^*}\left[\frac{\gamma_q(\beta_0+\beta_x\theta q^*)}{k\beta_r} + \frac{\beta_x\theta\left(\gamma_0+\gamma_q q^*\right)}{k\beta_r} - \frac{i_x\theta}{s-i_z}\right] > 0$$

if, we assume that $\left(\dfrac{i_x\theta}{s-i_z} - \dfrac{\beta_0\gamma_q+\beta_x\gamma_0\theta}{k\beta_r}\right) < 0$, the inequality being part of the sufficient conditions for existence derived above.

7 The economics and politics of social democracy

A reconsideration

Servaas Storm

The dilemma facing social democracy

Social democracy, the political force which has shaped post-1945 Western Europe more than any other political movement (Berman 2006; Judt 2010), is dying – or so it appears. In recent years, in European country after country, voter support for social-democratic parties, which had been hegemonic on the left, has collapsed. France's *Parti Socialist*, which received the support of 23.8% of the electorate in 1998 and peaked at 29.4% of voters in 2012, won only 9.5% in the parliamentary election in 2017; it is now France's fifth-largest political party. Support for the Dutch Labour Party (PvdA) fell dramatically, if not spectacularly – from a peak of 29% of the voters in 1998 to a mere 9.2% in 2017. In Germany, voter support for the SPD dropped from almost 41% in 1998 to 20.5% in 2017, which was its worst electoral result during the entire postwar period. Electoral support for social-democratic parties in Italy came down from 43% in 1996 to 23% in the 2018 elections, and the Greek PASOK party polled at just over 6% in 2015, down from 43.8% in 2000. Britain's Labour Party's last electoral win dates back to 2005 – almost a generation ago. The result has been a remarkable decline in the political relevance and influence of Europe's social-democratic parties (Marlière 2010).

The decline of social democracy in Europe is even more astonishing, because most voters, heavily hit by the fall-out of the 2008 global financial recession and the ensuing painful Eurozone crisis, and cognizant of the sharp increase in the gap between rich and poor, would in earlier times have turned to the social democrats. The reality is, they didn't. Part of the reason is voter opposition to post-crisis austerity policy in the EU, which was in many instances the responsibility of social-democratic parties participating in government. This has, without doubt, contributed to the weakening of the political Left. But there is more: the roots of the demise of social democracy stretch back further in time (Judt 2010). In fact, the beginning of its slump dates back to the 1970s (Marlière 2010). Average voting for social-democratic parties in the EU-12 countries – was 29.7% in the 1990s, which was below the 1980s average (31.1%) and well below the 1950s peak (33.2%). The decline continued, with average electoral support for social-democratic parties in the EU-12 being 26.6% during 2000–09 and dropping down to around 21% during 2010–19. This means that social democracy has been steadily losing votes over the past 40 years – and at an accelerating rate. While the decline in voter support was 1.5 percentage points in the 1970s and only 0.6 percentage points in the 1980s, this increased to 1.9 percentage points in the 1990s, to 2.6 percentage points in the early 2000s, and to around 5 percentage points in the 2010s. Compared to the 1950s and 1960s, social-democratic parties in the EU-12 have lost around 12 percentage points in electoral support – and in France, Greece, and the Netherlands, there is not much left of the social-democratic Left.

The long-run decline of electoral support for social democracy reflects, as this chapter argues, a failure of social-democratic parties in Europe to strike a convincing and effective balance between 'short-term practical relevance' and 'progressive, egalitarian reformism'. This is the inescapable dilemma facing European social democracy, as outlined by Amit Bhaduri (1993), in a brilliant but little-known contribution to a *festschrift* for K. N. Raj: short-term practical relevance requires social democracy to accept, at least partly, the very socio-economic and political conditions (of 'really-existing capitalism') which it purports to change in the longer run.

The dilemma arose historically in the 19th century, as universal suffrage became a feasible goal in many parts of Europe. Universal suffrage opened up a 'parliamentary', 'gradualist' pathway to social democracy as a feasible alternative to the more bumpy 'revolutionary' road. But going down the incrementalist-parliamentary path, as Bhaduri argues, implied transforming a confrontational 'class politics' into a cooperative 'coalition politics', based on class compromises, once it became clear that no social-democratic electoral majority could be created based on just the industrial working class. Such coalition politics constituted a *first* check on the social-democratic project.

In addition, the rules of the game set by property-owning democracies imposed a *second*, even more binding, constraint on any social-democratic economic programme, aiming for the nationalization of the means of production and a gradual transformation of ownership structures in general. Working within the rules of capitalism, social democracy had to abandon these goals. After all, the capitalist class has the power to strike back against attempts to nationalize the means of production by sharply reducing firm investment which, in turn, would reduce demand and employment in the short run and have negative impacts on long-run growth as well. This, then, is the dilemma: social-democratic policies must at the same time strengthen the productive power of capital and counteract the (political) power of capitalists. Once the goal of systemic transformation was abandoned and the commitment was made to maintain private property of the means of production, social democrats had to work, through the state, *within* the capitalist system, assuring its efficiency and the growth of productive capabilities, while (as far as possible) mitigating adverse distributional effects. Crucially, in all this, the state is not neutral, but 'governed by its class character' and inclined to protect the 'foundations' and 'authority structure' of the capitalist order (Kalecki 1943); to be clear, there is no 'hard' fiscal budget constraint within which social democracy had and has to formulate its political compromise, because states can borrow from (lender-of-last-resort) central banks. Rather, the 'hard' limit is based on what is deemed 'political acceptable' by national elites and establishment interests.

Cooperative capitalism: the 'wage-led' compromise

During the Great Depression of the 1930s, the twin constraints led to a drastic reorientation of European social-democratic thinking: away from the 'nationalization of the means of production' to the 'nationalization of consumption', as Swedish economist Bertil Ohlin (1938, pp. 4–5) put it. Reformism was abandoned – and capitalism accepted – on the condition that it be regulated and disciplined by the state, without any need to socialize the means of production (Table 7.1). Social democrats developed a full-fledged

Table 7.1 Social democracy as a historical phenomenon

Phases	*The social-democratic consent to capitalism*	*Macroeconomic theory*	*Policy focus*
c. 1890–end 1930s	Reformism: a gradualist, parliamentary road to transform capitalism into socialism	No clearly elaborated macroeconomic model	Nationalization of the economy and radical redistribution of property ownership structure
End 1930s–1970s	Keynesian demand management I: correcting the outcomes of capitalism through the 'nationalization of consumption'	Wage-led demand	Full-employment fiscal policy; build-up of welfare states
1970s–c. 1990	Keynesian demand management II: correcting the outcomes of capitalism by protecting firms' profitability	Profit-led demand	Wage restraint and tax reform to revive firm profits, investment and growth
c. 1990–present	New Labour/Third-Way: working not just to reproduce capitalism, but also to improve it by deregulation of financial and labour markets and imposing fiscal discipline on states	New Consensus (NAIRU) Macroeconomics	Inflation-targeting by independent central banks; fiscal policy rules and austerity; labour market deregulation

Source: Based on Przeworski (1985), Bhaduri (1993) and Storm and Naastepad (2012).

ideology of the 'welfare state', as the means to nationalize consumption and bring about mass-consumption-driven economic expansion. The fact is, writes Adam Przeworski (1985, p. 36), that

> social democrats everywhere soon discovered in Keynes' ideas, particularly after the appearance of his *General Theory*, something they urgently needed: a distinct policy for administering capitalist economies. The Keynesian revolution – and this is what it was – provided social democrats with a goal and hence the justification of their governmental role, and simultaneously transformed the ideological significance of distributive policies that favoured the working class.

The Keynesian turn was narrowed down to the argument that effective demand could be increased and unemployment reduced by redistributing income in favour of the lower-income groups (which have a higher propensity to consume). Carried to its logical extreme, higher wages and other pro-labour policies to manage aggregate demand could be shown to benefit the capitalist class as well – at least in principle; the configuration of structural conditions which bring about this outcome of 'wage-led growth' was formalized by Bhaduri and Marglin (1990).[1] Thus, during the 1950s and 1960s, Keynesian demand management (mostly through deficit financing of desirable lines of public spending) helped sustain a full employment regime, which featured high real wage growth, shortening of the working week, and the build-up of welfare states, but at the same time safeguarded adequate profit rates for firms, thereby offering an effective solution to the dilemma facing European social democracy (Marglin and Schor 1992; Glyn 2006). The Keynesian consensus of the 1950s and 1960s was unusually broad, including West-German 'social market' theorists, the governing Labour Parties in Britain and the Netherlands, social-democratic governments in Scandinavia and Austria, as well as the 'indicative planners' who shaped French public policy during the 1950s and 1960s. Its success was historically unprecedented (Marglin and Schor 1992); as political scientist Ralf Dahrendorf (1979, pp. 108–9) wrote in a post-mortem at the end of the 1970s, in "many respects the social democratic consensus signifies the greatest progress which history has seen so far. Never before have so many people had so many life chances."

A sharper economic understanding of the foundations of the 'golden age' of cooperative capitalism can be derived from a closer look at the following simple, but insightful, decomposition of the profit rate of firms (ρ), defined as the real return on their invested capital:

$$\rho = \frac{\Pi}{K} = \frac{\Pi}{X} \times \frac{X}{\overline{X}} \times \frac{\overline{X}}{K} = \pi \times u \times \kappa \tag{1}$$

Here $\pi = (\Pi/X)$ = the share of real profits (Π) in real manufacturing income (X), $u = (X/\overline{X})$ = capacity utilization, and $\kappa = (\overline{X}/K)$ = the 'normal' output-capital ratio in manufacturing. K is the capital stock (at constant prices) and $\bar{X}$ is 'normal' (trend) output. I assume that κ is a long-run constant (Storm 2019). Equation (1) can be extended using the following definition of the profit share π (Storm and Naastepad 2012):

$$\pi = 1 - \theta = 1 - w \times \lambda^{-1} \tag{2}$$

where Θ = the wage share, w = the real wage (per hour of work), and λ = labour productivity per hour worked. Substituting equation (2) into equation (1) gives:

$$\rho = \left(1 - w \times \lambda^{-1}\right) \times u \times \kappa \tag{3}$$

It can now be seen that the profit rate has three determinants: the real wage w, labour productivity λ, and capacity utilization u, which is determined by aggregate demand. Equation (3) brings out, in sharp relief, the dilemma facing social democracy: attempts to increase the real wage w for the working class raise the wage share, but they reduce the profit share and therefore decrease the profit rate (under the *ceteris paribus* assumption).

However, the golden age of cooperative capitalism managed to avoid (or overcome) this profit squeeze, because of four factors which more than offset the negative impact of higher wages on the profit rate. First, aggregate demand was 'wage-led' (Bhaduri and Marglin 1992), which meant that higher wages led to higher demand and hence to higher-capacity utilization; as equation (3) shows, higher utilization u raises the profit rate ρ (keeping other factors constant). Second, the pressure of high wages on the profit rate was reduced because higher demand and higher utilization led to higher labour productivity through the Kaldor-Verdoorn relation.[2] In terms of equation (3), this means that labour productivity (λ) increases in response to higher utilization (demand), and this in turn contributes to an increase in the profit rate (ρ). The third factor was that high wages were supported by fiscal policy intended to keep the economy (and u) close to full employment. The fourth and final factor was the high growth of world trade, enabled by the Bretton Woods system of stable exchange rates and limited cross-border capital mobility, which contributed to high export growth in most European economies (Marglin and Schor 1992). Fiscal policy was the critical factor, because it made possible (and stabilized) high productivity growth and hence high wage growth, helped by the overall wage-led nature of demand (Storm and Naastepad 2017).

The mechanism is illustrated in Figure 7.1 by the upward-sloping 'wage-led demand' curve: higher wages led to higher demand and faster economic growth as well as to higher productivity growth – and with the crucial support of fiscal support policy and high export growth, the profit rate could stay the same or even increase as wages increased along with utilization. By propping up demand, fiscal policy contributed to high rates of capacity

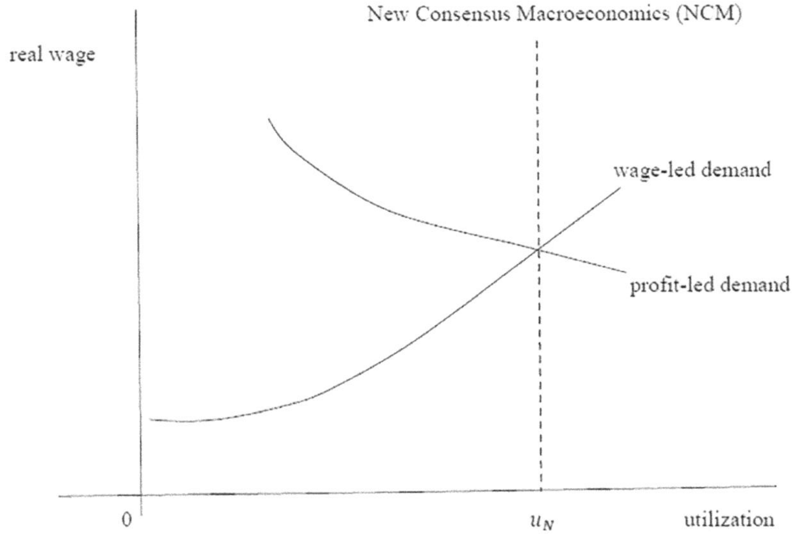

Figure 7.1 A morphology of social democracy

Note: u_N is the normal (or 'steady-inflation') rate of capacity utilization.

utilization and a stabilization of both the profit rate and employment. This way, the wage-led growth regime of the 'golden age' allowed social democracy to break free from the trade-off between higher wages and higher employment – allowing it to have the cake and eat it too.

Cooperative capitalism: 'profit-led' mongrel politics

The 'golden age of wage-led capitalism' did not prove durable, however: the compromise of the 1950s and 1960s broke down in response to the 'stagflation' of the 1970s. The reason for the breakdown was more political than economic: decades of (near) full employment had unleashed, as Michał Kalecki (1943) warned, forces which directly threatened the authority structure of capitalism – forces which became manifest in growing wage pressure, heightened worker militancy, calls for greater redistribution, and growing demands for a radical democratization of society, the economy and the workplace (Glyn 2006). The breakdown of the Bretton Woods system in 1971 added further fuel to stagflation, leading to heightened uncertainty for exporters, competitive exchange rate devaluations (triggered by the devaluation of the U.S. dollar), a slowing down of world trade growth, two oil-price shocks, and import-cost inflation (Halevi 2019). Demand growth began to decline, which in turn depressed productivity growth – and this drove up the wage share even more. The 'indiscipline' of workers, the collapse of the

Bretton Woods order, and the consequent 'profit squeeze' led governments, which in Kalecki's view cannot remain neutral in case of escalating class conflict, to protect the capitalist order by structural policy reform aimed at improving the 'climate' for private investment and finance.

The macroeconomic case for this kind of conservative-style demand management was founded on the notion of 'profit-led growth' in a Keynesian model of demand-led growth (Bhaduri and Marglin 1990, see Table 7.1). This regime of 'profit-led' capitalism is illustrated in Figure 7.1 by the downward-sloping 'profit-led' demand curve: higher wages depress aggregate demand (mostly because higher unit labour cost will reduce export and investment demand) and hence capacity utilization declines. Higher wages hurt profitability in two ways: profits per unit of output (π) go down, and demand-determined output (and, therefore, utilization u) goes down. Accordingly, a higher ρ requires that wages be reduced or that real wage growth is suppressed below the rate of labour productivity growth, because this increases both the profit share and utilization. This is illustrated by the downward slope of the 'profit-led' demand curve in Figure 7.1, which illustrates the trade-off between higher wages, on the one hand, and higher utilization, higher profitability, and higher employment, on the other hand (Esping Andersen 2000).

Given this trade-off, reviving private investment (and exports) became the focal point of a new wave of conservatism, which, championed by British Prime Minister Margaret Thatcher and US President Ronald Reagan, centred on wage moderation, monetarist inflation control (instead of full-employment-oriented fiscal policy), the deregulation of labour and financial markets, privatization, (corporate) tax reductions, globalization and (accompanying) military build-ups, and the scaling down of 'nanny' welfare states (Glyn 2006; Halevi 2019).

The collapse of wage-led growth and the crisis of stagflation brought back, with a vengeance, the dilemma of social democracy – in a profit-led system, profits must be protected from demand of the masses, because if profits are not 'sufficient', then eventually wages and/or employment must decline. In Karl Kautsky's (1925, p. 273) words, if "production does not continue, the entire society will perish, the proletariat included". In an open, profit-led economy, full employment demand management and radical redistributive policies are not in the material interest of wage-earners, because they result in high wages and poor international cost competitiveness, and therefore low profitability, sluggish investment, and stagnation (Przeworski 1985).

Social democrats completely internalized this lesson. West-German Bundeskanzler Helmut Schmidt (1976), a leading European social democrat, articulated it as follows:

> The profits of enterprises today are the investments of tomorrow, and the investments of tomorrow are the employment of the day after.
>
> (*Le Monde*, July 6, 1976)

Schmidt's argument – that current profits are the foundation of future jobs and future improvements of material conditions of workers – became the cornerstone of the post-1970s social-democratic consent of capitalism (Przeworski 1985, p. 43). While Schmidt's policy reorientation was conservative, social democracy's consent could still be justified within a system of cooperative capitalism (Bhaduri 1993). The reason is that it was still common understanding that aggregate demand mattered for profits and investment. Keynesianism was not dead yet. Social democrats could continue to argue in favour of fiscal stabilization (of the business cycle), (decent) minimum wages, collective wage bargaining, and welfare-state support for the unemployed, the disadvantaged and the elderly, because these 'Keynesian' interventions could be argued to contribute to stabilizing aggregate demand and protecting the profit rate.

Social democratic politicians – including Karl Schiller, the German SPD Minister of Economic Affairs, and Roy Jenkins, the British Labour President of the European Commission – were behind the creation of the European Monetary System (EMS) in 1979, a forerunner of the Euro. The EMS was intended to reduce exchange rate fluctuations within the European Economic Community (EEC), and especially to block Italy from pursuing its strategy of inflation and devaluation. The EMS also provided a shield against the depreciation of the US dollar (Halevi 2019). But the EMS put pressure to internally adjust on member countries having an external deficit, deflating their demand, cutting imports and (arguably) raising exports.[3]

Perhaps the clearest expression of this reorientation of social democracy within the EMS is the Dutch 'Polder Model' consensus on real wage restraint, carved in stone in the by-now near-mythical bipartite 'Agreement of Wassenaar' (of November 1982). In exchange for higher investment, more jobs and a redistribution of work, Dutch labour unions agreed, albeit reluctantly and with qualifications (Becker 2003), to keep wage growth below productivity growth so as to reduce Dutch unit labour cost and raise net exports (and utilization u in equation (3)). Wage growth restraint was also intended to bring about a higher profit share and hence a higher profit rate (as in equation (3)). It is true that the Dutch Labour Party (PvdA) initially opposed the agreement (when it was not in government), but already by the late 1980s and early 1990s (while in government), it claimed ownership of the agreement for a combination of reasons which are not difficult to fathom: the threat of Thatcher-Reagan conservativism, the failure of Mitterrand's flawed 'Keynesian experiment', and the fact that the agreement appeared to work. Dutch unemployment declined steeply in the 1980s and 1990s, exactly when unemployment in other EU countries remained high or even increased. The much-publicized 'Dutch employment miracle'[4] was widely attributed to the 'exemplary' Wassenaar agreement, by observers as diverse as Olivier Blanchard (2000), *The Economist* (2002) and the largest Dutch labour union, the FNV (see Becker 2003). The Dutch social democrats set the example to emulate, and from the late 1980s onwards, their European comrades followed suit, choosing to co-operate to reproduce capitalism and rather drastically tone down whatever was left of their initial reformist intentions – all on the assumption that their economies were profit-led and, hence, radical redistributive policies would not be in the interest of wage-earners, whose jobs and incomes depend on firm investment and, hence, on profits.

The 'Nasty Trade-Off' between growth and equality

Social democracy's compromise with 'profit-led' capitalism broke down in the early 1990s under the impacts of two powerful forces. The first one was the collapse of communism in the Soviet Union and much of Eastern Europe, which did unravel "the whole skein of doctrines which had bound the Left together for over a century", as Tony Judt (2010, p. 142) put it. From its origin, the social-democratic Left in Europe had projected itself as the reasonable alternative to revolutionary socialism, offering a respectable radical choice within the liberal polity. But with communism in ruins and the arrival of the 'end of history', Europe's social democracy, after already having consented to a bumbling stewardship of profit-led capitalism, had nothing distinctive to offer, except its "exhausted language" (Judt 2010, p. 144). "The worst thing about Communism is what comes after," wrote the Polish former dissident and newspaper editor Adam Michnik[5] – and for Western Europe's social-democratic Left, what came after was an empty space, shorn of a clear and ideological narrative which was sufficiently different from the Christian-democratic centre or from (social) liberalism.

The second force to undermine the compromise of the 1980s, no less important than the first, was the demise of Keynesianism. The victory of Thatcher-Reagan conservatism was far from inevitable, and it might not have happened, as Judt (2010, p. 96) argued, without a supporting intellectual revolution – one which succeeded in overthrowing the Keynesian consensus and turning 'government' into the problem, rather than the solution. This is the essence of the neoliberal turn in Europe's political formation: rather than entrusting the state, or the 'Staatsvolk' in Wolfgang Streeck's (2016) terminology, with the task to stabilize the unstable capitalist economy, the new (neoliberal) conservatism relegated to deregulated (financial) markets, or Streeck's 'Marktvolk', the task to maintain the stability of the social and political order. Markets are supposed to do this by imposing market discipline on corporations (which is argued to happen via shareholder pressure and the stock market), on individuals and households (through their engagement in labour markets and through debts), and on governments (which arguably are being disciplined by sovereign bond markets). The emergence of the state's private creditors, the 'Marktvolk', as disciplinarians of advanced capitalist states is arguably the key characteristic of this new political formation – which intensified distributional conflict over taxes, redistribution, and the repayment of the sovereign debts.

In 1981–83, European social democracy suffered a traumatic confrontation with the new neoliberal order, when François Mitterrand, the social-democratic President of France, who was elected on the promise of Keynesian demand stimulus, capitulated as soon as bond and currency markets started to protest. If Mitterrand were serious about his pledge to fight unemployment, writes Joseph Halevi (2019, p. 13), "he would have addressed the financial instability by a combination of sharp devaluations of the overvalued currency ('the Franc') and also by tightening capital controls". But he didn't and instead made, with remarkable speed and assiduousness, a '*tournant de la riguer*' as favoured by the *Trésor*: 'structural austerity', the outlawing of monetary financing, and 'competitive disinflation', where the latter means that nominal wage growth is deliberately suppressed below inflation – to reduce unit labour cost, arguably to boost cost competitiveness and raise the profit share of French firms. It needs no elaboration that French social democrats played major roles in the scaling up of austerity, the full marketization of sovereign debt, and competitive disinflation to policy dogma at the level of the EU and EMU (see Halevi 2019).

In macroeconomics, the 'intellectual revolution' gave birth to the New Consensus Macroeconomics (NCM) in the 1980s. NCM rejected Keynesianism by critiquing the Phillips curve – the supposedly precise and (until *circa* 1970, rather) stable trade-off between unemployment and inflation, which served to complete the 'Keynesian consensus' model and offered (monetary) policymakers the analytical apparatus to explore the impacts on output, unemployment, and inflation (see Storm 2018 for a review). In the NCM view, the stagflation of the mid-1970s proved that the Phillips-curve trade-off could exist only in the short run, for as long as actors in the economy were wrong about (actual and expected) inflation. In the longer run, once actors had learned from experience and correctly started to anticipate the rate of inflation, the NCM claims that the Phillips curve is vertical at a given rate of unemployment – the 'natural' rate of unemployment, also known as the non-accelerating inflation rate of unemployment (NAIRU). Accordingly, monetary policy could affect the unemployment-inflation trade-off in the short run, but economic activity could not deviate from its 'natural' level, as determined by the NAIRU, in the long run (Storm and Naastepad 2012). Likewise, in NCM, fiscal policy cannot have permanent, long-run, impacts without causing unmanageable accelerating inflation, which would force the central bank to increase the interest rate. Higher interest rates would, in turn, crowd out private sector investment – and unemployment would converge back to the NAIRU.[6]

The NCM position is illustrated in Figure 7.1 by the dashed vertical curve, which reflects the NCM assumptions that (i) there is a 'natural' rate of capacity utilization, u_N, which is determined by the NAIRU and from which the economy cannot permanently diverge when inflation is kept stable (at, say, 2%); (ii) there exists an equilibrium unemployment rate (the NAIRU), which is higher (lower) when the labour market is more (less) strictly regulated so as to strengthen the bargaining position of workers; and hence (iii) any increase in the wage rate in excess of labour productivity growth will raise inflation, but will have no permanent effect on economic activity (captured by u_N). Since fiscal policy does not – by assumption – have permanent effects on the growth of the economy, but only on inflation, it follows that it makes sense to restrict the policy space for fiscal policymakers by means of stringent fiscal policy rules. Keynesian economists became the 'laughing stock' and demand management was made anathema, as Robert E. Lucas (1980) explains in a quasi-obituary:

> Keynesian economics is dead . . . This is a sociological, not an economic observation, so the evidence for it is sociological. For example, you cannot find a good, under 40 economist who identifies himself and his work as 'Keynesian'. Indeed, people even take offense if referred to in this way. At research seminars, people don't take Keynesian theorizing seriously any more – the audience starts to whisper and giggle to one another. Leading journals aren't getting Keynesian papers submitted anymore.

Monetary policy suffered a similar fate. In the NCM view, monetary policy cannot have permanent impacts on growth and hence it should be strictly used to control inflation; this is best done by 'politically independent' central banks, run by technocrats who follow a monetary policy rule.

There is, in this approach, only one way to structurally raise growth and permanently reduce unemployment in a non-inflationary manner: namely, imposing structural reforms on the labour market, which lower the NAIRU. In terms of Figure 7.1, lowering the NAIRU will shift the vertical u_N curve to the right. The higher utilization raises the profit rate, also helped by a lower real wage, and this boosts investment and growth. This way, the NCM created the governing myth that governments and central banks should refrain from intervening actively, using fiscal and/or monetary policy instruments, to smooth short-run fluctuations or to steer the economy, but rather concentrate on creating the structural conditions for deregulated (labour) markets to grind out the 'natural' long-run equilibrium (Storm 2018).

The NCM has one profound policy message, which constitutes a radical denial of the promise of Keynesian demand management in a wage-led economy: macroeconomic policy faces an inescapable trade-off between 'growth' (or 'efficiency') and 'equality' (Esping-Andersen 2000). What it means in common parlance is that any policy intervention to reduce inequality, for instance by means of labour market regulation and welfare-state redistribution, carries a welfare cost, because it raises the NAIRU and hence *must* lower growth. Vice versa, any attempt to permanently raise economic growth means lowering the NAIRU by deregulating the labour market and downsizing the welfare state – which *must* raise inequality. Andrew Glyn (2006) appropriately called it the 'Nasty Trade-Off' between higher wages and more jobs – or, more generally, between economic growth and egalitarianism.

The collapse of communism deprived European social democracy from its ideological 'doppelgänger'. The death of Keynesianism left it clueless and without any effective policy levers to counteract the (political) power of capitalists. The ideological emptiness created by the collapse of communism and the demise of Keynesianism in favour of NCM was filled by 'Third Way' pragmatic compromising, strategic rebranding, and technological tinkering.

New Labour: Mrs. Thatcher's finest creation

The defining feature of New Labour of the 'Third Way' variety is its complete internalization of the idea that there exists an inescapable 'Nasty Trade-Off'. As a result, New Labour discarded fiscal policy activism in favour of rule-based fiscal austerity, supported (and in the case of Britain's New Labour, established) the independence of central banks (in effect, handing over the levers of monetary policy to unelected and democratically unaccountable technocrats), completely submitted to 'reactionary' financial interests (of the 'Marktvolk') by endorsing central-bank inflation targeting and deregulation of financial markets, and, in doing so, lost all sense of shared purpose. "Modern capitalism has no purpose except to keep the show going", wrote Joan Robinson (1971, p. 143), and the same could be said about New Labour.

It is often stated that New Labour is 'Thatcherism with a human face'. Mrs. Thatcher, who once called New Labour 'my finest creation', would likely have agreed. But so does Peter Mandelson, who was (before he was made a Baron) one of several key politicians involved in rebranding the British Labour Party as 'New Labour' and who held a number of Cabinet positions under Prime Ministers Tony Blair and Gordon Brown. In June 2002, Mandelson publicly stated, while addressing a select group of social-democratic luminaries including US President Bill Clinton, that social democrats must recognize that, when it comes to the tactics of economic modernization:

> Globalisation punishes hard any country that tries to run its economy by ignoring the realities of the market or prudent public finances. In this strictly narrow sense, and in the urgent need to remove rigidities and incorporate flexibility in capital, product and labour markets, we are all Thatcherites now.
>
> (Tempest 2002)

Prime Minister Blair could sound plausibly progressive merely by saying something positive about 'inclusive growth' or the desirability of broadly accessible public services, but the thrust of his 'Third Way' economic policies was to create a business- and finance-friendly economic environment (Osler 2002) – by means of the (semi-)privatization of public services (such as London's Underground), social dumping to attract foreign investors, tax cuts for the rich and social-benefit cuts for the (undeserving) poor, opting out of the European social charter, and unconditional support for financial globalization, harsh law-and-order policies, and deregulation of labour and financial markets, while turning a blind eye to rising income and wealth inequality (Glyn 2006; Marlière 2010). Blair and his aides consistently used Thatcherite rhetoric to strengthen his 'New Labour' credentials, such as the use of 'No turning back' and 'No, no, no'. In Labour's 1997 manifesto, Blair promised, in a special business section, that "Labour is now the party for business, the entrepreneurs' champion." Business influence within the Labour Party increased as trade unions were increasingly marginalized (Osler 2002).[7]

But it is not just Britain's New Labour. In the 1990s, it was widely felt that European social democracy needed a modern makeover, in particular by becoming more market-friendly. As a result, Europe's social democracy became a conservative force, both politically and economically – and most national governments adopted the strategy of blaming the EU and Brussels for unpopular policy reforms, which they themselves were (covertly) favouring. During 1997–2002, in France, Lionel Jospin, who led a coalition government of the 'gauche plurielle', privatized more public utilities than all the previous conservative governments combined (Marlière 2010); Jospin also publicly cautioned against wage increases and, a few months after his electoral victory, put his prime-ministerial signature on the Treaty of Amsterdam, which included the Growth and Stability Pact, as if he had already forgotten that he had campaigned on the promise to renegotiate the austerity inherent in the Pact. Similarly, SPD leader Gerhard Schröder, Germany's Armani-wearing and business-friendly Bundeskanzler, often called '*der Genosse der Bosse*', dismantled large parts of the German social welfare state, while deregulating the labour market with his Agenda 2010 (Odendahl 2017). In Italy, Walter Veltroni and Massimo d'Alema decimated the Left in a coalition with right-wing parties. At home and in the EU, social-democratic parties consolidated this neo-Thatcherite consensus, promoting 'markets' and 'community' – but as party members and voters discovered they could no longer meaningfully engage with politics when and where it mattered most, they started to switch off. To illustrate: in the 2002 French presidential elections, Jospin polled third, coming behind the National Front's candidate Jean Marie Le Pen.

Again, the Dutch social democrats had arrived there first. In his famous Den Uyl Lecture of December 1995, PvdA leader and Prime Minister Wim Kok spoke about the "liberating experience of shedding the ideological feathers" (Kok 1995). Trying to rebrand social democracy as some moderate version of Thatcherism, Kok proclaimed:

> We no longer speak of a social-democratic 'vision' or 'the alternative' of the PvdA. . . . There is no alternative for the societal constellation we have now and therefore it's no use to aim for one.
>
> (cited in Marijnissen 2009, p. 36)

The Dutch PvdA hoisted the white flag – in an unconditional surrender to TINA that there is no escape from the 'Nasty Trade-Off'. It internalized the

NCM mantra that traditional demand management by the state is no longer effective, nor can the problem of unemployment be solved by mere wage restraint. It meant that Kok felt forced to choose between 'Scylla' (protecting Dutch egalitarianism, but at the cost of low growth and high unemployment) and 'Charybdis' (promoting growth of incomes and jobs, but at the cost of greater inequality). He opted for the latter, prioritizing job growth over rising inequality.

In terms of Figure 7.1, job growth means that the u_N curve has to shift to the right – a shift associated with a non-inflationary step-up in economic growth, brought about by a decline in the NAIRU. This required, in line with the NCM view, a drastic deregulation of labour markets, implementing activating labour market programmes which offered positive ('carrots') and negative ('sticks') incentives pushing (more) people on to the labour market, and a considerable tightening of the access to social security systems, and pension and tax reforms (intended to incentivize working). These are thoroughly supply-side measures aimed at increasing (cheap) labour supply and raising the ease with which firms can hire and fire workers. Tellingly, the motto of the two consecutive Dutch governments (1994–2002) led by Prime Minister Kok was "jobs, jobs, jobs" – a motto he also gave to the report of the *Employment Taskforce* (2003), which he chaired in 2003 on behalf of the European heads of state. "Jobs, jobs, jobs" became the shared policy priority of all left-of-centre governments, which in the face of historically high rates of unemployment decided to step up job growth (Bonoli 2004). These social-democratic governments operated in the belief that fuller employment is possible only if one reduces the cost of labour and allows for low-wage flexible services jobs, as in the case of the labour market reforms of New Labour (Glyn 2006) and the Hartz-Reforms of the Schröder government (Odendahl 2017).

Table 7.2 presents the decline in the NAIRU (as estimated by the OECD) achieved during the rule of six New Labour governments in the EU. The NAIRU, just to be clear, is not the actual (observed) rate of unemployment but rather the (estimated) rate of unemployment associated with a steady-inflation growth path of the economy under consideration (see Storm and Naastepad 2012). France, Germany, and Italy had much higher NAIRUs than the Netherlands, Sweden, and the UK – a difference caused by the fact that their labour markets were more heavily regulated in favour of labour. The NAIRU is supposed to be a measure of structural unemployment, which changes only slowly, if at all – and if the NAIRU goes down, this must (in NCM theory at least) reflect structural deregulatory reform of an economy's labour market. As Table 7.2 shows, the NAIRUs came down in these six countries, and in most cases in no small measure. Reforms by the Kok governments (1994–2002) contributed to a decline in the Dutch NAIRU by 2.13 percentage points. Structural labour market reforms by Blair's governments (1997–2007) lowered the British NAIRU by 1.43 percentage points (over a period of ten years), while Jospin's reforms reduced the French NAIRU by

1.24 percentage points (in only five years). But by far the biggest reduction in the NAIRU was engineered by the Schröder government in Germany: after the introduction of the Hartz reforms, Germany's NAIRU came down from a peak of 9.49% in 2004 to 6.76% in 2010, a decline of 2.73 percentage points. The numbers in Table 7.2 underscore the considerable ambitions of Europe's New Labour governments.

These reforms created a larger 'disposable' labour force, a flexible reserve army of the underemployed, and, through this, raised inequality. This is clear from Table 7.2, which also presents changes in income inequality (as measured by the Gini coefficient of household disposable income) in the six countries over (roughly) the same period of time. Income inequality clearly increased across the board (Italy is the only exception here). In NCM logic, higher inequality is the collateral damage of lower unemployment (per the 'Nasty Trade-Off') – it is something New Labour was willing to accept, and remarkably, leisurely so. As Peter Mandelson put it, he "was relaxed about people getting filthy rich" (quoted in Marlière 2010). Many voters were not – and felt increasingly left behind by Labour's leadership.

Table 7.2 The trade-off between unemployment and inequality

	%-change in the NAIRU under New Labour:		*Social-democratic Prime Minister:*	*Gini coefficients: income*		
				Mid-1990s	*2008*	*Change*
France	-1.24%	From 9.87% in 1997 to 8.63% in 2002	Lionel Jospin (1997–2002)	0.28	0.29	0.02
Germany	-2.73%	From 9.49% in 2004 to 6.76% in 2010	Gerhard Schröder (1998–2006)	0.27	0.30	0.03
Italy	-0.05%	From 9.48% in 1996 to 9.43% in 2001	'Olive Tree' governments	0.35	0.34	-0.01
Netherlands	-2.13%	From 6.87% in 1994 to 4.74% in 2002	Wim Kok (1994–2002)	0.25	0.29	0.04
Sweden	-0.57%	From 7.49% in 1994 to 6.92% in 2006	Ingvar Carlsson/Göran Persson	0.21	0.26	0.05
UK	-1.43%	From 7.30% in 1997 to 5.87% in 2007	Tony Blair (1997–2007)	0.31	0.34	0.03

Source: NAIRU estimates are from: *OECD Economic Outlook Dataset*, No. 105, May 2019; (b) Gini coefficients of household disposable income are from: Bonesmo Fredriksen (2012).

Note: During 1997–2002, social democrats were in government in 12 out of 15 EU member states.

The economic consequences of New Labour

Although New Labour's compromise did succeed in reducing unemployment, it rather spectacularly failed to improve overall macroeconomic performance. Table 7.3 presents growth rates of real GDP, hourly employment, and (hourly) labour productivity growth in the same six European countries which appeared in Table 7.2. Real GDP growth during 2000–08 was considerably below growth in the 1990s in all economies listed in Table 7.3 (except Sweden) – notwithstanding the structural reforms introduced on New Labour's brief. The reason for the growth slowdown is ironic: as is shown by study after study, aggregate demand in these six economies is robustly 'wage-led' (Storm and Naastepad 2012, 2017). This means that the New Labour strategy of wage restraint and structural reform, coupled with strict rule-based fiscal austerity (Storm 2019), which was meant to reduce the NAIRU, raise the profit rate ρ, and push up utilization u_N, backfired. The reason: it did reduce demand and utilization and hurt both the profit rate and investment. In terms of Figure 7.1, the relevant curve is not the vertical u_N curve, proposed by NCM, but rather the upward-sloping ('co-operative Keynesian') wage-led demand curve. To paraphrase Mark Twain, the report of the death of Keynesianism seems to have been an exaggeration.

However, the macroeconomic damage done is larger. The labour market deregulation and supply-side measures to push more people into the labour market were, as noted earlier, successful: unemployment came down and

Table 7.3 Real GDP growth $\hat{x}$, hourly employment growth $\hat{\ell}$, labour productivity growth $\hat{\lambda}$, and the employment elasticity of growth η: six EU countries, 1990–99 and 2000–08

	1990–1999				*2000–2008*			
	$\hat{x}$	$\hat{\ell}$	$\hat{\lambda}$	η	$\hat{x}$	$\hat{\ell}$	$\hat{\lambda}$	η
France	1.78	−0.01	1.79	−0.01	1.58	0.54	1.04	+0.35
Germany	1.81	−0.23	2.04	−0.13	1.37	−0.12	1.49	−0.09
Italy	1.35	0.00	1.35	–	0.82	0.81	0.01	+0.99
Netherlands	3.08	1.36	1.72	+0.44	1.96	0.54	1.42	+0.28
Sweden	1.83	−0.23	2.06	−0.13	2.55	0.55	2.00	+0.22
UK	2.38	−0.18	2.56	−0.08	2.23	0.42	1.81	+0.19

Source: Storm and Naastepad (2017). Employment is measured in total hours worked; GDP is in constant prices. Employment and GDP data are from the Groningen Growth and Development Centre's total economy database. Data on real compensation per employee (GDP deflator, total economy) are from the AMECO Database. The employment elasticity η is calculated as the ratio of employment growth and real GDP growth.

labour force participation went up, which was exactly the intention. But at the macro level, the slowdown of economic growth and the increase in (hourly) employment growth imply, when taken together, a decline in labour productivity growth. This is what happened, as is shown in Table 7.3. Labour productivity declined in all countries, and most dramatically so in Italy (from 1.35% on average per year during the 1990s to zero during 2000–08). This slowdown of productivity growth puts welfare states under growing fiscal pressure (if we rule out monetary financing).

A summary indicator of the structural change that was socially engineered by New Labour's policies is the employment elasticity (η), estimates of which appear in Table 7.3. The employment elasticity gives the percentage increase in hours of work needed to generate an increase in real GDP of 1 percentage point. During the 1990s, the employment elasticity was negative in France, Germany, Sweden and the UK, which suggests that total hours of work declined while GDP was growing. The Netherlands, which had turned 'New Labour' years before the ideological turn became commonplace, is the only country where η is positive: to generate 1 percentage point growth of real GDP, the Dutch had to increase hours worked by 0.44 percentage points. The picture changes drastically after New Labour's reforms did work themselves out: the employment elasticity turned positive in France, Italy, Sweden, and the UK. This constitutes a major structural break with the past decades, when working hours fell with economic growth. Due to New Labour's intervention, workers now have to work 'harder' (more hours), rather than work 'smarter' (with higher productivity and reduced hours) to generate 1 percentage point of real GDP growth. It is impossible to read this as (social and/or emancipatory) progress – because what it reflects on the ground is the growth of low-productivity, low-pay, generally temporary 'alternative working arrangements', mostly in private services industries – arrangements which in post-Schröder Germany are often 'mini-jobs', in Italy are all fixed-term contracts (Storm 2019) and in the Netherlands post-Kok most often mean temporary self-employment.

We have reached the stage where central banks appear to worry more about the growing incidence of temp work and easily 'dismissible' workers, the fissuring of the workplace, the rise of precarious self-employment, and the consequent stagnation of wages, than social-democratic parties; for instance, the Dutch central bank (DNB 2018) sounded the alarm about the growing prevalence of self-employed workers, a phenomenon that was found to have also weakened the wage bargaining power of 'insider' permanent workers, who have to compete with flex workers who cost often only 60 percent of the wage cost of a permanent worker.

The stagnation of wage-led aggregate demand and the growing job and income insecurity, characteristic of the New Labour compromise, threatened to undermine its political legitimacy. The rapid growth of deregulated financial markets provided policymakers with an opportunity to defer this threat by enabling a strong growth of private borrowing, by households and firms, to keep 'the show going' by sustaining demand. Colin Crouch (2009) calls it "privatised Keynesianism", and its defining feature is the dramatic increase in the system's reliance on household and corporate debt to defer distributional conflicts and continue to meet the electorate's welfare expectations.

Finally, the failed New Labour compromise has caused unmeasurable political damage. This damage comes in two forms. First, big parts of social democracy's core constituency have defected to either the more extreme Left movement or to (extreme) right-wing populist parties. There is a growing polarization in the polity – with growth on the far left and even more on the far right. In Italy, France, and the UK, this polarization has already seriously destabilized the established political system – to (as yet) unknown effect. Germany, the Netherlands, and Sweden each have seen not just growing right-wing populism, but also a considerable shift of the political centre and 'accepted political discourse' to the right. Governing is becoming increasingly difficult under these polarized conditions. The other form of damage comes in more subtle ways: growing (income and wealth) inequalities have made class and status divisions more powerful, have considerably reduced (upward) social mobility, and strengthened residential segregation and segregation in education (Wilkinson and Pickett 2019). In contrast, in more equal societies, citizens trust each other, there is a greater willingness to help each other, and general attitudes to the social welfare state and taxation are more positive. As inequality rises, all this goes in reverse. Growing inequalities also lead to a bigger role for 'political money' to shape political decision-making (Ferguson, Jorgenson and Chen 2017).[8] Seen this way, the recent collapse in support for social democracy is a largely self-inflicted wound – and an unprecedented act of self-destruction.

What is to be done?

Social democracy learnt the wrong lessons from the stagflation of the 1970s and the failure to revive private investment and (profit-led) growth in the 1980s – and by embracing NCM thinking and internalizing the 'Nasty Trade-Off' as an inescapable feature of 'really-existing' capitalism, it contributed to locking economies into patterns of slow growth of the real economy – driven by debt-financed spending – and rapid growth of the financial sector – featuring rising inequality, more working poor, greater income and job insecurity, and declining social mobility. Europe's economies are turning into dual economies, split into a technologically dynamic high-wage (manufacturing) segment, which sheds jobs, and technologically stagnant low-wage services, operating as an employer of last resort (see Storm 2019). To see that this is not a sustainable outcome, one does not have to go back to Karl Marx but may consult Adam Smith (1776/1976, p. 88), who famously wrote that "No society can surely be flourishing and happy, of which the far greater part of the members are poor and miserable."

So, what is to be done? What sort of political economy framework can the Left propose to explain its objectives and justify its goals? For a start, social democrats should discard the now-discredited NCM thinking and draw the right lesson from Keynes (1936), namely that capitalism is inherently unstable and needs to be 'wisely managed' in order to become more efficient. Markets turned out to be 'bad masters' and now have to be turned into 'good servants'. Hence, rather than having 'markets' and 'Marktvolk' act as the disciplinarians ensuring social and economic order, we need states and social organization to impose stability on unruly markets, including through imposing cross-border capital controls (when and where necessary). Social democrats also have to understand that it makes no sense to let financial markets determine the fiscal capacity of the state – this is a fundamentally political decision which involves matching society's levels of taxation to its social (spending) ambitions and deciding on how to finance a public deficit (in case it arises). This is neither a plea for Big States nor for maximum monetary financing, but rather for meaningful deliberative democracy in which citizens have a say in politics when and where it matters most. It is a firm plea against the de-politicization of fiscal and monetary policy as well as against the corrupting influence of political money on democracy – which should have been obvious to social democrats anyway.

Second, social democrats must reject the ideology of the 'Nasty Trade-Off' for what it is: a conservative fantasy. The vertical u_N curve in Figure 7.1 does not exist (Storm and Naastepad 2012). European economies are wage-led, and this means that higher wages and progressive income redistribution do indeed improve macroeconomic performance and benefit both workers and firms, especially when supported by aggregate demand management. Social democrats ought to stand for both fair real wage increases and a credible commitment in macroeconomic policymaking to full employment (rather than low inflation) – demands which do not conflict with productivity growth and profitability (if properly managed). Likewise, welfare states and protective labour market institutions must not be considered a cost and a drain, but rather constitute efficient frameworks which, by helping nations to share the costs and benefits of globalization and technological progress, make firms more flexible and raise their international competitiveness. This is by no means a covert defensive call for a return to an idealized past (e.g. the 'golden age'); instead it is an evidence-based diagnosis of where we are and how we got there, and a recognition that there are alternatives to Thatcherism beyond the 'Thatcherism with a human face'. Capitalism needs to be managed, and if citizens do not do it (through the political process), then 'superstar' firms, big banks, big-tech companies, and billionaires will do it for us.

And lest we forget: the management of capitalism will soon become even more urgent – because the coming fourth industrial revolution (with robotics and artificial intelligence taking away jobs on an unprecedented scale) and the looming crisis of global warming will reopen the Social Question (Judt

2010): how is a democratic society to respond to high un- and underemployment, to sharply rising inequalities in pay, to wealth and social mobility, and to the mounting costs of climate damage and growing pressure from climate refugees? What can we do to share employment, and how do we finance jobs in socially meaningful but economically insufficiently profitable activities? What should be done to bring down carbon emissions, bring about the necessary technical progress in low-carbon forms of transportation and power generation, and step up zero-carbon renewable energy generation fast enough and in ways that ensure that the strongest shoulders carry the largest burden? Social democracy cannot leave it to 'markets' to find the answers to these burning questions – what is needed is 'social organization', collaboration, and co-ordination of decision-making within and between nations. A reinvented, self-critical social democracy, which has learned the right lessons from its own flawed history, can contribute to findings ways to respond to the challenges ahead in peaceful, equitable, and inclusive ways, appropriate to varying national contexts.

However, any reimagined social democracy worth the name must begin by imposing discipline on banks and financial markets – and by domestication, turn them from the powerful over-lords (who they currently are) into useful servants for the societal interest. This, in turn, requires a counter-revolution in economic thinking, one which overthrows the NCM in favour of more realistic (less utopian) and more humane approaches. NCM must be seen for what it is: stale 19th-century pre-Keynesian thinking, a parody of an accountant's nightmare, as John Maynard Keynes (1933) put it:

> Instead of using their vastly increased material and technical resources to build a wonder city, the men of the nineteenth century built slums; and they thought it right and advisable to build slums because slums, on the test of private enterprise, 'paid', whereas the wonder city would, they thought, have been an act of foolish extravagance, which would, in the imbecile idiom of the financial fashion, have 'mortgaged the future' – though how the construction to-day of great and glorious works can impoverish the future, no man can see until his mind is beset by false analogies from an irrelevant accountancy. Even to-day I spend my time – half vainly, but also, I must admit, half successfully – in trying to persuade my countrymen that the nation as a whole will assuredly be richer if unemployed men and machines are used to build much needed houses than if they are supported in idleness. For the minds of this generation are still so beclouded by bogus calculations that they distrust conclusions which should be obvious, out of a reliance on a system of financial accounting which casts doubt on whether such an operation will 'pay.' We have to remain poor because it does not 'pay' to be rich. We have to live in hovels, not because we cannot build palaces, but because we cannot 'afford' them.
>
> The same rule of self-destructive financial calculation governs every walk of life. We destroy the beauty of the countryside because the

> unappropriated splendors of nature have no economic value. We are capable of shutting off the sun and the stars because they do not pay a dividend. London is one of the richest cities in the history of civilization, but it cannot 'afford' the highest standards of achievement of which its own living citizens are capable, because they do not 'pay.'
>
> If I had the power to-day, I should most deliberately set out to endow our capital cities with all the appurtenances of art and civilization on the highest standards of which the citizens of each were individually capable, convinced that what I could create, I could afford – and believing that money thus spent not only would be better than any dole but would make unnecessary any dole. For with what we have spent on the dole in England since the war we could have made our cities the greatest works of man in the world.

Where can one find a better place to start re-imagining social democracy?

Notes

1 Aggregate demand is said to be 'wage-led' if it increases to a rise in the real wage rate. For this to occur, the increase in consumption demand (triggered by the higher wage) must more than offset the decline in investment and (net) exports, caused by the higher wage. Investment declines because the higher wage reduces the profit share. Net exports decline because the higher wage raises unit labour cost of production; to the extent that this raises prices, the international cost/price competitiveness of the country will be hurt. Aggregate demand is 'profit-led' if it falls in response to an increase in the real wage. See Bhaduri and Marglin (1990) and Storm and Naastepad (2012).

2 The Kaldor-Verdoorn relation states that faster growth of aggregate demand and output must cause an acceleration of productivity growth. First, demand growth allows an economy-wide deepening of the division of labour and more rapid learning-by-doing (in firms), both of which are processes which eventually are reflected in higher productivity growth. Moreover, to the extent that demand growth is investment growth, the new investments result in higher labour productivity, because the newly installed equipment embodies state-of-the-art technology and is therefore more productive than older vintages of capital stock. See Storm and Naastepad (2012, 2016).

3 Halevi (2019) provides the relevant political economy of the EMS and how it morphed into the Economic and Monetary Union (EMU).

4 Dutch unemployment was more than 11% of the labour force in 1982, or 2.1 percentage points *higher* than the average EU-15 unemployment rate in the same year. But by 1990, Dutch unemployment had come down to 5.1%, a full 2.1 percentage points *below* the EU-15 unemployment rate, and it declined further to only 3.1% in 2000, with the EU-15 unemployment rate stuck at 7.7% (Storm and Naastepad 2017).

5 Quoted in Judt (2010, p. 139).

6 In reality, the Thatcher-Reagan disinflation was done through sharp increases in interest rates and strong anti-labour policies (Marglin and Schor 1992; Glyn 2006). It took a decade or more for economies to adjust to the new policy regime – and this obvious failure to quickly adjust is difficult to square with the insistence of NCM on rational, optimizing, forward-looking behaviour by economic agents.

7 Osler (2002) documents how relations between New Labour and business were cemented through large donations to the party, often running to millions of pounds, from top executives and leading companies. Such generosity was reciprocated with peerages for major benefactors, while corporate supporters (including multinationals with questionable track records on union recognition, human rights and the environment) were given lucrative privatization contracts.
8 Ferguson *et al.* (2017) propose a "spectrum of political money", or eight ways, all legal but difficult to trace, through which outside money shapes political decision-making. These include payments to lawyers, politicians and foundations; money spent on lobbying and think tanks; formal campaign spending; the value of stock tips to political figures and public relations spending. See also Osler (2002).

References

Becker, U. 2003. 'Competitive corporatism? National and transnational elements in the Dutch "employment miracle".' In H. Overbeek (ed.). *The Political Economy of European Employment*. London: Routledge, pp. 154–175.

Berman, S. 2006. *The Primacy of Politics: Social Democracy and the Making of Europe's Twentieth Century*. Cambridge: Cambridge University Press.

Bhaduri, A. 1993. 'The economics and politics of social democracy.' In P. Bardhan, M. Datta-Chaudhuri and T.N. Krishnan (eds.). *Development and Change: Essays in Honour of K.N. Raj*. Delhi: Oxford University Press, pp. 59–67.

Bhaduri, A. and S. Marglin. 1990. 'Unemployment and the real wage: The economic basis for contesting political ideologies.' *Cambridge Journal of Economics* 14 (4): 375–393.

Blanchard, O. 2000. *The Dutch Jobs Miracle*. Available at: www.project-syndicate.org/commentary/bla5/English

Bonesmo Fredriksen, K. 2012. 'Income inequality in the European Union.' *OECD Economics Department Working Paper No. 952*. Paris: OECD. Available at: https://doi.org/10.1787/5k9bdt47q5zt-en

Bonoli, G. 2004. 'Social Democratic party policies in Europe: Towards a Third Way?' In G. Bonoli and M. Powell (eds.). *Social Democratic Party Policies in Contemporary Europe*. London: Routledge, pp. 197–213.

Crouch, C. 2009. 'Privatised Keynesianism: An unacknowledged policy regime.' *British Journal of Politics and International Relations* 11 (3): 382–399.

Dahrendorf, R. 1979. 'The end of the social democratic consensus.' In *Life Chances*. Chicago: University of Chicago Press.

DNB. 2018. 'Flexibilisering van de arbeidsmarkt gaat gepaard met daling arbeidsinkomensquote' ('Flexibilization of the labor market leads to decline in the wage share'). *DNBulletin*, February 1. Amsterdam: De Nederlandsche Bank.

The Economist. 2002. 'Model makers: A survey of the Netherland.' May 2.

Employment Taskforce. 2003. *Jobs, Jobs, Jobs: Creating More Employment in Europe*. Available at: www.ciett.org/fileadmin/templates/eurociett/docs/Kok_Report _2003 _Jobs_Jobs_Jobs.pdf

Esping-Andersen, G. 2000. 'Two societies, one sociology, no theory.' *British Journal of Sociology* 51 (1): 59–78.

Ferguson, T., P. Jorgenson, and J. Chen. 2017. '*Fifty Shades of Green: High Finance, Political Money and the U.S. Congress*.' Report for the Roosevelt Institute. Available at: https://rooseveltinstitute.org/wp-content/uploads/2017/05/FiftyShadesof-Green _0517.pdf

Glyn, A. 2006. *Capitalism Unleashed: Finance, Globalization and Welfare*. Oxford: Oxford University Press.

Halevi, J. 2019. 'From the EMS to the EMU . . . and to China.' *Unpublished Mimeo.*

Judt, Tony. 2010. *Ill Fares the Land: A Treatise on Our Present Discontents*. London: Penguin Books.

Kalecki, M. 1943. 'Political aspects of full employment.' *The Political Quarterly* 14 (3): 322–330.

Kautsky, K. 1925. *The Labour Revolution*. London: Allen & Unwin.

Keynes, J.M. 1933. 'National self-sufficiency.' *The Yale Review* 22 (4): 755–769.

Keynes, J.M. 1936. *The General Theory of Employment, Interest and Money*. London: Macmillan.

Kok, W. 1995. 'We laten niemand los.' *Den Uyl-Lecture*, December 11.

Lucas, R.E. 1980. 'The death of Keynesian economics.' *Issues and Ideas* (Winter issue).

Marglin, S.E. and J.B. Schor (eds.). 1992. *The Golden Age of Capitalism: Reinterpreting the Postwar Experience*. Oxford: Clarendon Press.

Marijnissen, J. 2009. *Tegenstemmen: Een Antwoord op het Neoliberalisme*. (Voting Against. A Reply to Neoliberalism). Amsterdam: L.J. Veen.

Marlière, P. 2010. 'The decline of Europe's social democratic parties.' *Open Democracy.org*, March 16. Available at: www.opendemocracy.net/en/decline-of-europes-social-democratic-parties/

Odendahl, C. 2017. 'The Hartz myth: Drawing lessons from Germany.' *CER Bulletin No. 115*. London: Centre for European Reform.

Ohlin, B. 1938. 'Economic progress in Sweden.' *The Annals of the American Academy of Political and Social Science* 197 (1): 1–6.

Osler, D. 2002. *Labour Party PLC. New Labour as a Party of Business*. London: Mainstream Publishing.

Przeworski, A. 1985. *Capitalism and Social Democracy*. Cambridge: Cambridge University Press.

Robinson, J. 1971. *Economic Heresies: Some Old-Fashioned Questions in Economic Theory*. London: Macmillan.

Schmidt, H. 1976. Interview. *Le Monde*, July 6.

Smith, A. 1976/1776. *An Inquiry into the Nature and Causes of the Wealth of Nations*. Chicago: University of Chicago Press.

Storm, S. 2018. 'The wrong track also leads someplace: Milton Friedman's presidential address at fifty.' *Review of Keynesian Economics* 6 (4): 517–532.

Storm, S. 2019. 'Lost in deflation: Why Italy's woes are a warning to the whole Eurozone.' *International Journal of Political Economy* 48, forthcoming.

Storm, S. and C.W.M. Naastepad. 2012. *Macroeconomics Beyond the NAIRU*. Cambridge, MA: Harvard University Press.

Storm, S. and C.W.M. Naastepad. 2017. 'Bhaduri-Marglin meet Kaldor-Marx: Wages, productivity and investment.' *Review of Keynesian Economics* 5 (2): 4–24.

Streeck, W. 2016. *How Will Capitalism End?* London: Verso.

Tempest, M. 2002. 'Mandelson: We are all Thatcherites now.' *The Guardian*, June 10. Available at: www.theguardian.com/politics/2002/jun/10/labour.uk1

Wilkinson, R. and K. Pickett. 2019. *The Inner Level: How More Equal Societies Reduce Stress, Restore Sanity and Improve Everyone's Well-being*. London: Penguin Random House.

8 What is the impact of an exogenous shock to the wage share?

VAR results for the US economy, 1973–2018

Deepankar Basu and Leila Gautham

The relationship between distribution, demand and growth has occupied a central place in contemporary debates within heterodox macroeconomics. Early models that built on the work of Michał Kalecki (collectively referred to as "neo-Kaleckian" models) emphasized the result that distributional changes tilting national income in favor of profits would depress both capacity utilization and the accumulation rate or growth rate. This decidedly underconsumptionist conclusion was put into question by the seminal contribution of Bhaduri and Marglin (1990), who showed that increases in the profit share, through positive effects on investment or the trade balance, might result in an increase in capacity utilization or the rate of growth. A large and growing literature has followed Bhaduri and Marglin's (1990) lead by attempting to empirically ascertain whether individual economies are profit-led or wage-led, the former referring to an economy where a shift in income towards profits boosts demand and growth, and the latter referring to the opposite scenario. We contribute to this literature by using a novel empirical strategy to credibly identify the effect of shocks to the functional distribution of income on aggregate demand and growth.

Existing empirical studies can be divided into broad groups: structural models that attempt to separately estimate the effect of distribution on different components of aggregate demand, and systems models that investigate the overall relationship between distribution and demand, while accounting for the endogeneity of distributional variables (Blecker 2011). We take the second approach and use vector autoregressions (VARs) to construct impulse response functions as a way to identify the effect of distributional shocks on demand and growth. VARs are powerful tools to explore interrelationships between macroeconomic aggregates while imposing minimal restrictions. But by themselves, i.e. without additional restrictions, they cannot tell us about how the economy might respond to distributional shocks. Existing studies that estimate the effect of distribution on demand have not paid much attention to the identification of shocks to distribution. We use a recursive strategy to identify the impact of shocks to the wage share on demand and growth for the US economy from 1973 to 2018. We impose a minimal set of assumptions and show that our results are robust to differences in specification. Our substantive contribution is therefore in providing convincing empirical estimates of the effect of shocks of distribution on demand and growth.

The rest of this chapter is structured as follows: the next section lays out a simple theoretical model outlining the relationship between distribution and demand in the context of an open economy that we use to guide our empirical strategy. In this section, we also review existing empirical studies with a focus on papers that estimate the effect of the wage share or profit share on capacity utilization using a VAR methodology. This is followed by a discussion of the VAR framework and the problem of identifying structural shocks. We then outline two identification strategies that we use to identify shocks to distribution: a pure recursive VAR, and a modified recursive VAR that builds on the seminal contribution of Christiano, Eichenbaum and Evans (1999). We discuss the application of both strategies to our research question, and we present an econometric model and a discussion of the restrictions that we impose to identify shocks to distribution. We then describe our data and present and discuss our main results.

Neo-Kaleckian models and empirical work

This section presents a basic neo-Kaleckian open economy model of the short run, extends it to account for medium-run dynamics and reviews some empirical literature relevant for our work. First, we present a basic short-run model of the goods market that outlines the standard post-Keynesian/neo-Kaleckian insight of how the functional distribution of income determines aggregate demand. This model assumes a given real exchange rate and functional distribution. Second, following Blecker (2011), we present a dynamic model of conflicting-claims inflation and a managed exchange rate, which solves for medium-run equilibrium levels of the wage share and real exchange rate. Our modelling framework serves to synthesize existing insights from the theoretical post-Keynesian literature and forms a backdrop for the discussion of the empirical literature that follows. The theoretical results also guide our own empirical strategy.

The baseline model

We model a one-sector open economy, where prices are set as a markup over average variable costs and labor is assumed to be the only variable input. Our pricing equation is therefore given as

$$P_t = (1 + \tau_t) W_t a_t$$

where P denotes prices, τ is the markup, W is the nominal wage and a denotes the inverse of labor productivity (subscripts for all variables denote the time period). Expressions for the wage share ψ and the real exchange rate q are therefore given by

$$\psi_t = \frac{W_t a_t}{P_t}$$

$$q_t = \frac{E_t P_t^F}{P_t}$$

where P^F denotes foreign prices and E denotes the nominal exchange rate (price of the foreign currency in terms of the domestic currency, for instance, \$/€). For the short-run goods market equilibrium, we assume that nominal wages, prices, labor productivity (and hence the wage share), exchange rates and foreign prices are given. The open economy national income accounting identity (omitting fiscal variables for simplicity) would therefore require that

$$\frac{S_t}{K_t} = \frac{I_t}{K_t} + \frac{TB_t}{K_t}$$

where S, I, TB, and K refer, respectively, to aggregate savings, gross investment, the trade balance and capital stock. As is standard in post-Keynesian models, our behavioral equations represent the savings rate and the investment rate as depending negatively on the wage share and positively on the rate of capacity utilization z, so we have

$$s \equiv \frac{S_t}{K_t} = s(\psi_t, z_t), s_\psi < 0, s_z > 0$$

$$g \equiv \frac{I_t}{K_t} = g(\psi_t, z_t), g_\psi < 0, g_z > 0$$

We assume the ratio of the trade balance to capital stock to be a positive function of the real exchange rate and a negative function of the capacity utilization rate,

$$b \equiv \frac{TB_t}{K_t} = b(q_t, z_t), b_q > 0, b_z < 0$$

Substituting for these relations in the national income identity, we get

$$s(\psi_t, z_t) = g(\psi_t, z_t) + b(q_t, z_t)$$

which allows us to solve for the equilibrium rate of capacity utilization as a function of the wage share and real exchange rate

$$z_t = z(\psi_t, q_t),$$

a linear version of which can be written as

$$z_t = a_0 + a_1\psi_t + a_2 q_t \tag{1}$$

Demand can be characterized as profit-led if the partial derivative of equilibrium capacity utilization with respect to the wage share is negative, and growth is profit-led if the partial derivative of the accumulation rate (as a function of the equilibrium rate of capacity utilization) with respect to the wage share is negative.

While prices, nominal wages and the exchange rate are given in the short run, we would expect them to adjust over the medium run. Following Blecker's (2011) adaptation of the conflict-driven inflationary process, we model the adjustment of prices by assuming that firms have a target markup rate (corresponding to a target wage share) that they attempt to achieve when setting prices, and that this target markup rate depends positively on the real exchange rate. We also assume that firms base their pricing decisions on past realizations of the wage share and the real exchange rate (which is a plausible assumption, as current realizations of the wage share and the real exchange rate depend on current prices and wages, and hence would not be known to firms). We can therefore model the dynamics of prices as

$$P_t = P_{t-1}\left[1 + p\left(\psi_{t-1}, q_{t-1}\right)\right]$$

with $p_\psi > 0$ (a higher wage share means that firms are further away from their target markup and adjust prices upwards) and $p_q > 0$ (a depreciation would improve competitiveness and induce firms to raise their prices).

Similarly, we assume that workers have a target real wage and that lower realized real wages in the previous period induce them to bargain for higher nominal wages in the present period. We can therefore think of nominal wage growth as depending positively on the difference between some target ω and the previous period realization of $\frac{W_{t-1}}{P_{t-1}^{\alpha} P_{t-1}^{F1-\alpha}}$, where α denotes the relative importance of domestic goods in the workers' consumption bundles. So, we have

$$W_t = W_{t-1}\left[1 + w\left(\psi_{t-1}, q_{t-1}\right)\right]$$

with $w_\psi < 0$ and $w_q > 0$.

Finally, we model nominal exchange rates as being managed by the central bank which has a target real exchange rate and adjusts nominal exchange rates to achieve that target

$$E_t = E_{t-1}\left[1 + e\left(q_{t-1}\right)\right]$$

with $e_q < 0$.

These three equations give us dynamic equations for the adjustment of the wage share and the real exchange rate:

$$\widehat{\psi_t} = \widehat{W_t} - x - \widehat{P_t} = w(\psi_{t-1}, q_{t-1}) - x - p(\psi_{t-1}, q_{t-1})$$

$$\widehat{q_t} = \widehat{E_t} + \widehat{P_t^F} - \widehat{P_t} = e(q_{t-1}) + p^F - p(\psi_{t-1}, q_{t-1})$$

where x and p^F denote the growth rate of labor productivity and the foreign price level, respectively, and are taken as given.

The steady state values of q and ψ therefore satisfy

$$w(\psi, q) - x - p(\psi, q) = 0 \quad (2)$$

$$e(q) + p^F - p(\psi, q) = 0 \quad (3)$$

Equations (1), (2) and (3) define the baseline neo-Kaleckian model that we estimate and use for the VAR analysis. While the baseline model is useful for initiating the analysis, it has three important limitations.

First, it takes the accumulation rate to be affected contemporaneously by the wage share and capacity utilization rate, and it does not allow for exogenous shocks to the accumulation rate. Rather, we would expect the accumulation rate to be exogenously given in the short run, with firms basing their investment decisions on past values of the wage share and capacity utilization rates; we also need to allow for exogenous shocks to have impacts on investment, primarily to capture the role of animal spirits in determining the accumulation rate. Second, the baseline model takes labor productivity growth to be exogenously given. Labor productivity would depend on the accumulation rate and also on the wage share: a higher wage share may induce firms to substitute away from labor through capital deepening. It would therefore be essential to allow for the endogeneity of labor productivity growth when attempting to estimate the interaction between the wage share and capacity utilization and accumulation. Finally, we would expect the setting of nominal wages and wage bargaining to depend on the unemployment rate. A more complete specification would therefore include three additional variables: the accumulation rate, the growth rate of labor productivity and the unemployment rate.

An extended neo-Kaleckian model

Given the problems of the baseline model, we need to incorporate additional variables into our analysis and develop an extended neo-Kaleckian model. First, we note that the rate of capital accumulation, g_t, is completely determined by variables in the previous period. This follows our understanding, alluded to earlier, that capital accumulation decisions are largely inherited from the past, they are not impacted by contemporaneous variables:

$$g_t = g(u_{t-1}, x_{t-1}, \psi_{t-1}, q_{t-1}, z_{t-1}) \tag{4}$$

The second modification is to endogenize labor productivity growth. We posit that the growth rate of labor productivity depends on the accumulation rate (thus allowing for Kaldor-Verdoorn learning-by-doing effects of investment on productivity growth) and also on the unemployment rate and the wage share, the latter two factors capturing the effects of labor-saving technological change:

$$x_t = x(g_t, u_t, \psi_t) \tag{5}$$

Next, we turn to the determination of real exchange rate. Our analysis in the baseline model had shown that, in a medium-run equilibrium, the real exchange rate is impacted by the wage share – capturing the effect of wage pressures on the relative price of domestic goods in the international market. To that mechanism we now add two more determinants: the unemployment rate and the rate of capital accumulation. The first is meant to capture the effect of labor market tightness, and the latter the impact of possible embodied technological change on relative prices. Bringing these together, we have

$$q_t = q(\psi_t, u_t, g_t) \tag{6}$$

The adjustment of prices is unchanged; however, we modify the nominal wage-setting process to depend on the current unemployment rate (which affects the bargaining power of workers) and previous period labor productivity growth (which affects real wages for a given wage share) in addition to the previous period values of the wage share and the real exchange rate:

$$W_t = W_{t-1}\left[1 + w(u_t, x_{t-1}, \psi_{t-1}, q_{t-1})\right]$$

The equation for the adjustment of the wage share is altered as follows:

$$\widehat{\psi_t} = w(u_t, x_{t-1}, \psi_{t-1}, q_{t-1}) - x(g_t, u_t, \psi_t) - p(\psi_{t-1}, q_{t-1}),$$

So that, in medium-run equilibrium, the wage share becomes a function of the unemployment rate and the rate of capital accumulation:

$$\psi_t = \psi(u_t, g_t) \tag{7}$$

We allow the unemployment rate to depend on the rate of capacity utilization and labor productivity growth in the previous period, as well as on the current rate of accumulation:

$$u_t = u(g_t, z_{t-1}, x_{t-1}) \tag{8}$$

Finally, the rate of capacity utilization, being an indicator of demand, is impacted by all variables contemporaneously:

$$z_t = z(g_t, u_t, \psi_t, q_t, x_t) \tag{9}$$

Equations (4) through (9) comprise the extended neo-Kaleckian model in this chapter.

We estimate both the baseline model – given by equations (1) through (3) – and the extended model – given by linear versions of equations (4) through (9). The advantage of estimating the baseline model is that it requires fewer assumptions and is easier to interpret; however, the inclusion of additional variables is necessary for a more complete specification, and we therefore also estimate the extended model.

Existing empirical literature

Empirical studies that examine the relationship between, on the one hand, distributional variables and, on the other, aggregate demand and growth, can be usefully divided into two categories: structural models (that attempt to separately estimate the different components of aggregate demand) and aggregative or systems models (that look at the overall relationship between distribution and demand). Examples of studies that attempt an econometric estimation of structural models include Hein and Vogel (2008), Stockhammer, Onaran and Ederer (2008), and Onaran, Stockhammer and Grafl (2011), among many others. As structural approaches typically regress the various components of aggregate demand (consumption, investment, exports, imports) on some measure of the functional distribution and other control variables, their estimates are biased to the extent that the wage/profit share is endogenous. Moreover, estimating separate econometric equations for each component of aggregate demand misses out on dynamic interactions between these components, making it hard to interpret their coefficients or even computing standard errors for important effects that involve parameters from different equations (an example of the latter is the total effect of the profit share on the growth rate of GDP reported in Table 10 in Hein and Vogel 2008).

Aggregative or systems approaches address the endogeneity of distribution and demand either through the use of instrumental variables or methods such as vector autoregressions (VARs). As our own method in this chapter falls under this category, we provide a brief overview of studies that attempt to estimate the relationship between demand and distribution using systems approaches, highlighting in each case what we see to be limitations or problems in their methodology. Stockhammer and Onaran (2004) look at accumulation, demand, distribution and unemployment for the UK (1970–1997), the US (1966–1997) and France (1972–1997) using a VAR analysis. They formulate a structural Kaleckian model for the interactions between these variables, and the model provides the motivation for restrictions on contemporaneous effects in their VAR analysis. While their analysis confirms key Keynesian insights such as the importance of the goods market in determining unemployment, they do not find any significant effect of the distributional variable on effective demand for any of the countries. They do not read this as supporting the absence of interaction between distribution and demand, but rather that the positive and negative effects of the profit share on effective demand roughly offset each other.

However, some of their key identifying restrictions appear to be arbitrary rather than motivated by theoretical priors. For example, they allow capacity utilization to have a contemporaneous effect on the profit share, but do not allow the profit share to have a contemporaneous effect on capacity utilization. This contradicts their own theoretical model: capacity utilization is assumed to be determined by the *current* value of the profit share (equation 5, Stockhammer and Onaran 2004, p. 424). It is possible that this restriction contributes to their finding that distribution does not play a role in determining goods market outcomes – by assumption, they do not allow distribution to have contemporaneous effects on utilization. A second problem is their failure to include real exchange rate dynamics in their analysis: as Blecker (2011) points out, an open economy with flexible markups would respond differently depending on the source of the increase in the profit share.

Barbosa-Filho and Taylor (2006) more narrowly analyze the interaction between capacity utilization and the labor share for the US economy (1948–2002) using a two-variable VAR. They find demand to be profit-led and distribution to be characterized by a profit squeeze, providing empirical support for the Goodwin model. Their conclusions are, however, based exclusively on estimates from reduced form VARs. For the reduced form errors to *not* exhibit contemporaneous correlation, the labor share must not have a contemporaneous effect on capacity utilization, and vice versa. If this does not hold, their estimates are appropriate for forecasting purposes but cannot be given a causal interpretation (Sims 1986). Other studies using VAR approaches generally appear to confirm these qualitative findings (profit-led demand and profit squeeze) (Carvalho and Rezai 2015; Kiefer and Rada 2014). Carvalho and Rezai (2015) split their US sample into two periods based on the degree of income inequality (pre- and post-1981) and estimate a recursive VAR for the labor share and capacity utilization. They do not, however, specify or justify the causal ordering they employ in the Cholesky decomposition that they appear to use. As impulse response functions from a recursive VAR are generally sensitive to the causal ordering that is imposed, this strengthens our view that estimations of demand and distribution have not paid much attention to the problem of identification.

A second, more substantive, problem is that with the exception of Stockhammer and Onaran (2004), the studies mentioned here estimate only bivariate VARs in capacity utilization and the wage/profit share. While this is a direct result of their focused attention on Goodwin-type dynamics, the simplicity of the model – which is certainly desirable in the case of a theoretical framework that intends to explain a particular dynamic process in capitalist economies – poses an important problem in econometric estimation: in particular, the issue of omitted variables and misspecification. In low-dimensional VARs, the effects of omitted variables are subsumed under "innovations" to included variables. If important variables are omitted from the system, the estimated impulse responses may be highly distorted and not have a structural interpretation (Lütkepohl 2005, 62). In the context of reduced form VARs in distribution and demand, as Skott (2017) persuasively argues, exogenous shocks may affect *both* demand and distribution, which means that we cannot uniquely ascertain the relationship between demand and distribution. A good example of this could be shocks that reduce wages in the context of flexible price markups: this would increase the profit share but would also affect aggregate demand through the channel of real exchange rates. If real exchange rates are not controlled for, the estimated effect of distribution on demand would be very different from what it would be if the source of the positive shock to the profit share was a rise in the markup rate. The estimated relationship therefore hinges on which source of the shock is more common. While there could be multiple such sources of shocks, it should not preclude any attempt at empirical estimation. Rather, a more careful consideration of the factors that affect both distribution and demand and a properly-specified model would allow us to get at more convincing estimates of the relationship between distribution and demand. Our methodology, which we describe in the next section, attempts to do precisely that. We therefore believe that our estimates improve significantly on both the estimations based on structural models and on existing aggregative studies.

VAR and the two identification strategies

A vector autoregression (VAR) is a linear model in which each variable is explained by its own lagged values and the past and/or current values of the other variables in the system. Since their introduction by Sims (1980), they have been widely used as a macro-econometric tool to capture dynamic interactions in multiple time series (Stock and Watson 2001). To briefly describe the problem: the starting point of a VAR analysis would be to select a set of variables suggested by the theoretical model and to regress each variable on its own lagged values and the lagged values of other variables. The resulting estimates from the reduced form model can be used to trace out the effect of a shock to one variable on the system. These dynamic response functions (called impulse responses), however, cannot be interpreted as causal because these variables are likely to correlated with each other, and we therefore cannot expect the shocks to be contemporaneously uncorrelated. Hence a shock to one variable would also have a contemporaneous effect on some other variable in the system through its own error term. The only way to generate economically meaningful impulse response functions is to work with orthogonal shocks, i.e. where each shock is contemporaneously uncorrelated with every other shock. However, there is no unique way to orthogonalize the reduced form errors. Identifying the full set of contemporaneous relations between all variables is impossible without imposing a sufficient number of restrictions.

To describe it formally, suppose our dynamic macro-econometric model is given by

$$AX_t = A_0 + A_1 X_{t-1} + \dots + A_p X_{t-p} + e_t$$

where $X_t = [\psi_t, q_t, z_t]'$ is a 3 × 1 vector of three variables – the wage share, the real exchange rate and the capacity utilization rate – of our baseline model, A is the matrix of contemporaneous relations between the variables, A_i is the matrix of relations between current values and lagged values and e_t are structural shocks. In addition to the linearity assumption and time-invariance of the coefficients, we assume that $\Sigma_e = E(e_t e_t') = I$ and $E(e_s, e_t') = 0$, $\forall s \neq t$. Given the endogeneity of the regressors, we cannot directly estimate this structural model. We instead estimate the reduced form model which is given by

$$X_t = B_0 + B_1 X_{t-1} + \dots + B_p X_{t-p} + u_t$$

The reduced form errors are not contemporaneously uncorrelated: $\Sigma_u = E(u_t u_t') = A^{-1} A^{-1\prime}$ and so the covariance matrix for the reduced form errors is not diagonal unless the matrix A is an identity matrix (in which case none of the variables have a contemporaneous effect on one another). The implication of this is that we cannot interpret impulse responses calculated from the reduced form VAR as the causal impact of a shock to one variable in the system. Recovering the structural VAR from the reduced form estimates would, however, require us to impose a sufficient number of restrictions. In our 3 × 3 VAR, for example, we can estimate the 3 × 3 Σ_u matrix. As it is symmetric, it contains 6 distinct values. As the A matrix has 9 distinct values, the system of equations given by $\Sigma_u = A^{-1} A^{-1\prime}$ is under-identified. In particular, we need three additional restrictions to recover the structural model (for an n-variable system, we would need $\frac{n(n-1)}{2}$ restrictions).

In general, strategies for identification can be classified into two broad groups: structural VARs and recursive VARs. A recursive VAR depends on a particular ordering of the variables and implies restrictions on which variables are allowed to have contemporaneous effects on other variables. In particular, the strategy for estimating a recursive VAR involves imposing a lower (or upper) triangular structure on the matrix A, which implies a strict ordering of the contemporaneous effects of variables in the VAR. An early example of a recursive VAR is Sims (1980). A key drawback of a recursive

VAR is that changing the ordering of variables alters the impulse response functions. A structural VAR uses economic theory to impose restrictions on contemporaneous links between variables that do not necessarily force A into a triangular structure (Bernanke 1986; Sims 1986; Blanchard and Quah 1989). While triangularization guarantees the existence of a unique solution, we do not necessarily have a solution in the case of a structural VAR even if we impose the required number of restrictions – because the system of equations that need to be solved, $\Sigma_u = A^{-1}A^{-1\prime}$, are nonlinear, and the restrictions just make the number of equations equal to the unknowns.

Baseline model: a pure recursive VAR

To estimate our baseline model, we employ a recursive VAR approach and use the model given in equations (1) through (3) to guide our causal ordering. The model suggests that both the real exchange rate q and the wage share ψ have a contemporaneous impact on the capacity utilization rate: therefore, we do not restrict the equation for the capacity utilization rate and allow it to be affected by current and lagged values of all three variables. However, our model does suggest that capacity utilization does not have a contemporaneous effect on either the exchange rate or the wage share: this gives us two zero restrictions on the matrix A. In order to identify the system, we need a third restriction: theory does not suggest a particular causal ordering between q and ψ. We are therefore left with two possible orderings: $\psi \rightarrow q \rightarrow z$ and $q \rightarrow \psi \rightarrow z$, where "$\rightarrow$" denotes causal impact running from the left to the right, for a recursive VAR identification.

Using e_t and u_t to denote structural and reduced form shocks, respectively, the first ordering would suggest that the equation $Au_t = e_t$ takes the form

$$\begin{bmatrix} a_{11} & 0 & 0 \\ a_{21} & a_{22} & 0 \\ a_{31} & a_{32} & a_{33} \end{bmatrix} \begin{bmatrix} u_t^{\psi} \\ u_t^{q} \\ u_t^{z} \end{bmatrix} = \begin{bmatrix} e_t^{\psi} \\ e_t^{q} \\ e_t^{z} \end{bmatrix}$$

which suggests that shocks to capacity utilization are not allowed to affect current values of the real exchange rate and the wage share, and shocks to the real exchange rate are allowed to affect current values of the wage share. The second ordering would suggest that the equation $Au_t = e_t$ takes the form

$$\begin{bmatrix} a_{11} & 0 & 0 \\ a_{21} & a_{22} & 0 \\ a_{31} & a_{32} & a_{33} \end{bmatrix} \begin{bmatrix} u_t^{q} \\ u_t^{\psi} \\ u_t^{z} \end{bmatrix} = \begin{bmatrix} e_t^{q} \\ e_t^{\psi} \\ e_t^{z} \end{bmatrix}$$

which suggests, again, that shocks to capacity utilization are not allowed to affect current values of the wage share and real exchange rate, and shocks to capacity utilization do not affect current values of the real exchange rate. We estimate both orderings and compare them to ascertain the robustness of our results.

Extended model: CEE recursive VAR

The extended model introduces three variables in addition to the wage share, real exchange rate and capacity utilization rate and also suggests how contemporaneous links between these variables could be modelled, as we have discussed in the earlier section on an extended neo-Kaleckian model. Since there are a total of 720 possible orderings among the six variables in our system, a strategy based on recursive identification and comparisons among the impulse response functions from the different orderings is infeasible. Another possible approach would be to impose restrictions on the A matrix and estimate the full set of structural shocks, as used in, for instance, Bernanke (1986) or Sims (1986). The disadvantage of this approach is that it requires us to specify many more restrictions – in this case a total of 15 restrictions – than can be justified by theoretical considerations alone. Moreover, as we have indicated earlier, this approach does not guarantee the existence or uniqueness of the impulse response functions. Hence, we turn to an alternative identification strategy developed by Christiano, Eichenbaum and Evans (1999) (henceforth CEE).

The CEE methodology is a modified recursive VAR approach. Its power lies in the fact that it guarantees existence and uniqueness of the impulse response functions without requiring a full set of causal ordering among the variables in the VAR. The main disadvantage of the CEE method is that it can identify the structural shocks associated with only one variable in the VAR. For us, this is not a problem because our interest is in identifying only the shock to distribution (measured by the wage share) and its impulse response functions. More precisely, since our variable of interest is ψ, the only assumptions necessary to uniquely identify the effect of a structural shock to ψ are to partition all the other variables into two sets: a set of variables of X_{1t} that are causally prior to ψ_t, and a set of variables of X_{2t} that are not causally prior to ψ_t (that is, they do not have a contemporaneous effect on either X_{1t} or ψ_t). If we have k_1 variables that are causally prior to ψ_t and k_2 that are not causally prior to ψ_t, this implies that the identification of the structural shocks through the equation $\Sigma_u = A^{-1}A^{-1\prime}$ restricts the matrix A to be of the form

$$\begin{bmatrix} A_{11} & 0 & 0 \\ A_{21} & a_{22} & 0 \\ A_{31} & A_{32} & A_{33} \end{bmatrix}$$

where A_{11} is a $k_1 \times k_1$ matrix, A_{21} is $1 \times k_1$ matrix, A_{31} is a $k_2 \times k_1$ matrix, A_{32} is a $k_2 \times 1$ vector and A_{33} is a $k_2 \times k_2$ matrix. The pioneering contribution of Christiano, Eichenbaum and Evans (1999) was to show that all the matrices A that satisfy the above block triangular structure and solve the equation $\Sigma_u = A^{-1}A^{-1\prime}$ imply the same value for a_{22}. In effect, therefore, CEE show that imposing a particular causal ordering among X_{1t} and X_{2t} is not necessary in order to uniquely identify a_{22} (and the elements of the vector A_{32}), and therefore the impulse response functions associated with a shock to ψ.

Hence, our identifying restrictions in the CEE approach are the following:

a the rate of accumulation and the unemployment rate are causally prior to the wage share (this means that the wage share does not have a contemporaneous impact on the rate of accumulation or the unemployment rate);
b the wage share is causally prior to the real exchange rate, the rate of labor productivity growth and the capacity utilization rate (this means that the real exchange rate, the rate of labor productivity growth and the capacity utilization rate do not have contemporaneous impacts on the wage share, and by the previous assumption, on the rate of accumulation and the unemployment rate).

Note that we do not impose *any restrictions* on the contemporaneous relationships between the rate of accumulation and the unemployment rate, and neither do we impose *any restrictions* on the contemporaneous relationships between the real exchange rate, the growth rate of labor productivity and the capacity utilization rate.

Data

Unless mentioned otherwise, the frequency of all data is quarterly, and the time period is from the first quarter of 1973 to the fourth quarter of 2018. Our starting period is constrained by the availability of data on the real exchange rate. For series that have been seasonally adjusted, we use the seasonally adjusted data. We summarize the construction and sources for the six key variables that we use in our VAR analysis and briefly discuss results from unit root tests on these variables.

Variable definitions

Wage share

The wage share variable ψ is the percentage share of compensation of employees in net value added – that is, $\frac{\psi}{100} = \frac{W_n}{Y_n}$, where Y_n is the net value added of the corporate business sector in current dollars and is obtained from the National Income and Product Account (NIPA), and W_n is the compensation of employees in the corporate business sector (corresponding to rows 3 and 4 of NIPA Table 1.14, Gross Value Added of Domestic Corporate Business in Current Dollars, respectively).

Real exchange rate

The variable for the real exchange rate q is obtained from the Real Trade Weighted US Dollar Index series provided by the Board of Governors of the Federal Reserve System. This is a monthly series of a weighted average of bilateral real exchange rates of a broad group of major US trading partners, where weights are based on annual data on international trade. It is therefore a geometrically weighted average of $\frac{e_{j,t}p_t}{p_{j,t}}$, where $e_{j,t}$ is the price of the US dollar in terms of foreign currency j, and p_t and $p_{j,}t$ are price indexes for the US and for economy j, respectively. Quarterly averages were obtained from the monthly series.

Capacity utilization rate

The capacity utilization rate z is constructed as 100 times the ratio of real GDP to potential GDP. Real GDP is a seasonally adjusted quarterly series in chained (2012) dollars and is obtained from the NIPA (corresponding to row 1 of NIPA Table 1.1.6, Real Gross Domestic Product, Chained Dollars). Potential GDP is obtained from Congressional Budget Office estimates of real potential GDP in chained (2012) dollars.

Accumulation rate

The accumulation rate g is constructed by dividing gross domestic private non-residential fixed investment (current dollars, seasonally adjusted) by the current cost net stock of private non-residential fixed assets (current dollars). The fixed asset series is annual – quarterly series are not obtainable. The conversion from annual to quarterly data is made by means of linear interpolation. Private non-residential fixed investment is obtained from the NIPA and private non-residential fixed assets are obtained from the BEA's Fixed Assets Accounts (corresponding to row 2 of NIPA Table 5.3.5, Private Fixed Investment by Type, and row 4 of Fixed Assets Accounts, Table 1.1, Current-Cost Net Stock of Fixed Assets and Consumer Durable Goods, respectively).

Labor productivity growth rate

Measures of labor productivity are taken from the BLS's series of real output per hour index for the non-farm business sector (corresponding to the BLS Series ID: PRS85006093). The BLS constructs this series by using BEA's estimates of real non-farm business sector output and dividing this by hours of labor input from BLS's Current Employment Statistics (CES) program, which provides monthly survey data on total employment, and employment and average weekly hours of production.

Unemployment rate

These data are from the BLS's seasonally adjusted monthly civilian unemployment rate, which is the number of unemployed persons as a percentage of the labor force, restricted to the non-institutional civilian population of age 16 and above (this corresponds to the BLS Series ID: LNS14000000). Monthly data was averaged to get the quarterly series. This series pertains to the whole economy rather than just the private sector.

Descriptions and properties of the time series variables

As a preliminary step to our econometric analysis and to ensure that our specification is correct, we check for the degree of integration for our six variables. From the time series plots for each of our six variables which is shown in Figure 8.1, none of the variables display a time trend. We perform an augmented Dickey-Fuller (ADF) test and a Kwiatkowski-Phillips-Schmidt-Shin (KPSS) test to check for the presence of a unit root. Both tests are specified to allow for a drift term but not a time trend (given the lack of a trend observed in the time series plots). The results from the ADF test and the KPSS test are summarized in Table 8.1. The null hypothesis for the ADF test is that the time series has a unit root: we are able to reject the null for g and u at the 5% level of significance, and for x and z at the 1% level of significance. The ADF fails to reject the null for u and ψ, even at the 10% level. The null hypothesis for the KPSS test is that the series is stationary. It confirms the results from the ADF test in that we cannot reject the null that x, g, and z are stationary even at the 10% level. The KPSS test also cannot reject the null that q is stationary at the 10% level. However, the KPSS test does not reject the null that u is stationary at the 5% level and rejects the null that ψ is stationary at the 1% level. We therefore conclude that three time series (g, x, z) are stationary while three series are marginally stationary (u, ψ, q). In the following section, our VAR specification takes all six variables in levels; however, for the purpose of robustness, we also show some of our key results using three variables (u, ψ, q) in differenced form.

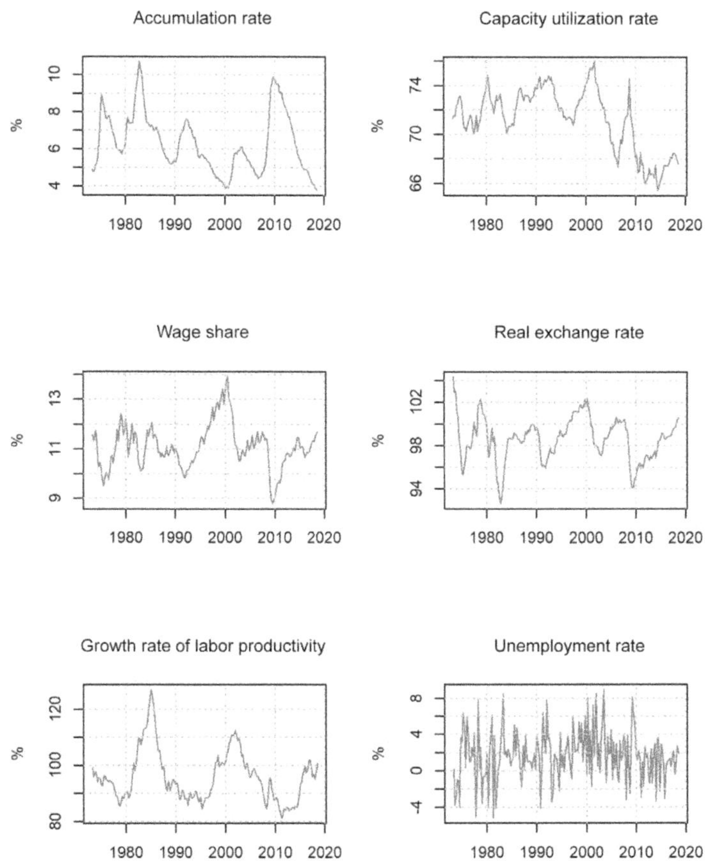

Figure 8.1 Time series plots of the variables in the VAR analysis for the period 1973Q1 to 2018Q4

Table 8.1 ADF and KPSS test results

	ADF	*KPSS*
u	Reject at the 5% level	Not reject at the 5% level
x	Reject at the 1% level	Not reject at the 10% level
g	Reject at the 5% level	Not reject at the 10% level
z	Reject at the 1% level	Not reject at the 10% level
q	Not reject at the 10% level	Not reject at the 10% level
ψ	Not reject at the 10% level	Reject at the 1% level

Note: All tests include a drift/constant term but no time trends. The null hypothesis for the ADF test is that the series has a unit root. The null for the KPSS test is that the series is stationary. The lags for the ADF test were chosen by AIC criterion.

Results

Baseline model: a pure recursive VAR

As explained earlier in this chapter, we first estimate the reduced form VAR in the wage share, real exchange rate and the capacity utilization rate:

$$X_t = B_0 + B_1 X_{t-1} + \ldots + B_p X_{t-p} + u_t$$

where $X_t = [\psi_t, q_t, z_t]'$. We use a lag length of two quarters, which is the optimal lag length as given by the Akaike information criterion (AIC). We include a constant, but not a time trend, as the time series plots do not suggest that any of the variables trend over time. The correlation matrix for the reduced form residuals (the matrix $\Sigma_u = E(u_t u_t')$) is shown in Table 8.2. There is substantial correlation among the residuals to justify treating them all as part of a system.

In order to identify the structural shocks from the reduced form errors, we proceed to estimate a recursive VAR using two alternative causal orderings: the causal ordering $\psi \rightarrow q \rightarrow z$ and the causal ordering $\psi \rightarrow q \rightarrow z$, and the results from each are presented next.

Causal ordering $\psi \rightarrow q \rightarrow z$

The recursive VAR implied by this causal ordering does not allow the capacity utilization to have a contemporaneous effect on either the real exchange rate or the wage share and does not allow the real exchange rate to have a contemporaneous effect on the wage share. This imposes a lower triangular form on the matrix A, which allows us to uniquely identify A using the matrix of reduced form residuals shown in Table 8.2 in the equation $\Sigma_u = A^{-1}A^{-1\prime}$. Table 8.3 shows the forecast error variance decomposition for all three variables based on this causal ordering. For instance, about 27% of the 10-quarter-ahead forecast error variance of the capacity utilization rate is accounted for by shocks to the wage share, while 48% of the 10-quarter-ahead forecast error variance for the wage share is accounted for by shocks to the capacity utilization rate. For both the capacity utilization rate and the wage share, variation in the real exchange rate accounts for less than 2% of error variance for any forecast horizon.

Table 8.2 Correlation matrix of reduced form residuals

	ψ	q	z
ψ	1.00000	-0.01274	-0.44751
q	-0.01274	1.00000	-0.03987
z	-0.44751	-0.03987	1.00000

Table 8.3 Forecast error variance decomposition for the system $\psi \rightarrow q \rightarrow z$

Forecast error in	*Quarters ahead*	*Proportion of forecast error variance accounted for by shocks to*		
		ψ	q	z
z	10	0.27	0.01	0.72
	15	0.28	0.01	0.71
	20	0.28	0.01	0.70
q	10	0.00	0.99	0.00
	15	0.00	0.99	0.01
	20	0.00	0.99	0.01
ψ	10	0.52	0.00	0.48
	15	0.36	0.01	0.63
	20	0.29	0.02	0.69

The impulse response functions that are generated using the structural shocks are shown in Figure 8.2, with 95% confidence intervals that are generated by bootstrapped standard errors (100 runs). Panel A shows impulse responses for all three variables due to a 1-standard deviation increase to the structural error associated with the wage share. The effect of a rise in ψ on q is small and negative (a real depreciation) but is not statistically significant. However, an increase in ψ has a negative effect on the capacity utilization rate that is statistically significant and long-lasting (it persists for more than 15 quarters). This result indicates that aggregate demand can be characterized as being profit-led. Panel B shows impulse response functions due to a 1-standard deviation increase in the structural error associated with the real exchange rate. That the effect of a shock to the real exchange rate on the wage share and the capacity utilization rate is small and not significant is not surprising, as the US is a large, relatively closed, economy. We observe, however, that an appreciation of the real exchange rate has a small but positive effect on the wage share, which confirms our theoretical expectations that real appreciations force reductions in the markup rate and hence an increase in the wage share. Panel C of Figure 8.2 shows that a positive 1-standard deviation increase in the structural error associated with the capacity utilization rate has a positive and long-lasting effect on the wage share, indicating the presence of a profit squeeze.

Causal ordering $q \rightarrow \psi \rightarrow z$

The recursive VAR implied by this causal ordering does not allow the capacity utilization to have a contemporaneous effect on either the real exchange rate or the wage share but – unlike the previous model – allows the real

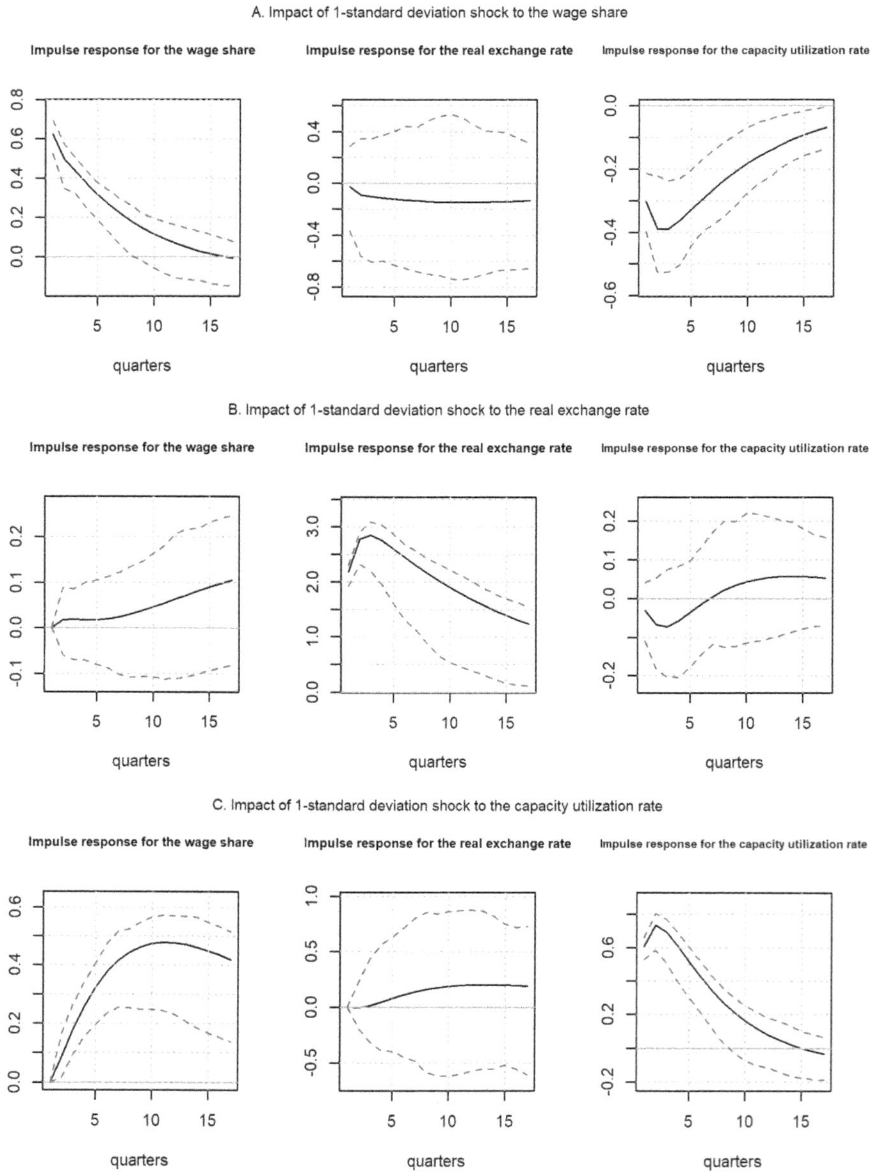

Figure 8.2 Impulse response functions based on the causal ordering ($\psi \rightarrow q \rightarrow z$)

exchange rate to have a contemporaneous effect on the wage share but does not allow the wage share to have a contemporaneous effect on the real exchange rate. We find that our main qualitative results are robust to the change in the specification: a positive shock to the wage share has a

Table 8.4 Forecast error variance decomposition for the system $q \rightarrow \psi \rightarrow z$

Forecast error in	*Quarters ahead*	*Proportion of forecast error variance accounted for by shocks to*		
		Q	ψ	z
z	10	0.01	0.27	0.72
	15	0.01	0.28	0.71
	20	0.01	0.28	0.70
q	10	1.00	0.00	0.00
	15	0.99	0.00	0.01
	20	0.99	0.00	0.01
ψ	10	0.00	0.52	0.48
	15	0.01	0.36	0.63
	20	0.02	0.29	0.69

long-lasting and negative effect on the capacity utilization rate (profit-led demand), while a positive shock to the capacity utilization rate has a positive effect on the wage share (profit squeeze).

Extended model: CEE recursive VAR

To implement the CEE identification, we first estimate a reduced form VAR for all six variables of our extended model. We estimate

$$X_t = B_0 + B_1 X_{t-1} + \ldots + B_p X_{t-p} + u_t$$

where $X_t = [g_t, u_t, \psi_t, q_t, x_t, z_t]'$. We then partition X_t into three sets of variables: the set $X_{1t} = [g_t, u_t]'$ whose variables are causally prior to ψ_t, and the set $X_{2t} = [q_t, x_t, z_t]'$ whose variables are not causally prior to ψ_t (that is, they do not have a contemporaneous effect on either X_{1t} or ψ_t). We utilize the causal ordering $g_t \rightarrow u_t \rightarrow \psi_t \rightarrow q_t \rightarrow x_t \rightarrow z_t$ to construct impulse response functions for each of the variables due to a 1-standard deviation shock to the wage share using a Cholesky decomposition. As the results from the CEE recursive VAR allow for the most general and complete specification, we show our results for the main specification which estimates all variables in levels, and also a second specification which estimates three variables (the unemployment rate, the wage share and the real exchange rate) in first differences and the other variables in levels.

Figure 8.4 shows impulse response functions for all six variables due to a 1-standard deviation positive shock to the wage share (all variables estimated in levels). The confidence bands are somewhat wider, compared to

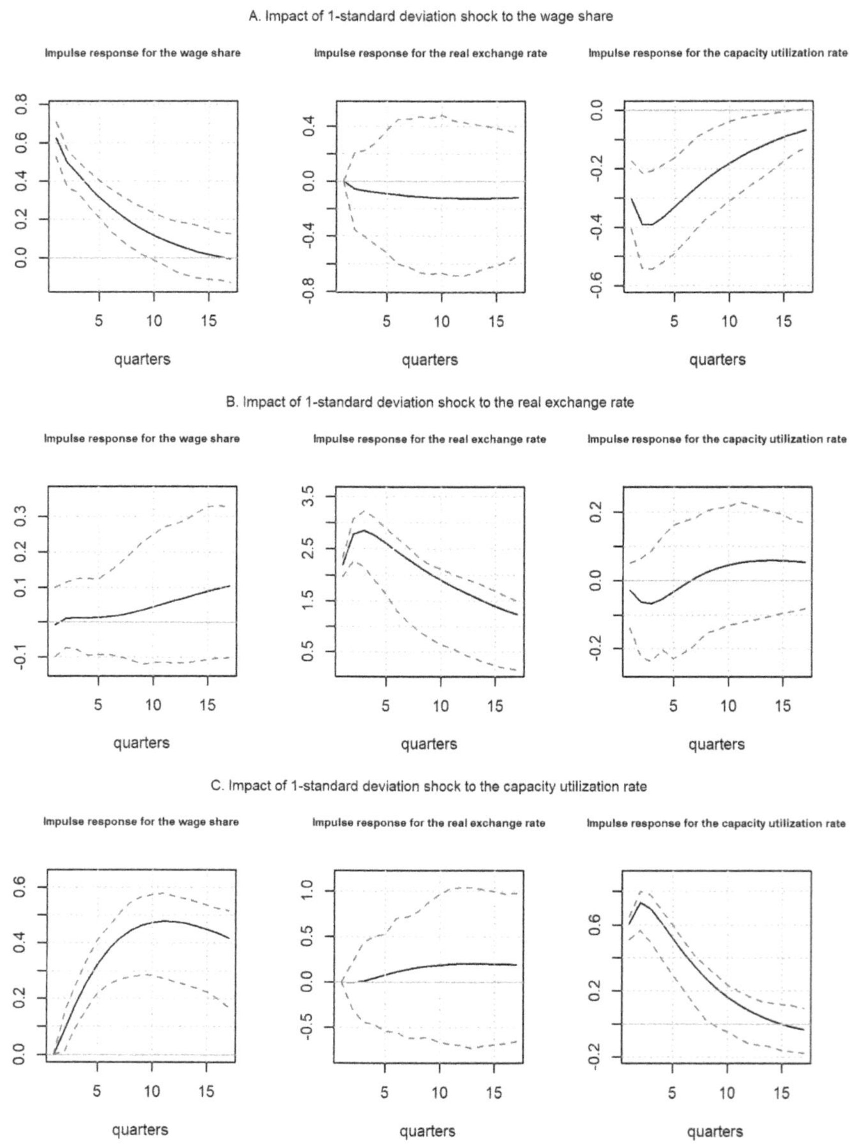

Figure 8.3 Impulse response functions based on the causal ordering ($q \rightarrow \psi \rightarrow z$)

the baseline VAR, because the number of variables is greater – however, an increase in the wage share continues to have a negative and long-lasting effect on the capacity utilization rate, confirming the previous result that demand is profit-led. We find that growth is also profit-led: the accumulation rate also undergoes a long-lasting and negative effect in response to the increase in the

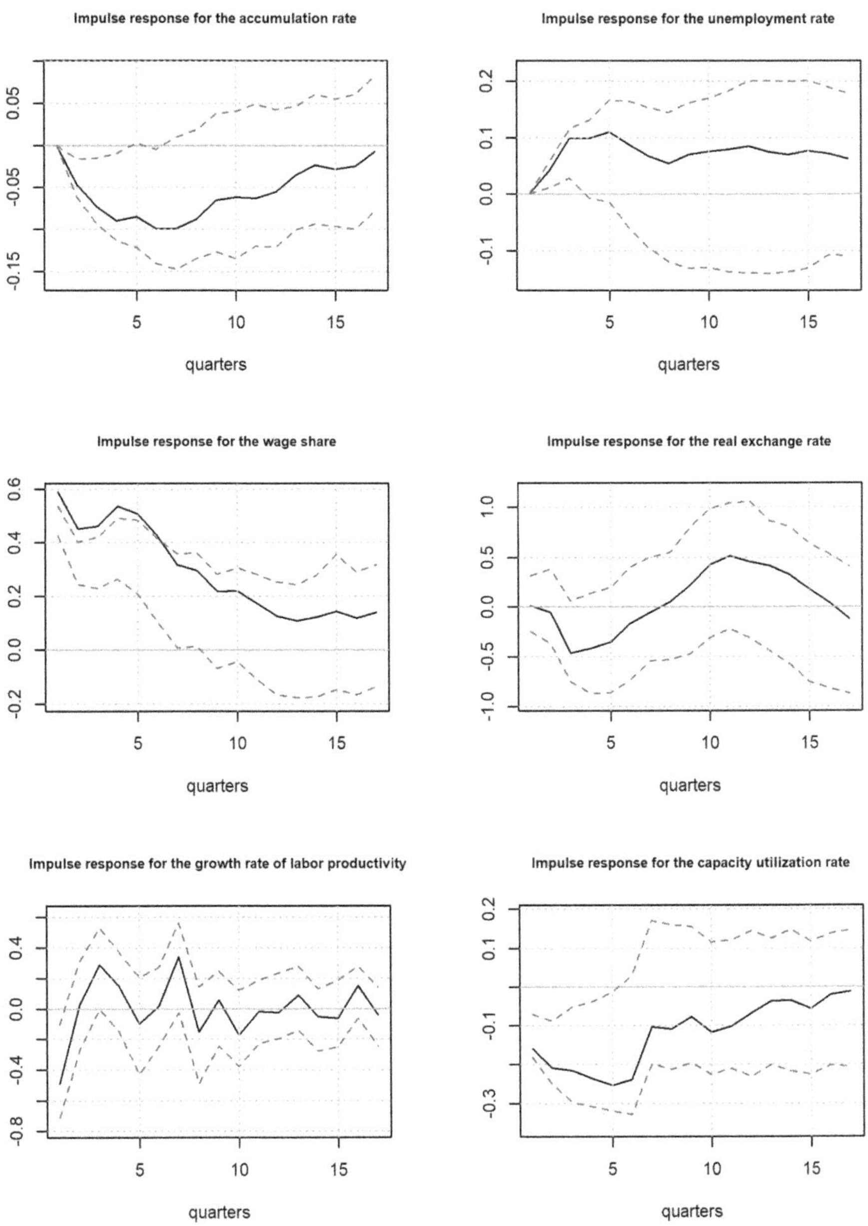

Figure 8.4 Impulse response functions for a 1-standard deviation shock to the wage share (all variables in levels)

wage share. In addition, the increase in the wage share increases the unemployment rate – as would be expected by the profit-led nature of demand. There is a negative effect on the growth rate of labor productivity – however, this operates for a very short period of time. As in the baseline model, there is no significant effect of the increase in the wage share on the real exchange rate. Figure 8.5 shows that estimating the unemployment rate, the wage

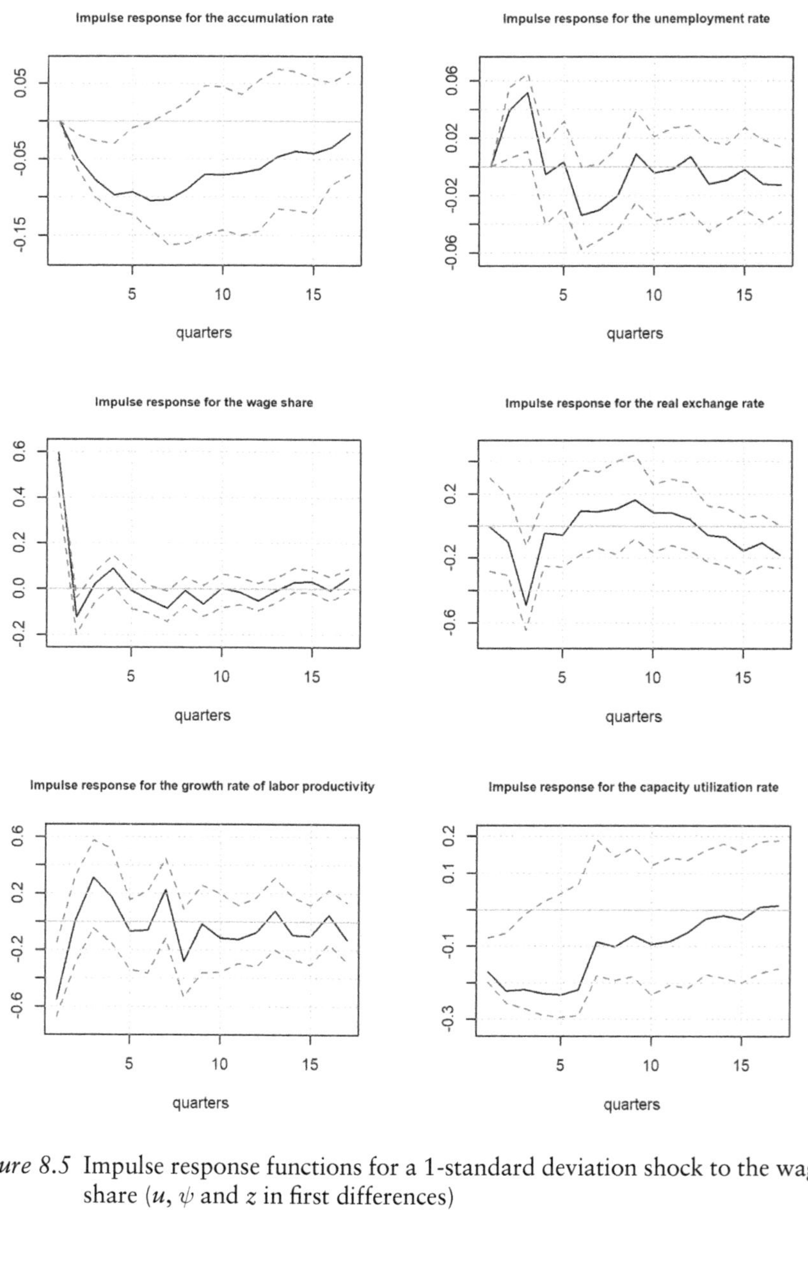

Figure 8.5 Impulse response functions for a 1-standard deviation shock to the wage share (u, ψ and z in first differences)

share and the real exchange rate in first differences does not alter our results: we continue to find that a positive shock to the wage share has a long-lasting and negative effect on the capacity utilization rate and the accumulation rate.

Taken together, our results strongly suggest that the US economy, in the period 1973 to 2018, is characterized by both demand and growth being profit-led. Our simple recursive VAR in the wage share, real exchange rate and capacity utilization rate shows that a positive shock to the wage share has a negative, long-lasting effect on the utilization variable. In an extended variable VAR that includes variables for the accumulation rate, unemployment rate and labor productivity growth rate, we continue to find that a positive shock to the wage share has a long-lasting negative impact on growth and demand. Our results are robust to both the inclusion of additional variables and to differences in specification (first differences instead of levels).

Conclusions

The seminal contribution of Bhaduri and Marglin (1990) established the theoretical possibilities of profit-led and wage-led demand and growth in heterodox macroeconomic models. This suggested that the impact of distributional changes on demand and growth were ambiguous for any capitalist economy. Hence, identification of the nature of demand and growth became an empirical question. In this chapter, we have contributed to the empirical literature on profit-led and wage-led demand and growth by presenting credible estimates of an exogenous shock to distribution (measured by the wage share) using a novel empirical strategy developed by Christiano, Eichenbaum and Evans (1999).

We begin our analysis in this chapter by laying out a basic open economy neo-Kaleckian model to think about the relationship between distribution and demand (or growth). The basic model gives us relationships among three endogenous variables: the capacity utilization rate, the real exchange rate and the wage share. We extended the basic model by incorporating three additional variables: the accumulation rate, the unemployment rate and the growth rate of labour productivity. The basic and the extended theoretical models motivate our empirical analyses.

We use a VAR framework for estimation since it allows for the most general way to model the co-movements among a group of variables over time. The basic theoretical model is used to estimate a three-variable VAR using recursive identification. The extended theoretical model is used to estimate a six-variable VAR using the Christiano, Eichenbaum and Evans (1999) identification strategy. Impulse response functions from the three-variable VAR show that the US economy was profit-led in terms of demand and that it witnessed profit squeeze. Impulse response functions from the six-variable VAR confirm and strengthen that result: a 1-standard deviation positive shock to the wage share had a long-lasting negative effect on both the capacity utilization rate and the accumulation rate.

The policy implications of these results do not, of course, vitiate the case for redistributive policies that tilt the functional distribution of income in favor of labor on social grounds. Rather, by identifying the consequences of such shifts through a robust econometric framework, our study would help frame more effective redistributive policies. A major caveat to our results is their limited applicability to developing countries. One-sector models, of the kind that we have presented here, neglect the coexistence of dual economies and labor surpluses that are characteristic of developing countries: two-sector models with a traditional sector that provides an elastic supply of labor to the modern sector would provide the foundation for a more appropriate characterization of developing countries (for instance, see Ros 2013).

References

Barbosa-Filho, Nelson H., and Lance Taylor. "Distributive and demand cycles in the US economy: A structuralist Goodwin model." *Metroeconomica* 57, no. 3 (2006): 389–411.

Bernanke, Ben S. *Alternative Explanations of the Money-Income Correlation*. No. 1842. Cambridge, MA: National Bureau of Economic Research, Inc. 1986.

Bhaduri, Amit, and Stephen Marglin. Unemployment and the real wage: The economic basis for contesting political ideologies. *Cambridge Journal of Economics* 14, no. 4 (1990), 375–393.

Blanchard, Olivier J., and Danny Quah. "The dynamic effects of aggregate demand and aggregate supply." *The American Economic Review* 79, no. 4 (1989): 655–673.

Blecker, Robert A. "Open economy models of distribution and growth." *A Modern Guide to Keynesian Macroeconomics and Economic Policies*. Cheltenham, UK: Edward Elgar. 2011: 215–239.

Carvalho, Laura, and Armon Rezai. "Personal income inequality and aggregate demand." *Cambridge Journal of Economics* 40, no. 2 (2015): 491–505.

Christiano, Lawrence J., Martin Eichenbaum, and Charles L. Evans. "Monetary policy shocks: What have we learned and to what end?" *Handbook of Macroeconomics* 1 (1999): 65–148.

Hein, Eckhard, and Lena Vogel. "Distribution and growth reconsidered: Empirical results for six OECD countries." *Cambridge Journal of Economics* 32, no. 3 (2008): 479–511.

Kiefer, David, and Codrina Rada. "Profit maximising goes global: The race to the bottom." *Cambridge Journal of Economics* 39, no. 5 (2014): 1333–1350.

Lütkepohl, Helmut. *New Introduction to Multiple Time Series Analysis*. New York: Springer Science & Business Media. 2005.

Onaran, Özlem, Engelbert Stockhammer, and Lucas Grafl. "Financialisation, income distribution and aggregate demand in the USA." *Cambridge Journal of Economics* 35, no. 4 (2011): 637–661.

Ros, J. *Rethinking Economic Development, Growth and Institutions*. New York: Oxford University Press. 2013.

Sims, Christopher A. "Are forecasting models usable for policy analysis?" *Quarterly Review* (1986): 2–16.

Sims, Christopher A. "Macroeconomics and reality." *Econometrica: Journal of the Econometric Society* (1980): 1–48.
Skott, Peter. "Weaknesses of 'wage-led growth'." *Review of Keynesian Economics* 5, no. 3 (2017): 336–359.
Stock, James H., and Mark W. Watson. "Vector autoregressions." *Journal of Economic Perspectives* 15, no. 4 (2001): 101–115.
Stockhammer, Engelbert, and Özlem Onaran. "Accumulation, distribution and employment: A structural VAR approach to a Kaleckian macro model." *Structural Change and Economic Dynamics* 15, no. 4 (2004): 421–447.
Stockhammer, Engelbert, Özlem Onaran, and Stefan Ederer. "Functional income distribution and aggregate demand in the Euro area." *Cambridge Journal of Economics* 33, no. 1 (2008): 139–159.

Part II

Classical political economy

Conflict and exploitation

9 'Superhuman efforts' and the theory of value and distribution

Sraffa on Pareto[1]

Heinz D. Kurz

I had the privilege of being a colleague of Amit Bhaduri as a member of the teaching staff of the annual Trieste International Summer School at the Centro di Studi Economici Avanzati. The school was organised by Sergio Parrinello in cooperation with the late Pierangelo Garegnani and Jan Kregel in the 1980s and early 1990s. To me it was a unique experience that had a huge impact on my intellectual life and work. The School brought together scholars with a critical orientation towards what was then the mainstream (and by and large still is today). Its purpose was both critical and constructive, designed to find out whether scholars coming from different intellectual traditions could join forces and work out a coherent alternative explanation of the working of the economic system, of facts and trends, and derive from it sound economic policies. The currents of thought present in Trieste were: Keynesians of various orientations, including Sidney Weintraub, Hyman Minsky and Jan Kregel; Kaleckians, most notably the late Joseph Steindl and Amit; scholars starting from Piero Sraffa's reformulation of the classical economists' approach to the theory of value and distribution, in particular the late Krishna Bharadwaj, Garegnani, Bertram Schefold and Ian Steedman; Marxists, including Edward J. Nell; but also economists with institutionalist and evolutionary leanings.

I counted myself as belonging to the "Sraffian" camp with a lot of sympathy for certain other traditions. On numerous occasions I was able to discuss matters of common interest with Amit and I always benefited from his deep knowledge and pungent judgement. It was a marvellous time for me, which I remember both with joy and melancholy.

At the time we had only Sraffa's published works at our disposal, especially his 1925 and 1926 articles, the Ricardo edition (Ricardo 1951–1973) and his 1960 book (Sraffa 1925, 1926, 1960). What was missing was an access to his numerous unpublished notes and papers and his correspondence.[2] We could see the tip of an iceberg, but not the iceberg. Garegnani, who was very close to Sraffa over many years and whom Sraffa had appointed as his literary executor, explained Sraffa's contribution to us – its roots, content and purpose. So did Luigi Pasinetti, who had also been in close contact with Sraffa and participated in some of the summer schools. But none of them had seen the huge amount of preparatory notes and manuscripts that were eventually to culminate in *Production of Commodities by Means of Commodities*. For obvious reasons, Garegnani's interpretation dominated the discussions. While I never saw him argue that Sraffa's production equations were inspired by, or derived from, Marx's production price equations in Volume III of *Capital*, or from Marx's schemes of reproduction in Volume II, he expressed the view that Marx had stopped only one step short of a proper solution to the problem of value and distribution in terms of the surplus approach proposed by the classical economists (see Garegnani 1984). Others were less circumspect and contended boldly that the Marxian roots of Sraffa's 1960 treatise were obvious.

In 1995 Garegnani invited me to join a group of scholars he had put together in order to prepare the edition of Sraffa's works and correspondence, and in the following year he asked me to become the General Editor of the edition, because he felt that he could not do it. After some reflection I accepted, proposing Christian Gehrke and Neri Salvadori as additional scholars to help with the edition. (Garegnani had already involved a number of other scholars close to him.) The three of us then began to study systematically Sraffa's papers, which turned out to be very difficult and demanding. However, we eventually made progress and were able to clear the clouds that obscured Sraffa's literary remains. In several contributions we presented our findings. We argued, among other things, that there is no evidence in support of the claimed Marxian lineage of Sraffa's equations of production and provided compelling evidence from Sraffa's papers and annotations in the books in his library in support of our case; see, most recently, Gehrke and Kurz (2018) and Gehrke, Kurz and Salvadori (2019).

While our papers provided numerous hints as to the sources Sraffa tapped and the inspirations he drew from them, for good reasons we did not provide a direct answer to the following question that continues to bother scholars dealing with Sraffa's contribution: What are the "origins" of Sraffa's equations? In our view, the answer is obvious: the equations are Sraffa's and nobody else's. However, since Sraffa elaborated them in a critical confrontation with the analyses of several economists, past and then contemporary, it is perhaps interesting to note whether his papers and books contain traces to views and concepts contained in the literature Sraffa scrutinised. Here I focus attention essentially only on one of the authors and doctrines Sraffa had studied: Vilfredo Pareto's contribution to general equilibrium theory and his criticism of what he called the "literary economists", which include Marx. Sraffa consulted the works of Pareto from an early time onwards, which is reflected in his notes and papers and in his annotations in works by Pareto in his library (see also Kurz 1998; Gehrke and Kurz 2006). To be clear, I do *not* argue that *the* "origin" of Sraffa's equations is to be found in Pareto. Nor do I argue that his equations can be traced back to a single source only. I simply provide evidence in support of the fact that Sraffa studied meticulously Pareto's contributions and that some of the thoughts and even expressions used by the Lausanne economist reverberate in Sraffa's papers and his 1960 book – neither more nor less.[3]

The composition of this chapter is as follows. In the next section, I argue that searching for the "origin" of Sraffa's equations is a somewhat mistaken endeavour. Next, I put forward evidence in support of Sraffa's critical scrutiny of Pareto's doctrine. I then trace some of the concepts and formulations we encounter in Sraffa's papers, which echo Pareto's writings, after which I offer conclusions.

The "origin" of Sraffa's equations

In an attempt to come to grips with the roots of Sraffa's reformulation of the classical economists' surplus approach to the problem of value and distribution, Giancarlo de Vivo and Giorgio Gilibert sought to identify the "origin" of Sraffa's equations. De Vivo, for example, contended that "the origin of the equations formulated by Sraffa in 1927 . . . is to be found in Marx's reproduction schemes" (De Vivo 2019: 95).

Christian Gehrke, Neri Salvadori and I disputed this view in several contributions; see most recently Gehrke et al. (2019). There is no need to repeat our argument and the evidence put forward in its support. Rather, I ask: what can possibly be meant by "*the* origin" of a set of equations, and how can it be identified beyond reasonable doubt? Two answers are close at hand. First, in the literature one encounters systems of equations that are identical or very similar to Sraffa's or can easily be reformulated to make them to be so. Second, it is possible to identify a piece of literature that has clearly prompted Sraffa to elaborate his own equations, because what is stated in it *verbatim* is simply given a formal expression.

The first answer faces the following problem: systems of equations that are equal or similar to Sraffa's can be found in the writings of numerous economists including classical authors, Marx and marginalists of various orientations, including Léon Walras and Vilfredo Pareto. This is hardly surprising since Sraffa's equations express the equality between prices and normal costs of production of commodities plus normal profits at a competitive rate of return on the capitals invested. What Sraffa has taught us is that information about the quantities of commodities produced and used up and about one of the distributive variables (the wage rate or share or, alternatively, the rate of profits) is enough to determine relative prices and the remaining distributive variable; no other givens are needed. Unless Sraffa in his published or unpublished writings specified whether he started from some particular equations contained in the literature, the "origin" of his own equations is clouded in darkness. Alas, no document from his writings has been identified in this regard and, I am sure, can possibly be identified.

Hence, there remains the second answer. However, this runs the severe risk of degenerating into pure speculation unless its advocates are able to refer to documents in Sraffa's writings, which establish clearly and unequivocally that he obtained his inspiration from some particular source. In the best possible case one would be able to explicitly and positively point out the source and its author. In a somewhat less clear-cut case one could draw the attention to the fact that Sraffa was struggling with the same analytical problems as some other author and used the same notions and concepts as the latter. If none of these conditions is met, things are uncertain and probably cannot be decided conclusively. Sraffa's equations cannot then be unambiguously traced back to some unique "origin".

Yet this is precisely the situation: up until now nobody has been able to present documents which provide compelling evidence that Sraffa started from Marx's schemes of reproduction, let alone the labour value version of them (as De Vivo originally contended). Moreover, when elaborating what he called his "First Equations", which refer to economic systems without a surplus, and his "Second Equations", which refer to systems with a surplus, Sraffa did not use Marxian terms such as "reproduction", "surplus value" or "rate of profit", but rather spoke of "self-replacing systems" and "rate of interest".[4] It is interesting to note that marginalist authors such as William Stanley Jevons, Eugen von Böhm-Bawerk and Irving Fisher typically used the concept of rate of interest instead of rate of profit. We also know (see the evidence provided in Gehrke and Kurz 2006: 99–101) that Sraffa at around the time when he elaborated his equations in the late 1920s studied carefully the writings of these authors. Still more importantly, he was, of course, familiar with the writings of the marginalist authors Alfred Marshall and Maffeo Pantaleoni and Vilfredo Pareto long before he assumed an academic position in Cambridge. This is clearly documented in terms of books by them he had in his private library, some heavily annotated. In short, Sraffa in the late 1920s can safely be assumed to have been abreast with the leading economics literature at the time.

The fact that those who sought to be able to trace Sraffa's equations back to Marx's reproduction schemes failed to provide any cogent evidence from his writings in support of their interpretation does not mean that no clarity can be reached with regard to the roots of Sraffa's early constructive and interpretive work. However, the answer is much less simplistic than what some interpreters have insinuated. As Sraffa's papers document impressively, he was extremely well read in the economics literature (and beyond it) and identified meticulously any idea or concept he had encountered in it and found worth employing in his own research. This means that the path of Sraffa's thinking can be reconstructed with a remarkable degree of precision.

In this chapter I focus on a single aspect of his huge intellectual enterprise: Sraffa's views on the contributions of the Lausanne economist Vilfredo Pareto. After having dealt a serious blow to Marshall's partial equilibrium theory (Sraffa 1925, 1926), it was only natural for Sraffa to turn to Pareto, the then leading general equilibrium theorist. What did he have to offer with regard to two problems Sraffa had identified in his 1926 paper? These concerned, first, the determination of cost of production of commodities in competitive conditions (Sraffa 1926: 540–541) and, second, the "process of diffusion of profits throughout the various stages of production and of the process of forming a normal level of profits throughout all the industries of a country" (1926: 550). These two problems he had put on one side in his criticism of Marshall's partial analysis, which was concerned only with "the formation of the prices of single commodities" and not of an entire system of interdependent prices and the establishment of a general rate of profits in competitive conditions. In the book ("mio libro") Sraffa was intent to write since the late 1920s, he had to tackle especially these problems. Prior to him, marginalist authors also had been concerned with these problems, Pareto being arguably one of the most sophisticated amongst them. There was no doubt that Sraffa had to come to grips with what Pareto had achieved, and what not. Sraffa abhorred the self-deception of subjective originality and was keen to acknowledge whatever had already been put forward by others.

Sraffa's studies of Pareto

Sraffa had studied contributions by Pareto, most importantly the *Cours d'économie politique* (1896–1897) and the *Manuale* (1906), already at an early time, long before he was appointed to a lectureship in Cambridge in 1927. In his private library there are several books and essays by Pareto, many of which are annotated, some heavily. His concern with Pareto's approach to economics considered as a "natural science", founded upon facts, and his general equilibrium theory is also reflected in numerous references to them in Sraffa's preparatory notes and manuscripts that led up to his 1960 book. Sraffa was particularly interested in what Pareto had to say about:

- The failure of the older, i.e. non-mathematical, economists to deal with interdependences in the theory of value and distribution;
- The need to approach the problem in terms of simultaneous equations;
- The need to re-interpret the concepts of cause and effect vis-à-vis relations of mutual dependence;
- The unimportance of utility and disutility in the concept of general economic equilibrium;
- The replacement of the cardinal by an ordinal concept of utility.

Sraffa acknowledged that in some respects Pareto's contribution constituted an important step beyond earlier formulations of marginalist theory and that one can learn quite a bit from it. This did not mean, however, that he adopted Pareto's vision of economic equilibrium as reflecting "the opposition of tastes and obstacles".

On the concept of equilibrium and the role of utility

Sraffa was especially intrigued by Pareto's view that utility has no role to play in an investigation of a state of equilibrium. In a document contained in a folder called "London Summer 1927", he stated: "How useless the notions of utility and disutility are in the study of equilibrium . . . Explain the notion of *equilibrium*, and its relation to *causes*: much to be found in Pareto" (D3/12/3: 1; Sraffa's emphases).[5] At the time when he composed the note, Sraffa was still concerned with the question of the classical authors whether or not the values (alias prices) of commodities could be reduced to some "ultimate measure of value". In this way, the classical authors from William Petty to Adam Smith and David Ricardo tried to cope with the heterogeneity of commodities, deprived as they were of the necessary tool of simultaneous equations. Sraffa at the time distinguished between two kinds of approaches to the problem of value and distribution, one concerned with the process via which equilibrium gets established, the other with the properties of equilibrium. He wrote:

> Should Pareto's doctrine of general equilibrium be classed as belonging to the first or to the second theory of value? It surely is mainly concerned with the mechanism through which equilibrium is reached, and is not in quest of an ultimate standard. But on the other hand, could it be denied that it may legitimately be used in *challenging the existence of any such standard*?
>
> (D3/12/3: 25; emphasis added)

He then asked how the equilibrium is affected by some change in the data and stressed:

> If we change those other quantities the shape of the utility curve of one commodity would entirely change: the utility of bread, when we have eaten potatoes or not, is entirely different. Inter-destructive. Thus we cannot at all say that utility is ultimate cause of value.
>
> Of course we might "imagine" the utility of each commodity to be a function of thousands of variables i.e. all commodities: and we might say that the equilibrium of all commodities is simultaneously determined by one system of equations. This is Walras' and Pareto's system. But another difficulty arises: the only way of measuring utility is the money test, which obviously in this case is inapplicable. This would not matter very much: after all, even in our system of plane curves, we have never been able to construct a statistical real one. What matters is that a method of measurement, even if inapplicable in practice, has a very great theoretical importance even if rough and approximate as money test; in fact it helps us to conceive, we could not otherwise.
>
> This is so true, that Pareto himself (though personally not giving up the belief in utility) *has found it necessary to make his general system independent of utility and base it on empirical indifference (i.e. demand) curves.*
>
> (D3/12/3: 67–69; emphasis added)

Pareto's claim regarding the dispensability of the notion of utility in his scheme of general equilibrium is scrutinised more than once in Sraffa's papers. He commented, for example, in Italian on the following remark in the French edition of the *Manuale* (Pareto 1909):

> Pareto, Manuel, App. p. 558
>
> Il y a lieu de remarquer que l'équilibre vient d'être déterminé sans faire usage des notions d'*utilité* (ophelimité), de prix, etc.
>
> (D3/12/9: 93; see also D3/12/10: 39)[6]

Sraffa objected that just a few lines before this passage, Pareto had made the individual consumer move to the point at which the indexes of ophelimity stopped to increase and started to decrease. Sraffa was at a loss to see how these indexes could be taken not to represent utility. Apparently, the consumer had to decide where that point was. Sraffa added: "In altre parole l'esperienza è l'α e l'ω di questa teoria: ma chi l'ha fatta l'esperienza?" (D3/12/9: 93).[7] Hence Sraffa was not convinced by Pareto's claim that the latter's concept of equilibrium actually did not employ the notion of utility.

The question was: is an attempt to elaborate such a concept, and therefore a theory determining relative prices and income distribution without recourse to subjective notions, doomed to failure – is it a search for a will-o'-the-wisp? According to Sraffa's intuition, it was not, and in late 1927 he was able to confirm this in terms of his "First" and "Second Equations". His critical scrutiny of Pareto's contribution marked apparently a crucial step in this regard.

The theory of value of the mathematical and the "literary" economists

In several of his writings Pareto distanced his approach from what he called the "literary" economists, meaning non-mathematical scholars unable to formulate the theory of value and distribution in terms of a system of simultaneous equations. Pareto did so in the *Manuale* and prior to it in an essay, in German, entitled "Anwendungen der Mathematik auf Nationalökonomie" ("Applications of Mathematics to Economics"), published in *Encyklopädie der mathematischen Wissenschaften* in 1902 (Pareto 1902), and in his two-volume treatise *Les systèmes socialistes*, published in 1902 and 1903, respectively (Pareto 1902–1903). In the treatise the issue is dealt with in chapters VI and VII (pp. 263–400) of Volume 1.[8] Essentially the same arguments recur in all three publications. Here we focus attention on the 1902 essay.[9]

Sraffa, who read German, heavily annotated Pareto's paper.[10] We focus on the annotated passages. He agreed with Pareto that utility cannot be measured and put a straight line in the margin of the following statement: "The only measurable magnitudes that are considered are *the commodities themselves*" (1902: 1111; emphasis added). This, Pareto was convinced, renders "our thinking that leads to the basic equations rigorous" (ibid.). Sraffa ticked the remark in the margin. The equations are designed to express the needs and wants of people, on the one hand, and the "obstacles" to be overcome in order to satisfy them, on the other. Pareto then launched an attack at the "literary" economists:

> Economists that do not know mathematics are in the situation of people, who wish to solve a system of equations without knowing what a system of equations or even a single equation is. Basically the procedure to which they have recourse consists in assuming that all equations except one are met and then study the changes in the quantities, which are connected to these equations. In this way one arrives occasionally at useful studies of some detail, but not at an *understanding of the system as a whole.*
>
> (1902: 1114; emphasis added)

Sraffa put a straight line in the margin of the last sentence.[11]

Pareto continued by exposing his system of equations:

> Let $p_1, p_2, \ldots$ be such commodity prices, $q, \ldots$ the prices of labour [wages], i, the rate of interest, $r, \ldots$ the prices of land rent, and a_1, $a_2, \ldots$ certain parameters, then mathematical economics proves that the unknowns $p_1, p_2, \ldots, q, \ldots, i, r, \ldots$ are determined by a system that has as many equations:
>
> $$F_1(p_1, p_2, \ldots; q, \ldots; i; r, \ldots; a_1, a_2, \ldots) = 0$$
> $$F_2(p_1, p_2, \ldots; q, \ldots; i; r, \ldots; a_1, a_2, \ldots) = 0, \text{ etc.}$$
>
> From this it follows that the unknowns $p_1, p_2, \ldots$ can be determined only after *all* the parameters $a_1, a_2, \ldots$ are known. The non-mathematical economist are however concerned with problems like this: What is the "cause" of the value (price)? What is the cause of interest? And so on. However, such problems are indeterminate, because they are based on arbitrary hypotheses. It is not possible to identify *that* parameter, which, for example, "determines" p_1, and it is a barren dispute, when some claim that the parameter is a_1, others however that it is a_2, and so on. Or, to provide an example of a different kind, it is contended that costs of production "determine" the selling price. If we designate the former as x and the latter as y, then under certain conditions of economic organisation the equation $x = y$ is one of those that represent economic equilibrium.

Sraffa put a straight line in the margin from "What is the 'cause'" to "selling price". Pareto continued: "The obfuscation of such a simple fact by sentences like: 'costs of production determine the selling price' may lead to fallacies and sophisms."[12] Sraffa ticked the statement in the margin.

We encounter an echo of Pareto's view in Sraffa's book, yet for good reasons with explicit reference to *basic* products only; that is, products that are needed directly or indirectly in the production of all products: "in the case of a basic product the prices of its means of production depend on its own price no less than the latter depends on them" (1960: §7). Therefore Sraffa refrained from employing the concept of "cost of production" and used instead the notions of "value" and "price". With regard to non-basic products one could, however, still speak of prices being regulated essentially by costs of production (of basic products).

Pareto added that "the general equations of economic equilibrium show at a first glance a truth that the classical economists already knew partly, namely that prices are only means to an end, that is, to establish relationships between pleasures and obstacles" (1902: 1115). He then pointed out that a maximum of ophelimity can be brought about both by the cost-minimising behaviour of producers in conditions of perfect competition confronted with a choice of technique, and by rules judiciously imposed by a socialist state.[13] Sraffa put a straight line in the margin of the respective passage.

Pareto's considerations did not fully clarify his claim that the "only measurable magnitudes that are considered are the commodities themselves". And while Pareto insisted that utility was no such magnitude, in his argument he employed it clandestinely as if it was. And if the classical economists already knew "partly" the proper solution to the problem at hand, which part precisely did they know and which not?

Sraffa's "First" and "Second Equations" contained an answer to the two problems mentioned earlier. Sraffa showed that utility and subjective factors more generally play no role and quantities of commodities are indeed the only parameters postulated. Pareto's approach to the problem suffered from the fact that while utility had been thrown out by the front door, it had come back again through the back door. And Sraffa managed to show that the approach to the problem of value and distribution advocated by "the old classical economists from Adam Smith to Ricardo" (1960: v) could be brought to fruition and given a logically coherent form. This requested the use of simultaneous equations, as Pareto had insisted.[14]

We now turn to the *Manuale*.

The Manuale

Sraffa annotated intensively his personal copy of the *Manuale*. From his handwriting we may conclude that he did so at an early time of his academic career, that is, long before 1928. And while his papers of 1925 and 1926 (Sraffa 1925, 1926) were first and foremost concerned with a critique of Marshall's partial equilibrium analysis, Pareto is explicitly referred to in the former and implicitly in the latter. Sraffa concluded the 1926 paper in terms of a passage we have already quoted earlier in this chapter concerning the establishment of a general rate of profits. In the following we collect elements from (the English version) of the *Manuale* (Pareto 1971) that can be taken to have found an echo in Sraffa's constructive work.

Pareto defines equilibrium as a state of rest that satisfies the condition "that no movement occurs" (1971: 110). Pareto was convinced that thanks to the use of mathematics, economics "acquires the rigor of rational mechanics; it deduces its results from experience, without bringing in any metaphysical entity", with the conditions of a problem being "interpreted algebraically by equations" (1971: 113). Goods A, B, C, etc., are being produced and consumed, some of them serving as means of production. A "state of equilibrium" is a "point where *certain quantities of goods*, having certain prices, *are being transformed, by exchange or otherwise, indefinitely*" (1971: 165; emphasis added). In such a state, provided "competition is complete, equilibrium can take place only where . . . cost of production is equal to the selling price" (1971: 168). Pareto illustrates his argument in terms of numerical examples, in which commodities are productively transformed into each other, that is, production is a circular flow. The situation under consideration recurs in Sraffa's work as a state of "self-replacement".

Earlier economists did not know how to deal with the problem in a consistent way. Pareto accused them of assuming "more or less implicitly, that all the conditions (equations) minus one were satisfied, and they then had only a single unknown to determine by means of known quantities. That was a problem that was not beyond the power of ordinary logic" (1971: 171–2; see also Pareto 1902–1903, vol. II: 288–9) He insisted, however, that this successivist solution was inacceptable since "Price or *value in exchange* is determined *at the same time* as economic equilibrium, and the latter arises from the opposition between tastes and obstacles" (1971: 176; second emphasis added).

Sraffa: equilibrium without the "forces" Pareto invoked

Sraffa accepted the first part of the statement but not the second, which refers to the "forces" that according to Pareto establish equilibrium. These forces Sraffa considered to be dubious. He was therefore concerned with investigating the properties of equilibrium without any reference to the forces Pareto had invoked. In a document drafted in 1942, shortly after resuming his constructive work again, which he had to interrupt because of the Ricardo editorial project, Sraffa stressed:

> This paper deals with an extremely elementary problem; so elementary indeed that its solution is generally taken for granted. The problem is that of *ascertaining the conditions of equilibrium of a system of prices & the rate of profits, independently of the study of the forces which may bring about such a state of equilibrium.* Since a solution of the second

> problem carries with it a solution of the first, that is the course usually adopted in modern theory. The first problem however is susceptible of a *more general treatment, independent of the particular forces assumed for the second*; and in view of the *unsatisfactory character of the latter*, there is advantage in maintaining its independence.
>
> (D3/12/15: 2, emphases added)

The reference to "modern theory" can safely be taken to mean in particular the contribution of Pareto.

A most interesting aspect of Sraffa's approach is that at an early time he was convinced that equilibrium theory can basically cover both the core of the classical and of the marginalist theory. In a long document also contained in the folder "London Summer 1927", Sraffa explained his assessment of equilibrium theory. He started with a comparison between Marshall's partial equilibrium theory and the value theory in classical political economy, especially Ricardo:

> The introduction of the concept of equilibrium, which wiped out the primitive notion that there had to be somewhere or other one single ultimate cause of value, besides the immense scientific importance which it had in itself, brought with it the great practical advantage that, *being to a certain extent compatible with both schools of thought* [classical and marginalist] (*since it embodied their doctrines*), it closed the old controversy and brought back the T[heory] [of] V[alue] from the field of politics to that of economic theory. This was no[t] only the consequence of the conciliation represented by the "scissors", but also of the fact that it put as the principal problem to be solved by T.V., not the question of the causes of value of all commodities together, but the determinants of the value of *one* article considered separately, and regarded as independent from all the others.
>
> (D3/12/3: 9; first two emphases added)

After some further deliberations in this regard, he came to speak about the determination of (relative) prices on the one hand and the determination of income distribution on the other, and he insisted that they are fundamentally different. But he had to admit not least with reference to Pareto's general equilibrium theory that the factors affecting income distribution are reflected in the system of prices that supports the resulting distribution. He wrote:

> At present we have a separate theory of distribution: we do give to it a very great importance, but we recognize that besides it there is a different, but also very important question – the fixing of prices of single articles. Besides it has been found that the two questions [the determination of the values of commodities as a whole and of the price of a single commodity] cannot be treated simultaneously: different general

> assumptions and different methods of analysis are required. This splitting up of questions, this power of abstraction and isolation is a feature of every scientific progress. We know that the ultimate forces which regulate the division of product of industry between factors are the same that regulate the price of hats (drawback: we are apt to forget them: use of Pareto's general equilibrium): but we also recognize that the frictions, the obstacles through which those forces have to work [are] so great, that their effect, when they reach what we may call the capillary blood-vessels of the economic body their action is so much different in degree as almost to be a difference in kind from what their action is in the main streams. The hypothesis [*sic*!] on which the analysis of price fixing is based are fundamentally different from those of distribution. Certain subtle features which are essential act upon the first, may be neglected when considering the broad lines of the general equilibrium: while the dominating elements of the latter may be regarded as not affected by (and therefore not reacting) by the microscopic changes of the latter.
>
> (D3/12/3: 11)

The problem was to bring the two aspects – distribution and prices – together under a single umbrella in a coherent way. At the time Sraffa did not yet have a fully convincing answer and struggled with the problem, trying out various ideas. Here is not the place to enter into a detailed discussion of the path he took in the late 1920s and early 1930s. For a summary account of it, see Gehrke and Kurz (2006) and Kurz (2012). It suffices to point out that for a while he felt that he could settle the issue in terms of an approach to the problem of the sharing out of the product amongst the different claimants in terms of the concept of "withdrawing". The basic idea of this (which Sraffa had encountered in Adam Smith, Anonymous *and Pareto* 1971: 231) is the following: workers, land owners and capital owners could threaten society by withdrawing the respective productive resource they possessed from production. The remuneration they received in terms of wages, rents and profits society had to pay to make the respective proprietors of the productive resources drop the threat. However, Sraffa soon understood that this idea could not be sustained and abandoned it.

Let us now go back to Pareto and have a closer look at his criticism of the "literary" economists.

The "synthetic notion of economic equilibrium"

Not possessed of the tool of simultaneous equations and the knowledge of how to solve them, these economists were on the lookout for what they called an "ultimate measure of value" to which all commodities could be reduced and thus made commensurable. Pareto rejected this idea and made fun of it: "We have had incarnations of Buddha, here we have incarnations of value." He went on: "What indeed can this mysterious entity be? . . .

And, what is still more important, how is it measured?" He concluded: "it is useless to entangle ourselves with these metaphysical entities" (1971: 177 n.17). And then:

> There exists no entity resembling what the literary economists call *value*, and which is *objectively dependent on a thing*, as would be the density or any other such *physical property of that thing* [A]. Neither does that entity exist in the form of "the estimation" which one or several individuals make of that thing [B]. *Nor is the consideration of certain obstacles to production enough to give it existence* [C].
>
> If this vague and indeterminate thing which the literary economists call *value* has any relation to prices, we can assert that it depends on *all* the circumstances, none excepted, which have an influence on the determination of economic equilibrium [D].
>
> (1971: 179; the final two emphases are by Pareto)

I have given letters to the various statements that interest us here. Statement A is clearly directed at the classical economists and Marx. Statement B is directed at advocates of cardinal utility theory, such as Eugen von Böhm-Bawerk ([1884] 1921: 386), who had argued that the common thing that renders heterogeneous commodities commensurable was not "abstract labour" (Marx), but "use value jelly" or "use values *in abstracto*". Apparently Pareto rejected both views for the same reason. Sraffa disputed statement C and Pareto's particular version of the concept of "determination" implied by statement D, as we shall see.

In the sequel, Pareto insisted:

> The thing indicated by the words value in exchange, rate of exchange, price, does not have *one* cause; and it can be declared henceforth that any economist who looks for *the cause* of value shows thereby that he has understood nothing about the synthetic phenomenon of economic equilibrium.
>
> (1971: 179; Pareto's emphases)[15]

The *synthetic notion of economic equilibrium* has far-reaching consequences:

> the mutual dependence of economic phenomena . . . makes the use of mathematics indispensable for studying these phenomena; ordinary logic can serve well enough for studying the relations of cause and effect, but soon becomes impotent when it is a matter of relations of mutual dependence.

He added: "The latter, in rational mechanics and in pure economics, necessitate the use of mathematics" (1971: 180).

Chapter V of the *Manual* deals with "The Obstacles". Pareto called "Things which are not consumed, or which are consumed slowly in the act of production . . . CAPITAL" (1971: 217). It deserves to be noted that in his notes and papers, Sraffa repeatedly uses the words "things" or "cose" (in Italian). Pareto stressed: "production is nothing else but the transformation of certain things into certain other things" (1971: 278) (a view Sraffa also endorsed). He mentioned joint production (e.g. 1971: 216 and 244) and analysed the use of fixed capital (e.g. 1971: 223 and 227). And he discussed the problem of the choice of technique when alternative methods of production are available to produce the same commodity. "Income from capital" he called "NET INTEREST", and he stressed that it is "an entity whose origin is not so obvious" (1971: 230). Some received explanations of interest he found wanting and concluded that the existence of net interest has its origin exclusively in the fact that "capital has been appropriated" – that is, there is private property of the means of production. The obstacles to production, he insisted, depend on the social organisation and emphasised: "net interest on capital has its origin in the social organization" (1971: 231). But later in the text he argued, somewhat contradicting himself, that it is the scarcity of capital that accounts for interest.

Pareto stressed that the coefficients of production actually observed depend not only on technical features but also, in competitive conditions, on the choice of cost-minimising producers. In this context he launched a frontal attack at a "completely erroneous theory . . . called *definite proportions*" (1971: 239; Pareto's emphasis). This theory has been "borrowed from chemistry, which indeed has recognized that elements combine in strictly defined proportions". Here the reference is apparently to John Dalton's atomic theory. Pareto denies the claim that it is applicable to economics: "But, much to the contrary, the factors of production of political economy can, within certain limits, combine in any proportion whatsoever" (1971: 239). And they typically will, "varying with the prices [of things], which give certain profit maxima" (1971: 240). Pareto concluded: "In sum, these coefficients cannot be determined independently of the other unknowns of economic equilibrium; they are in a relation of mutual dependence with the other quantities which determine economic equilibrium" (1971: 240–241).

"Superhuman efforts"

To the passage just cited, Pareto appended a footnote, which apparently was of particular interest to Sraffa, as will become clear in the following section:

> The literary economists – being not only incapable of solving a system of simultaneous equations which alone allows one to acquire an idea of the mutual dependence of economic phenomena, but even of merely comprehending what it is – make *superhuman efforts* to treat separately phenomena which they do not know how to consider in their

state of mutual dependence. This is the reason why they have conceived vaguely metaphysical theories of *value*; this is the reason why they have attempted to *determine* selling price by cost of production; this is the reason why they have created the theory of *definite proportions*; and again this is the reason why they continue to propound a mass of erroneous propositions.

(1971: 241, n. 7; the first emphasis is added)

Reverberations in Sraffa's papers and his book

We now turn briefly to reverberations of Pareto's considerations in Sraffa's preparatory notes and manuscripts for his 1960 book and in the book itself. Perhaps most interesting, in a document entitled "Metaphysics", dated 26 November 1927 (D3/12/4: 14–17), Sraffa entered straightforwardly into a discussion of Pareto's point of view. This was the day when Sraffa experienced a breakthrough in his endeavour to come to grips with the problem of value. On that very day Keynes had "approved" of Sraffa's first equations. As Keynes wrote in a letter to his wife Lydia Lopotkova two days later, the breakthrough made Sraffa so excited that he could not sit down in his study room; he had to walk up and down all the time. His breakthrough in terms of his "First Equations" involved an answer to Pareto's accusation that the theories of the classical economists and Marx were nothing but "vaguely metaphysical theories of *value*" and necessarily so, because they lacked a proper understanding of the mutual dependence of economic phenomena – the "synthetic notion of economic equilibrium" – and the tool necessary to deal with it – simultaneous equations.

Sraffa's document shows that while he agreed with several of Pareto's observations, he did not agree with the latter's strict antinomy of metaphysics and mathematical economic theory. Even the mathematical economist's theory was imbued with some metaphysics, whether or not he or she was aware of it. The relationship between economic doctrines and metaphysics was invariably more complicated than Pareto had thought. Sraffa insisted that "a difference in metaphysics can make to us absolutely unintelligible an otherwise perfectly sound theory". At the same time he stressed "how little our metaphysics affect the truth of our conclusions, and how the same truths can be expressed in two widely divergent forms". He concluded: "Our metaphysics is in fact embodied in our technique; the danger lies in this, that when we have succeeded in thoroughly mastering a technique, we are very liable to be mastered by her" (D3/12/4: 15). As regards the same metaphysics underlying different theories, he referred to Marx's view that only human labour produces values and pointed out: "the same metaphysical notion . . . [was] held by such an anti-Marxian as [Edwin] Cannan". The upshot of Sraffa's argument is that vis-à-vis the bewildering variety of relationships between metaphysics and tools, Marx was to be credited with having rediscovered the classical theory again, which had been buried under thick layers of interpretation, or rather, misinterpretation. He had accomplished this, Sraffa stressed, "either by accident or by *superhuman effort*" (D3/12/4: 17; emphasis added).

It can safely be assumed that Sraffa borrowed from Pareto the term "superhuman effort" and in this way indicated that he engaged in a critical discussion with the latter's view of the classical economists and their followers. This is also implicit in Sraffa's constructive work at the time. In a system without a surplus, the production equations in the case of n products being produced by means of n single-product methods of production can be written (in obvious notation) in the following way:

$$A_a p_a + B_a p_b + \ldots + N_a p_n = A p_a$$
$$A_b p_a + B_b p_b + \ldots + N_b p_n = B p_b$$
$$\cdots\cdots\cdots\cdots\cdots\cdots\cdots\cdots\cdots\cdots$$
$$A_n p_a + B_n p_b + \ldots + N_n p_n = N p_n$$

where $\Sigma_i A_i = A$, $\Sigma_i B_i = B, \ldots, \Sigma_i N_i = N$. The input amounts comprise not only necessary means of production, but also necessary means of sustenance in support of workers. In the case of no surplus, all n commodities are *basic* products (Sraffa 1960: 6); that is, each and every commodity enters directly or indirectly in the production of each and every of the n commodities, either as a means of production or a means of sustenance. These simultaneous equations can be solved with the help of linear algebra.

In terms of the properties of this system that he investigated, Sraffa implicitly commented upon two contradictory propositions by Pareto. First, Pareto was wrong in maintaining against the classical economists that "the consideration of certain obstacles to production" are "[not] enough to give [value] existence". The system of equations shows on the contrary that what Sraffa called "physical real cost", that is, information about the necessary quantities of means of production and means of sustenance of workers required to overcome the "obstacles" of production, is all that is needed in order to determine the exchange values of commodities. Secondly, Sraffa at the same time confirmed that equilibrium can in fact be ascertained "without making use of the notions of utility (ophelimity), prices, etc.". This Pareto had maintained correctly but then failed to show.

It is significant to note that Sraffa at the time used a mathematical textbook written for students of chemistry and the natural sciences (Chini 1923). The significance lies in the fact that it can be related to Pareto's reference to chemistry and what he called the "completely erroneous" theory of "definite proportions". Again, contrary to Pareto's claim, in the previously noted equations the input–output system is taken to be given and definite. In this case the contention that the theory is "completely erroneous" cannot be sustained. In the case in which there is a choice of technique, for example, the proportions cannot be known *a priori*; we must first request a solution to this choice. Once it is decided, there is again a system of production with definite proportions and the previous argument applies *a fortiori*.

The above system of $n - 1$ independent equations can be solved using the well-known tools of linear algebra. But Sraffa also put forward another (and related) tool that can be said to mimic the classical author's search for an "absolute measure of value". In an attempt to render heterogeneous commodities commensurable with one another, William Petty had suggested to reduce each commodity to a certain amount of some composite commodity, which was used directly and indirectly in its production. After some deliberation he suggested to take "the days food of an adult Man, at a Medium" as the sought measure. Sraffa in his early papers called the tool under consideration the "method of substitution" and later the "Reduction method". It is the method used by the classical economists in their quest for an "ultimate measure of value". He illustrated the method *inter alia* in terms of the following example:

> For the first equations (without surplus) it is obviously true that the amount of *B* that a unit of *A* fetches in exchange is equal to the amount of *B* that directly or indirectly has been used up, in successive stages, in the production of a unit of *A*. The method would be that, if in 1*A* enter 3*B* + 2*C*, we would put aside the 3*B*; find that in 2*C* enter 1*B* + 2*D* . . . put aside the 1*B* and find how many *B* enter into 2*D* etc. etc. *The series is infinite but the sum is finite.*
>
> (D3/12/7: 30–31, emphasis added)

Obviously, in systems without a surplus, this method can be applied to each and every one of the *n* products. The exchange ratios of commodities that guarantee the "self-replacement" of the system can therefore be conceived as reflecting the relative total amounts of any one of the products used up in production. Hence Pareto was wrong on maintaining that no physical "content" of commodities can be ascertained. The problem was rather that each commodity could be reduced to as many commodities as there are in the system as a whole, and if composite commodities such as Petty's "the days food" are allowed, then also to them![16] The view that only a single (composite) commodity can perform the role under discussion is mistaken.

Even in systems *with* a surplus, one can still ascertain the amount of some basic product needed directly and indirectly in the production of a commodity. But, flukes aside, the exchange ratios of commodities no longer reflect only the total amount of the chosen basic product used up in production, but in addition to physical real costs the sharing out of the surplus product in terms of wages and profits. Sraffa stressed this fact in several of his notes. He discussed, in particular, systems of production with a (uniform) "rate of interest" and pointed out in 1928 that this rate and relative prices depend on real wages.

Concluding remark

In this chapter we focused on one of the focal points of Sraffa's (re-)constructive work: Pareto's general equilibrium theory. Pareto had chastised the classical economists and Marx for not having formulated their approach to value and distribution in terms of systems of simultaneous equations. Instead they are said to have made "superhuman efforts" to cope with the problems they faced by seeking a single or composite commodity that served as an ultimate measure of value. This measure would reflect the material "content" of each and every commodity and was taken to render heterogeneous commodities commensurable. Alas, according to Pareto these authors followed a will-o'-the-wisp, because there was no such thing. At the same time he somewhat surprisingly maintained that in defining the concept of equilibrium, there was no need to have recourse to the notions of utility or disutility: it could be defined exclusively in terms of commodities. Apparently Pareto was not aware that there is a tension between the two propositions.

Sraffa brought this tension into the open. He first pointed out that Pareto did not stick consistently to his second claim but in fact abandoned it without noticing he had done so. The claim, however, was correct and could be established rigorously. This Sraffa did in terms of his first and second equations, that is, systems of production without and with a social surplus product, which he developed in late 1927 and in 1928. By accomplishing this, Sraffa obtained a result that also answered Pareto's first point. Prices in both systems, and in the second also the interest rate, depend only on the amounts of the various commodities used up (means of production and means of sustenance) and produced (gross outputs), that is, on the material metabolism of society. There is no need, and indeed no possibility, to have recourse to (marginal) utility or disutility. Physical real cost of production is all that matters. Interestingly, all commodities can be "reduced" to well-specified amounts of any one of the basic products needed directly and indirectly in their production. Hence commodities can be conceived as embodying definite amounts of any one of the basic products in the system. Commodities had "content", so to speak.

As Sraffa had pointed out at an early time, there is "much to be found in Pareto". But much of what he found he could not just accept and adopt, but first he had to correct or complete or simply use as an inspiration to elaborate a coherent theory of value and distribution. Cleary the "origin" of Sraffa's equations of production is not in Pareto. But Pareto's criticism of the "literary" economists provided Sraffa with a welcome opportunity to make up his own mind as regards alternative approaches to the theory of value and distribution and to develop some of the concepts upon which he was eventually to erect his own analytical construction in his 1960 book. In it he returned to the "standpoint of the old classical economists from Adam Smith to Ricardo", but with an understanding of the issues at hand that had benefited significantly *inter alia* from his critical examination of Pareto's "synthetic" notion of equilibrium.

Notes

1 I am most grateful to Christian Gehrke for valuable comments on an earlier draft of this paper. I should also like to thank him and Neri Salvadori for many years of close collaboration. Any remaining errors or misconceptions are, of course, my responsibility.
2 Sraffa died on 3 September 1983, but his papers were opened to the public only more than a decade later.
3 Incidentally, and from a purely formal point of view, Sraffa followed Pareto (and other authors, including Wittgenstein) by subdividing his book in §§s.
4 The "First Equations" recur in Chapter 1, "Production for Subsistence" and the "Second Equations" in Chapter 2, "Production with a Surplus", §§ 4–5, of Sraffa (1960).
5 The references to Sraffa's papers follow the catalogue prepared by Jonathan Smith, archivist, of the Wren Library, Trinity College, Cambridge, UK.
6 English translation: "It ought to be mentioned that the equilibrium is going to be determined without making use of the notions of utility (ophelimity), prices, etc."
7 English translation: "In other words, experience is the alpha and omega of this theory: but who made the experience?"
8 The treatise is reprinted in Volume V of Pareto's *Oeuvres complètes*.
9 The essay had apparently been translated into German, but the translation is "bumpy", to put it mildly. The translation from German into English is mine.
10 It is perhaps interesting to mention that the copy Sraffa used, Pareto had originally dedicated to Vito Volterra, who was on friendly terms with Sraffa.
11 Pareto's following discussion of "total ophelimity", reflecting his idea that the maximising behaviour of individuals yields a maximum satisfaction of needs and wants of society as a whole, Sraffa for a short while took up in his papers in terms of a search for the maximum total value of the social product (see, for example, D3/12/6: 6–7) but then abandoned the idea, because it did not lead him anywhere.
12 In a footnote Pareto referred to Walras and to his *Cours* (§594, 598–600)
13 This idea was further developed by Enrico Barone and played an important role in the debate about the possibility of market socialism.
14 This applies to the case of a given system of production without a choice of technique, whereas with such a choice the adequate tool are *in*equalities, as John von Neumann emphasised and Sraffa implied *verbatim*, without using inequalities; see Kurz and Salvadori (1993).
15 It is interesting to note that Pareto accused even Walras of occasionally falling victim to what we may dub the *single-cause doctrine of value* (see 1971: 179–180). While he does not refer to Carl Menger, Eugen von Böhm-Bawerk, Friedrich von Wieser or any other representative of "Austrian economics", it is clear that his criticism is directed especially at this doctrine.
16 Sraffa's Standard commodity is a particular composite commodity that reflects the material content *in abstracto* of commodities of a given system under consideration.

References

Böhm-Bawerk, E. v. [1884] 1921. *Kapital und Kapitalzins. Erste Abtheilung: Geschichte und Kritik der Kapitalzinstheorien*. Innsbruck: Wagner.

Chini, M. (1923). *Corso speciale di matematiche con numerose applicazioni ad uso principalmente dei chimici e di naturalisti*. Livorno: Raffaello Giusti Editore-Libraio-Tipigrafo.

De Vivo, G. (2019). Marx and Sraffa: a comment on Gehrke and Kurz. *Review of Political Economy*, 31(1): 95–99.

Garegnani, P. (1984). Value and distribution in the classical economists and Marx. *Oxford Economic Papers*, 36(2): 291–325.

Gehrke, C. and Kurz, H. D. (2006). Sraffa on von Bortkiewicz: reconstructing the classical theory of value and distribution. *History of Political Economy*, 38(1): 91–149.

Gehrke, C. and Kurz, H. D. (2018). Sraffa's constructive and interpretive work, and Marx. *Review of Political Economy*, 30(3): 428–442.

Gehrke, C., Kurz, H. D. and Salvadori, N. (2019). On the "origins" of Sraffa's production equations: a reply to de Vivo. *Review of Political Economy*, 31(1): 100–114.

Kurz, H. D. (1998). Against the current: Sraffa's unpublished manuscripts and the history of economic thought. *The European Journal of the History of Economic Thought*, 5(3): 437–451.

Kurz, H. D. (2012). Don't treat too ill my Piero! Interpreting Sraffa's papers. *Cambridge Journal of Economics*, 36: 1535–1569.

Kurz, H. D. and Salvadori, N. (1993). Von Neumann's growth model and the "classical" tradition. *The European Journal of the History of Economic Thought*, 1(1): 129–160.

Pareto, V. (1896–1897). *Cours d'économie politique*. Two vols, vol. I 1896, vol. II 1897. Lausanne: F. Rouge.

Pareto, V. (1902–1903). *Les systèmes socialistes*. Two vols, vol. I 1902, vol. II 1903. Paris: Giard & Brière.

Pareto, V. (1902). Anwendungen der Mathematik auf Nationalökonomie. In *Encyklopädie der mathematischen Wissenschaften*. vol. I, No. 7. Leipzig: B. G. Teubner, pp. 1094–1120.

Pareto, V. (1906). *Manuale di economia politica con una introduzione alla scienza sociale*. Milan: Società editrice libreraria.

Pareto, V. (1909). *Manuel d'economie politique*, French translation of the Italian original. Paris: Giard & Brière.

Pareto, V. ([1927] 1971). *Manual of political economy*, translated from the French edition of 1927. New York: Augustus M. Kelley.

Ricardo, D. (1951–1973). *The works and correspondence of David Ricardo*. 11 vols. edited by Piero Sraffa with the collaboration of Maurice H. Dobb. Cambridge: Cambridge University Press.

Sraffa, P. (1925). Sulle relazioni fra costo e quantità prodotta. *Annali di Economia*, 2: 277–328.

Sraffa, P. (1926). The laws of returns under competitive conditions. *Economic Journal*, 36: 535–550.

Sraffa, P. (1960). *Production of commodities by means of commodities*. Cambridge: Cambridge University Press.

10 Rosa Luxemburg, Mikhail Tugan-Baranovsky and the current state of economic crisis

Tracy Mott and P. Sai-wing Ho

Amit Bhaduri is well-known for his contributions to macroeconomic theory in a Kaleckian-Keynesian framework. This chapter relates to such a perspective by extending the ideas of Michał Kalecki's (1991 [1967]) paper, "The Problem of Effective Demand with Tugan-Baranovsky and Rosa Luxemburg," which describes the strengths and weaknesses of Mikhail Tugan-Baranovsky's and Rosa Luxemburg's theories of macroeconomics in a capitalist economy. In this chapter we will look once more at these ideas and at Kalecki's insights concerning them to see if these can tell us more about the problems of today's world.

We will ask if Luxemburg's ideas and Kalecki's critique can give us a deeper understanding of the "East Asian models" of economic development followed historically by Japan and China. We will ask if Tugan-Baranovsky's proposed answer to the effective demand problem can be usefully compared to some aspects of the method of development followed by the Soviet Union. We will look at Kalecki's concerns about the limits to the use of fiscal policy and at Joseph Schumpeter's proposals for dealing with unemployment, and then we will ask if Kalecki's remarks about social control over profit margins could be a way to achieve the type of flexibility needed to deal with the macroeconomic problems seen in existing capitalist and socialist economies.

Rosa Luxemburg – the "queen of the underconsumptionists"

Luxemburg's (2003 [1913]) argument is based on the understanding that capitalist economies suffer inexorably from "underconsumption." That is, there is a shortfall in effective demand, and therefore we have unemployment, because of limited purchasing power in the hands of wage-earners. This must mean that spending out of profits on consumption plus investment is not sufficient to purchase the product that can be produced at full employment. The idea that consumption out of profits is low is not hard to maintain, but her argument that there is insufficient investment spending out of profits is also due to underconsumption in that investment spending is depressed because consumption is not high enough to make sufficient investment spending profitable. She then goes on to argue that this means that the only possible solution is for the capitalist economies to find "external markets" in underdeveloped countries and non-capitalist sectors at home in which to sell their products.

Kalecki pointed out that Luxemburg made a mistake by identifying *total* exports, rather than just the export *surplus*, as a source of effective demand. His major criticism of her argument, however, was that she had not treated with full importance the possibility of government spending financed by borrowing or by profits taxation as providing the desired effective demand. She did recognize that such government expenditures, particularly on armaments, served as an "external market" which could provide demand for goods and services, though she didn't give this the attention it deserved and made a similar mistake to that related to exports in seeing the total of such government expenditures as creating demand without considering how the spending would be financed.

Kalecki noted that Luxemburg's schema would also require the export of capital to the economies buying the export surplus to finance it. In addition, Luxemburg framed her argument as saying that what was required were exports to the non-capitalist parts of the world. Kalecki pointed out that this meant that, as the world's economies became capitalist, we would no longer be able to achieve such.

The "East Asian model"

The country which was most noticeably building an economy with a large external focus during the 20th century was Japan. Japan had been able to escape colonial penetration in the 19th century from Western Europe or the United States, partly because it was not possessed of any significant quantity of desirable natural resources and partly because it benefited from the intentions of the US to limit the influence of the European powers, particularly Great Britain, in the Far East. Indeed, Japan's push to industrialize was somewhat spurred by wanting to ensure its ability to be strong enough to meet any potential Western military threats that might arise or the commercial threats that actually did appear.[1]

The military and industrial apparatus thus constructed in Japan encouraged the following of the imperialist road to development. This was given a further push in the 1930s by the fact that Japan suffered more than most of the industrialized countries from the Great Depression, and this, plus the country's lack of natural resources, inspired Japan to the attempt to create its "Greater East Asia Co-Prosperity Sphere."

This ultimately led to the Pacific theatre of World War II, with Japan's ultimate defeat. After the war, Japan had to turn to dealing with effective demand questions to a significant degree by producing for external markets, and, we should note, in the capitalist world rather than the non-capitalist world, as Luxemburg had thought to be necessary.[2] The only military source of demand was limited to whatever came from the US occupation forces plus the build-up for the Korean conflict, as the constitution imposed by the Allies forbade Japan from maintaining any significant military establishment. The export strategy required low labor costs, first realized by means of lower wages. In the 1950s and 1960s, Japan's exports were cheap trinkets and gadgets, and the term "Made in Japan" came to signify in the US that something was cheap. Over time, though, Japan's mercantilist industrial policy saw that the profits from its export surplus were channelled into investment in steel and automobile manufacturing and advanced electronic components with which to make radios, televisions, stereos, and eventually computers. By the 1970s, "Made in Japan" became synonymous with high quality. Its cost advantage now came from high productivity.

The strategy of the "Japanese model" of economic development was copied by South Korea, Taiwan, and the other "Asian tigers," and eventually by the People's Republic of China, after its turn to a "socialist market economy" in 1979. Indeed, this "East Asian model" seems to have been the only successful economic development strategy of the 20th and 21st centuries.

Obviously, not every country can run an export surplus. The limits to maintaining effective demand by means of external markets are that you have to find such markets to penetrate and that you have to maintain a cost advantage. Japan's economy in the 1990s fell into a financial bubble which burst, but the various East Asian competitors following the Japanese strategy may well be the biggest obstacle to Japan's continued success at it.

South Korea, Taiwan, and others began to develop a cost advantage over Japan in several product sectors, and China eventually came to play this this game, too, especially after its accession to the WTO, and most recently with its "Belt-and-Road Initiative." Chinese successes and problems with this strategy may be very illustrative of the problems which Kalecki identified in it. Much of China's success has come from its ability to export to the US and, to a lesser extent, Europe. Vis-à-vis the US, this has necessitated that China keep its currency from appreciating too much against the US dollar, which in turn has meant that China has had to use a good deal of its export profits to buy US securities, in effect to loan the US the money to buy Chinese products.[3] China also has faced complaints from the US about its undervalued currency and its mercantilist policies, and today China is also beginning to see lower-cost rivals threaten its export dominance as well. Whatever problems China has or will have in continuing this strategy, it does have the promise of a huge internal market as wages rise to allow it to switch to producing for domestic consumption. Also, its huge state sector and power may allow it to follow whatever degree it likes of the Tugan-Baranovsky strategy that we look at next.[4]

Mikhail Tugan-Baranovsky – investment spending *ad infinitum*

Tugan-Baranovsky's (1901) approach to the problem of effective demand, as we know, claimed that a capitalist economy need not worry about production for consumers if their purchasing power was insufficient. It could rather continue to produce capital goods to make capital goods to maintain effective demand. Kalecki's criticism, of course, was that such a method of providing adequate demand to support growth would be unstable in that any deviation in investment spending below the proportion that would maintain growth at the existing rate would lead to overproduction and thus insufficient demand.

We believe that Tugan-Baranovsky's theoretical framework for maintaining expanded reproduction in a capitalist economy, however, has been carried out in practice, ironically not in a capitalist economy, but in the Soviet model of socialism. When the Bolsheviks came to power, the economy was in a very underdeveloped state, and the country was almost immediately plunged into a civil war. After various fits and starts, some forced by exigencies, some due to experiments, the Soviets decided to obtain an agricultural surplus by forcible collectivization and to use it to industrialize by emphasizing the production of capital goods to make capital goods. This may have made a lot of sense as a matter of an industrialization strategy for an economy needing to accumulate such capital goods both for the purposes of developing industrial production capacity and for a country faced with serious military threats.[5]

The Soviet model and its problems

The problems of the Soviet economy of course had nothing to do with insufficient aggregate demand, the solution that Tugan-Baranovsky said could be alleviated by such a policy. As economic development proceeded, one would suppose that this strategy would eventually lead to a shift towards increasing the proportion of capital goods to produce consumer goods and then to the production of greater proportions of consumer goods themselves in the economic plan. This, however, did not happen in the Soviet case. The Soviet economy was able to produce the military equipment necessary for the country to do perhaps more than its part in the defeat of Nazi Germany, along with suffering more than its share of the devastation, human and material, of the war. The scale of production increased, and the Soviets were able to accomplish impressive technical projects, but they were not able to make much of a change in the proportions of industry making capital goods to make capital goods vs. capital goods to make consumption goods vs. consumption goods.

Mario Nuti (1981) has described the Soviet economy and those which followed its model as being like a car stuck in first gear, building up huge revolutions per minute, but being unable to shift into higher gear when less take-off was needed. Much of this seemed to be because of the need for managers to meet plan-directed output levels by whatever means possible, disregarding cost and quality considerations while concealing reserves and overestimating requirements. The planning bureaucracy realized this and demanded more, along with penalizing success by raising quotas when it occurred. The ability to shift priorities towards consumption was largely stifled.

There was no problem of effective demand, as the system worked as Tugan-Baranovsky had described it in that respect. The problem was the opposite – excess demand, which, however, did not lead to price inflation because prices were fixed. The Soviet version of socialism was a shortage economy.

We know that Kalecki criticized the Soviet model on the grounds that it attempted to achieve growth rates that were too high. Kalecki's criticism of capitalism's failure to provide adequate effective demand held that, given the price-cost markup, which divides incomes broadly between wages and profits, a fall in investment spending would lower aggregate demand unless markups fell, redistributing income from profits to wages. In a socialist economy, he thought that markups could be lowered when investment fell. In the Soviet model, however, this did not happen because investment spending never fell. This avoids the effective demand problem, but only by creating a different problem. In both capitalism and Soviet-style socialism, though, we have seen a type of underconsumption due to real wages' being too low.

How can we manage aggregate demand successfully?

Kalecki realized that "Keynesian" fiscal policy could solve Luxemburg's effective demand failures, but he had doubts about fiscal policy as a solution for effective demand problems because he believed that there were limits to its being used, as spelled out in his famous article, "Political Aspects of Full Employment" (Kalecki, 1990 [1943]). The main political problems which Kalecki identified with the use of fiscal policy were that business interests would dislike government spending to achieve full employment because (1) this would give government rather than business influence over economic conditions, which would remove a check that business otherwise has over government policies they may dislike, (2) such spending might compete with or take over areas which otherwise would be served solely by business, and (3) the *maintenance* of full employment by government spending would undermine labor discipline.

Kalecki saw that attempting to avoid these problems by lowering interest rates or taxes would not be able to provide *continual* full employment, as this would come to require negative interest rates and taxes eventually. His conclusion was that government policy would be used to mitigate slumps, now that its use had been realized and experienced in World War II, but this would then be withdrawn rather than used to maintain full employment, leading to the "political business cycle." He also mentioned in the article the ability to overcome these objections by fascist states, which need not fear political resistance, even though business would be less threatened, since government spending is used there primarily for military spending.

The experience of the use of fiscal policy after World War II very much followed as Kalecki had predicted. Countries such as the USA, given the excuse to do so by the "Cold War," maintained a significant level of government spending for military purposes. Even though this spending was largely financed by taxation, it still served as support for higher levels of spending and so employment than might have existed otherwise. The US benefited, at least up to the 1970s, from also being the least-cost producer of many industrial and agricultural products. Though the country did run an export surplus during those years, the US was seen largely as a "closed economy," since its volume of international trade was small relative to its total GDP.

International exchange rates were then fixed under the Bretton Woods Agreement. Economies which were significantly "open" did have to worry about balance of payments deficits forcing them under the Bretton Woods rules to adopt austerity to maintain the promised exchange rate parity, or devaluation which might lead to inflationary pressures that undid much of the competitive advantage offered by the devaluation. Even the U.S. developed a balance of payments problem, due to capital outflows, by the 1960s, when France began demanding gold for the dollars it was accumulating, eventually leading to the demise of Bretton Woods.

Without properly flexible markups, the Luxemburg solution to the effective demand problem fails, unless adequate external markets can be found. This requires appropriate trade deficits financed by the surplus economies. For adequate external markets to be found in the world economy taken as a whole, the deficit economies have to run government budget deficits. If we attempt to have adequate government spending in any country, though, we will have the political resistance which Kalecki predicted, and which we have seen in practice, supported politically by fear of price inflation and/or loss of international competitiveness by the national economy. The socialist alternative that has been tried benefited from the Tugan-Baranovsky solution to the effective demand problem but suffered from the inability to change the share of investment vs. consumption. That is, the Soviet model did not face the problem of insufficient investment, which lower markups would cure by increasing consumption demand. Instead, it could not decrease capital spending and increase consumption spending when that would have been desirable.

Looked at in this way, the problem in both economies has been the problem of flexibility. In the socialist economy, the lack of flexibility in output and employment leads to shortages of consumer goods. In the capitalist economy, the necessity to vary output and employment with aggregate demand leads to unemployment. The attempts to prevent unemployment with fiscal policy in capitalism also can decrease the amount of variation in the output mix in ways that interfere with Schumpeterian "creative destruction" and so cause some longer-term inefficiencies, as noted, for example, by Hyman Minsky (1985), but the lost profit and wage incomes are surely worse. Is there a way to modify capitalism, bringing it closer to the ideals of socialism, without arriving at the Soviet-type shortage economy?[6]

Schumpeter (1975 [1942], pp. 69–71), a one-time teacher of Minsky and the apostle of creative destruction, argued that the level of wealth in a capitalist economy should make us able to provide "adequately for the unemployed *without impairing the conditions of further economic development*" (emphasis in original), disapproving of doing so by "Keynesian" aggregate demand management but rather by capitalistic improvements in the care for the sick and aged and public provision of certain basic commodities in "an otherwise unfettered capitalism." This method might deal well with the problem of weeding out inefficiencies, but it could quite easily run into the problem of getting stuck in the down phase of the cycle for too long. We do see that recessions have been much shorter since we have become aware of monetary and fiscal responses, at least when we have been willing and able to use them. Also, taking care of the unemployed by public provisioning that does not give them remunerative work has the danger of codifying the creation of an underclass of "warehoused" people.

Income distributional issues

Schumpeter's approach might allow the flexibility necessary for a high degree of creative destruction, but we think that Kalecki's notions regarding markup flexibility would be better for the income distributional problems capitalism can develop. If we look at the current state of affairs in the capitalist world, we think we see the limits to capitalism's ability to solve its own problems for reasons pointed out by Kalecki and Minsky. Kalecki's political business cycle argument has showed us why fiscal policy cannot succeed, and we have seen that its use in the post-World War II OECD countries has become limited since the 1970s, with inflation-fighting since then having been carried out by maintaining a higher average level of unemployment, which has also kept real wages from keeping up with productivity growth and contributed to the build-up of household and corporate debt, following on Minsky's ideas.[7]

The paradox is that only a socialist economy would have the ability to enforce the markup flexibility which a capitalist economy requires if it is to produce at full capacity with full employment, while the socialist economies that have existed have been unwilling or unable to do this. What is really called for, we would submit, is social control over profit margins. This was also advocated by John Maynard Keynes when he wrote, "If the State is able to determine the aggregate amount of resources devoted to augmenting the instruments [of production] and the basic rate of reward to those who own them, it will have accomplished all that is necessary" (Keynes, 1964 [1936], p. 378).

Two pages later, Keynes (1964 [1936], p. 380) added a statement saying that such policies would seem horrific to "a contemporary American financier," but it is surely this sort of opposition which has led to the less-than-desirable functioning of both capitalism and socialism as we have known them. Nuti (1981) argued that the solution to reform in the existing socialisms of the 20th century was political rather than economic, and this is the case, *mutatis mutandis*, in today's capitalisms, which discovered "stagnation policy," as Josef Steindl (1990 [1979]) described it, in the 1970s and cannot agree to take enough simple "Keynesian" stimulus measures to deal with what has been called the "great recession" from which we are now trying to recover.

If the problem, though, is "underconsumption" due to insufficient purchasing power in the hands of wage earners, the remedy can only be higher real wages, which can only come when productivity gains do not go solely to profits and/or profit margins are lowered. In a socialist economy, profits are clearly there only for the purpose of directing resources into investment. When less investment is needed or desired, profits should fall in either type of economy. In capitalism, where profits are supposed to be the reward for providing capital for investment, if it is successful, the aggregate effects of a decrease in markups on profits in a closed economy is basically positive only if the propensity to save out of wages is greater than the propensity to invest out of output. (See the Technical appendix.) An individual firm will be better off if it does not lower its markup when investment spending falls, but all firms may well be worse off.

The desire to have social control over markups follows from these considerations. If this method is not pursued, we will face the attempts to solve these problems by the search for export markets (Luxemburg) or the pursuit of investment for the sake of having something to spend on (Tugan-Baranovsky). As Keynes (1964 [1936], p. 129) wrote, we could bury bank-notes in old bottles so that companies would hire people to dig them up, if we weren't willing to finance socially useful work. Or, we could listen to the many economists who tell us that any government-financed spending is bad and possibly leads to inflation.

If we do maintain high employment by "Keynesian" creation of effective demand by means of government spending, over time, inflation in a capitalist world or shortages in a socialist world will occur. In the capitalist economy, of course, the arguments in Kalecki (1990 [1943]) will come into play, and the danger of losing international competitiveness will also bring calls for austerity. With social control over markups, however, we have a way to ensure that rising wages or profits don't raise prices.

At the end of his *General Theory*, Keynes asked, "Is the fulfillment of [my] ideas a visionary hope?" (Keynes, 1964 [1936], p. 383). Kalecki (1991 [1967], p. 458) saw that the visions of Luxemburg and Tugan-Baranovsky, as he put it, "despite slips in their arguments, contributed to the understanding of the perverse world in which we are living." Can we use their contributions and Kalecki's insights concerning them to help us see more about the problems of this world?

Notes

1 Paul Baran (1962 [1957], pp. 158–161) discusses this, for example.
2 Some (e.g., Andrea Boltho [1996]; Titus Awokuse [2005]) have argued that econometric analysis shows that Japan's growth during those years cannot be characterized unambiguously as "export-led." To say that Japan had adopted "mercantilist" policies of discouraging imports and encouraging exports à la Luxemburg is clear, though.
3 Cf. Kalecki (1991 [1967], p. 456). "Only to the extent to which the capitalist system lends to the non-capitalist world (or the latter sells its assets) is it possible

to place abroad the surplus of goods unsold at home." We should substitute for "capitalist system" and "non-capitalist world," we believe, "exporting economy" and "importing economy." We might also remember the role of British capital in financing the development of the USA.

4 Its use of debt to finance so much of its state-led investment, however, has created problems.
5 See, for example, Baran (1962 [1957], pp. 261–271).
6 Nuti (1981) says that the drawbacks of the Soviet system were felt more sharply in the more-developed Eastern European economies.
7 See Mott (2010, chapter 11) for the exposition of how shortening recessions with policy actions can also lead to a "Minsky knife-edge" due to a tendency for private debt ratios to rise over time.
8 This is a variation on any number of Kaleckian models, such as Donald Harris (1974).

References

Awokuse, Titus (2005). "Export-led Growth and the Japanese Economy: Evidence from VAR and Directed Acyclic Graphs," *Applied Economics Letters* 12, pp. 849–858,

Baran, Paul (1962 [1957]). *The Political Economy of Growth*, New York: Monthly Review Press.

Boltho, Andrea (1996). "Was Japanese Growth Export-led?" *Oxford Economic Papers* 48, pp. 415–432.

Harris, Donald (1974). "The Price Policy of Firms, the Level of Employment, and the Distribution of Income in the Short Run," *Australian Economic Papers* 13, pp. 144–151.

Kalecki, Michał (1990 [1943]). "Political Aspects of Full Employment," in Jerzy Osiatyński ed., *Collected Works of Michał Kalecki*, Vol. I, Oxford, UK: Clarendon Press, pp. 347–356.

Kalecki, Michał (1991 [1967]). "The Problem of Effective Demand with Tugan-Baranovsky and Rosa Luxemburg," in Jerzy Osiatyński ed., *Collected Works of Michał Kalecki*, Vol. II, Oxford, UK: Clarendon Press, pp. 451–458.

Keynes, John Maynard (1964 [1936]). *The General Theory of Employment, Interest, and Money*, New York: Harcourt, Brace & World.

Luxemburg, Rosa (2003 [1913]). *The Accumulation of Capital*, London and New York: Routledge.

Minsky, Hyman (1985). "The Financial Instability Hypothesis: A Restatement," in Philip Arestis and Thanos Skouras eds., *Post Keynesian Economic Theory*, Sussex, UK: Wheatsheaf Books, pp. 24–55.

Mott, Tracy (2010). *Kalecki's Principle of Increasing Risk and Keynesian Economics*, London: Routledge.

Nuti, Mario (1981). "Socialism on Earth," *Cambridge Journal of Economics* 5, pp. 391–404.

Schumpeter, Joseph (1975 [1942]). *Capitalism, Socialism, and Democracy*, New York: Harper.

Steindl, Josef (1990 [1979]). "Stagnation Theory and Stagnation Policy," in *Economic Papers 1941–88*, New York: St. Martin's Press, pp. 107–126.

Tugan-Baranovsky (1901). *Studien zur Theorie und Geschichte der Handelskrisen in England*, Jena: Verlag von Gustav Fischer.

Technical appendix

We can see much of the argument that follows in terms of the following mathematical model:

Nominal national income = $pY = W + \Pi + pT = pC + pI + pG$.
Workers employed, $L = bY$, where b = the inverse of productivity, or workers per unit of output.
Total wages, $W = \bar{w}L$, where $\bar{w}$ = the money wage per unit of time.
Injections = leakages gives $pI + pG = s_\Pi \Pi + s_w W + pT$.
Unit labor costs = wage per worker ($\bar{w}$) ÷ output per worker (productivity) = $\bar{w}b$
Price level = unit labor costs × % markup ($\bar{\phi}$), so $p = \bar{\phi}\bar{w}b$

real wage = $\dfrac{\bar{w}}{p} = \dfrac{1}{\bar{\phi}b}$.

Investment, $I = I_0 + \alpha\left(\dfrac{\Pi}{p}\right) + \gamma Y$.

$Y^* = \dfrac{\bar{\phi}(I_0 + A - T)}{(s_\Pi - \alpha)(\bar{\phi} - 1) + s_w - \gamma\bar{\phi}}$, where real autonomous spending, A, which here is export surplus plus real government spending plus any autonomous consumption spending, and p times real taxes, T.

$$\left(\frac{\Pi}{p}\right)^* = \frac{(\bar{\phi} - 1)(I_0 + A - T)}{(s_\Pi - \alpha)(\bar{\phi} - 1) + s_w - \gamma\bar{\phi}}.$$

Consumption spending is taken to be mostly out of wages, while investment spending is mostly financed from profits. National income is mainly divided between wages and profits by price-cost markups. Markups cover overheads, etc., as well as profits. Inputs bought from other firms net out in the aggregate.[8]

Now if we differentiate Y with respect to $\bar{\phi}$, we will get

$$\frac{\partial Y}{\partial \bar{\phi}} = \frac{-(I_0 + A - T)(s_\Pi - \alpha - s_w)}{\left[(s_\Pi - \alpha)(\bar{\phi} - 1) + s_w - \gamma\bar{\phi}\right]^2},$$

which is < 0 if $s_\Pi > \alpha + s_w$.

If we differentiate real profits, Π/p, with respect to $\bar{\phi}$, we have

$$\frac{\partial(\Pi / p)}{\partial\bar{\phi}} = \frac{(A-T)(s_w-\gamma)}{\left[(s_\Pi-\alpha)(\bar{\phi}-1)+s_w-\gamma\bar{\phi}\right]^2},$$

which is > 0 if $s_w > \gamma$.

If we have an open economy, we need both to include exports and imports directly into the model as well as to allow changes in prices also to have an effect on them. The simplest way to do this with the present model is to divide our parameter A into a term C_0 for autonomous consumption, a term G for the level of government spending, and a term for the real export surplus or deficit, which we will take to be determined by a parameter η times p plus a parameter m (the marginal propensity to import) times Y. Substituting for the endogenous variable p its equal, the exogenous variables $\bar{\phi}\bar{w}b$, and including the effect of mY, we will now have

$$Y^* = \frac{\bar{\phi}(I_0+C_0+G-T-\eta\bar{\phi}\bar{w}b)}{(s_\Pi-\alpha)(\bar{\phi}-1)+s_w+\bar{\phi}(m-\gamma)}, \text{ and}$$

$$\left(\frac{\Pi}{p}\right)^* = \frac{(\bar{\phi}-1)(I_0+C_0+G-T-\eta\bar{\phi}\bar{w}b)}{(s_\Pi-\alpha)(\bar{\phi}-1)+s_w+\bar{\phi}(m-\gamma)}.$$

Now, though the sign of $\frac{\partial Y}{\partial\bar{\phi}}$ will still be negative as long as $s_\Pi > \alpha + s_w$, the sign of $\frac{\partial(\Pi/p)}{\partial\bar{\phi}}$ will depend upon the sign of $m-\gamma$. That is, though the existence of a high marginal propensity to import relative to the influence of changes in national income on investment cannot by itself cause a rise in markups actually to increase national income, it can contribute to making a rise in markups increase profits. The more open the economy, then, the more room there is for a conflict between wages and profits.

Another new development with the opening of our model economy is that we now can see effects on national income from changes in the money wage. A rise (fall) in $\bar{w}$, unless equally or more than offset by a fall (rise) in $\bar{\phi}$, will now reduce (increase) national income, and employment as well.

This reminds us that the effect of increases in $\bar{\phi}$ should now be affected by whether they come at the expense of money wages or prices. If higher markups come about due more to lower money wages than to higher prices, the magnitude of the harm to national output and employment will be less. Another matter that we need to consider in the open economy case is that changes in interest rates will now have a stronger effect on output, employment, and prices because of their effects on foreign exchange rates.

11 Some reflections on 'primitive accumulation'

Rune Skarstein

The fall of communism in the Soviet Union and Eastern Europe did not mean "the end of history", as Francis Fukuyama suggested in 1992. Instead, in a state-supported process of economic deregulation and globalisation, called neoliberalism, capitalism became more aggressive than it had ever been since the Second World War. Phenomena such as privatisations of public property, "outsourcing", rolling back of welfare states, increasing inequality of incomes and wealth, and – not least – expropriations of large populations for their land and other natural resources became central issues in the academic discourse as well as in the media. For an increasing number of people around the world, it has become evident: The liberal view that the triumph of capitalism implies only winners and no losers is fundamentally wrong. Some of these changes, especially land grabbing in Asia, Africa and Latin America, gave rise to a revival of interest in Marx's analysis of "so-called primitive accumulation".

In several publications Amit Bhaduri has analysed the Indian states' cooperation with and active support of corporations in forced dispossession of people from traditional livelihoods in the countryside for rapid industrialisation: "The government displaces people from land usually through legal 'notification', and the acquired land and the related natural common property resources, like grazing lands, forests, rivers, mountains and coastlines, are allotted to corporations at highly subsidized rate" (Bhaduri 2018). Bhaduri shows that adivasis, dalits and poor farmers are the main victims of this process (Bhaduri 2009, 2010). In one of his publications he presents a formal model displaying various interconnections that characterise corporate-led growth where rapid industrialisation implies forced dispossession and uprooting of a large number of people from their traditional livelihoods in the countryside and creates higher growth with greater joblessness and poverty (Bhaduri 2018).

In this chapter I will first give a brief account of Marx's theory of "so-called primitive accumulation". Next I will show that far from all land acquisitions can be called primitive accumulation, and I will discuss two recent criticisms and extensions of Marx's theory. This is followed by a summary of essential aspects of the "classical form" (Marx) of primitive accumulation leading to capitalism in England. Finally, I will consider whether the phenomenon Bhaduri analyses can be categorised under Marx's primitive accumulation.

Marx's concept of primitive accumulation

Marx's question in chapters 26–28 of the first volume of *Capital* is, how did the capitalist mode of production originate, and how does it expand? He argues that one fundamental precondition for the capitalist mode of production is an accumulation which precedes that mode of production. In an ironic allusion to Adam Smith, he uses the term "so-called primitive accumulation", in German "sogenannte ursprüngliche Akkumulation".[1] In *Grundrisse*, written in 1857–58, he uses the term "so-called *provisional accumulation* of capital" (Marx 1939/1973: 433; emphasis in original). In the pamphlet *Lohn, Preis und Profit* (1865), he notes that what the economists describe as "previous or original accumulation" should in his view rather be called "original expropriation".

In the mentioned chapters of *Capital I* (Marx 1867/1976: 873–904), he notes that "the whole movement" of capital accumulation

> seems to turn around in a never-ending circle, which we can only get out of by assuming a primitive accumulation . . . which precedes capitalist accumulation; an accumulation which is not the result of the capitalist mode of production but its point of departure.
>
> (ibid.: 873)

The "point of departure" of capitalism is robbery of the immediate pre-capitalist producers of their means of production and livelihoods, of land, forests, water and other resources, so that they become vagabonds and beggars or, at best, people dependent on selling their labour power as members of the reserve army of labour: "In actual history, it is a notorious fact that conquest, enslavement, robbery, murder, in short, force, play the greatest part. . . . As a matter of fact, the methods of primitive accumulation are anything but idyllic" (ibid.: 874). He goes on to specify some essential aspects of primitive accumulation:

> The process, therefore, which creates the capital-relation can be nothing other than the process which divorces the worker from the ownership of the conditions of his own labour; it is a process which operates two transformations, whereby the social means of subsistence and production are turned into capital, and the immediate producers are turned into wage-labourers. . . . So-called primitive accumulation, therefore, is nothing else than the historical process of divorcing the producer from the means of production. . . .
>
> In the history of primitive accumulation, all revolutions are epoch-making that act as levers for the capitalist class in the course of its formation; but this is true above all for those moments when great masses of men are suddenly and forcibly torn from their means of subsistence, and hurled into the labour market as free, unprotected and rightless

> proletarians. The expropriation of the agricultural producer, of the peasant, from the soil is the basis of the whole process. *The history of this expropriation assumes different aspects in different countries, and runs through its various phases in different orders of succession, and at different historical epochs*. Only in England, which we therefor take as our example, has it the classical form.
>
> (Marx 1867/1976: 875–876, my italics)

Marx leaves no doubt that the state plays a major part in enforcing primitive accumulation. The methods of primitive accumulation

> all employ the power of the state, the concentrated and organized force of society, to hasten, as in a hothouse, the process of transformation of the feudal mode of production into the capitalist mode, and to shorten the transition. Force is the midwife of every old society which is pregnant with a new one. It is itself an economic power.
>
> (ibid. 915–916)

Thus, one important aspect of primitive accumulation is the expropriation of the pre-capitalist immediate producers from their means of production and livelihoods, transforming land and other natural resources into commodities. Another decisive aspect of the same process is that also labour is turned into a commodity. With regard to England, Marx writes that, "the great feudal lords . . . created an incomparably larger proletariat by forcibly driving the peasantry from the land, to which the latter had the same feudal title as the lords themselves, and by usurpation of the common lands". The expropriated populations will have "nothing to sell but their labour power", and they are thus ready to be exploited by capital, as wage labourers.

In other words, Marx's message is that the accumulation of capital depends on land and other natural resources as its material basis, as well as on labour power to add value to material "inputs". For the capitalist mode of production to expand, the immediate producers therefore have to be expropriated from their land and other natural resources, being turned into a "reserve army of unemployed", i.e. both land and labour power are made ready to be integrated into the circuit of capital. Marx emphasised that this process may originate in societies with quite different forms of pre-capitalist property (Marx 2014).

With regard to England, "the question remains: where did the capitalists originally spring from? For the only class created directly by the expropriation of the agricultural population is that of the great landed proprietors". A prolonged process of class struggles between peasants and feudal lords, wars between groups of lords and conflicts between lords and the Crown, all of which started with the shortage of serfs after the Black Death, gave rise "to the form of the farmer properly so called, who valorizes his own capital by employing wage-labourers, and pays part of the surplus product . . . to the landlord as ground rent" (Marx 1867/1976: 905).

Like most modern historians, Marx was convinced that the capitalist mode of production originated as agrarian capitalism in England. Modern historians have added a wealth of material and numerous new interpretations of details to the analyses of the transition from feudalism to agrarian capitalism in England (e.g. Brenner 1977, 1985; Hilton 1969, 1977; Perkin 1968; Postan 1975; Wrigley 2004, 2006; Dimmock 2015). However, in chapters 27–30 of *Capital I*, I have not found any central argument which is in significant disagreement with the results presented by the researchers referred to here.

Marx's objective was to investigate and specify the necessary and sufficient conditions for the capitalist mode of production to be established. These conditions will have to be fulfilled whenever the capitalist mode of production expands into new regions. Or, as we have already quoted Marx: "The history of this expropriation assumes different aspects in different countries, and runs through its various phases in different orders of succession, and at different historical epochs." Thus, in my view, it is not a reasonable interpretation of Marx that he considered primitive accumulation only as a finished historical process, as David Harvey among others seems to mean.

A more reasonable understanding of Marx is that primitive accumulation will be repeated whenever capitalism increases its territory, by conquering and destroying pre-capitalist modes of production, in a process called "development" in the modern mainstream literature. Marx emphasises that because this process takes place outside the circuit of capital and is a process of conquering land and labour for the accumulation of capital, "force, play the greatest part". In other words, primitive accumulation is a deeply political process. As long as capitalism does not encompass all natural resources and all labour power, there is scope for further expansion of the capitalist mode of production. In other words, primitive accumulation is not history, but an ongoing process where the capitalist mode of production is expanding by destroying pre-capitalist modes of production, today in the name of "development".

We have seen that Marx identifies three necessary and sufficient conditions for the establishment of the capitalist mode of production:

1. The expropriation of the agricultural producers, of the peasants, from the soil "is the basis of the whole process".
2. The immediate producers are "forcibly torn from their means of subsistence, and hurled into the labour market as free, unprotected and rightless proletarians". These populations freed from the bondage and servitude of feudalism will have "nothing to sell but their labour power", and they are thus ready to be exploited by capital, as wage labourers.
3. There is a class of owners of monetary wealth who intend to make investments and hire wage-workers in order to produce surplus value/profit.

Not all dispossessions represent primitive accumulation

These three conditions do, of course, not imply that all types of land acquisition or other forms of expropriation/dispossession are primitive accumulation. Marx himself refers to the Roman land grabbing in ancient Italy as one example. In *Grundrisse* he reiterates that,

> What enables money-wealth to become capital is the encounter on one side, with free workers; and on the other side with the necessaries and materials etc., which previously were in one way or another the *property* of the masses who have now become object-less, and are also free and purchasable.
>
> (Marx 1939/1973: 505)

However, the Roman masses were not free and purchasable, but were slaves or peasants in bondage and servitude under the landowners. Marx continues:

> [T]he *mere presence of monetary wealth*, or even a kind of supremacy on its part, is in no way sufficient for this *dissolution into capital* to happen. Or else Rome, Byzantium etc. would have ended their history with free labour and capital, or rather begun a new history. The *original formation* of capital does not happen, as is sometimes imagined, with capital *heaping up* necessities of life and instruments of labour and raw materials, in short the objective conditions of labour. Rather its *original formation* is that through the historical process of dissolution of the old mode of production, value existing as money-wealth is enabled, on one side to *buy* the objective conditions of labour; on the other side to exchange money for the *living labour* of the workers who have been set free.
>
> (ibid. 506–507; emphasis in original)

Roudart and Mazoyer give clear-cut accounts of the land acquisitions in ancient Rome and in the Spanish colonisation of South America. Let us take a look at those two examples.

Between the fifth and the third century BC, Rome conquered the entire Italian peninsula, as well as the southern part of Hispania. In the process,

> the Romans expropriated a large part of these territories, generally the best land, declaring it to *ager publicus* – that is to say agricultural land belonging to the Roman people. The Romans also confiscated mines, salt works, and the treasuries of the peoples, enslaving hundreds of thousands of prisoners of war.
>
> Governed by the Senate, the Roman state rented out the greater part of this *ager publicus* in the form of large estates to rich individuals, most of whom were already landowners, senators or knights. . . . As the state had fallen heavily into debt to support its wars . . . it sold whole sections

> of *ager publicus* or ceded full ownership by way of repayments. . . . Large agricultural estates called *latifundia* were thus created, most often through the seizure of conquered land, which was leased out or sold as property. There came into existence a highly influential landed oligarchy. . . . A single individual could control dozens, hundreds, or even thousands of hectares of land. . . . The necessary labour was generally provided by slaves, or by poorly-paid free peasants or by colonists, who were a category of tenant farmers allocated a plot of land in exchange for a share of their harvest, possibly reaching as much as two-thirds.
>
> (Roudart and Mazoyer 2015: 3–6)

Thus, instead of leading to capitalism, the enormous land acquisitions in the Roman Empire resulted in a latifundia system which was to a large extent run by slave labour. Something similar happened also after the Spanish conquest of South America.

"Spain followed a policy of conquest imperialism, exterminated the Aztec and Inca elites and their priesthood, and seized their property" (Maddison 2007: 91). The Spanish crown rewarded the conquistadores with formal grants of *encomienda*, which encompassed a certain area of land with its inhabitants. The main aims of Spanish rule

> were to transfer a fiscal tribute (in precious metals) to Spain and to hispanicize and catholicize the indigenous population. . . . A 20 per cent tax (*quinto real*) was levied on the value of silver. Proceeds of the *quinto* and other levies permitted large state transfers to Spain.
>
> (Maddison 2007: 90, 92)

In half a century, the indigenous populations in Spanish America were almost eradicated by arduous slave labour and European diseases brought by the conquistadores; or they were simply killed. Based on his own observations, the priest Bartolomé De las Casas gave an authentic account of the crimes of the Spaniards. In 1542 he reported that,

> At a conservative estimate, the despotic and diabolical behaviour of the Christians has, over the last forty years, led to the unjust and totally unwarranted deaths of more than twelve million souls, women and children among them, and there are grounds for believing my own estimate of more than fifteen million to be nearer the mark.
>
> (De Las Casas 1542/2004: 12)

Charles Gibson notes that, "The most painstaking modern studies record a decline in New Spain from about 25 million in 1519 to slightly over one million in 1605" (Gibson 1967: 63). In despair over the fate of the Indian population De las Casas was the first to suggest imports of slaves from Africa. "The continent was repopulated by the arrival of nearly eight million

African slaves between 1500 and 1820 and about two million European settlers" (Maddison 2007: 88).

Here is an extract from Roudart's and Mazoyer's account:

> [The conquistadores] began by pillaging the treasures of the defeated indigenous societies. Then they set about exploiting the gold and silver mines. From the outset of the conquest, the royal authorities confiscated the conquered territories and distributed them as *encomiendas*, immense feudal fiefdoms – to expedition leaders, soldiers, royal officials and clerics, as well as compliant dignitaries among the indigenous peoples. . . . The *encomenderos* were responsible for exploiting the wealth of these fiefdoms while protecting, civilising and evangelising resident native populations. . . .
>
> [The] Crown undertook in the late sixteenth century gradually to replace this system with *haciendas*. These very large estates could cover several tens of thousands of hectares, with the *hacendado* enjoying sole ownership of the soil and the subsoil, as under ancient Roman law. This form of land tenure was a fundamentally alien notion to the native American societies, for whom possession of the land could only be collective.
>
> A number of these haciendas were based on the old encomiendas, to which the territories purchased from the Spanish Crown had been added, while others were . . . granted by the Crown for services rendered or sold, to conquistadores or compliant native chiefs. The Catholic Church which benefited from large numbers of donations, became the biggest landowner. The fate of the indigenous populations was little different from before: they were confined to restricted areas, known as *reducciones*, . . . while being collectively subject to payment of tribute to the *haciendas*, in labour or in kind. Tribute in kind was gradually replaced by taxation in cash, which obliged the farmers to work even harder for their sole employers, the *hacendados*, for a paltry wage. . . .
>
> Large-scale land grabbing also took place in Brazil, the vast territory that fell to the Portuguese Crown by the terms of the Treaty of Tordesillas (1494) between Spain and Portugal. Initially, the territory was divided into 15 hereditary captaincies allocated to nobles, who were responsible for exploring, exploiting and administering them. The Portuguese Crown then conceded vast tracts of land, called *seismarias*, to individuals on long leases. Large plantations were set up, with a labour force consisting of slaves captured from amongst the indigenous populations. . . . Over time, however, slave labour became scarcer and more expensive as the indigenous population had collapsed and survivors had fled to the interior or taken refuge in missions. Slaves then began to be imported from Africa.
>
> (Roudart and Mazoyer 2015: 8–9)

Angus Maddison notes that,

> In New Spain, the best land was controlled by hacienda owners. . . . New Spain had a privileged upper class, with a sumptuary lifestyle. Differences in status – as hereditary aristocracy, privileged groups of clergy and military with tax exemptions and legal immunities – meant that there was much less entrepreneurial vigour than in the British colonies. The elite in New Spain were rent seekers with a low propensity to productive investment.
>
> (Maddison 2007: 101, 102)

Enormous quantities of gold and silver, as well as products such as maize, potatoes, tomatoes, cocoa and tobacco, flowed into Spain and Portugal, and further into the rest of Europe, from the new colonies in South America. During the Spanish colonial rule, about 1,700 tons of gold and 73,000 tons of silver were shipped into Spain (Maddison 2007: 91). These inflows which were based on whopping and brutal land acquisitions, led to a significant rise in the consumption among the higher classes, in South America as well as in Spain and Portugal. However, the land acquisitions did not represent primitive accumulation in Marx's sense. They did not transform the economic basis into a capitalist mode of production, either in South America or in Europe, but rather led to prolonged economic stagnation on the Iberian Peninsula:

> The inflow of silver had a limited impact in strengthening the Spanish economy. Some of it financed the construction of baroque churches and palaces. Much more went to finance Spain's hegemonial commitments in Europe. The government waged an eighty-year war trying to reconquer the Netherlands. It launched a huge Armada in 1588 in an attempt to invade England. It had to defend its territorial possessions in Italy, parts of northern France, Franche Comté and the southern Netherlands (Belgium). From 1580 to 1640 it ruled Portugal.
>
> (Maddison 2007: 92–93)

From "accumulation by dispossession" (David Harvey) to "regimes of dispossession" (Michael Levien)

David Harvey raises two points of criticism against Marx's notion of primitive accumulation. First, he claims that Marx "does not consider this possibility except in the case of the creation of an industrial reserve army through technologically induced unemployment" (Harvey 2005: 143). However, as we have seen, Marx actually argues that the most fundamental aspect of primitive accumulation is expropriation of the immediate pre-capitalist producers from their livelihoods and means of production, making them accessible for capitalist exploitation.

Second, Harvey holds that Marx considers so-called primitive accumulation as a finished historical process that does not take place any more (ibid.: 144). Implying that Marx had another view, he argues that, "All the features of primitive accumulation that Marx mentions have remained powerfully present within capitalism's historical geography up until now" (ibid.: 145). He argues that Marx's assumptions "relegate accumulation based upon predation, fraud and violence to an 'original stage' that is considered no longer relevant". To emphasise that his view diverges from that of Marx, he writes: "Since it seems peculiar to call an ongoing process 'primitive' or 'original' I shall . . . substitute these terms by the concept of 'accumulation by dispossession'" (ibid.: 144). However, as we have already noted, Marx emphasised that, "The history of this expropriation [of the immediate producers] assumes different aspects in different countries, and runs through its various phases in different orders of succession, and at different historical epochs." Nowhere does Marx consider primitive accumulation as a finished historical process. While Marx's concept of primitive accumulation deals with the necessary *preconditions* of the capitalist mode of production, Harvey's "accumulation by dispossession" is a very broad concept, encompassing a big bundle of phenomena, some internal and others external to the capitalist mode of production. In his narrative, fundamentally different institutions or social groups are "dispossessed". For example, he includes expropriation of land and other natural resources from peasant populations, conversion of common or state property into private property, privatisation of collective social assets such as pensions and healthcare, dispossession of land for the establishment of factories, dams, SEZs, slum demolitions, mining projects, privatised infrastructure, real estate projects, the loss of pension funds due to the collapse of Enron, the speculative raiding carried out by hedge funds and other major institutions of finance capital, privatisations of different types of public utilities or assets such as water supply, selling off of publicly owned companies, etc. (Harvey 2005: 145–161). In sharp contrast to Marx's concept of primitive accumulation, Harvey claims that accumulation by dispossession is "primarily economic rather than extra-economic" (Harvey 2006: 159). Harvey's view implies that numerous *internal aspects of the capitalist process itself* can be labelled "accumulation by dispossession".

On the other hand, he refers to Rosa Luxemburg's view that with accumulation (reproduction on an expanded scale), capitalism depends on markets in non-capitalist economies to realise the whole surplus value (Luxemburg 1923/1970: 272–288). He argues that:

> The implication [of Luxemburg's theory] is that non-capitalist territories should be forced open not only to trade (which could be helpful) but also to permit capital to invest in profitable ventures using cheaper labour power, raw materials, low-cost land and the like. . . . Since privatization

> and liberalization of the market was the mantra of the neo-liberal movement, the effect was to make a new round of "enclosure of the commons" into an objective of state policies. Assets held by the state or in common were released into the market where overaccumulating capital could invest in them, upgrade them, and speculate in them. New terrains for profitable activity were opened up, and this helped stave off the overaccumulation problem, at least for a while.
>
> (Harvey 2005: 139; 2006: 158)

Michael Levien counters Harvey's view that accumulation by dispossession is capital's response to overaccumulation: "While contemporary land grabs may be considered accumulation by dispossession, we should understand this as a political process of state redistribution and not a functional response to over-accumulation" (Levien 2015: 148). He argues further, in my view with good reason, that Harvey not only fails "to provide a clear definition of accumulation by dispossession", but also "overlooks . . . how and why states restructure themselves to dispossess land for different purposes and different classes in different periods" (Levien 2015: 149). Levien's alternative view is that "Dispossession is organised into socially and historically specific regimes, we can call this a regime of dispossession" (ibid.). He defines a regime of dispossession as

> an institutionalised way of expropriating land from their current owners or users. It has two essential components: a state willing to dispossess for a particular set of economic purposes that are tied to particular class interests; and a way of generating compliance to this dispossession. . . . one must distinguish between dispossessing land for public infrastructure and dispossessing land directly for private capital. . . . Assuming that state willingness to dispossess flows automatically from the "needs" of capitalism elides important variation and also renders dispossession inevitable. . . . Regimes of dispossession vary to the extent to which they must rely completely on coercion or can additionally draw on normative and material inducements to separate people from their land.
>
> (ibid.: 150)

Levien uses the concept of different "regimes of dispossession" in his analysis of India. He argues that there was a shift of regime from the era of state-controlled capitalism, starting after independence and lasting until the end of the 1980s, to free-market neoliberalism since the early 1990s. Under state-controlled capitalism, the major projects driving dispossession were infrastructural works managed and funded by the public sector, and involving commitment to labour-intensive growth and balanced regional development. Large amounts of arable land were expropriated for constructing roads and railways, building dams in river valleys, modernising agriculture, mining minerals and expanding heavy industry.

He further argues that following economic liberalisation, these "developmentalist priorities" were replaced by the willingness of states to confiscate farmers' land on behalf of big corporations for any private purpose alleged to contribute to economic growth, including for real-estate development. Moreover, the abolition of industrial licencing as part of economic liberalisation intensified the competition among states to attract investment, so that the ability of state governments to dispossess farmers of their land for private corporations became "a key criterion of their economic competitiveness". Levien notes that the competition between states also creates incentives to acquire land cheaply, which is mostly achieved by compensating farmers poorly (Levien 2015: 150–153).

Like Harvey, Levien does not distinguish between, on the one hand acquisition of land from peasants or tribal peoples making their livelihoods in a pre-capitalist environment, and on the other hand, market-integrated farmers, other commercial landowners or the capitalist state.

By now it should be clear that Marx on the one side and Harvey/Levien on the other have fundamentally different objectives. So-called primitive accumulation was the conceptual core in Marx's attempt to identify and specify the *preconditions* for the capitalist mode of production, and – as we have seen – he noted that, primitive accumulation "assumes different aspects in different countries, and runs through its various phases in different orders of succession, and at different historical epochs". For Marx, the territorial expansion of the capitalist mode of production is by necessity based on primitive accumulation which implies destruction of pre-capitalist modes of production and livelihoods.

By contrast, Harvey/Levien's objective is to investigate "accumulation by dispossession" as such and *in general*, where Levien emphasises the necessity of specifying the different institutional contexts of this process and therefore prefers the concept of "regimes of dispossession". To me it seems strange that the two authors apparently consider dispossession exclusively as an internal aspect of the capitalist process. Because, as we have seen, for example, dispossession of peasants' or indigenous peoples' land and other resources is not a phenomenon particularly characteristic of capitalism.

My criticism is not that "accumulation by dispossession" or "regimes of dispossession" cannot be useful concepts. What I would criticise is that Harvey/Levien ignore Marx's theoretical objective, which is fundamentally different from theirs, and establish their own concepts in a misconceived criticism of Marx.

England: "the classical form" (Marx) of primitive accumulation

In England, the first capitalist nation, the feudal mode of production approached its limits in the second half of the 13th century. Reclamation of mores and other forms of expansion of the agricultural area had been exhausted. Land and labour productivity was falling at the same time as the landlords increased their class power and their pressure on the peasants by raising land rents and other taxes including labour dues on the demesne.[2] Robert Brenner summarises the situation as follows:

> In leading to the systematization of serfdom, the self-centralization of the lordly class through the monarchical state gave English lords economic opportunities unavailable to most of their counterparts in France or, or elsewhere in Western Europe. . . . In England in the late thirteenth century, perhaps . . . 40–50 per cent of the population was unfree. . . . According to Postan, in the thirteenth century unfree peasants, whose lands covered around one-third of England's cultivated surface, handed over, on average, some 50 per cent of their output to the lords. In comparison, according to Bois, French customary peasants in Normandy could be expected to pay the lords only about 10 per cent of their produce. English demesne land covered a third of cultivated surface, perhaps three times the proportion covered by demesnes in France, a particularly important contrast given the rising rents of the period.
>
> (Brenner 1996: 263–264, 271)

In England towards the end of the 13th century, the large share of demesne land was linked with the persistence of enforced servile labour as an important part of total dues: Rodney Hilton notes that, "Labour services were at their peak, and it did not matter whether they were performed or temporarily commuted for money as far as the economic burden on the holding was concerned" (Hilton 1969: 24). This can explain that "an important feature" of peasant risings "was that they frequently involved the claim that they were not, and should not be, serfs but free men" (Hilton 1969: 25). The dominance of labour services "frequently led to common action" of protesting servile peasants (Hilton 1977: 88–92).

E.A. Wrigley estimates that the population of England and Wales reached 5.75 million in 1300. He writes that:

> There can be little doubt that arable land use in medieval times reached its apogee c. 1300 And it is reasonable to suppose that . . . the arable area would have been extended as far as prevailing techniques permitted. . . . It is sometimes taken as a rule of thumb that a population chiefly dependant on cereals for sustenance will need about one quarter of grain per person per annum. The 1300 figure of 8.62 bushels is close to this level (eight bushels = one quarter). The population . . . numbers had tended to outgrow food output, so that the balance between production and reproduction had become precarious. . . . Early in the fourteenth century the scale of mortality during the famine years 1315–17 in part reflected the severity of this tension, though no doubt the exceptional weather conditions would have caused great hardships and many deaths in any

> case. During the ensuing quarter-century there was marked population decline in much of eastern England, and perhaps more generally, before plague effected a radical reduction in numbers that was not repaired for several centuries. The situation in c. 1300, therefore, represents the point at which England was closer to a state of "bare subsistence" than at any other period in subsequent history.
>
> (Wrigley 2006: 437–438, 440, 441, 457).

Spencer Dimmock notes that,

> The relative political strength of the lords over the peasantry in England is above all revealed by the fact that when their income did finally begin to decline due to the crisis around 1300 . . . they were still able and willing to generate compensatory income through increasing servile dues; and their success is written in the legal victories over the peasants in the early fourteenth century. . . . Lords sought to extract more surplus from the peasantry even though peasants in 1320 were paying more than ever to the lords. Entry fines and marriage fines offered lords the best source for profit, and these rose in the 1310s when the peasants could least afford them.
>
> (Dimmock 2015: 85)

The initial outbreak of the Black Death in 1348–49 killed about a third of the population in England and Wales. The subsequent outbreaks kept the population down, and still in 1600 the population was only about 4.2 million, 27 per cent lower than the 5.75 million in 1300 (Wrigley 2004: 42, and f.n. 19, p. 50). The demographic catastrophe led to a dramatic change of the relations of power between classes, and the landlords' control of the peasantry was substantially weakened.

The servile status of peasants had been recognised and enforced by the Crown. But the question of whether or not a peasant was defined as unfree still continued to be settled by reference to that peasant's status on his own manor vis-à-vis his own lord. Moreover, according to custom, a peasant could in general establish his freedom by remaining away from his manor for at least one year (Brenner 1996: 272). The sharply reduced numbers of tenants, servile and free, implied an immense labour shortage causing competition between lords to keep and recruit peasants. Large numbers of servile peasants left their manors to seek freedom from servitude and work under better conditions in other manors. Robert Brenner summarises:

> When English peasants deserted their manors *en masse* from the 1390s onwards, they did so to take advantage of the free zone available in other manors all across England, a zone that had been maintained by the English state but which was now consolidated, paradoxically, by English lords. English serfdom thus declined not by virtue of any

> abolition of the category, but rather by the peasantry's evacuation of that category.
>
> (Brenner 1985: 272)

However, as R.H. Hilton points out, "the first reaction of the lords was repression rather than accommodation". A greater burden of rent and a more intensive exploitation of demesne labour was being imposed on the peasants.

> Such burdens could, of course, only be imposed by using the various means of coercion that the landowners had at their disposal. These included the old restrictive laws of servile villeinage and the new laws designed to keep down wages and to restrict the mobility of labour.
>
> (Hilton 1969: 36)[3]

With "new laws" Hilton refers to the *Ordinance and Statutes of Labourers* of 1351 which should prevent wage increases and gave clear preference to the lords who had the first call on their serfs' labour.[4] To begin with, the wages were held down to some extent. But the shortage of labour and the increasing competition for workers between landlords made the government powerless to support servitude and keep down wages. From 1340–59 to 1380–99, the real wages of agricultural labourers in term of wheat rose by 60 per cent. On the other hand, in estates where data are available, land rents fell by more than 40 per cent between 1370 and c. 1450 (Hilton 1969: 38–39, 41).

The flights of serfs and persistent shortage of labour increasingly forced the landlords to lease out their demesnes. From c. 1350 until late 1400, the lords transferred 25 per cent of the cultivated area of the English manors in the form of "leases to thousands of peasants from the wealthiest stratum". These thousands of "new men", referred to as yeomen, had become prominent by the end of the 15th century (Dimmock 2015: 146). Robert Brenner summarises his explanation of the lords' turn to predominantly leasing their land as follows:

> Lacking the ability to reimpose some system of extra-economic levy on the peasantry, the lords were obliged to use their remaining feudal powers to further what in the end turned out to be capitalist development. Their continuing control over the land – their maintenance of broad demesnes, as well as their ability to prevent the achievement of full property rights by their customary tenants and ultimately to consign these tenants to the status of leaseholders – proved to be their trump card.
>
> (Brenner 1985: 293)

Gradually a market for leases with market-determined rent developed. The lords leased out demesne land, abandoned holdings and land from lapsed tenements which remained in their hands. To begin with, land was often leased out in small parcels. Later, the demesnes were leased out as a whole and other holdings were often consolidated before being leased out to one well-to-do tenant farmer. The length of lease contracts varied from 6 to 40 years and even more: "On the whole, there was probably a general tendency towards the end of the fifteenth century to long leases, acquired by the payment of considerable fines" (Hilton 1969: 44–46).

Interestingly, Robert Allen notes that many landlords preferred short lease contracts, at least to begin with, because they hoped to turn back to the arrangements before the plague. They considered the lease contracts as a temporary measure which should not establish a long-run precedent (Allen 1992: 65). This indicates that the turn to leasehold and the consequent transition to capitalism was not at all intended by the landlords. Rather, it was the unintended result of the class struggle between peasants and landlords where landlords used their feudal power to secure their landed properties (cf. also Dimmock 2015: 27).

The great peasant uprising in 1381 represents a turning point. The peasants struggled for land and freedom. They won their freedom, but the landlords succeeded in keeping the land. By mid-1400, serfdom had practically disappeared in England, but the resumption of population growth from the early 1400s onwards strengthened the power of the landed nobility, and the peasantry became again increasingly more exploited.

We have seen that leasing of land was one of the landlords' measures to maintain their feudal power and control over the land. Another, and decisive, measure was enclosures. The first wave of enclosures started as a direct aftermath of the Black Death and the subsequent outbreaks of the plague. Dimmock emphasises that,

> It is enclosure as dispossession, either directly by eviction, or indirectly by the generation of large farms out of vacant land in the post-Black Death period which restricted the supply of land when the population rose in the sixteenth century, that is key for the origin of capitalism.
>
> (Dimmock 2015: 134)

At times in conflict with the Crown, big landlords, including the Church and monasteries, enclosed vast areas of abandoned as well as still cultivated holdings, and also some common land. The enclosed land was turned into less work-demanding sheep pastures. Tenants with lease contracts hired wage labourers as fence-builders, herdsmen, slaughterers and shearers. In this way the landlords mitigated the shortage of labour, and they succeeded in maintaining control over their land and reinforcing their property rights. According to Dimmock, "the main flood of enclosure . . . took place between 1440 and 1520" (Dimmock 2015: 141).

Through the wool exports to the Flemish market, the landlords established close networks with the urban bourgeoisie (Tawney 1912/1967: 185–197).

Gradually, the process which started with the enclosure of abandoned holdings led to displacements of numerous small peasants from their plots of cultivated land, and even from their pastures and from firewood resources in the commons. This process was so comprehensive that, between c. 1450 and 1525, about 10 per cent of the villages in the southern part of the Midlands were destroyed (Allen 1992: 66, 163–167). Dimmock refers to a list of 58 depopulated villages in Warwickshire between 1485 and 1491 (Dimmock 2015: 141). In 1500 an estimated 45 per cent of the cultivable area of England was already enclosed (cf. Dimmock 2015: 133, 135). Peasants' protests against enclosures, such as the widespread rebellion of 1549, were brutally defeated.

The second wave of enclosures (from c. 1660 to the late 1700s) is often called "parliamentary enclosure", because it was backed by law enacted by Parliament where only the landed nobility was represented. In that wave the development of agrarian capitalism was completed. A main aspect was enclosure of the remaining open fields and most of the commons, and amalgamation of relatively small peasant holdings into large farms, to be leased out to tenant farmers for cultivation using wage labour.

Under pressure from competition and the landlords' rent hunger, the tenant farmers sought to reduce costs through the typical capitalist form of technical change, viz. *labour-saving innovations*.[5] In the process, large numbers of peasants were evicted from their holdings, and the number of employed per acre fell to about half of what it was in 1600. As a result, average labour productivity in English agriculture more than doubled between 1600 and 1800, while land productivity increased far more modestly (Wrigley 2004: 43). Through this process, a large industrial reserve army was created:

> By enclosure it was argued in 1663, people were added to the manufacturing population who previously did not increase the store of the nation but wasted it . . . A wage-earner who had lost his common rights would be much more dependent on his employer than one who had not. Enclosure, Adam Moore argued in its favour, "will give the poor an interest in toiling, whom terror never yet could enure to travail".
>
> (Hill 1991: 51–52)

Providing several examples, Robert Allen argues that the amalgamation of holdings into large farms implied a "landlords' revolution", which actually represented the consolidation of agrarian capitalism. He concludes that:

> Not only were most rural people becoming exclusively dependent on wage income, but the demand for that labour was falling. Enclosures and large farms were the cause of the rise in productivity, but they also caused low wages and unemployment for the majority of the population, and high rents for the rich minority. *Inequality and productivity growth were inextricably linked.*
>
> (Allen 1992: 8, 21; my italics)

Allen holds that industry, including proto-industries, absorbed very little of the labour force evicted from agriculture (Allen 1992: 239–262). The migration of people from England to the "New World", including North America, possibly contributed more to alleviating the problem of unemployment and poverty caused by the emergence of agrarian capitalism in England. According to the first US Census of 1790, 1.87 million persons were of English ancestry. This figure corresponds to 32 per cent of the estimated population of England in 1751.[6]

Karl Polanyi notes that the intellectual support for enclosures "appears to take for granted the essence of purely economic progress which is to achieve improvement at the price of social dislocation", and that it hints at how the poor man is "doomed by the rich man's desire for a public improvement which profits him privately". He adds that enclosures turned the majority of the displaced peasants "from decent husbandmen into a mob of beggars and thieves" (Polanyi 1957: 34–35).[7]

Contemporary India: development by dispossession or primitive accumulation?

In an analysis focusing on India, Amit Bhaduri argues that the political independence of the former colonies meant only a change of direction in the hunt for natural resources in these areas, meaning also a change of direction in primitive accumulation:

> As countries that were once formal or informal colonies gain political independence, the more successful among them join the march of civilisation in the name of "development" only to become colonisers themselves . . . If a lack of strength does not allow them to conquer other lands and people, regions inside the country are identified for the hunt of natural resources. Imperialism turns inwards, and the latecomers in the race wage war against their own citizens, but this time in the name of developing them. Nevertheless, with the hunt for resources turning inwards history begins to repeat itself, but this time perhaps as a farce. Development again becomes a class project despite the attempts at giving it the face of a nationalist project.
>
> (Bhaduri 2010: 12)

The establishment of corporate-led hydropower plants and mining, as well as industry projects within Special Economic Zones (SEZs) in India is based on forced displacement of very large numbers of people making their livelihood in a pre-capitalist environment. The internally displaced persons (IDPs) and project-affected persons (PAPs), dispossessed of livelihood and habitat, are the true victims of land acquisitions. According to one estimate, the acquisition of 25 million ha of land for industrial sites, hydropower plants, mines and highways had resulted in around 60 million IDPs/PAPs from the early

1950s up until 2004. This total land area included 7 million ha of forests and 6 million ha of other common property resources (Fernandes 2011: 303). Another recent study estimates that 70 million people have been forcibly relocated since the 1950s (cf. Breman 2019: 227).

The main victims of these land acquisitions are the two groups of people at the bottom of the social ladder: the *adivasis* and the *dalits*. The adivasis, who have their homeland in some of the most resource-rich regions of India, form about 8.5 per cent of the total population but account for 40 to 50 per cent of those dispossessed. Dalits (c. 16 per cent of the population) are also disproportionally high among victims (Bhaduri 2018: 20, f.n. 1). Together, these two groups are among the poorest in rural India (Bhaduri 2010: 13). The "tribal" proportion among the IDPs/PAPs has been put at 40 per cent. Studies also show that more than 20 per cent of IDPs/PAPs are *dalits* (Fernandes 2011: 305). The so-called rehabilitation of the IDPs/PAPs has been negligible (Asher and Atmavilas 2011: 322, 331). The affected families are often not even paid the "compensation" they were promised for the loss of land (Dhagamwar 2011: 223). One report points out that almost 30 years after the massive Bhakra-Nangal hydropower project was completed, only 730 of the 2,108 displaced families had been resettled (Dharmadhikary 2005).

As well as destroying the livelihood of large tribal and lower-caste sections of the population, the acquisition of land causes distress to small farmers, who are very often displaced to less fertile land. As Fernandes points out: "An obvious result of landlessness is joblessness, because the land the IDPs/PAPs lose to the project is their sustenance, both in the form of food and work. So its loss deprives them of both" (Fernandes 2011: 309). Hence landlessness equates to impoverishment, and impoverishment forces many IDPs/PAPs into debt or labour bondage, or into child labour, prostitution and crime. Displacement also leads to increased pressure on the remaining non-privatised land (ibid.: 310–311).

The corporate industries have not provided the expropriated and poor farmers with decent new employment opportunities. The growth of employment in the organised industrial sector has been minimal (or non-existent) since the market reforms started (Singh 2006). Instead, the displaced people migrating to urban areas in search of a livelihood are brutally exploited:

> Subcontracting to the unorganized sector along with casualization of labour on a large scale become convenient devices to ensure longer working hours without higher pay. Self-employed workers, totalling 260 million, expanded fastest during the high-growth regime, providing an invisible source of labour productivity growth
>
> (Bhaduri 2009: 69)

The process of land acquisitions and displacement of the local people for "development" purposes has accelerated since the mid-1990s, under the neoliberal "reform" regime. To the extent that this process represents an invasion of the capitalist mode of production into a pre-capitalist society, it is obviously primitive accumulation.

Let me only note that Bhaduri uses the term "creative destruction" almost synonymously with "development by dispossession" (Bhaduri 2018: 19, 20). This term was coined by Joseph Schumpeter to describe a process internal to capitalism, viz. the "process of industrial mutation . . . that incessantly revolutionizes the economic structure *from within*, incessantly destroying the old one. This process of Creative Destruction is the essential fact about capitalism" (Schumpeter 1954: 83, italics in original). In line with Schumpeter, Chris Freeman describes "the disequilibrating and innovative process of creative destruction, the central feature of capitalism – and the very reason for its survival and adaptation" (Freeman and Loucã 2002: 62). I think that the term "creative destruction" should be limited to the meaning given to it by Schumpeter, and that it is not appropriate for an analysis of "development by dispossession".

A final comment

The historical and contemporary experiences of primitive accumulation make it essential to elaborate an alternative policy for a fundamentally different model of development – one that gives voice and power to the population at the lowest local level to control their land, their resources and their livelihoods; and one that implies a far more equal distribution of the fruits of our earth. I dare to call such a model a form of democratic socialism.

Notes

1 With the term "so-called primitive accumulation" Marx refers ironically to Adam Smith's view, in *Wealth of Nations*, of "original accumulation of stock". Smith argued that "the accumulation of stock must, in the nature of things, be previous to the division of labour" (Smith 1776/1986: 371–372) He depicted a harmonious process in which some workers laboured more diligently than others and gradually built up wealth, eventually leaving the less diligent workers to accept living wages for their labour. Marx characterised Smith's view as "insipid childishness".

2 Demesne is land on the landlord's manor not held by serfs or free tenants but directly administered for the lord by an agent using the peasants' compulsory and unpaid labour services.

3 A villein was a customary tenant, in England regarded as unfree from the 13th century.

4 Cf. https://en.wikipedia.org/wiki/Statute_of_Labourers_1351.

5 An important aspect of labour saving was the increased use of horses in agriculture, as well as outside agriculture. E.A. Wrigley shows that in agriculture, horses replaced human labour, e.g. in freight work (pulling of carts) and soil tillage. Increased use of horses combined with improved implements for horse-draught (carts, ploughs, harrows) appears to have been the most important labour-saving innovations. In 1800, English agriculture (including Wales) had three times more horsepower than in 1300 on virtually the same area of cultivated land of ca. 4.5 million hectares (Wrigley 2006: 456).

6 Cf. http://en.wikipedia.org/wiki/1790_United_States_Census.

7 See also Hill (1991: 39–56).

References

Allen R.C. (1992). *Enclosure and the Yeoman*. Clarendon Press, Oxford.

Asher, Manshi and Yamini Atmavilas (2011). 'Special Economic Zones: The New "Land" Mines'. Edited by Hari Mohan Mathur, *Resettling Displaced People: Policy and Practice in India*. Routledge, New Delhi/London.

Bhaduri, Amit (2009). *The Face You Were Afraid to See: Essays on the Indian Economy*. Penguin Books, New Delhi/London.

Bhaduri, Amit (2010). 'Recognise This Face?', *Economic and Political Weekly*, No. 47, pp. 10–14.

Bhaduri, Amit (2018). 'A Study in Development by Dispossession', *Cambridge Journal of Economics*, Vol. 42, No. 1, pp. 19–31.

Breman, Jan. (March–June, 2019). 'Development's Shadow', *New Left Review*, pp. 223–228.

Brenner, Robert (1977). 'The Origins of Capitalist Development: A Critique of Neo-Smithian Marxism', *New Left Review*, No. 104, pp. 25–92.

Brenner, Robert (1985). *The Brenner Debate: Agrarian Class Structure and Economic Development in Pre-Industrial Europe*. Edited by T.H. Aston and C.H.E. Philpin. Cambridge University Press, London/New York. First article in the book published as 'Agrarian Class Structure and Economic Development in Pre-Industrial Europe', *Past and Present*, 70 (February 1976), pp. 30–74.

Brenner, Robert (1996). 'The rises and declines of serfdom in medieval and early modern Europe', in: M. L. Busch (ed.), *Serfdom and Slavery: Studies in Legal Bondage*, Longman, London and New York, 1996.

De Las Casas, Bartolomé (1542/2004). *A Short Account of the Destruction of the Indies*. Penguin Classics, London. The original Spanish text is available on internet: *Brevísima relación de la destrucción de las Indias*, an e-book published by Biblioteka Digital Ciudad Seva at: www.ciudadseva.com/textos/otros/brevisi.htm

Dhagamwar, Vasudha (2011). 'From Narmada to Nandigram: The Never-Ending Clamour for Land as the Only Route to Resettlement'. Edited by Hari Mohan Mathur, *Resettling Displaced People: Policy and Practice in India*. Routledge, New Delhi/London.

Dharmadhikary S. (2005). *Unravelling Bhakra: Assessing the Temple of Resurgent India*. Manthan Adhyayan Kendra, Barwani, India.

Dimmock, Spencer (2015). *The Origin of Capitalism in England 1400–1600*. Haymarket Books, Chicago, IL.

Fernandes, Walter (2011). 'Development-Induced Displacement in the Era of Privatisation'. Edited by Hari Mohan Mathur, *Resettling Displaced People: Policy and Practice in India*. Routledge, New Delhi/London.

Freeman, Chris and Francisco Louçã (2002). *As Time Goes By: From Industrial Revolutions to the Information Revolution*. Oxford University Press, Oxford.

Gibson, Charles (1967). *Spain in America*. Harper Perennial, New York.

Harvey, David (2005). *The New Imperialism*. Oxford University Press, Oxford.

Harvey, David (2006). 'Comment on Commentaries', *Historical Materialism*, Vol. 14, No. 4, pp. 157–166.

Hill, Christopher (1991). *The World Turned Upside Down*. Penguin Books, London.

Hilton, Rodney (1969). *The Decline of Serfdom in Medieval England*. Macmillan/St. Martin's Press, London.

Hilton, Rodney (1977). *Bond Men Made Free: Medieval Peasant Movements and the English Rising of 1381*. Methuen & Co., London.

Levien, Michael (2015). 'From Primitive Accumulation to Regimes of Dispossession: Six Theses on India's Land Question', *Economic & Political Weekly*, May 30, 2015, pp. 146–156. Levien has elaborated his theses more in detail in his book *Dispossession without Development: Land Grabs in neoliberal India*. Oxford University Press, New York, 2018.

Luxemburg, Rosa (1923/1970). *Die Akkumulation des Kapitals*. Verlag Neue Kritik, Frankfurt.

Maddison, Angus (2007). *Contours of the World Economy, 1–2030AD*. Oxford University Press, Oxford.

Marx, K. (1867/1976). *Capital*, Vol. 1. Penguin Books, Harmondsworth.

Marx, K. (1939/1973). *Grundrisse: Foundations of the Critique of Political Economy (Rough Draft)*, Penguin Books, Harmondsworth.

Marx, K. (2014). *Formen, die der kapitalistischen Produktion vorhergehen*, Zenodot Verlagsgesellschaft, Berlin. (There are numerous editions of this booklet, starting with Dietz Verlag, (East) Berlin, in the 1950s.)

Perkin, H.J. (1968). 'The Social Causes of the British Industrial Revolution', *Transactions of the Royal Historical Society*, 5th Series, Vol. 18, pp. 123–143.

Polanyi, Karl (1957). *The Great Transformation*. Beacon Press, Boston, MA.

Postan, M.M. (1975). *The Medieval Economy and Society*. Penguin Books, Harmondsworth.

Roudart, Lawrence and Marcel Mazoyer (2015). 'Large-Scale Land Acquisitions: A Historical Perspective', *International Development Policy*, series No. 6, Geneva. Accessible on internet: https://journals.openedition.org/poldev/2088

Schumpeter, Joseph A. (1954). *Capitalism, Socialism and Democracy*. Unwin University Books, London. Fourth edition, sixth impression.

Singh, S. (2006). 'Agriculture, Agrarian Crisis and Employment: Some Views', *Indian Journal of Labour Economics*, Vol. 49, No. 4, pp. 757–778.

Smith, Adam (1776/1986). *The Wealth of Nations: Books I–III*. Penguin Books, London.

Tawney, R.H. (1912/1967). *The Agrarian Problem in the Sixteenth Century*. Harper &Row Publishers, New York/London.

Wrigley, E.A. (2004). *Poverty, Progress and Population*. Cambridge University Press, Cambridge.

Wrigley, E.A. (2006). 'The Transition to an Advanced Organic Economy: Half a Millennium of English Agriculture', *Economic History Review*, Vol. LIX, No. 3, pp. 435–480.

12 A model of the Marxist rent theory

Debarshi Das

In the Marxist framework, the theory of rent is central to the understanding of production of surplus value in agriculture as well as its distribution. Discussion of rents of various kinds occupies a substantial portion of the third volume of *Capital*. Yet, Marx's rent theory has received "fewer comments and developments, by followers and critics alike, than other major parts of his 'system'" (Mandel, 1990). This is puzzling. Developing economies like India have a vast agricultural sector providing livelihood to a large segment of the population. These countries do not lack the presence of political movements animated by the Marxist vision. Yet one does not find many attempts to understand their agrarian economy by deploying Marx's rent theory.[1]

There can be two possible reasons for this absence. First, it has been observed that the rent theory is one of the most difficult parts of Marxist economics (Mandel, 1990). There have been conflicting claims over interpretations of his theory as well (Fine, 1979). This signals an analytical terrain whose contours are disputed. Not surprisingly, few structures have been built on the uncertain ground.

The second reason is the assumption of the framework. The first chapter on rent in *Capital III* (chapter 37) made it clear that the discussion was applicable to an agrarian economy where the capitalist mode of production has established itself.[2] This would preclude many of today's third world countries. For instance, agricultural production of India is characterised by production relations which can scarcely be called capitalist. The classical pattern of agrarian capitalism that took shape in England was characterised by the triad of landowning rent-earner, tenant capitalist farmer and wage-earning agricultural worker. Such is not the defining feature of Indian agriculture.

Our purpose in this chapter is to address this gap. The paper would attempt to deploy the Marxist rent theory in the Indian context. Although the capitalist mode of production does not characterise Indian agriculture, the chapter would argue that deployment of Marx's rent theory, with qualifications, can be fruitfully done in the Indian context. However, before applying the theory, we would frame it in an easily understandable schematic manner.

The chapter would begin by presenting a model subsuming the three kinds of rent that Marx discussed. In his expositions Marx relied on arithmetical examples (mostly) to illustrate the general tendencies. Arithmetical examples invite at least two troubles. First, they are specific to the numbers chosen. Second, as the examples are number-specific, it is difficult to put the different components of the theory together in an overarching framework. The use of algebra could prove to be helpful in this regard.

This is not an unprecedented endeavour. A notable work in this direction is by Basu (2018), to which this chapter owes a great deal. However, our approach has some differences with Basu's approach. Capital can be divided into infinitesimally small units in Basu's paper, enabling him to apply differential calculus. In contrast, in Marx's examples, capital investments appear as discrete blocks. There could be theoretical reasons behind this (investments, which are embedded with specific technologies, could be indivisible below a limit). In this chapter, following Marx, we have taken capital in discrete blocks.

The rest of the chapter is organised as follows. In the next section, I discuss the two forms of differential rent. In subsequent sections, I take up the absolute rent and present a mathematical model subsuming these three kinds of rents in a single structure. I then offer brief comments on the relevance of rent theory to contemporary Indian agriculture and conclude with closing remarks.

Differential rents

Two important thinkers who left an impression on Marx were Adam Smith and David Ricardo. To Smith, rent was a monopoly price: "the rent of the land . . . is naturally a monopoly price" (Smith, [1776] 1970, p. 249). Rent arose at a particular historical juncture when land became private property. Smith observed, "[a]s soon as the land of any country has all become private property, the landlords, like all other men, love to reap where they never sowed, and demand a rent even for its natural produce" (Smith, [1776] 1970, p. 152). Marx approvingly quoted this passage in *The Theories of Surplus Value* (1963). In the same work Marx took Ricardo's definition of rent to task for its ahistoricity. Rebutting Ricardo's famous assertion that "[*r*]*ent* is that portion of the produce of the earth, which is paid to the landlord for *the use* of the *original and indestructible powers of the soil*", Marx remarked, "it has no 'original' powers either, since the land is in no way 'original', but rather the product of an historical and natural process".

But, Marx was influenced by Ricardo's theory of rent as well. The notion of differential rent formulated by Ricardo found reflection in Marx's *first and second form of differential rent*. In this theory Ricardo had emphasised the objective basis of rent. This objective basis could be higher soil fertility, for instance. Similarly, Marx sought to formulate his theory of rent on a material foundation. But he did not borrow blindly from the Ricardian ideas.

He insisted on the monopoly power exercised by landlords, without which rents cannot exist. Differential rents are categorised into two categories: the first form of differential rent (*DR I*), and the second form of differential rent (*DR II*).

Differential rent I

Differential rent I arises due to difference in soil quality, or due to difference in the location of the land plot. This is illustrated through an example. Suppose there are two land plots of equal size: land 1 and land 2. Land 1 is more fertile than land 2. With the same amount of capital, land 1 would produce more crop than land 2. If the price remains low, it may not be worthwhile for a farmer to cultivate land 2 because revenue from the harvest of land 2 would be below the cost. If price is high and land 2 is cultivated, then in land 1 an excess of revenue over cost and the normal profit would be generated. This excess is termed as "surplus profit". If the old lease of plot 1 continues, the capitalist farmer of land 1 would pocket the surplus profit. It is an addition over his normal profit. When the lease of land 1 is renewed, the landlord would include the surplus profit as rent in the new lease agreement. The surplus profit is thus transformed into "capitalist ground-rent". The supernormal high profit that the capitalist farmer earned earlier would cease to exist. Hence no difference in profit rates across plots would remain.

The notion of differential rent, apparently, depends on difference of soil fertility. But this overlooks the implicit condition that landlords have monopoly right or "landed property". On the relation of landed property and surplus profit which transforms into rent, Marx (1981[1894], p. 786) observed,

> This surplus profit exists even if there is no landed property . . . It [landed property] is not the cause of this surplus profit's creation, but simply of its transformation into the form of ground-rent.

Differential rent II

Unlike what has been assumed earlier in this section, generally speaking, land plots can have different volumes of capital investment. Marx handled this complication by considering that multiple units of the same magnitude of capital (usually £2.5) are invested. Some plots receive more units of capital and thus have greater volume of capital.

Multiple units of capital invested on lands may generate *DR II*. Let us illustrate this by rephrasing Marx's example in chapter 40 of *Capital III*. Let us assume that three units of capital of equal magnitude are applied consecutively on the same land. These three units of capital have different yields: they produce y_1, y_2, y_3 respectively, where $y_1 > y_2 > y_3$.[3] The last dose of capital is applied only if the price of crops is high enough to cover the cost as well as the normal profit on capital. If the price is at such a high level, the first and second doses of capital would produce surplus profit. When the lease is renewed, this surplus profit accrues to the landlord as *DR II*.

DR II is similar in nature to *DR I*. In *DR I*, output from two different lands are compared. Since other things – including capital – remain the same, *DR I* is attributed to fertility difference. In *DR II*, different units of capital produce different outputs. The site of capital investment may be the same, as in the previous example. But they may be different as discussed in chapter 44 of *Capital III*. *DR II* is a generalisation of *DR I*. For, in the final analysis, investment of capital prompts production of output – whether the land is the same or not is not of primary concern.

Two conceptual issues are in order before we proceed further. First, we shall use the phrase "total price of production" to denote what Marx called "price of production". This is capital outlay plus the normal profit on the capital. We shall use the phrase "unit price of production" to denote price of production *per unit* of output. Second, the unit price of production of the *marginal* capital, not the unit price of the *average* capital, governs the price of crop. Taking the price of production of the marginal capital as the benchmark one can estimate the *DR II* (see Appendix 1).

Absolute rent

So far it is assumed that absolute rent (*AR*) does not exist. The notion of *AR* itself was a critique of the Ricardian theory.

> Does an *absolute rent* exist? That is, a rent which arises from the fact that capital is invested in agriculture rather than manufacture; a rent which is quite independent of *differential rent* or *excess profits* which are yielded by capital invested in better land?
>
> It is clear that Ricardo correctly answers this question in the *negative*, since he starts from *the false* assumption that *values* and *average prices of commodities are identical.*
>
> (Marx, 1863, italics in the original)

The basis for absolute rent is low "organic composition of capital" in agriculture. As it is standard in the Marxist value theory, the aggregate capital is divided into two parts: constant capital (*C*) and variable capital (*V*). *C* includes outlays made for machines, equipment, raw material and the like, whereas *V* accounts for wage bill of workers. For reasons of technological backwardness or otherwise, the agricultural capital has lower *C* per unit of *V* (Marx, [1894] 1981, p. 894). In other words, production in the rest of the economy is more capital intensive. From the point of view of India and other LDCs, this is not an outlandish supposition.

Difference in the organic composition implies that the same volume of capital produces different volumes of surplus value. Therefore rate of profit in agriculture differs from the economy:

> [T]he surplus-value produced in agriculture by a capital of a given size . . . is greater than for an equally large capital of the average social composition.
>
> (Marx, [1894] 1981, p. 894)

The rate of profit in agriculture is higher than the social average since surplus value stems from variable capital and agriculture has more variable capital per unit of constant capital. In general, the additional surplus earned by capital in a sector tends to get distributed across sectors due to competition between capitals. Price in agriculture would fall due to competition. How far shall it fall? The fall will be to the extent that the rate of profit gets equalised across sectors. This uniform rate of profit is the "average rate of profit". The prices that are obtained by imputing this uniform, average rate of profit on capitals are "prices of production". In the agricultural sector, value is higher than its price of production.

The aforementioned spontaneous flow of capital gets stalled due to the presence of landed property. Landed property restricts capital inflow, thereby crop output remains low and market price remains high. This difference between market price and price of production gets extracted by landlords in the form of *AR*.[4]

Since the agricultural sector does not take part in the sharing of the aggregate surplus value of the economy, the total value produced by it must be equal to its total revenue. In other words, price and value per unit of output are equal for capital of average productivity in agriculture. For the least productive capital in agriculture, where value per unit of output is higher than average value, value exceeds price.[5]

Let us summarise. Cultivation under the capitalist mode of production requires that price of crops cover cost and normal profit. We have termed this price as the unit price of production. Existence of landed property warrants that landlords be paid rent. *DR I* arises from difference in productivity of any land from the land yielding normal profit, assuming lands have been invested with the same volume of capital. As more capital is invested, productivity of successive capitals may drop. Price has to rise in order to enable the additional investments. Under such a condition, a non-marginal piece of land gets rent from two sources. First, it is more productive than the marginal land and therefore yields *DR I*. Second, investments made on the land could be more productive than the marginal capital. This is the source of *DR II*. Finally, with the assumption of lower organic composition of capital in agriculture, a third factor influences the price: low organic composition of capital in agriculture and landed property. This is the source of *AR*.

In Figure 12.1 *A*, *B*, *C*, *D* and *E* indicate five different lands of descending fertility. They are of the same size, and the same capital has been invested on them. The heights of the rectangles indicate the revenue from crops. If the price of crop changes, the heights change proportionately. Production from *A*, *B*, *C* and *D* are enough to satisfy the demand. *D* is therefore the marginal

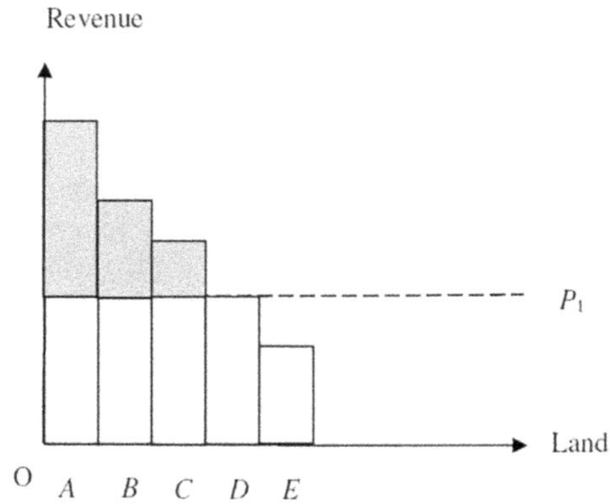

Figure 12.1 Differential rent of the first form (*DR I*)

land. Its *total* price of production, say P_1, the height of the rectangle at *D*, determines the governing market price: market price, $p_1 = \frac{P_1}{Output\,of\,D}$. p_1 is thus the *unit* price of production of *D*. At this price *A*, *B*, *C* generate surplus profit since their revenue is more than P_1. The surplus profit (*DR I*) of each land is indicated by grey-coloured rectangles above the horizontal line P_1. *E* is not under cultivation since its revenue is below P_1. As greater demand arises, price would go up, and output of *E* could be required to satisfy the additional demand. In this new condition, all inframarginal lands will earn more *DR I* since each rectangle will be taller due to price rise.

Figure 12.2 depicts *DR II*. Two lands, land *A* and land *B* are under cultivation. On each land successive units of capital have been applied. The height of each rectangle represents revenue from output produced by each unit of capital. Three units of capital in land *A* and two units in land *B* are sufficient to satisfy demand. The third capital on *A* is the marginal capital, as it is the least productive of all five units of capital. Its total price of production, i.e., the height of the rectangle at 3, will determine the market price. Market price, i.e., the unit price of production, is, say, $p_2 = \frac{P_2}{Output\,of\,capital\,3}$. At this unit price of production, the first two capitals of both lands earn surplus profits. These surplus profits are indicated by the grey rectangles. For each land, the summation of areas of the rectangles is the differential rent. For land *B*, *DR II* is simply the sum of the two grey rectangles above 1 and 2 in panel 2. For land *A*, however, the differential rent, which is the sum of grey rectangles in panel 1, is composed of *DR I* and *DR II*. *DR I* is given by the difference in the revenue from the first capitals of *A* and *B* (indicated by the dark grey rectangle).[6] When *DR I* is subtracted from the differential rent of

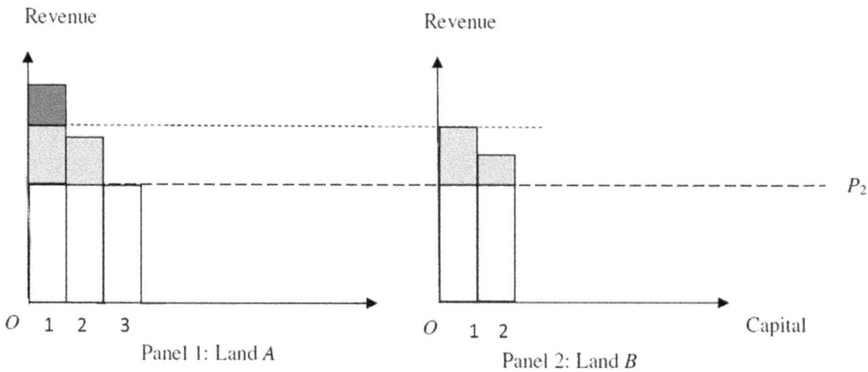

Figure 12.2 Differential rent of the second form (*DR II*)

land *A*, *DR II* is obtained. Note that, compared to the situation where there is no *DR II*, here crop price is higher.

Finally, *AR* requires that the agricultural sector's surplus value does not get eroded through competition. This principle of preservation of value determines the price. Suppose there are l units of capital employed in agriculture; each has the same organic composition, and each produces value worth v. Suppose Y is the aggregate output produced by these l units of capital. Then *AR* would warrant that the price, p_3, be given by the condition,

$$p_3.Y = l.v$$

Thus agricultural output must be sold at a price that guarantees that the value produced in agriculture remains within it. But, there is no certainty that p_3 be greater than or equal to p_2 (the price that guarantees normal profit to the least productive capital in agriculture). If p_3 is less than p_2, then capital may move out of the agricultural sector. Hence we need the condition $p_3 \geq p_2$. We shall return to this point in the next section.

A model

In this section the three aforementioned rents would be integrated in a mathematical model. Suppose there are n lands of same size, denoted by 1, 2, . . . n, with output levels $y_1, y_2, \ldots y_n$, where, $y_1 > y_2 > \ldots > y_n$. Each land is invested with k amount of capital. k is the minimum indivisible amount of capital at the present state of technology, and it is taken to be the unit of capital. The entire value of k gets transferred to the crop produced, i.e., the rate of depreciation is 100%. The price of crop is denoted by p. The normal rate of profit is assumed to be r^*. We assume r^* is economy's overall profit rate r_s, i.e., $r^* = r_s$.

DR I

Suppose,

$$p_n.y_n - (1 + r^*)k = 0 \tag{1}$$

In other words, the marginal land, that is, the n-th land, earns no surplus profit (we are abstracting from *AR* here). p_n is the unit price of production of the n-th land. At p_n price all n lands are worth cultivating. For any land i, the *DR I* is given by,

$$DR\ I_i = p_n.y_i - (1 + r^*)k \tag{2}$$

From equations (1) and (2), it's clear that at price p_n, *DR I* is non-negative for all lands. From the 1st to the n-th land, the *DR I*'s follow a descending order.

Using equation (1), equation (2) is rewritten as,

$$DR\ I_i = p_n\,(y_i - y_n) \tag{3}$$

DR II

Let us suppose lands 1, 2, . . . n have been invested with $l_1, l_2, \ldots l_n$ units of capital. Output produced by the j-th capital on the i-th land is denoted by y_i^j, where j can take values 1, 2, . . . l_i. Therefore the output produced by the marginal capital on the i-th land is $y_i^{l_i}$. Estimation of *DR II* depends on the price of production of the marginal capital (see Appendix 1 for an illustration). Suppose the m-th land has the least productive investment ($1 \le m \le n$). In other words, in the m-th land, the last unit of capital (l_m-th) is the least productive of all capitals.

$$y_m^{l_m} = \text{Min}(y_1^{l_1}, y_2^{l_2}, \ldots, y_n^{l_n})$$

Let us assume that the unit price of production of the l_m-th capital be $p_m^{l_m}$.

$$p_m^{l_m}.y_m^{l_m} = (1 + r^*)k \tag{4}$$

Note from equations (1) and (4) it follows, $p_m^{l_m} > p_n$, since $y_n > y_m^{l_m}$

Now, for land i, each capital invested on it is at least as productive as the marginal capital. Hence each capital earns a surplus profit at the price, $p_m^{l_m}$. The differential rent of land i is the sum total of these surplus profits. Differential rent of i is thus given by,

$$DR_i = p_m^{l_m}\left[\sum_{j=1}^{l_i} y_i^j - l_i.y_m^{l_m}\right] \tag{5}$$

With this change in price, the expression of $DR\ I_i$ in equation (3) has to be modified. This is given by equation (6).

$$DR\,I_i = p_m^{l_m}[y_i^1 - y_n^1] \tag{6}$$

If *DR I* is subtracted from the total differential rent, *DR* in equation (5), one obtains *DR II*. Rearranging terms, from equations (5) and (6) we get,

$$DR\,II_i = p_m^{l_m}[y_n^1 - y_m^{l_m}] + p_m^{l_m}[\textstyle\sum_{j=2}^{l_i} y_i^j - (l_i - 1).y_m^{l_m}] \tag{7}$$

DR II of the *i*-th land is the summation of: (i) difference in productivity between the first capital of the worst land and the worst capital, and (ii) difference in productivity of other capitals on the *i*-th land with the worst capital. It is easy to see that $DR\,II_i$ is non-negative, because each of the terms in the square brackets in equation (7) is non-negative.

AR

We start with a proposition pertaining to the governing price in the agricultural sector.

Proposition 1: *If r_a and r_s are the rate of profit in agriculture and the average social rate of profit, Y is the aggregate level of agricultural output, l is the sum total of units of capital engaged in agriculture and $y_m^{l_m}$ is the output produced by the least productive capital in agriculture, then,* $(1 + r_a) \geq (1 + r_s)\dfrac{\frac{Y}{l}}{y_m^{l_m}}$

The proof is provided in Appendix 2. The main idea behind the proposition was discussed in the previous section on absolute rent. The agricultural sector has a lower organic composition of capital than the rest of the economy and it does not participate in the equalisation of rate of profit. It preserves the surplus profit in the form of rent. This principle of preservation of rate of profit yields a price p_3. There is another price, p_2, which ensures that the least productive capital in agriculture gets invested. The condition $p_3 \geq p_2$ has to be satisfied, otherwise capital in the least productive agricultural land would not be invested. The proposition is another way of stating this condition.

Let us consider the marginal capital. *AR* of this capital is the difference between value and the total price of production, imputed at the social rate of profit r_s. Thus absolute rent is given by,

$$AR = p_3.y_m^{l_m} - (1 + r_s)k \tag{8}$$

Using [H] in Appendix 2, one can see that *AR* is non-negative.

For any land *i*, total rent R_i is the sum total of all surplus profits earned by all capitals invested on it. So, it is given by

$$R_i = p_3.\textstyle\sum_{j=1}^{l_i} y_i^j - (1 + r_s)l_i.k \tag{9}$$

Here l_i is the number of units of capital invested on the i-th land. By [G], AR of the least productive capital is non-negative, i.e., $p_3.y_m^{l_m} - (1+r_s)k \geq 0$. Hence R_i is positive.

Evaluating differential rent DR_i at p_3, we get from equation (5),

$$DR_i = p_3[\sum_{j=1}^{l_i} y_i^j - l_i.y_m^{l_m}]$$

Rewriting equation (9), we get,

$$R_i = p_3.\sum_{j=1}^{l_i} y_i^j - p_3.l_i.y_m^{l_m} + p_3.l_i.y_m^{l_m} - (1+r_s)l_i.k$$
$$= DR_i + l_i.AR \text{ (by (8))}$$

So,

$$AR_i = l_i.AR = R_i - DR_i = l_i[p_3.y_m^{l_m} - (1+r_s)k] \qquad (10)$$

The absolute rent of a land is units of capital invested on it multiplied by the absolute rent earned by the least productive capital. AR earned by the least productive capital is the same as earned by any other capital. This is not surprising because all capitals have the same value and the same organic composition.

The three elements of rent are now put together below. Since p_3 is the price, we modify equations (6) and (7) as given in equations (6') and (7').

$$DR\ I_i = p_3.[y_i^1 - y_n^1] \qquad (6')$$
$$DR\ II_i = DR_i - DR\ I_i = p_3[\sum_{j=1}^{l_i} y_i^j - l_i.y_m^{l_m}] - p_3.[y_i^1 - y_n^1] \qquad (7')$$
$$AR_i = l_i.[p_3.y_m^{l_m} - (1+r_s)k] \qquad (10)$$

[E] in Appendix 2 gives the value of p_3. If the data of output, capital and degree of exploitation are known, one can use these three equations to estimate the three kinds of rents.

Marxist rent theory and Indian agriculture

In the Marxist framework land is owned by the landlord, from whom the capitalist farmer leases it in lieu of payment of rent. The capitalist farmer employs agricultural workers to produce surplus value. That Indian agriculture is far from attaining such a state is a widely shared observation, and this position is supported by empirical evidence (Patnaik, 1983; Basu and Das, 2013; Das, 2016). Petty farms, having less than one to two hectares of land and relying on family labour, dominate the agrarian scene. The small peasants usually own the land they cultivate, rather than lease it.

In theory, a process of "peasant differentiation" is supposed to ensue from this state. Superior productive power of large farms and the force of accumulation are to put the small farms out of business. Historically, multifarious routes have been traversed by different societies. These paths were clubbed under two broad categories, the Prussian and the American path, by Lenin (1907). The first entails gradual evolution of feudal lords into capitalist farmers, or capitalism from above. The second path is capitalism from below: peasants evolve into capitalist farmers, in some cases through revolution.[7] In reality, in India, the share of small farms in terms of number, and their land area have been rising steadily over time. To be sure, there are patches where the top deciles of the farms have gained in terms of assets, and even land. In those areas the capitalist relations of production has progressed. But this is far from a general feature (Das, 2015).

But, the theoretical tools mentioned earlier can still be applied in such a peasant proprietor-dominated economy. The creation of value does take place in such an economy. Existence of *value*, to wit exchange value, requires that production is carried out for the purpose of exchange.[8] This condition is widely satisfied. Existence of *surplus value* requires separation of labourers from the means of production; the latter are owned by capitalists who, by ensuring that value of the labour power stay less than the value produced by labourers, exact the difference as surplus value.[9] But, Marx was not consistent in applying the idea of surplus value to exclusively capitalist agriculture. For instance in *Capital III* he alludes to surplus value in the context of "small-scale peasant ownership" economy.[10] Surplus value in these cases is only notional, not actual. The value of labour power can be estimated by imputing the wage rate prevailing elsewhere to the hours performed by the peasant family.

Once the Marxist analytical tools are applied to Indian conditions, a second question arises. Rent acted as a barrier to capital inflow into agriculture. The landlords took away a part of the surplus profit which otherwise would have accrued to the capitalist farmer. In practice, this barrier functions through landlords' restricting the supply of land to prospective leasers by charging high rent. In the peasant proprietorship economy, in contrast, the petty peasants do not pay rent, as they themselves own the land. If there is no rent to pay, there is no rent barrier. In such a circumstance, the momentum of capital investment should quicken. But, evidence does not indicate fast accumulation.

Although Marx did not spend much time on peasant proprietor-dominated agrarian economy, his followers did so as they attempted to apply Marx's theory. Commenting on a situation of falling ground rent, Kautsky ([1899] 2007) observed that declining ground rent led to, "a crisis in agriculture which . . . is chronic in character, especially in those areas where, as in most countries, *the landowner and farmer are one and same individual*, so that a loss to the landowner is also a loss to the farmer" (italics added). This observation is useful in understanding the predicament of Indian peasants. The peasant, being the owner of the land, earns the rent in an implicit manner. In a condition of declining ground rent, her income falls. But why does the ground rent fall in the first place?

From the discussion in the previous two sections, it follows that as market price falls, different kinds of rents tend to decline. By limiting the supply of land – thereby raising crop price – the big landlords try to ensure that the market price stays above the price of production. But whether they would succeed in doing so depends on the balance of class forces. When the balance is a tilting against them and towards the big bourgeoisie, when there are fewer restrictions on the import of agricultural commodities, when landholdings are getting subdivided and fragmented – the landlords have few instruments to keep the price high and earn rent.[11] The dampened price hurts all owners of land, not only the big landlords. Petty peasants, constituting the largest pool of landowners, lose out.

Petty farmers also lose out as earners of profit. As the price of crop collapses, the farmers may not even get the average rate of profit, which capitalists of the economy normally earn. Instead of being higher than the price of production, crop price may plummet below it. The fact that the profit rate in Indian agriculture is alarmingly low, negative in the case of some crops, indicates that such a state of affairs could actually be existing.[12] A low profit rate adversely affects the condition of farm labourers as well. It's possible that a low crop price may benefit them as buyers of crop (food grain, for example). But a depressed state of cultivation implies low demand for labour, which diminishes prospects of finding jobs. The petty peasant, relying on wage income to supplement the meagre income from land, suffers.

Conclusion

Marx's rent theory is a painstakingly rendered body of scholarship. It is consistent with his theory of value. In spite of its relevance, few scholarly works have attempted to examine Indian agriculture using the Marxist framework. This chapter has sought to integrate different pieces of rent theory in a single model. In Marx's theory, landed property acted as a barrier to capital inflow. In an economy like India where small peasant proprietors dominate, a similar phenomenon of lack of inflow of capital could be present. But this lack of accumulation stems from a different set of pre-conditions. The tilt of balance of class power against land owners depresses crop prices. This discourages investment in farming. Capital accumulation remains slow. The dismal condition of peasants continues.

Notes

1 Few exceptions, such as Patnaik (1983), exist.
2 "The analysis of landed property in its various historical forms lies outside the scope of the present work . . . We assume therefore that agriculture, just like manufacturing, is dominated by the *capitalist mode of production*" (Marx, [1894] 1981, p. 751, emphasis added).
3 This implies diminishing marginal productivity. But the assumption of diminishing marginal productivity is not necessary for *DR II*.

4 To be precise the formula *AR* = value – price of production, is correct under the assumption that value and price are same. In general, *AR* is the gap between market price and the price of production, provided price is not above value. In other words,

AR (per unit) = Min (value, market price) – price of production (per unit), if Min (value, market price) > price of production
= 0, otherwise.

5 In the section on *AR* later in this chapter, it will be demonstrated that a condition on the difference of organic compositions is essential. This condition is similar to Assumption 3 in Basu (2018).

6 In estimating *DR I* the capital invested on each land is taken to be 1 unit. This may appear arbitrary. However, estimation of *DR I* requires only that the *same capital* be invested on each land, with the quantity of capital remaining unspecified. Here the *same capital* is taken to be 1 unit.

7 Lenin (1907) observed:

> [T]wo paths of objectively possible bourgeois development we would call the Prussian path and the American path, respectively. In the first case feudal landlord economy slowly evolves into bourgeois, Junker landlord economy . . . In the second case there is no landlord economy, or else it is broken up by revolution . . . the peasant predominates, becomes the sole agent of agriculture, and evolves into a capitalist farmer.

This categorisation could be seen as an extension of what Marx ([1894] 1981, p. 452) said of transition in general.

8 "What exclusively determines the magnitude of the value of any article is therefore the amount of labour socially necessary, or the labour-time socially necessary for its production" (Marx [1887] 1976, p. 130). This applies irrespective of the nature of mode of production.

9 Marx ([1887] 1976, p. 251) introduced the notion of surplus value in chapter 4 of *Capital I*: "The complete form of this process is therefore M-C-M', where M' = M+ΔM, i.e. the original sum advanced plus an increment. This increment or excess over the original value I call 'surplus-value'".

10 "Here the peasant is the free proprietor of his land, which appears as his main instrument of production, as the indispensable field of employment for his labour and his capital. No lease-price is paid in this form; thus rent does not appear as a separate form of *surplus-value*" (Marx [1894] 1981, p. 940, italics added).

11 See Chatterjee (2008), for instance, on the falling heft of landlords vis-à-vis the big bourgeoisie in India.

12 The Commission for Agricultural Costs and Prices reported the return farmers earned over C_2, a comprehensive estimate of cost of cultivation, in the 2014–15 kharif season. For a number of crops, the rate of return was negative (table 5.1, Government of India, 2017). For paddy, the most popular crop in India, the return was a measly 8%. One can contrast this with the high profit rates earned in the organised manufacturing sector (Basu and Das, 2018). Agarwal and Agarwal (2017) reported that low profitability was a major reason why a bulk of farmers in India wanted to quit farming.

References

Agarwal, B and A Agarwal (2017): "Do Farmers Really Like Farming? Indian Farmers in Transition", *Oxford Development Studies* 45(4): 460–478.

Basu, D (2018): *Marx's Analysis of Ground-Rent: Theory, Examples and Applications*, Working Paper 2018-04, Department of Economics, University of Massachusetts Amherst, retrieved on April 25, 2018 (www.umass.edu/economics/publications/2018-04.pdf).

Basu, D and D Das (2013): "The Maoist Movement in India: Some Political Economic Considerations", *Journal of Agrarian Change* 13(3): 365–381.

Basu, D and D Das (2018): "Profitability in India's Organized Manufacturing Sector: The Role of Technology, Distribution and Demand", *Cambridge Journal of Economics* 42(1): 137–153.

Chatterjee, P (2008): "Democracy and Economic Transition in India", *Economic and Political Weekly* 45(16): 53–62.

Das, D (2015): "Changing Distribution of Land and Assets in Indian Agriculture", *Review of Radical Political Economics* 47(3): 412–423.

Das, D (2016): "Agricultural Investment in India in Recent Decades: A Political Economic Note of Its Causes and Consequences", p. 286–299 in *Economic Challenges for the Contemporary World: Essays in Honour of Prabhat Patnaik*, edited by M. Das et al. New Delhi: Sage Publishing.

Fine, B (1979): "On Marx's Theory of Agricultural Rent", *Economy and Society* 8(3): 241–278.

Government of India (2017): *Price Policy for Kharif Crops: The Marketing Season 2017–18*, Commission of Agricultural Costs and Prices, Ministry of Agriculture, retrieved on April 25, 2018 (https://cacp.dacnet.nic.in/ViewReports.aspx?Input=2&PageId=39&KeyId=598).

Kautsky, K ([1899] 2007): "The Capitalist Character of Modern Agriculture", p. 187–226 in *The Agrarian Question in Marx and His Successors, Vol. I*, edited by U. Patnaik. New Delhi: LeftWord Books.

Lenin, V I (1907): *The Agrarian Programme of Social-Democracy in the First Russian Revolution, 1905–1907*, retrieved on April 25, 2018 (www.marxists.org/archive/lenin/works/1907/agrprogr/ch01s5.htm#v13pp72-238).

Mandel, E (1990): "Karl Marx," p. 1–38 in *Marxian Economics*, edited by J Eatwell, M Milgate and P Newman. London, retrieved April 25, 2018 (www.marxists.org/archive/mandel/19xx/marx/ch05.htm).

Marx, K (1863): *Theories of Surplus-Value*, retrieved August 25, 2018 (www.marxists.org/archive/marx/works/1863/theories-surplus-value/ch11.htm#s1).

Marx, K ([1887] 1976): *Capital, Vol. I*. London: Penguin Classics.

Marx, K ([1894] 1981): *Capital, Vol. III*. London: Penguin Classics.

Patnaik, U (1983): "Classical Theory of Rent and Its Application to India: Some Preliminary Propositions, with Some Thoughts on Sharecropping", *The Journal of Peasant Studies* 10(2–3): 71–87.

Smith, A ([1776] 1970): *The Wealth of Nations*. London: Penguin Classics.

Appendix 1

Unit price of production of marginal capital as the governing price

Different doses of capital are of varying productivity and have different unit prices of production. Is it the average unit price of production of all capitals, or the unit price of production of the marginal capital, which governs the price? An arithmetic example is given in Table 12.1 to elaborate.

Two successive doses of capital each worth 50 monetary units are applied on the same land. The normal rate of profit is assumed to be 20%, hence the total price of production of each dose of capital is 60 = (50 × 1.2). The outputs from these two doses are 4 and 2 units respectively. The unit price of production of the first and the second doses of capital therefore are $15\left(=\frac{60}{4}\right)$ and $30\left(=\frac{60}{2}\right)$ respectively. If the prevailing market price is 30, i.e., the unit price of production of the marginal capital, then the 1st capital will earn surplus profit of 60. This is *DR II* according to our definition.

Alternatively, one may consider the average unit price of production of both capitals put together. In all, 6 units are produced with a total price of production of 120. Thus on average the unit price of production is $20\left(=\frac{120}{6}\right)$. At this price, the revenue of the 1st capital is $80(=20\times 4)$, whereas its total price of production of the 1st capital is 60. Thus there is a surplus profit of 20. This is counterbalanced by the deficit of 20 of the 2nd capital (its total price of production is 60, the revenue is 40, so there is a deficit of 20). The land therefore does not yield rent. This contradicts the conclusion of the previous paragraph that rent is 60.

How to resolve this? One may ask the following questions. If the prevailing price is 30 (the first case), will a landlord be able to extract 60 as rent from the land with no surplus profit left? The answer is yes. The tenant would gladly accept the deal of paying 60 as rent. She will invest two doses of capital worth 100, earn 20% profit and pay the landlord 60, as Table 12.1 demonstrates. Second, if the prevailing price is 20 (the second case), will a landlord get zero rent with *no extra surplus profit* left? The answer is no. With 20 as the crop price, the farmer would accept the lease and invest only the first capital (for the second capital, the marginal cost, 60 exceed marginal

Table 12.1 *DR II* when two units of capital are applied on the same land

Capital	*Output (units)*	*Capital advanced*	*Rate of profit*	*Unit Price of production*	*Total price of production*	*Revenue at price 30*	*Surplus profit*	*Rent*
1st	4	50	20%	15	60	120	60	60
2nd	2	50	20%	30	60	60	0	0

benefit, 40). She will earn a revenue of 80. His total price of production is 60; with 0 rent, he would be left with a surplus profit of 20. This is not a sustainable situation. So, the price is governed by the unit price of production of marginal capital.

Appendix 2

Proof of proposition 1

Surplus value (S) is formed by the unpaid labour of workers. Surplus value is in proportion to variable capital (V). We assume, following Marx, that the ratio, $\frac{s}{v}$, the degree of exploitation, is constant across production activities. Let,

$$e = \frac{s}{v} \qquad \text{[A]}$$

We assume that the organic composition of capital in all agricultural activities is same, and it's given by α,

$$\alpha = \frac{C_a}{V_a} \qquad \text{[B]}$$

C_a, V_a and S_a are the constant, variable capital and surplus value of agricultural investment of 1 unit. It is assumed that α is lower than the organic composition of the rest of the economy. The average social organic composition is assumed to be β, $\alpha < \beta$.

The rate of profit, r, in general, is given by,

$$r = \frac{s}{c+v}$$

S is the surplus value produced by employing C and V amount of constant and variable capital.

$$\text{Or, } r = \frac{\frac{s}{v}}{\frac{c}{v}+1}$$

Let us recall r_a and r_s are the rates of profit in agricultural sector and the average rate of profit respectively. Using the above formula of r,

$$r_a = \frac{e}{\frac{C_a}{V_a}+1}$$

Or,

$$r_a = \frac{e}{\alpha + 1} \text{ (using [B])} \qquad \text{[C]}$$

Similarly, $r_s = \dfrac{e}{\dfrac{C_s}{V_s} + 1}$, where C_s and V_s are the value of constant and variable capital of the economy as a whole.

Or,

$$r_s = \frac{e}{\beta + 1}$$

Since $\alpha < \beta$,

$$r_a > r_s \qquad \text{[D]}$$

Let, the sum total of units of capital investments in agricultural sector be l, i.e., $l = \sum_{i=1}^{n} l_i$. Let Y be the sum total of output from all capital investments.

$$Y = (y_1^1 + y_1^2 + \cdots + y_1^{l_1}) + (y_2^1 + y_2^2 + \cdots + y_2^{l_2}) + \cdots + (y_n^1 + y_n^2 + \cdots + y_n^{l_n})$$

Let, $l.v = p_3.Y$

Here v = value produced by 1 unit of capital. p_3 ensures that revenue from the output produced by all units of capital be equal to the aggregate value.

$$\text{Or, } p_3 = \frac{l}{Y}.v$$

Now, $v = V_a + C_a + S_a = V_a\,(1 + \alpha + e)$

Moreover,

$$r_a = \frac{e}{\alpha + 1}$$

Implying, $e = r_a\,(1 + \alpha)$. Substituting, we get,

$$p_3 = \frac{l}{Y}.V_a(1 + \alpha)(1 + r_a) \qquad \text{[E]}$$

On the other hand, price p_2 ensures that the marginal capital earns the social rate of profit, r_s. p_2 is given by,

$$p_2 = \frac{1}{y_m^{l_m}} V_a(1 + \alpha)(1 + r_s) \qquad \text{[F]}$$

Price p_3 cannot be less than p_2. For, if it is less than p_2, then the marginal capital will earn a rate of profit less than elsewhere and will not get invested.

$$p_3 \geq p_2 \tag{G}$$

Using [E] and [F], we get,

$$\frac{l}{Y}.V_a(1+\alpha)(1+r_a) \geq \frac{1}{y_m^{l_m}} V_a(1+\alpha)(1+r_s) \tag{H}$$

Simplifying,

$$(1+r_a) \geq (1+r_s)\frac{\frac{Y}{l}}{y_m^{l_m}} \tag{H'}$$

By [D], $r_a > r_s$. We know that the marginal capital produces less output than the average output produced by capital, $\frac{Y}{l} > y_m^{l_m}$. For [H'] to be satisfied r_a has to be sufficiently higher than r_s. In other words, the organic compositions must be sufficiently different.

Part III

Duality and underdevelopment

13 Rural poor or peasant-proletarians

Agrarian change and labour markets in Eastern United Provinces in the colonial period

Ramaa Vasudevan

The link between regional disparities in patterns of accumulation in agriculture and underlying class relations across India has been an important focus of Amit Bhaduri's research. Bhaduri (1973) entered the debate on the mode of production in Indian agriculture in the 1970s and 1980s, with the argument that the agrarian economy was characterized, predominantly, by semi-feudal production relations. Bhaduri (1976, 1981, 1985), put forward the thesis that the imposition of the rent demands of the colonial state and the imbrication of sections of the rural economy into the commodity circuits of colonial trade, established the interplay of the processes of normal and forced commercialization. While the former was associated with market incentives and incipient capital accumulation in the rural economy, the latter process was characterized by compulsions faced by cultivating peasant burdened by debt and rack-rents. These distinct processes led to the emergence of the 'rich peasant' or progressive landlord in case of the normal processes of commercialization, and the consolidation of the hold of the traditional landlord and merchant-moneylenders in the case of forced commercialization.

Bhaduri (1985) draws on the divergent experiences of the western and eastern parts of the North Indian state of Uttar Pradesh (UP; formerly United Provinces in the colonial period) to illustrate his thesis. Using this analysis of the contrasting trajectories of agrarian transformation in Eastern and Western UP as my point of departure, I shift the focus from the evolution of the market for land, and the dispossession and differentiation of the peasantry, to the development of the market for labor and the transformation of the strategies for enforcing labor through a comparative historical analysis of two adjoining districts of Gorakhpur and Basti in Eastern UP.

Eastern UP embodies much of what characterizes agrarian backwardness: low land-man ratios, precarious dependence on monsoons, and institutional constraints on the emergence of a peasant elite. The limited resources of the small peasant, no doubt, provide the basis for subordination through the mechanisms of forced commercialization, as noted by Bhaduri (1981). However, the peculiarities of the agricultural labor process also underscore the paradoxical need for labor enforcement strategies in the labor surplus agrarian economy, where the small size of the holdings poses a constraint on expanding productivity and output. The consolidation of holdings enables both the extension of the social division of labor and the mechanization of the labor process. But where holdings are sub-divided and fragmented, increasing productivity through the development of cooperative forms of labor use and the social productivity of labor are precluded by the persistence of small holdings. The expansion of production depends, in the absence of technological innovation, on intensification of control and supervision, even as peasant households that seek to retain elements of control over the process of production and resist the imposition of wage relation as a form of social control. Debt and interlinked contracts thus come to play an integral role in the strategies for controlling and enforcing labor.

The emergence of labor markets is, of course, entwined in the distinct processes of commercialization that Bhaduri (1981, 1985) points to. However, apart from revenue demands and the expansion of cash-crop cultivation, the colonial period impinged on the rural economy in another critical way. The emerging enclaves of capitalist enterprise – plantations, tea-gardens and export-oriented industry – drew on the labor-surplus rural economy to fulfill their growing needs for a labor force. Colonial migration was highly segmented (Das Gupta 1981; de Haan 1995), and intermediaries were crucial to the functioning of these migrant flows. A key argument of this chapter is that the distinct pattern of migration from the two districts shaped the specific paths of evolution of their labor markets.

Gorakhpur was characterized by the dominance of cyclical (or circular) migration to colonial industrial centers (particularly in Bengal), which enabled the emergence of the peasant proletarian – a class of peasants with small uneconomic holdings whose survival strategy depended on hiring out their labor and migration. Permanent indenture and contract migration to the overseas sugar colonies and the tea gardens in Assam, which predominated in Basti, in contrast, did not forge similar links between the colonial capitalist enclaves to where the small peasant families migrated, and the rural hinterland from where they had originated. The labor market was dominated not by peasant proletarians but the rural poor constituted primarily by the impoverished small peasant.

This investigation of the agrarian transition in Gorakhpur and Basti begins with a brief outline of the antecedent production relations that confronted colonial commercial and settlement policies, before presenting the broad contours of changes that occurred in the rural economy in the late colonial period. This account informs the analysis of the evolution of labor markets and distinct migration patterns in the two districts.

Production conditions in the last decades of the nineteenth century

To trace the distinct trajectories of agrarian transition in the two districts as it got integrated in the commercial circuits of colonial India, we need to begin by outlining the antecedent institutional arrangements within which labor was embedded. Accounts of the Gorakhpur region bear testimony to the prevalence of forms of agrestic servitude and casual labor in the early nineteenth century (Siddiqui 1973, p. 52).

Of particular importance in this region was the ploughman or harwaha. Traditionally, the harwaha was a permanent farm servant who performed a variety of agricultural tasks (apart from ploughing) for the landlord. The organization of production involved the allocation of small plots of land to the harwaha. The rest of the land was apportioned to the various tenants. These tenant farmers were responsible for cultivating these plots of land, and procuring the necessary supply of labor for peak season operations like harvesting from the village harwaha families. The harwaha received a share of the produce – bhata – from the land under cultivation. The share varied from one-fifth in the more recently reclaimed regions, to one-sixth in the more populated regions to the south (Hooper 1892, p. 38) The bhata was enshrined within the customary responsibility of the landlord to ensure the reproduction of the harwaha household.

This traditional bond between the master and servant, related to caste-based notions of the 'degrading' aspects of handling the plough and restrictions on access to land, was the basis of labor organization and enforcement. The subordination of the farm servant was delinked from, and prior to the process of land allocation. The antecedent structure of labor relations was embedded in reciprocal rights and obligations between master and servant that were exploitative but that also granted the farm-servant some security and conditional property rights (Breman 1974).

The modes of control and access to land in the 'pattidari' (and 'bhaiachara') tenure characteristic of the region, reflect a pattern of landholding by co-parcenary sharers. Proprietary rights were determined by graded interests in rights to the produce of land (Siddiqui 1973). Tenurial rights were defined in terms of area corresponding to the tillage of a plough and is possibly related to the holding under cultivation by a harwaha family. The norm of a single rate per ploughshare implied that "means have to be taken to ensure that lands apportioned to each are equal in value" (Hooper 1892, p. 37). Each holding of land was comprised of a series of sub-blocks, such that each of these series had its share in different types of land in the village, in proportion to the number of plough cattle possessed.

This ensured that

> everyone got a share of every bit of land in every part of the village . . . No one among the cultivating body, whether he be landlord or tenant is allowed to pick out the good land for himself.
>
> (Hooper 1891, pp. 35–37)

This tenurial system resulted in the extreme subdivision of the land into tiny fields with the average size of such plots being no more than one-fifth of an acre (Hooper 1892, p. 37).

Looking beyond the absence of absolute proprietary rights, the tenurial system represented distinct and hierarchical claims to the product of land. Property rights were not defined in terms of fixed, spatially demarcated territorial boundaries. In fact, plots were periodically exchanged and redistributed. Landlordial power derived from the extent of cultivation and the number of ploughs controlled by the landlord. Partitioning or alienation of these holding rights was accompanied by the relocation or transfer of harwahas. Such transfers reflected the recalibration of the power of the landlord rather than a commodification of labor or the laborer. At the same time, the persistence of cultivators with conditional rights to land constituted a barrier to proletarianization of agricultural labor. These tenurial systems were less prominent in Gorakhpur district, with 'imperfect pattidaris' comprising less than half of the tenures, and pure pattidaris about 5% (Cruickshank 1891, pp. 6, 47).[1]

The distinctive antecedent structure of property rights and forms of social existence of labor implies that the investigation of the dimensions and extent of agrarian transformation needs to go beyond the process of peasant differentiation and dispossession (Shah 1985). The impact of inelastic cash revenue demands and the changing notions of property rights with the imposition of settlement policy by the British are also contingent on the extent to which means of social control of labor were being transformed.

Commander's (1983) study of traditional patronage relationships in colonial India suggests that these relations are not antagonistic to market forces but are sensitive to demographic pressures, labor migration, land colonization and new avenues of employment. The dissolution of the harwaha bond also involved a qualitative transformation of underlying social relations that went beyond the erosion of patronage elements, as land shares got increasingly subdivided, with mounting demographic pressure. The limits of the extensive margins of cultivation with the reclamation of wastelands necessitated new modes of labor appropriation as a way of tying cultivators and labor, paving the way for transformation of social relations. The extent and manner of transformation would also vary across regions.

Agrarian transition at the turn of the century

The region faced increasing pressure on land (Table 13.1), even as the colonial revenue demands and the new possibilities of commerce increased with the advent of railways in the 1890s. The distinct paths of agrarian transition in the districts of Gorakhpur and Basti can be seen in the differences in the relative position of the occupancy tenant, the pattern of debt and the evolution of the labor market.

By the 1890s the subdivision of land had proceeded to a greater extent in Basti compared to Gorakhpur. The average holding per proprietor during the 1891 land settlement was 11.36 acres in Gorakhpur and 17 acres in Basti, while the average size of the cultivated holding was 2.45 acres and 2 acres in

Table 13.1 Population density and land use

Year	*Population density*		*Cultivable waste/cultivated area (%)*	
	Gorakhpur	*Basti*	*Gorakhpur*	*Basti*
1891	656	656		
1901	655	655	25.05	23.64
1911	706	706	21.02	21.25
1921	721	721	20.61	20.03
1931	787	787	19.01	18.59
1941	712	712	19.23	17.55

Source: Census of India: United Provinces of Agra and Oudh, Season and Crop Report United provinces of Agra and Oudh.

Note: Cultivable waste refers to uncultivated culturable area other than fallow land.

Table 13.2 Tenurial distribution of cultivated area (%)

Tenure	*Year*	*Gorakhpur*		*Basti*
		West	*East*	
Owner proprietor	1891	25	23	27
	1919	28	23	34
Occupancy tenants	1891	36	48	27
	1919	48	58	38
Other tenants	1891	39	29	46
	1919	24	19	28

Source: Hooper (1892), Cruickshank (1891), Knox (1919), Stewart (1919).

the two districts respectively. The average size of the fields in Gorakhpur was 0.66 acres, and only 0.33 acres in Basti (Cruickshank 1891, p. 6).

The area under occupancy tenancy doubled in Gorakhpur between 1870 and 1890 settlements. In Basti in the same period the area increased by only about 50% (Cruickshank 1891, p. 11). In terms of share of area under tenancy, the share of occupant tenancy increased from 31% to 55% in this period in Gorakhpur, and from 30% to 37% in Basti. The growth and consolidation of occupancy rights was greater in Gorakhpur compared to Basti (Cruickshank 1891, p. 11), and continued through the turn of the century (Table 13.2). By 1919 the occupancy tenant cultivated about 48% of the cultivated area in West Gorakhpur, and 58% in East Gorakhpur. While there was a rise in the share of occupancy tenants in Basti too, the owner-proprietors appear to have strengthened their position in this district. The circumstances of non-occupancy tenant

Table 13.3 Distribution of land according to size class of revenue payments (1948)

Revenue class (Rs)	*Basti*		*West Gorakhpur*		*East Gorakhpur*	
	Revenue	*No. of Zamindars*	*Revenue*	*No. of Zamindars*	*Revenue*	*No. of Zamindars*
Below 25	24.3	86.61	24.0	89.47	22.4	87.74
25–250	34.9	12.54	30.0	9.66	31.4	11.38
250–1000	13.8	0.71	14.7	0.66	14.2	0.73
1000–5000	10.1	0.12	18.3	0.18	9.7	0.13
Above 500	16.8	0.02	13.0	0.02	22.3	0.02

Source: Uttar Pradesh Zamindari Abolition Report (1948).

in Basti, however, "suffered a big change for the worse . . . They were compelled to give an unusual amount of free labor, which occasionally involved cultivating the whole of the zamindar's land before he starts to work on his own" (Clow 1919, p. 14). In addition, the landlord in Basti also claimed extensive feudal privileges. (Clow 1919, p. 14).

The skewed nature of landholdings can be inferred from the distribution of revenue paying categories, with the caution that the categories are not coterminous with land control (Table 13.3). The size class paying less than Rs 250 was about 99% of all zamindars in both districts, but contributed a slightly larger share to revenue in Basti (59.2%) compared to Gorakhpur (about 54% in both eastern and western parts of the district). The top two classes, paying more than Rs 1000, contributed a slightly larger share to revenue in Gorakhpur (31.3% in West Gorakhpur and 32% in East Gorakhpur) compared to Basti (26.8%), with relatively comparable shares in the number of zamindars (0.2% in West Gorakhpur, 0.15% in East Gorakhpur and 0.14% in Basti). These figures suggest a relatively higher revenue burden on larger-size classes in Gorakhpur compared to Basti. This is reflected in the larger share of debt for unavoidable reasons (for consumption requirements or fulfillment of rental obligations) in Gorakhpur compared to Basti (Report of the United Provinces Provincial Banking Enquiry Report [henceforward UPBER] 1929–1930, Vol. I, p. 140).

Growth in area cultivated under occupancy rights occurred alongside a significant expansion of wheat and sugarcane cultivation in Gorakhpur. Acreage under sugarcane expanded by 79% between 1901–1905 and 1941–1945, that under wheat by 180%. In Basti, cane cultivation acreage increased by 28% and that of wheat by 65% (Season and Crop Reports 1901–1905, 1941–1945). The growth of cane cultivation also meant a more intensive deployment of labor. Amin (1984) investigates the role of cane as a cash-raising, debt-servicing crop requiring larger cash outlays for cultivation, that exacerbated the dependence of the cultivator peasant in Gorakhpur. The fact that it was lucrative made it attractive collateral for loans. Thus, the culture of cane, indigenous refining and later modern mill-refining, involved the cultivator in Gorakhpur in the need for credit through a system of advances from local peasants and landowners (Amin 1984). In Basti, however, cane cultivation and the production of indigenous raw sugar was both less developed and less integrated with sugar refining (Amin 1984, p. 61).

While the average holding in the region was uneconomic, the resort to subsidiary occupations and the high proportion of highly skilled agricultural castes (Kurmi caste in particular) helped cushion the fall into deep poverty and debt (UPPBER 1929–1930, Vol. I, p. 27). The percentage of debt-free landlords and tenants in Gorakhpur was 51% in 1930 compared to 73% in Basti. About 59% of debt in Gorakhpur was encumbered (debt greater than one year's rent), while 20% was encumbered in Basti. The system of advances to cultivators was dominated by the landlords and rich peasants. The landlord provided 54% of loans in Gorakhpur and about 51% in Basti (UPPBER 1929–1930, Vol. 1, p. 192) . It was reported that,

> The agriculturist for the most part borrows from the more prosperous neighbor – the Kurmi tenant, the Brahmin zamindar and the Thakur pattidar, whilst the professional moneylender or mahajan plays a very insignificant part in agricultural finance.
>
> (UPPBER 1929–1930, Vol. 2, p. 162)

The burden of debt was more pronounced in Gorakhpur, in particular among cultivators of holdings of between 5 and 10 acres (Table 13.4). The debt-burden and the incidence of debt among laboring and menial castes and market gardening castes is also higher in this district[2] (Table 13.5).

Table 13.4 Debt burden/debtor across size class of holdings (Rs)

Size class (acres)	*Basti*	*Gorakhpur*
Below 5	70	91
5–10	116	319
10–20	708	645
Above 20	2107	811

Source: Report of the United Provinces Provincial Banking Enquiry 1929–1930, Vol. 1.

Table 13.5 Debt burden/debtor across caste groups (Rs)

Size class (acres)	*Basti*	*Gorakhpur*
High caste	530 (41%)	405 (54%)
Agricultural castes	181 (23%)	194 (48%)
Market gardening castes	31 (30%)	101 (75%)
Laboring and menial castes	35 (31%)	114 (61%)

Source: Report of the United Provinces Provincial Banking Enquiry 1929–1930, Vol. 1, p. 145.

Note: Incidence of debt (indebted/indebted + debt-free) in parentheses.

The pattern of debt throws light on the precise nature of the social relation that debt mediated. With the growth of labor-intensive cane cultivation, debt became an important means of subordinating labor and appropriating surplus (Amin 1984). Control of access to credit and land came to play an important role in establishing and intensifying the subordination of labor. Thus grain-loans (bisar) for seed or subsistence, which were incurred by laboring castes and cultivators of small holdings, were an important way of intensifying and enforcing labor deployment in Gorakhpur. These loans involved a loan of seed before sowing, with the stipulation that it would be returned in kind at the harvest at a 25% or even a 50% rate of interest. When the landlord provided the grain loan, the profits from the grain loan were larger and more easily realizable than rent.

This practice was less pronounced in Basti (UPPBER 1929–1930, Vol. I, p. 91) and the grain advance was generally provided without interest (UPPBER 1929–1930, Vol. I, p. 107). However, the practice of potai (rent loans) in Basti suggests a precarious position of the tenant cultivator. Potai refers to the practice of taking a loan (in lieu of rent) from the landlord when payments are due, and repaying this at the time of the harvest at a 25% rate. This 'loan' enabled a permanent enhancement of recorded rents through usury, since the cultivator had to invariably take a fresh loan when the next installment was due (Amin 1984, p. 76).

Debt also served as a mode of attachment of labor. The harwaha at the turn of the century was a virtual serf:

> who for an advance of cash have bound themselves their wives and children to work for the master until the money is repaid. Of course. the money is never paid. But the condition of the ploughman is not one of actual slavery. . . . When the harwaha was dissatisfied he simply runs away and takes up service elsewhere.
>
> (Hooper 1892, pp. 39–40)

The Banking Enquiry Report notes the presence of forms of debt peonage where debt was repaid in service and was used to attachment labor much later in 1929. The evidence also distinguishes this role in the two districts:

> In (Basti), for instance, the debtor contracts to give his own services or those of some member of his family free for a whole year. In the Tarai and Gorakhpur, on the other hand, the service is occasional and appears to be in lieu of interest. In Gorakhpur, for instance, the debtor must plough his creditor's fields with his own bullocks once in each crop-season, or, if he has bullocks, perform some other field-work for two days
>
> (UPPBER 1929–1930, Vol. I, p. 91).

At the same time, the debt burden among cultivators of larger landholdings above 20 acres in Basti is more than two and a half times that in Gorakhpur

(Table 13.3). This is also the case for the debt burden among high castes and agricultural castes. The less vulnerable position of the agricultural caste cultivator allowed them to extend cultivation to larger holdings. In Basti, however,

> It is well-nigh impossible for most of these high caste farmers (under circumstances in which they are placed and under traditions and customs to which they are slaves) to save anything out of their agricultural income . . . The few among them who have amassed some money and are practicing money-lending as an occupation subsidiary to their agricultural pursuits got it from sources other than agriculture.
>
> (UPPBER 1929–1930, Vol. I, p. 162)

Thus, in Basti, a higher share of about 47% of the debt was incurred for unproductive objectives – social functions, litigation or repayment of old debt compared to Gorakhpur where the share was estimated at 32% (UPBER 1929–1930, Vol. I, p. 140).

The Banking Enquiry Report records that a significant amount of borrowing was from more prosperous tenants and landlords in the village. Landlords and tenant comprised a smaller proportion of credit in Basti (62%) compared to Gorakhpur (71%) (UPPBER 1929–1930, Vol. I, p. 144). Among the agricultural castes, the kurmis came to play a very important part in the transformation of the agrarian economy and in the agricultural finance of the region – and Gorakhpur in particular. Noted for their 'industry and economy in social and domestic expenses', the kurmi cultivator incurred debt primarily for productive purposes and was "always anxious to take a mortgage on a bigha or two and thus make a profitable investment to increase his income" (UPPBER 1929–1930, Vol. II, p. 162). Kurmis had expanded landholding rights across the region, but the increase was more pronounced in Gorakhpur, in particular in Eastern Gorakhpur (Knox 1919, p. 19).

While high-caste brahmins and rajputs remained the most important landholders in the region, agricultural castes, in particular the kurmi cultivators, increased their share from around 11.5% to 14% in this period in Eastern Gorakhpur (Table 13.6). Caste cohesion, involvement in credit, trade and cartage, and other supplemental sources of income contributed to this increase. Ownership of bullocks was also important in the context of intensification of cultivation (cane in particular). Further, the practice of tenants transferring a bigha or so of their holdings in lieu of repayment of loans enabled an expansion of the kurmi creditor's control over land (UPPBER 1929–1930, Vol. II, p. 190). In the context of the expansion of cane cultivation and its integration with sugar refining, the rich peasants and landowners, in particular the kurmis (who also owned bullocks and carts) came to control the transport and marketing of the raw sugar and cane. As the mills relied on landlords and rich peasants for the procurement of cane,

Table 13.6 Distribution of land according to caste (%)

Caste	*Basti*		*West Gorakhpur*		*East Gorakhpur*	
	1891	*1919*	*1891*	*1919*	*1891*	*1919*
Brahman	33.58	35.20	29.13	27.65	29.67	22.43
Rajput	29.77	29.32	19.14	17.64	16.43	27.68
Bhuinhar	4.23	4.33	4.92	4.02	17.22	17.38
Kayasth	6.70	5.71	8.26	7.63	4.64	4.11
Vaish	3.43	3.88	10.95	11.38	2.87	3.70
Kurmi	2.32	2.44	6.43	7.12	11.56	13.92

Source: Hooper (1892), Cruickshank (1891), Knox (1919), Stewart (1919).

these groups exploited this position to further entrench their power over the other smaller peasants.

Between 1931 and 1937 the number of mills in Gorakhpur grew from 9 to 23, alongside the eclipse of the indigenous raw sugar production. Basti had just one sugar mill in 1931, and four in 1937 (Amin 1984, p. 294). Cane cultivation grew through the 1930s in response to this demand. In 1940, it is reported that about 63% of the cane was sent to sugar mills in Gorakhpur district, compared to only 29% in Basti (Amin 1984, p. 296).

What emerges from this investigation is the greater extent of the transformation of the basis of power and subordination in Gorakhpur, where the dominance of sections of occupancy tenant (the richer kurmi cultivator) and landlord became linked to the cultivation of cane on smaller farms and the supply of cane to the emerging sugar industry. The majority of smaller peasants growing cane remained dependent on the richer peasant and landlords for both credit and the access to the market (Amin 1984). Integral to this transition was the need for strategies to appropriate surplus through the subordination and intensification of labor. The vestiges of the traditional modes were more persistent in Basti.

In terms of Bhaduri's (1981, 1985) thesis, it could be argued that the dominance of the process of forced commercialization inhibited the emergence of a rich peasant in Basti. This was reflected in the continued dominance of the traditional landlords and the persistence of the traditional system of tenurial rights. In contrast, the expansion of cane cultivation and the growth of occupancy rights was conducive to the emergence of a rich peasant class that came to dominate the agricultural market, credit and land in Gorakhpur. This dominance enabled the appropriation of surplus from the smaller peasants through interlinked modes of exploitation.

These differences in the paths of agrarian transition in the two districts are also reflected in the evolution of the labor market. The persistence of coparcenary pattidari tenures, the associated mechanisms of patronage-based exploitation and the rise of the occupancy rights over small holdings pose a barrier to the process of expropriation that is integral to the evolution of an agricultural laboring class from the dispossessed peasant (Prakash 1984).

Forms of social existence of labor

The erosion of the traditional systems of property rights and control of labor outlined in these two districts was conditioned by the manner and extent to which access to credit and land became instrumental in enforcing control over labor, even without the concentration or consolidation of landholding. The induction into broader commercial circuits and the revenue demand of the colonial state would transform the material basis for maintaining a retinue of permanent farm servants – the harwahas.

The mutation of traditional notions of property rights and the dissolution of the traditional patronage-client system which bound the harwaha to the landholder was not the simple outcome of the incursion of market rationality or the accentuation of demographic pressures. It is, instead, explicable through the articulation of these factors through changing balance of class forces. There is no simple linear path from agrestic servitude through debt-bondage to wage labor.

The dissolution of the traditional relations of labor subordination was reflected in the increasing resort to debt as a mode of attachment of labor. While the traditional system was geared to ensuring a requisite supply of labor for the cultivation of land, the new forms, in particular debt, were deployed to control labor and interlink modes of extracting surplus. We have already highlighted the use of grain loans and the system of advances to intensify labor use and extract surplus from small poor peasants in Gorakhpur. The transformation of the harwaha from agrestic serf to a debt peon has also been noted. The landlords also allotted small plots of land to the harwaha for their own subsistence cultivation as a mode of attachment. The responsibility for subsistence was transferred to the harwaha family, and the manipulation of the size of holding became instrumental in the subordination of labor. The harwaha also depended on the 'master' for access to bullocks for ploughing the land. However, the scope for material provisioning outside the wage contract enabled resistance to the imposition of the wage contract as a form of social control.

While there was a decline in permanent farm servants (the harwaha) as a proportion of total farm servants in both districts from 1881 to 1921 (Table 13.7), the share remained relatively smaller in Gorakhpur. The practice of permanent farm servants was more resistant to the process of casualization in Basti.

Further, from Tables 13.8 and 13.9 we can glean the magnitude of involvement in the labor market in the two districts from the census data. The shares of agricultural workforce involved in both cultivation and the labor market were higher in Gorakhpur, though the share declined between 1911 and 1931. This is indicative of the capacity of the small peasant to resist cutting

Table 13.7 Percentage share of farm servants to agricultural laborers

Year	*Gorakhpur*	*Basti*
1881	46.2	59.3
1901	29.8	62.3
1921	33.2	50.6

Source: Census of India: United Provinces of Agra and Oudh

Table 13.8 Percentage of cultivators cum laborers in agricultural workforce (male)

Year	*Gorakhpur*	*Basti*
1911	11.3	1.7
1921	10.4	4.3
1931	5.6	4.5

Source: Census of India: United Provinces of Agra and Oudh.

Note: Includes tenants and proprietors cultivators with agriculture as a subsidiary occupation and agricultural workers with cultivation as a subsidiary occupation.

Table 13.9 Incidence of rural labor (male)

	Percent of agricultural workforce		*Percent of cultivators*	
	Gorakhpur	*Basti*	*Gorakhpur*	*Basti*
1881	14.16	22.14	17.72	31.07
1901	20.17	18.23	16.16	16.90
1911	22.09	14.61	29.71	17.88
1921	19.30	12.40	24.13	14.86
1931	20.19	14.44	26.14	17.86

Source: Census of India: United Provinces of Agra and Oudh

Note: Figures for 1881 and 1901 do not include cultivators with a subsidiary occupation as agricultural labor.

ties to land in Gorakhpur, and the attenuation of this capacity through the period. The incidence of rural labor in the agricultural workforce, and as a share of cultivators, increased in Gorakhpur between 1881 and 1911 and remained at around 20% in the next two decades (Table 13.9). In Basti the share dropped between 1881 and 1911. The declining share of permanent farm servants along with the rising share of rural labor in rural economy also suggests a greater degree of casualization of the labor contract in Gorakhpur.

While the growth of the casual labor force would have fostered the transformation of the traditional modes of attachment that tied the harwaha

Table 13.10 Wages of ploughmen and unskilled labor

Year	*Index of ploughman's wage (1906 = 100)*		*Index of unskilled workers wage (1906 = 100)*		*Ploughman's wage as percent of wage of unskilled labor*	
	Gorakhpur	*Basti*	*Gorakhpur*	*Basti*	*Gorakhpur*	*Basti*
1906	100	100	100	100	106.7	88.9
1911	120	96	120	117	106.7	73.1
1916	140	110	140	117	106.7	83.8
1928	200	160	180	183	118.5	77.6
1934	140	110	160	117	93.2	62.2
1939	120	160	160	133	80.0	106.7
1944	120	160	80	100	160.0	142.2

Source: Reports of the Wage Census of United Provinces, Chaturvedi 1944.

Note: The monthly wages of the harwaha are compared with that of unskilled labor under the assumption of full employment (monthly wages = daily wage × 30).

to the landowner, rising wages reinforced the resort to casual field labor. Table 13.10 shows that ploughmans' wages rose more sharply in Gorakhpur until the price wage collapse set off by the Great Depression.[3] The increased demand for labor, due to the extension of cane cultivation in the 1930s, may have led to the fall in the wages of unskilled field labor in Gorakhpur in this period being less sharp. Maintaining a harwaha was more expensive than hiring casual, unskilled labor in this district, and it was noted that

> Petty landholders are in a precarious position. The harwahas even defy their commands without the slightest regards.
>
> (Mathur 1930, p. 30)

Basti continued, until the 1930s, to operate in a context where the earnings of the permanent farm servant were lower than that of the daily unskilled labor. The traditional system would be characterized by more infrequent wage negotiations and might have been underwritten by some form of implicit contract, that assured off-season employment at lower than market wages (Roy 2007).

The evolution of the labor market involved the incomplete dispossession of sections of the peasantry and the erosion of traditional patronage relations through which surplus was extracted. The constraint on expanding the scale of production, in the context of a predominance of small holdings, structured the relations of dependency that were integral to intensifying labor use as a way of expanding the extraction of surplus.

Thus, the consolidation of occupancy rights and the emergence of a rich peasant in Gorakhpur also buttressed the ability of the harwaha to command a higher remuneration and resist traditional landlordial control. This played a role in shaping the strategies adopted (casualization and interlinked contracts) to enforce subordination. In the northern parts of Basti where the traditional system persisted beyond the turn of the century, the traditional landlords had continued to maintain their dominance. The transformation of social relations in this district was less pronounced.

The development of a labor market alongside the preservation of a core of permanent farm-servants are both linked to the specificities of the process of commercialization and the manner in which it articulated through the changing configuration of power in the agrarian economy. Evidence from UP before the Royal Commission of Agriculture reported that

> there is a growing class of landless labor whose employment is uncertain, and who shift from fields to mines and from mines to plantations . . . Every circumstance which has weakened the economic position of the small holder has increased the supply of agricultural laborers – the loss of common rights in the rural economy, the disuse of collective enterprise, the subdivision of holdings, the increase in the class of rent receivers, free mortgaging and transfer of land and the decline of cottage industries.
>
> (Royal Commission on Agriculture 1928, p. 388)

Subdivision of holdings and a preponderance of small uneconomic holdings necessitated recourse to supplementary earnings through other occupations or through the labor market. At the same time small holdings discouraged the employment of permanent farm servants, in particular when rising prices made the harwaha harder to maintain, and

> There is an exodus of agricultural labor from the holdings of cultivating landowners . . . Long period contracts are gradually superceded and field laborers instead of serving the same master from generation to generation, prefer to work for daily wages or on the piece work system.
>
> (Royal Commission on Agriculture 1928, p. 397)

What is missing in the analysis so far is an account of how agrarian transition is shaped by the linkages established between these two districts and the emerging centers of capital in industrial centers and plantations in colonial India. These linkages are of particular significance, as this region came to constitute an important catchment for long-distance migration in the late colonial period. The path of agrarian transition is not independent of the manner in which the rural economy was drawn into the ambit of distant capitalist centers in overseas colonies and within colonial India.

Migration and the transformation of labor markets

The early colonial period, when the peasantry became imbricated in the colonial circuits of commerce, was characterized by the concern with revenue and land settlement policy. By the end of the nineteenth century, as industrialization took root in India, the colonial government turned its focus to the problems of supplying labor to these emerging centers of capitalist enterprises. This is evident in the series of commissions that were set up to investigate the question of the conditions of labor in this period.

Long-distance migration flows came to play a significant role in Gorakhpur and Basti in the later decades of the nineteenth century. Labor from this region was found in the coolie lines of West Indian sugar plantations, the Assam tea gardens, the jute mills around Calcutta and the coalfields of Bihar. Demographic pressures, compounded by droughts and famines, no doubt played a role as 'push factors' in the emergence of migration flows from these districts. The role of colonial policy in determining the pull factors that shaped patterns of migration from Gorakhpur and Basti, however, bears investigation.

What is significant is that the pattern of migration that developed from these two contiguous districts were distinct. Basti was more integrated to the flows of indentured labor to the sugar colonies in British Guinea, Fiji, Natal and Mauritius, and later to the tea plantations in Assam. Gorakhpur in contrast was more embedded in the cyclical/circular migrant streams to the industrial centers around Calcutta and later the regional coal fields.

The high phase of overseas colonial migration, after the abolition of slavery in 1834, persisted well till the end of the century, until its suspension in 1921. The acute crisis of labor supply in the sugar plantations engendered the colonial policy of indentured labor from the eastern districts of UP. Labor from Eastern UP comprised about 83% of the overseas emigration from the port of Calcutta in the last decades of the nineteenth century (Saha 1970, p. 25). The long and tortuous passage to the colonies, the innumerable abuses and malpractices in recruitment, the conditions of hard unrelenting labor in the plantations, the difficulties of the return journey and the attenuation of ties with the home village have been well documented (Tinker 1974; Saha 1970). Basti sent a larger number of indentured labour overseas than Gorakhpur (Table 13.11).

Table 13.11 Registered emigrants sailing from Calcutta for British Colonies

Year	*Gorakhpur*	*Basti*
1891–1900	7568	21234
1901–1910	5708	31173
1911–1917	1857	7467

Chaudhury (1992) notes that while Basti was an important source of labor for the overseas colonies, it sent a much smaller number to distant places within India. The flows to overseas colonies came from sections of the population who were less privileged, and less connected with inland destinations and therefore more susceptible to the suasions of the recruiters. While emigrants from Basti were drawn from impoverished laboring and cultivating castes, there is no evidence of the bonded permanent farm servants being involved in this emigrant stream.

The pressure from the anti-indenture lobby within India and the evidence of the rampant abuses in the modes of recruitment led to the dismantling of the overseas indentured labor flows. Already, changing colonial priorities had created a demand for cheap labor in the tea plantations in Assam. In the face of a scarcity of local labor, these tea plantations resorted to a system of long-distance recruitment with penal contracts that were indistinguishable from indenture (Das Gupta 1981, p. 1791). 'Coolie catching' fastened on and refashioned the existing mechanism of overseas recruitment, and an illegal system of recruitment flourished as an appendage to the legal system (Behal and Mohapatra 1992). A key figure was the recruiter – arkatti – who scoured the countryside and used a variety of coercive means, even deceit and chicanery, to mobilize labor from the weekly village markets and send them to the labor depots (UPSA, Industry Department, File 118/1913: Enquiry into alleged irregularities in certain districts in UP in connection with recruitment for Assam Tea Gardens). Drawn from the impoverished laboring castes, picked up by the arkatti from bazaars or the roadsides, lacking knowledge or connections to the distant destination, the recruit was easy prey to the recruiter and also less able to resist the stringent conditions and the penal contracts associated with work in the tea gardens. The coolie "had no property and generally wished to escape from his past" (Foley 1906, p. 4).

The garden sardar system (that became more prevalent after 1926) sought to replace the coercive recruitment practices of the arkatti, and instead use kinship and village networks to bring people from the home village to the tea gardens. Instead, the sardar either became a puppet in the hand of the debarred recruiter or engaged some of those debarred from recruiting (Das Gupta 1981). These recruiters sought the aid of the zamindars, who provided finance to recruit while compensating themselves with the commissions paid (UPSA, Industry Department, File 179/1915: Assam Labor Enquiry).

The district Magistrate of Basti reported that

> In the absence of all restrictions, recruiters debarred from colonial emigration take up work for the garden sardars and incidentally the smuggling of opium is also taken up.
>
> (Annual Report of the working of the Assam Emigration Act of 1901, for the year ending 1919)

Gorakhpur sent out fewer migrants to Assam (Table 13.12).

Table 13.12 Inland emigration to Assam plantations

	Gorakhpur	*Basti*
1907–1908	3727	7583
1912–1913	–	2674
1913–1914	–	2111
1914–1915	594	1597
1915–1916	769	1533
1924–1925	724	742

Source: Census of India: United Provinces of Agra and Oudh; Report of the Working of the Assam Labor and Emigration Act of 1901 (various years).

The widespread abuses associated with the penal contracts and the recruitment system for the tea gardens, and the shift in colonial strategy from a steady supply of cheap labor from distant regions to ensuring the viability of the plantations in a period of plunging prices, led to a dismantling of the arkatti system and its final abolition in 1926. Long-distance emigration from the region to the tea gardens also dwindled (Behal and Mohapatra 1992).

By the end of the century, the development of industrial centers in Bombay and Calcutta created a new demand for labor. The jute mills around Calcutta were oriented primarily to the export markets and had to adapt production to the fluctuating levels of export demand. While the mills depended primarily on local labor till around the 1890s, as the demand for labor grew, migrants were drawn into the workforce. In 1896 itself, the colonial policy urged the importation of labor from UP as a way to solve the acute shortage of labor for the jute mills (Fremantle 1906, p. 41). The problem at the turn of the century was that, despite the high population density and the difficulties of subsisting the small holdings in the neighboring states of UP and Bihar, labor supply was still a problem for the mills in Bengal.

Fremantle's investigation of the problem of labor supply was preoccupied by the relatively unrealized potential of Eastern UP as a source of labor. He noted that "the standard of living of the Gorakhpuri is now lower than that of the man from Chupra, the adjoining district in Bengal which sends a large proportion of its surplus labor into the world" and hoped that "the Gorakhpuri will in time fall in line . . . and go to work in Calcutta" (Fremantle 1906, p. 46). That this region constituted a promising field of recruitment industry in Bengal seemed evident in light of "the fact that Basti district supplied in the last decade the largest number of emigrants in the colonies" (Fremantle 1906, p. 46). The colonial administrators came to emphasize administrative support to recruitment from these districts. Foley (1906, p. 3) pointed to the employer's lack of awareness of the best catchment areas for labor and the appropriate strategies for recruiting and retaining labor. Evidence before the Royal Commission on Agriculture also reported that where the local landlords command the agricultural labor supply, labor are more difficult to obtain for industrial purposes (Royal Commission on Agriculture 1928, p. 397).

Unlike migration to the colonies or to Assam, which often involved the migration of the entire family, migration to the industrial centers was of a cyclical nature, involving primarily males. The migrant would return to the village for harvesting and for the marriage season, creating a seasonal shortage of labor. At the same time, remittances from migration became crucial to the small peasant's capacity to hold on to land, as the small holdings would be left to be managed by other family members or mortgaged to richer cultivators (Stewart 1919, p. 18). Even so, Fremantle (1906, p. 34), while investigating the problem of shortages of labor for the Bengal mills, notes that

> The system by which mills depend for their labour chiefly on a class of temporary immigrants seems preferable to the formation of a regular mill population divorced from the soil.

A similar view is echoed in Foley's (1906) report on labor in UP.

Cyclical migration became integral to the need for flexible supply of labor in the jute mills, and the industry was characterized by chaotic conditions and high turnover of labor (Das Gupta 1976; Chakrabarty 1983; de Haan 1999). At the fulcrum of the calibration of the requisite supply of labor in the face of changing demand was the jobber – the sardar – who played a critical role in controlling labor supply through a network of kinship relations. (Chakrabarty 1983, 1989; Chandavarkar 1981, 1994; Bates 2000). Chakrabarty (1983) notes the existence of surplus labor *within* the jute mills, which according to factory inspector employed 100% more hands than that required to work in a similar mill in Dundee. A floating pool of labor that thronged the factory gates every day were crucial to ensuring the continuity and flexibility of labor supply, enabling the mills to employ additional workers at short notice, or to lay them off when demand flagged. The limited scale of enterprise and low level of technology necessitated institutional adaptations like the sardar system to engineer the subordination of labor within the factory.[4]

By the onset of the Depression, the labor force in the jute industry had stabilized. At the same time the slowdown in demand had led to reorganization and rationalization of the industry. A system of labor registration and the introduction of the Badli Control Act in 1937, along with the appointment of labor officers as recommended by the Royal Commission on Labor, led to a curtailment of the role of the sardar in regulating labor and arranging for substitutes through the network of workers under his control. Surplus labor that had existed within the jute industry was in effect transferred *out of the industry* and into an informal pool of casual unskilled labor *within the urban economy*. However, the pattern of cyclical migration endured.

The cyclical migration flows to the industrial center in Bengal are structurally quite distinct from the permanent migration to the colonies and Assam tea gardens in that it represented a sharper rupture from the rural hinterland from which the migrant was drawn. The cyclical migration that supplied labor to the jute mills, in contrast, entailed the persistence of a stronger connection to the village. Yang (1979) and de Haan (1997, 1999) argue that sections of the peasantry that migrated could repay debts and even enhance resources, thus reinforcing the structure of small holdings in the village.[5] However, the ties to land and the rural economy also allowed wages to remain low and accentuated the weak position of the industrial worker who remained dependent on the village connection for survival. Thus, the rural economy subsidized the cost of labor for the capitalist sector (Omvedt 1980; Sen 1999).[6] At the same time these village ties could be crucial in providing support and sustenance to the worker during prolonged strike actions or lock-outs (Das Gupta 1976).

The distinct manner in which the rural economy came to be linked to the capitalist enclaves and the particular requirements of these centers shaped nature of migration flows (Das Gupta 1983; de Haan 1995). The indentured and contract labor flows from Basti did not have a significant impact in eroding the traditional forms of subordination of labor, and the practice of maintaining permanent farm servants was more persistent. The labor market that emerged can be characterized as being constituted primarily by the *rural poor*, including the impoverished peasant and the farm servants. Migration from Gorakhpur was predominantly cyclical migration to Bengal. Thus, migration flows from Basti surpassed that from Gorakhpur, until 1911 (Table 13.13). However, by 1921 when migration to the plantations and tea gardens had dwindled, Gorakhpur began to send a larger stream of emigrant workers. This migrant flow was directed towards the jute mills and remained closely tied to the rural economy.[7] The labor market, in contrast to that in Basti, is based on a class of what could be termed as *peasant-proletarians*.

Table 13.13 Net emigration flow

Year	*Net emigrants*	
	Gorakhpur	*Basti*
1901	-118,000	27,000
1911	-15,000	52,000
1921	42,000	36,000
1931	96,000	14,000

Source: Census of India: United Provinces of Agra and Oudh.

Note: The negative sign denotes a net immigration into the district.

The management of labor supply in the early phase of the development of capitalist enclaves in colonial India depended on the role of intermediaries. While there is a debate on whether the indentured and contract labor that emigrated to the colonies and Assam were voluntary or coerced (Yang 1979; de Haan 1997), the force and chicanery involved in the recruitment process is indisputable. The mode of recruitment depended on organizational networks created from outside the village community, sometimes with the mediation of the landlord who could exert some control over the process and even profited from it (through commissions from the outside recruiter). The rural poor who constituted the rural labor market were, however, not linked to the emigrant laborer in the plantations, and they remained tethered to the traditional landlord.

The sardari mode of recruitment deployed by the jute industry, in contrast, was more dependent on the village networks of peasant-proletarians who returned to their villages. Debt also played a more critical role in the compulsion to migrate and as a means of social control within the village. To that extent it preserved the link between the village and the urban center. While the labor force was primarily drawn from the small peasants struggling to survive on uneconomic holdings in both districts, the peasant in Gorakhpur was drawn into the circuit of capital accumulation in the industry. This cyclical migration can be understood as the specific form which the jute mill owners need for a flexible labor supply and which the workers need to ameliorate the uncertainty and low wages in the industry by retaining their connections in the village, and over which their small plots of land were reconciled.

Alongside the processes of forced and normal commercialization that Bhaduri highlighted, attention needs to paid to the distinct way in which migration linked the rural economy to the colonial capitalist centers. The persistence of this rural connection represents the specific path of the evolution of labor markets and the centrality of the peasant proletarian.

Conclusion

This chapter has put forward an account of two distinct processes through which the rural labor market evolved in the colonial period. While revenue settlement demands and the imperatives of commercialization shaped the unfolding process of agrarian transition, an equally important external force was the policies adopted by the colonial government to ensure the supply of labor to the growing capitalist enclaves. Basti witnessed a preponderance of the process of forced commercialization that limited the emergence of the rich peasant. At the same time, the permanent migration to the colonies and tea gardens did not by itself help weaken the traditional forms of attachment of labor, even as the small cultivator faced impoverishment and was increasingly dependent on the rural labor market. In contrast, the pursuit of cane cultivation in Gorakhpur, which depended on the more intensive use of labor, implicated the small peasant in a relation of dependence to the emerging rich peasant. Cyclical migration to Bengal became pivotal to the peasant-proletarian household.

There are constraints on accumulation in agriculture through the enforcement and intensification of labor in a context where the under-formation of the markets for both land and labor are reinforcing each other within a structure of surplus labor and extreme subdivision of landholdings. This leads to what Byres (1981) calls the phenomenon of "partial proletarianization". The desperate dependence on land to ensure survival is the basis for the incomplete dispossession of the peasant-cultivator, who is also forced to rely on alternative means of livelihood to supplement the inadequate earnings from the marginal holdings of land. This perpetuates perverse exchange relations, interlinked modes of exploitation of mobilization of labor and a limited scope for productive accumulation (Bharadwaj 1985). The persistence of small holdings and the use of leasing out of small holdings and credit relations as a mode of tying labor is a reflection of these constraints in more recent times.[8]

It is in this context that migration came to play a crucial role in the process of agrarian transformation. The development of the plantations and industry fueled a demand for labor that was fulfilled through recruitment mechanisms structured around intermediaries, who played an integral role in mobilizing surplus labor in the rural economy. Despite the compulsions to seek additional avenues of employment, the small peasants sought to retain control over their small holdings and a pattern of cyclical or circular migration emerged. This surplus labor facilitates accumulation and the subordination of labor in the nascent industries in colonial India, but at the same time it enables the peasant proletarian to resist complete expropriation of the village landholding. Thus, labor surplus in the rural hinterland reinforces the 'surplus' informal labor pool in the urban center.

This history casts a long shadow and urban centers today face a growing pool of unskilled informal labor with durable connections to the stagnant rural economy. The social relations in the agrarian economy limit the scope for improvements in productivity through consolidation of landholdings and mechanization, leading to persistent stagnation. Stagnant agriculture further entrenches the pattern of circular migration that is flooding the informal labor markets in urban centers.

Acknowledgements

This chapter has its origins in my MPhil research guided by the late Sakti Padhi and K.P. Kannan at the Center for Development Studies, Trivandrum, many years ago. They both played an invaluable role in its conception. I am grateful to Debarshi Das and Deepankar Basu for organizing the Festschrift honoring Amit Bhaduri. This Festschrift prompted me to revive and develop this line of research that had been inspired by Amit Bhaduri's seminal work on agrarian relations. My thanks to all the participants of the Festschrift conference for their comments and feedback.

Notes

1 In the north of Gorakhpur, zamindari (rather than pattidari) predominates, as the former cultivating proprietors have been swept away, or formerly waste or uncultivated land has been given to the families of the present holders as grants (Cruikshank 1891, p. 7).
2 Laboring and menial castes include bhar, chamars and pasis; agricultural castes include ahirs, kurmis and lodhas; market gardening castes include malis, koeris and muraos.
3 Evidence placed before the Royal Commission on Agriculture also suggests that as rising prices made grain payments more expensive, farmers increasingly resorted to cash wages and casual labor, leading to a change in the customary relations that tied the permanent farm servant. It would also induce greater pressure to renegotiate wages. (Royal Commission on Agriculture Vol V 1928, pp. 394–395).
4 Sarkar (2003) notes how the technologically more advanced TISCO steel factory set up in the colonial period did not use the sardar system to recruit skilled workers, though such intermediaries were used to recruit unskilled labor.
5 For a different conclusion, consider the evidence of landless migrant family of Tulsi from Gorakhpur. He arrived in Calcutta in 1928 and began work in Anglo India Jute Company where he earned Rs 4.5 a week, while his wife earned less than Rs 3. After two years in Calcutta they had managed to repay only Rs 40 of a debt of Rs 100 that they had incurred in their village and had no desire to go back to the village (Report of the Royal Commission on Labor 1930, 125–6)
6 Migration also linked rural economies in different parts of India. Bates (1984) investigates inter-regional migration between tribal districts in Chota Nagpur with the prosperous wheat and cotton cultivating regions in western India.
7 Remittances were also more significant in Gorakhpur. Remittances to Gorakhpur were double those to Basti through 1910 (Mathur 1930).
8 Lerche's (1999) fieldwork in Eastern UP in the nineties notes the prevalence of the tiseri system in the nineties where small leases of land were deployed by the landowners to tie labor, and even enforce the performance of unpaid labor by family members, in particular in periods of seasonal out-migration. Srivastava's (1989, 1999) fieldwork in the nineties also points to the use by landowners of interlocking credit and lease markets other forms of extra-economic coercion to mobilize labor in Eastern UP, especially where laboring households' options of outside employment were limited.

References

Amin, S. 1984. *Sugarcane and Sugar in Gorakhpur*. Oxford University Press, Delhi.

Bates, C. 1984. Regional dependence and rural development in Central India: the pivotal role of migrant labor. *Modern Asian Studies*, 19,3: 573–592.

Bates, C. 2000. Coerced and migrant laborers in India: the colonial experience. *Edinburgh Papers in South Asian Studies*. 13 Centre for South Asian Studies, University of Edinburgh.

Behal, R.P. and P.P. Mohapatra. 1992. Tea and money versus human life: the rise and fall of the indenture system in the Assam tea plantations 1840–1908. *Journal of Peasant Studies*, 19,3–4: 142–172.

Bhaduri, A. 1973. A study in agricultural backwardness under Semi-feudalism. *Economic Journal*, 83, 329: 120–137.
Bhaduri, A. 1976. The evolution of land relations in Eastern India under British rule. *Indian Social and Economic History Review*, 13,1: 45–58.
Bhaduri, A. 1981. Class relations and the pattern of accumulation in an agrarian economy. *Cambridge Journal of Economics*, 5,1: 33–46.
Bhaduri, A. 1985. Class relations and commercialization in Indian agriculture: a study in the post-independence agrarian reforms of Uttar Pradesh. In K.N Raj, N. Bhattacharya, S Guha and S. Padhi eds., *Essays in commercialization of agriculture in India*. Oxford University Press, Bombay: 306–318.
Bharadwaj, K. 1985. A view on commercialization in Indian agriculture and the development of capitalism. *Journal of Peasant Studies*, 12,4: 7–25.
Breman, J. 1974. *Patronage and exploitation: changing agrarian relations in south Gujarat, India*. University of California Press, Berkeley, CA.
Byres, T.J. 1981. The new technology, class formation and class action in the Indian countryside. *Journal of Peasant Studies*, 84: 405–454.
Chakrabarty, D. 1983. Conditions for knowledge of working class conditions: employers, governments and the jute workers of Calcutta, 1890–1940. In R. Guha ed., *Subaltern studies, Volume II*. Oxford University Press, New Delhi.
Chakrabarty, D. 1989. *Rethinking working-class history: Bengal, 1890–1940*. Oxford University Press, New Delhi.
Chandavarkar, R.N. 1981. Workers and politics in the mill districts of Bombay between the wars. *Modern Asian Studies*, 15,3: 603–647.
Chandavarkar, R.N. 1994. *The origins of industrial capitalism: business strategies and the working classes in Bombay, 1900–1940*. Cambridge University Press, Cambridge, UK.
Chaudhury, P. 1992. Labour migration from the United Provinces, 1881–1911. *Studies in History*, 8,1: 13–41.
Clow, A.G. 1919. *Final report of the settlement in Basti district 1915–19*. Superintendent of Government Press, Allahabad.
Commander, S. 1983. The jajmani system in Northern India: an examination of its logic and status across two centuries. *Modern Asian Studies*, 17,2: 283–311.
Cruickshank, A.W. 1892. *Final report of the settlement in Gorakhpur district in 1891*. Allahabad.
Das Gupta, R. 1976. Factory labour in Eastern India: sources of supply, 1855–1946. Some preliminary findings. *Indian Economic and Social History Review*, 13,3: 277–329.
Das Gupta, R. 1981. Structure of the labour market in colonial India. *Economic and Political Weekly*, 16,44–46: 1781–1806.
De Haan, A. 1995. Migration in eastern India: a segmented labor market. *Indian Economic and Social History Review*, 32,1: 51–93.
De Haan, A. 1997. Unsettled settlers: migrant workers and industrial capitalism in Calcutta. *Modern Asian Studies*, 31,4: 919–949.
De Haan, A. 1999. The badli system in industrial labour recruitment: managers' and workers' strategies in Calcutta's jute industry. *Contributions to Indian Sociology*, 33,1–2: 271–301.
Foley, B. 1906. *Report on labour*. Bengal Secretariat Press, Calcutta.
Fremantle, S.H. 1906. *Report on the Supply of labor in the United Provinces and in Bengal*. Revenue Department, United Provinces, Lucknow.

Hooper. 1892. *Final report of the settlement in Basti district in 1891*. Superintendent of Government Press, Allahabad.

Knox, K.N. 1919. *Final report of the settlement of the revision of settlement in Gorakhpur district, tahsils Padrauna, Hata and Deoria in 1919*. Superintendent of Government Press, Allahabad.

Lerche, J. 1999. Politics of the Poor: Agricultural Laborers and Political Transformations in Uttar Pradesh, In T.J. Byres, K. Kapadia, and J. Lerche eds., *Rural Labour Relations in India*, Frank Cass, London, pp. 182–241.

Mathur, J.K. 1930. *The pressure of population and its impact on the rural economy in Gorakhpur district*. Department of Agriculture, Allahabad.

Omvedt, G. 1980. Migration in colonial India: the articulation of feudalism and capitalism by the Colonial State. *Journal of Peasant Studies*, 7,2: 185–212.

Prakash, S. 1984. Models of peasant differentiation and aspects of agrarian economy in colonial India. *Modern Asian Studies*, 19,3: 549–571.

Report of the Royal Commission on Agriculture in India. 1928. Vol. VII: Evidence taken in the United Provinces. Government of India, Central Publication Branch, Calcutta.

Report of the Royal Commission on Labor in India. 1930. Volume V: Evidence Bengal Presidency. His Majesty's Stationary Office.

Report of the United Provinces Provincial Banking Enquiry. 1929–1930. Government of India, Central Publication Branch, Calcutta.

Report of the United Provinces Zamindari Abolition Committee. 1948. Central Publication Branch Government of India, Calcutta.

Roy, T. 2007. Globalization, factor prices and poverty in colonial India. *Australian Economic History Review*, 47,1: 73–94.

Sarkar, S. 2003. The return of labor to South Asian history. *Historical Materialism*, 12,3: 285–313.

Saha, P. 1970. *Emigration of Indian labour 1834–1900*. Peoples Publishing House, Delhi.

Sen, S. 1999. *Women and labour in late colonial India. The Bengal jute industry*. Cambridge University Press, Cambridge.

Shah, M. 1985. The kaniatchi form of labor. *Economic and Political Weekly*, 20,30: 65–78.

Siddiqui, A. 1973. *Agrarian change in a northern Indian state: Uttar Pradesh*. Clarendon, London.

Srivastava, R. 1989. Interlinked modes of exploitation in Indian agriculture during transition: a case study. *Journal of Peasant Studies*, 16,4: 493–522.

Srivastava, R. 1999. Rural labor in Uttar Pradesh: emerging features of subsistence, contradiction and resistance. *Journal of Peasant Studies*, 26,2–3: 263–315.

Stewart, D.M. 1919. *Final settlement report in the western portion of the Gorakhpur district 1919*. Superintendent of Government Press, Allahabad.

Tinker, H. 1974. *A new system of slavery: the export of indentured labor overseas: 1830–1920*. Oxford University Press, London.

Yang, A. (1979). Peasants on the move: a study of internal migration in India. *Journal of Interdisciplinary History*, 10,1: 37–58.

14 Rising inequality and dualism in the US economy

Evidence and potential explanations

Ivan Mendieta-Muñoz, Codrina Rada and Rudi von Arnim

This chapter discusses two important features of the US economy over the past seven decades: the shift in the trend of the labour share of income and the rise of structural dualism. Dualism, a concept that originates in development economics, refers to the coexistence of sectors and economic activities that differ in terms of their growth performance and organization of production. Starting with Lewis (1954)'s seminal paper, the typical dual economy model consists of a modern, high-growth sector and a subsistence, stagnant sector. Lewis's contribution has inspired a rich literature in development economics. Its objective has been to identify the conditions and sectoral interactions that would transform the economy into a mature one with only modern, high-labour-productivity activities (Bhaduri and Skarstein, 2003).

Until the 1990s, the topic of structural change has been discussed mostly within the context of developing countries. This is despite stylized facts, identified by Kuznets, on the regularity with which countries across the development spectrum experience changes in their economic structures. An exception perhaps is Baumol (1967) who, for a long time, provided the only formal theory of structural change for advanced economies. Baumol's model is one of unbalanced growth. It postulates that the normal process of tertiarization observed in developed economies will eventually lead to stagnation. Baumol (1967) links structural change to the growth rate of the economy but assumes, as discussed here and in the next sections, no changes in income distribution, as real wages across sectors grow at the rate of average labour productivity. Contrary to this assumption, the growth rates of labour compensation and labour productivity have diverged over the past several decades in the US economy, leading to a decline in the labour share. Thus, the second topic of this chapter is the change in the labour share trend in the postwar period. Given this brief outline of the issues at hand, we have two objectives for this chapter. First, we describe how changes in income distribution and structural dualism relate to each other in the data for the US economy; and, second, we reflect, drawing on the work of Lewis and Baumol with insights from Bhaduri's work on dual economies, how these two phenomena are connected to economic performance.

Key results can be summarized as follows. First, growth of real compensation and labour productivity dominate the overall change in the labour share both in the short term and over longer time horizons. Second, the manufacturing sector plays a critical role throughout the entire postwar period. Initially, strong real compensation gains relative to labour productivity growth increase the labour share. In the later period, the accelerating collapse of employment in manufacturing coincides with strong growth of labour productivity, which in turn consistently exceeds that of real compensation. Third, sectors with rising employment shares feature on average lower real compensation and lower labour productivity growth, and furthermore higher labour shares. These structural changes thus imply downward pressure on labour productivity growth, and at the same time buffer the overall decline of the labour share.

Based on these results, we hypothesize that the U.S. economy is increasingly becoming a dual economy, where high-productivity sectors – such as manufacturing – and high-pay sectors – such as finance and professional services – coexist with low-pay and low-productivity sectors that employ most workers. This hypothesis has been recently put forth by others; for important contributions, see Storm (2017) and Temin (2017). However, their analyses focus on labour productivity growth (or total factor productivity growth) and wage inequality, rather than the functional distribution of income. Similar to Storm (2017), we seek to connect observed changes in the (functional) distribution of income and the structure of the economy to the hypothesis of secular stagnation. The centrally important insight here is that the forces of stagnation are certainly not (only) of Baumolian type. The mechanism suggested in Baumol (1967) assumes homogenous labour in a competitive labour market and *upward real wage convergence*: in the dynamic sector, nominal wages grow with labour productivity growth, whereas nominal wages *and* prices rise in the stagnant sector. As a result, growth rates of sectoral real consumption wages equilibrate and match that of aggregate labour productivity, leaving the labour share unchanged. Our empirical findings confirm the phenomena of the cost disease, but not this mechanism. Instead, dynamic sectors show slowing real wage growth, as surplus labour is absorbed in stagnant sectors with lower real wages. Hence, profit shares in dynamic activities rise due to weak real wage growth, whereas stagnant sector profit shares are supported only by price increases. This pattern, as suggested in Taylor and Ömer (2018), is consistent with a "reverse–Lewis" shift, where the existence of surplus labour in stagnant sectors puts a significant drag on real wage growth in dynamic sectors.

Aside of this introduction, the following section presents the Divisia decomposition technique as applied to the components of the labour share across sectors. Next, we summarize the results for the postwar period and the sub-samples of golden age and neoliberal era presented in Mendieta-Muñoz et al. (2020). We then analyse these findings in the context of structural change and Baumol's and Lewis's ideas on two-sector models. We conclude with an extension à la Kaldor that reflects on the role of demand, drawing on several papers by Amit Bhaduri on structural change and the interaction between income distribution and growth.

A Divisia index decomposition of the wage share

Before we discuss the decomposition methods and results for the US economy, let us briefly clarify how we measure structural change and the labour share of income. We will broadly refer to the former in terms of changes in the structure of the economy as captured by changes in sectoral shares of employment and value added. The decomposition approach presented below clearly shows the close connection between structural change and changes in the labour share. As discussed by Mendieta-Muñoz et al. (2020), several problems typically arise in measuring the labour share. First, it is not clear what properly can be counted as compensation for work. Are the salaries of the superstar CEOs really *labour* income, or are such flows rather rents and hence profit-like income? Further, it is not clear what portion of income from self-employment should be treated as remuneration for work. And, it is not obvious which economic activities should or should not be included in an accounting of the total. We follow closely their methodology and work with a measure of the labour share that (i) focuses on private economic activity, (ii) is based on gross income flows, (iii) excludes real estate and the associated imputed rental income, (iv) applies the corporate payroll share to non-corporate income streams, and (v) excludes taxes on production and imports.

Figure 14.1 shows that at the aggregate level the labour share gained ground until about 1970 and then levelled off for the decade. Since the 1980s

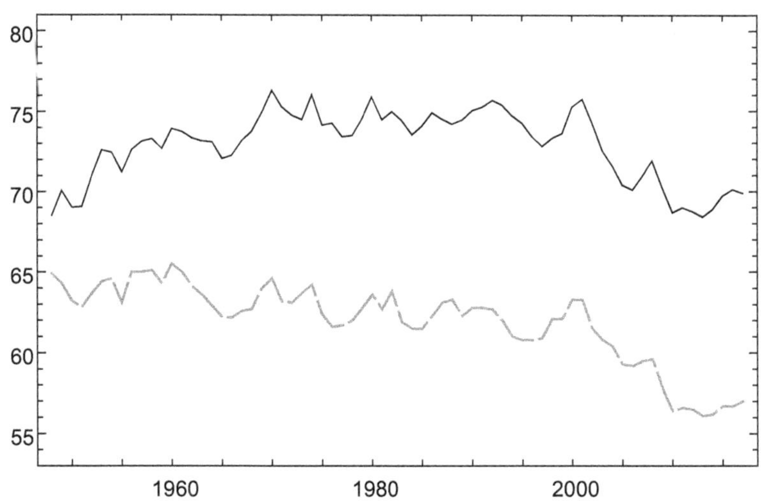

Figure 14.1 BLS headline measure of the labour share in the nonfarm business sector (grey solid) versus our measure (black solid)

Note: The BLS measure treats non-corporate labour income by assuming that hourly wages in the corporate sector and self-employment are the same. This amounts to adjusting the payroll share, which can be calculated unambiguously as the ratio of labour compensation to total income, by the ratio of self-employment hours to corporate labour hours.

it has followed a downward trend. This later period, known as the neoliberal era, has featured institutional changes and rapid deregulation that some claim has chipped away at the bargaining power of labour. So, what are the main sources of these changes in the aggregate labour share?

We take the aggregate labour share to be a Divisia index that captures changes in sectoral quantities of output and employment, as well as sectoral prices of goods and services and labour compensation. Index decomposition analysis dates back to the 1970s when it was used to assess the effect of changes in the structure of industrial production on energy demand. Decomposition techniques have since been refined and applied widely across disciplines including economics. Development and growth economics in particular have been concerned with the interaction of changing economic structure and economic growth ever since the mercantilists, and more formally since Leontief's seminal contribution on input–output analysis (Dietzenbacher and Los, 1998). Critically, the Divisia index decomposition has the desirable theoretical property of being a symmetric and additive indicator of relative change (Ang, 2004). Its discrete representation as a Törnqvist index is also a good approximation of the Fisher ideal index that lies behind data provided by the Bureau of Economic Analysis, our source of data for the exercise in this paper (Dumagan, 2002).

In the following paragraphs, we detail the decomposition technique for the labour share, which is generally defined as the ratio of nominal values of the wage bill and value added. If there are *i* sectors, the labour share can be written as:[1]

$$\psi = \frac{\sum_{i=1}^{n} \omega_i L_i}{\sum_{i=1}^{n} P_i X_i} \tag{1}$$

where ω_i, L_i, P_i and X_i are the nominal wage, employment, price level and quantity of output at the sectoral level. Multiplying equation (1) by *PL*/*PL*, we get:

$$\psi = \frac{\sum_{i=1}^{n} \omega_i L_i}{PL} \frac{PL}{\sum_{i=1}^{n} P_i X_i} = \omega / \varepsilon \tag{2}$$

where ω and ε are the average real wage and productivity. These can in turn be disaggregated:

$$\omega = \frac{\sum_{i=1}^{n} \omega_i L_i}{PL} = \sum_{i=1}^{n} \omega_i \lambda_i \tag{3}$$

$$\omega = \frac{\sum_{i=1}^{n} P_i X_i}{PL} = \sum_{i=1}^{n} \frac{P_i X_i}{PL_i} \frac{L_i}{L} = \sum_{i=1}^{n} p_i \omega_i \lambda_i \tag{4}$$

where ω_i, ε_i, λ_i and p_i indicate real compensation or the nominal wage deflated by the general price level P, labour productivity, employment share and terms of trade at the sectoral level. Using equations (3) and (4), the aggregate labour share can be written as:

$$\psi = \frac{\sum_{i=1}^{n} \omega_i \lambda_i}{\sum_{i=1}^{n} p_i \varepsilon_i \lambda_i} \tag{5}$$

The overall labour share can now be decomposed into several contributing factors. Changes in the sectoral real wage and labour productivity amount to shift effects; changes in the structure of the economy as measured by the employment shares are perceived as structural or share effects while changes in the terms of trade are market structure effects.

Assuming that all variables are continuous, differentiating equation (5) with respect to time, t, and dividing both sides by ψ yields:

$$d\ln(\psi)/dt = \Sigma\varphi_i[d\ln(\omega_i)/dt + d\ln(\lambda_i)/dt] - \Sigma\theta_i[d\ln(p_i)/dt + d\ln(\varepsilon_i)/dt + d\ln(\lambda_i)/dt] \tag{6}$$

The weights φ_i and θ_i are the nominal share of sector's i wage compensation in total wage compensation and the sector's i share in total value added.[2] Integrating equation (6) over the interval $[t - n,t]$ gives the Divisia decompositions of the growth rate of the economy-wide labour share:

$$\begin{aligned} \ln\frac{\psi_t}{\psi_{t-n}} = & \int_{t-n}^{t} \sum \phi_i \left[d\ln(\omega_i)/dt\right] + \int_{t-n}^{t} \sum \phi_i \left[d\ln(\lambda_i)/dt\right] \\ & - \int_{t-n}^{t} \sum \theta_i \left[d\ln(p_i)/dt\right] - \int_{t-n}^{t} \sum \theta_i \left[d\ln(\varepsilon_i)/dt\right] \\ & - \int_{t-n}^{t} \sum \theta_i \left[d\ln(\lambda_i)/dt\right] \end{aligned} \tag{7}$$

Applying the exponential to equation (7), we get:

$$D_T = D_\omega D_\lambda D_p^{-1} D_\varepsilon^{-1} \tag{8}$$

where the terms represent contributions from real compensation ω, employment structure λ, relative prices p and labour productivity ε to the total change D_T, respectively:

$$D_\omega = \exp\left[\int_{t-n}^{t} \sum \phi_i \left[d\ln(\omega_i)/dt\right]\right] \tag{9}$$

$$D_\lambda = \exp\left[\int_{t-n}^{t} \sum (\phi_i - \theta_i)\left[d\ln(\lambda_i)/dt\right]\right] \tag{10}$$

$$D_p = \exp\left[\int_{t-n}^{t} \sum \theta_i \left[d\ln(p_i)/dt\right]\right] \tag{11}$$

$$D_\varepsilon = \exp\left[\int_{t-n}^{t} \sum \theta_i \left[d\ln(\varepsilon_i)/dt\right]\right] \tag{12}$$

To match the discrete format of the data, we can write the components of the decomposition in discrete terms:

$$D_\omega = \exp\left[\sum \left(\phi_{i,t} + \phi_{i,t-n}\right)/2\ln\left(\omega_{i,t}/\omega_{i,t-n}\right)\right] \tag{13}$$

$$D_\lambda = \exp\left[\sum \left[\left(\phi_{i,t} + \phi_{i,t-n}\right)/2\ln - \left(\theta_{i,t} + \theta_{i,t-n}\right)/2\right]\ln\left(\lambda_{i,t}/\lambda_{i,t-n}\right)\right] \tag{14}$$

$$D_p = \exp\left[\sum \left(\theta_{i,t} + \theta_{i,t-n}\right)/2\ln\left(p_{i,t}/p_{i,t-n}\right)\right] \tag{15}$$

$$D_\varepsilon = \exp\left[\sum \left(\theta_{i,t} + \theta_{i,t-n}\right)/2\ln\left(\varepsilon_{i,t}/\varepsilon_{i,t-n}\right)\right] \tag{16}$$

The sectoral components of real wage and labour productivity have the same effect on the aggregate labour share as the aggregate real wage and aggregate labour productivity in equation (2). A positive change in the real wage in sector i raises the labour share, while a positive change in the sector's labour productivity lowers the labour share. The real wage component is weighted by the sector's share in the wage bill, while labour productivity has the sector's share in value added as the weight.

The interpretation of the structural component – equation (14) – is more nuanced. If a sector's share of employment declines, $ln(\lambda_i)$ is negative. However, if the sector's labour share is below the aggregate labour share, the weight is negative, since $\varphi_i - \theta_i = \psi_i/\psi - 1$. It follows that the aggregate labour share increases when employment shares decline for sectors with lower-than-average labour shares. This apparent improvement in the labour share is not necessarily a good thing if the sector that sheds labour (in either relative or absolute terms) is a sector with higher-than-average real wage and labour productivity. In this case the change in the structure of the economy takes place towards sectors with higher labour share yet a lower productivity and therefore a lower real wage in absolute terms. We will return to these issues later, in the discussion of results.

The last component of the decomposition is the change in the terms of trade captured by equation (15). A positive value means that the sector's price level grew faster than the general price level and, as a result, the sector contributed negatively to the aggregate labour share. Intuitively, sectors with rapidly rising price levels contribute more in relative terms to a rise in the general price level and therefore to a lower real wage. As an example, there would be no effect of individual sectoral terms of trade on the wage if price levels in all sectors grew at the same rate. This would also imply that the general price level P grows at the uniform sectoral rate. At the aggregate level, changes in the sectoral terms of trade reflect changes in the structure of the economy. As shown by Diewert (2010), the contribution from the relative price component exceeds unity, and thus reduces the aggregate labour share, if sectors with relatively high labour productivity also have fast-growing prices relative to the rest of the economy. The following section provides detailed results of this method, applied to the sectoral labour share for the US private sector.

Results

Consider Figure 14.2, which reports details on annual contributions to the annual change in the aggregate labour share from manufacturing (MAN) and education and health services (EHS). These are highlighted here in order to emphasise the central role that structural changes away from manufacturing and towards services activities play in the decline of the aggregate labour share. Manufacturing features strong cyclicality, though the variance of its contribution appears to have decreased with deindustrialization. Panel (c) of Figure 14.2 shows a strong downward trend of the contribution of manufacturing's real compensation component across the entire postwar period, driven both by the sustained fall in the sector's employment share and the decline in real wage growth. Further, panel (e) documents the on-average *positive* effects of both relative price and employment structure changes in manufacturing on the labour share. The terms of trade have moved against manufacturing as its relative price of output has fallen dramatically. Although barely visible on this scale, the contribution of the employment component is on average negative (and significant) prior to 1979, and on average positive, and larger (and significant) after 1979: the collapse of the labour share in manufacturing during the latter era – clearly taking off with the Great Moderation, and clearly preceding the "China shock" of the early 2000s – implies that continued deindustrialization acts as a buffer on the aggregate decline in the labour share, as labour moves out of (into) a sector with a lower (higher) labour share.

Similarly, the sustained rise of the employment share of EHS, from about 3 percent in 1948 to more than 15 percent after the Great Recession, buffers the overall decline in the labour share – since the latter averages 93% (!) during the neoliberal era. Recall the discussion of the structural component in the previous section: the contribution of the employment component to the aggregate labour share is positive if the sectoral labour share is larger than the aggregate *and* the employment share is rising, or if the sectoral labour share is smaller than the aggregate *and* the employment share is falling. The latter is true for manufacturing, the former for EHS. The contribution from the relative price component, in turn, is strongly negative. The well-known and sustained increases in the cost of healthcare provision and tuition at colleges and universities factor in here, and we will return to it in the next

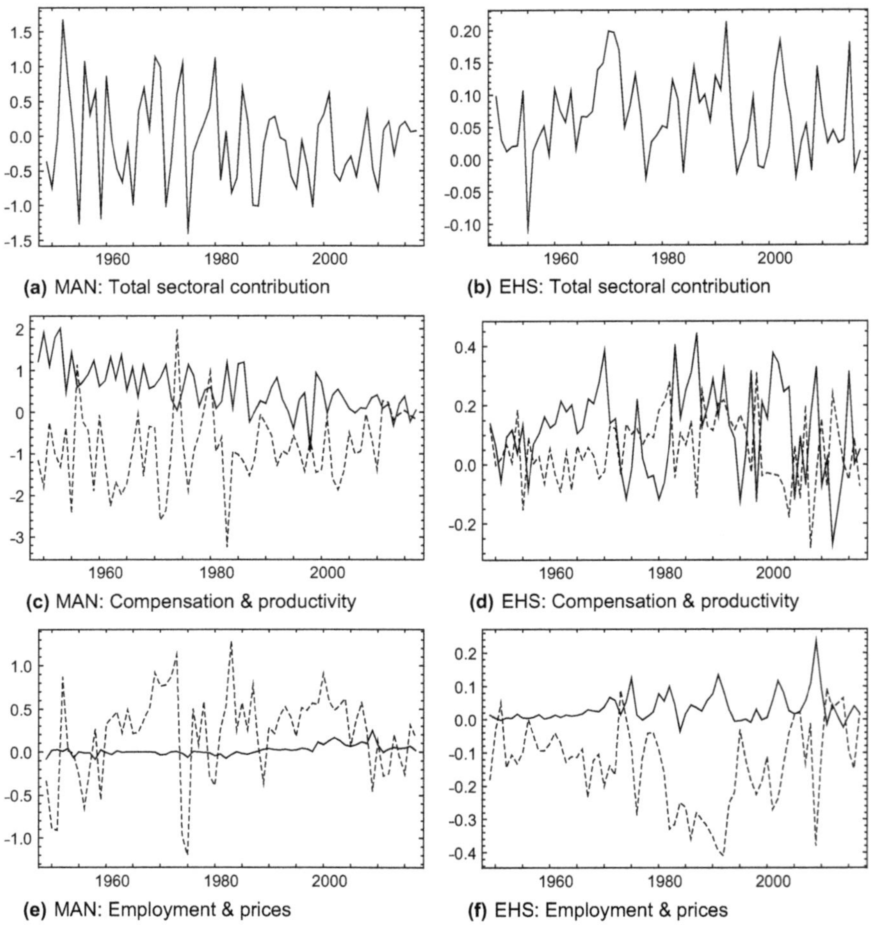

Figure 14.2 Sectoral component contributions in manufacturing (MAN) and education and health services (EHS)

Note: The figure provides detailed results of the Divisia index decomposition for two selected sectors. The top panels show total sectoral contributions, middle panels contributions of real compensation (solid) and labour productivity (dashed), and bottom panels contributions of employment structure (solid) and relative prices (dashed). The sum across the four sectoral component contributions equals the total contribution in the top panels.

section in a discussion of Baumol's disease. Though the sectoral contribution of EHS appears small, it is one of only two sectors' total contribution that is statistically significantly different from zero. The second aggregates professional and business services (PBS).

Let us now look at the two periods in greater detail. We define the golden age as the period from 1948 to 1979, and the neoliberal era as the period from 1979 to 2017.[3] Figure 14.3 summarises key results on the underlying

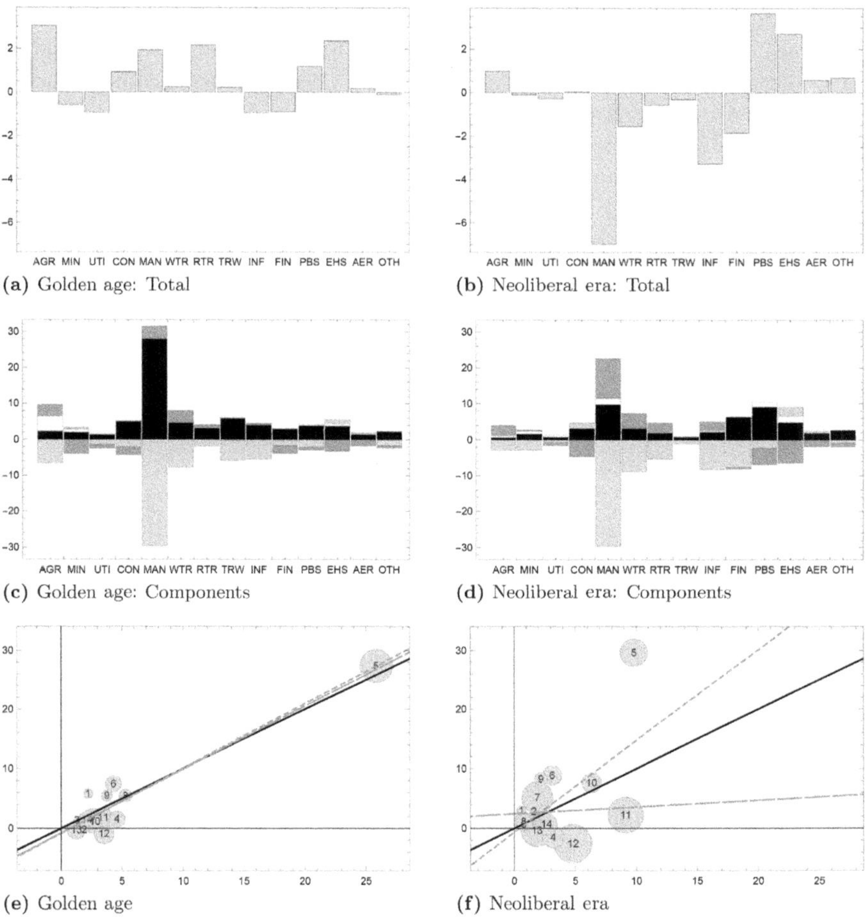

Figure 14.3 Sectoral contributions across "golden age" and "neoliberal era"

Note: The top two panels show total sectoral contributions, and the middle two panels sectoral component contributions: real compensation is black; employment structure white; labour productivity light grey and relative prices dark grey. The bottom row focuses on the sectoral contributions of real compensation (horizontal axis) vs. labour productivity (vertical axis). Bubble sizes represent employment share at the end of the respective period. The solid line has a slope of 1, the dashed line is an OLS regression and the long-dashed line an OLS regression *excluding manufacturing* (5).

patterns of structural change. In a nutshell, the labour share rose during the golden age due to matching real wage and productivity gains across sectors, and it fell during the neoliberal era due to real wage gains falling short, especially in manufacturing. The top row reports total sectoral contributions, and the middle row sectoral component contributions – so that the sum across the four components in each sectoral bar in the middle panel is equal to the bar height in the top panel. The golden age exhibits a sense of balance. While some sectors contribute negatively, others contribute positively. Across sectors, contributions from the real compensation component are roughly proportional to that of productivity. In sharp contrast, the neoliberal era is marked by large *negative* contributions from MAN, WTR, INF and FIN, and large *positive* contributions from PBS and EHS. The middle panel shows that across sectors, contributions from labour productivity components exceed that of real compensation. This gap is especially dramatic in MAN, WTR, RTR and INF but in FIN as well.

The importance of the manufacturing sector for the overall change of the labour share cannot be overstated. The very large contribution from MAN to the aggregate labour productivity component in both periods – holding steady at 46 and 44 percent, respectively – is one side of this coin, and the difference in the sector's contribution to the aggregate real compensation component – falling from 40 to 20 percent – is the other. The bottom row of panels further focuses on these two critical components for all sectors. While sectoral differences are apparent during the golden age, with manufacturing as a strong outlier, the neoliberal era sees a dramatic increase in dispersion.

The impact of relative price changes on the labour share differs starkly between "stagnant" Baumolian service sectors and the rest of the economy. Panels (c) and (d) of Figure 14.3 show negative contributions from changes in relative prices in CON, PBS, AER, EHS and OTH; and positive contributions for RTR, INF, MAN and WTR in the positive quadrant above the line. Put simply, stagnant service sectors experienced sustained relative price increases in both periods, and an acceleration of these trends in the neoliberal era. In contrast, manufacturing and some services, often considered susceptible to productivity increases through the use of information technology, experienced sustained relative price decreases in both periods, and an acceleration thereof in the more recent period. It is of course no surprise that weak productivity performance and relative price increases are correlated, and vice versa. Lastly, consider the impact of the change in the employment structure. Data shown here complements the earlier discussion: manufacturing is the only sector whose employment component contribution to the labour share change switches from negative during the golden age to positive during the neoliberal era. Again, stagnant service sectors stand out, with high, positive and (in the case of PBS, AER and EHS) increasing contributions from the structural shifts in employment.

In summary, it is widely recognised that the overall change in the labour share is driven by within-sector changes, predominantly payrolls. The findings here suggest, however, that the nature of structural change is indeed quite strongly related to this overall change. At the centre of it is a sustained decline of employment and a widening compensation–productivity gap in "dynamic" sectors on the one hand, and a sustained rise of employment without a compensation–productivity gap in "stagnant" sectors. In the following section, we discuss these results in the context of the seminal theories of Baumol and Lewis.

Discussion

Various explanations for the decline in the labour share have been put forth in the recent literature. Karabarbounis and Neiman (2014) and Piketty (2014), assign changes in factor income shares to a non-unitary elasticity of substitution between labour and capital, and capital intensity changes. Their neoclassical model maintains perfect competition in product and factor markets, and rising capital intensity to either capital-augmenting technological change or a decline in the price of new capital goods.[4] Elsby et al. (2013) conduct a similar analysis of sectoral sources of the decline in aggregate labour share and confirm the discrepancy between compensation and productivity growth for manufacturing, trade and transportation. They also evaluate the predictions of the neoclassical model for the US economy and conclude evidence in its favour is rather weak. A shift to capital-intensive techniques of production is not the main cause behind the decline in the labour share, and neither is the decline in unionization of workers. Instead, these authors suggest that sectors with the largest import exposure have faced the biggest decline in the payroll share. Using data on commuting zones, Autor et al. (2013) reach a similar conclusion: trade-exposed labour markets have been affected negatively both in terms of employment and compensation. These findings appear to hold for other countries. Rada and Kiefer (2016) show similar results on the basis of panel data analysis for thirteen OECD countries. Unlike Elsby et al. (2013), these authors also find that union density remains a fairly robust correlate of the labour share even when including an index of globalization.

Structural change remains a sideshow within this growing literature. This is in part due to the fact that the decomposition exercises do not identify structural change as a main source of change in the labour share. In other words, the labour share has not declined because workers moved to sectors with relatively lower labour shares. Rather, intra-industry dynamics dominate. Yet, a key observation is that structural change has indeed been important: dynamic sectors tend to shed labour, and stagnant sectors tend to absorb labour. (See the top row of panels in Figure 14.4.) The negative correlation between change in employment share and labour productivity growth persists throughout the entire period, with the qualification that the golden age saw five progressive sectors that still absorbed labour, compared to only one – PBS – during the neoliberal era. A different picture emerges for the two periods when comparing the change in employment share and the sectors' relative labour productivity, see the bottom row of diagrams in Figure 14.4: during the golden age, labour moved to sectors with higher-than-average productivity *levels*, while the reverse has happened in the neoliberal era. The question is if this dynamic matters indeed for the evolution of the functional

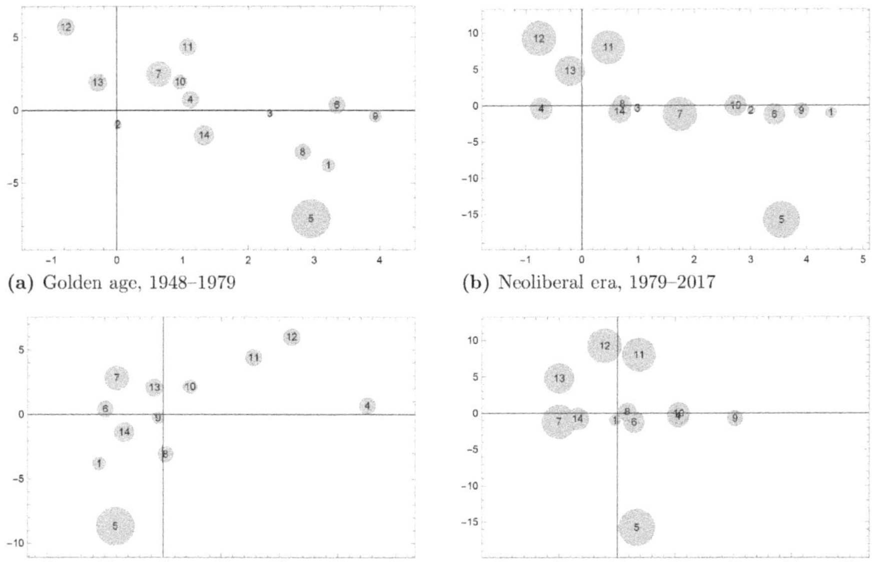

(a) Golden age, 1948–1979
(b) Neoliberal era, 1979–2017
(c) Golden age, 1948–1979
(d) Neoliberal era, 1979–2017

Figure 14.4 Structural change

Note: The figure illustrates patterns of structural change in the US post-war period. Panels (a) and (b) depict the average annual growth of labour productivity (horizontal axis) vs. the change in the sectoral employment share in percentage points. Panels (c) and (d) show average relative labour productivity on the horizontal axis, against the change in the sectoral employment share in percentage points.

distribution of income, through channels not readily observed in the statistics obtained from the decomposition. It certainly has an effect on the growth of the economy if only through the use of workers in less productive activities.

Furthermore, terms of trade clearly matter: stagnant service sectors such as EHS, AER and OTH have seen a rise in relative prices, while manufacturing, information and trade sectors have seen a decline in relative prices. Are we, therefore, simply experiencing Baumol's disease? To evaluate this question, the first task is to briefly review the cost disease hypothesis as put forth by Baumol (1967). First, assume that activities can be meaningfully categorized as either progressive (p) or stagnant (s), and that all costs aside of wages can be ignored. More importantly, assume further that real (consumption) wages across sectors equilibrate: in the progressive sector, nominal wages grow at the rate of productivity growth and prices remain constant; whereas in the stagnant sector, nominal wages grow at the same rate, while labour productivity remains unchanged. These changes in nominal unit costs are passed on to prices. If, in addition, demand for the stagnant sector's output is sufficiently price inelastic and income elastic; *and as a result thereof or due to government intervention the output shares of the sectors remain constant*, all labour will have to be transferred to the stagnant sector. As a consequence, the growth rate of the economy will fall to zero and relative (nominal unit labour) costs of the stagnant sector will rise without limit.

As Baumol points out, the cost disease does not require that wages increase with productivity. Two cases are possible. The one outlined earlier sees wages increasing with productivity in progressive sectors, and prices and wages increasing at that rate in stagnant sectors. The second possibility is that nominal wages do *not* increase, but instead progressive sector prices decline in line with productivity. In either case, the aggregate *real* consumption wage increases with aggregate productivity and there are no distributive effects. Put simply, the critical implication of Baumol's mechanism is that the labour share is constant, while the economy reaches stagnation.[5]

An alternative narrative builds on Lewis (1954), Kalecki (1976) and Kaldor (1978). Lewis's dual economy, as shortly described in the introduction, is characterised by the coexistence of modern and subsistence economic activities. In the Lewis model, marginal labour productivity in the latter is zero, so that transfer of labour to urban, modern employment does not change subsistence agricultural output or costs. In turn, the real wage in terms of consumption goods of urban workers does not need to rise. Growth and accumulation are therefore facilitated by a steady supply of cheap labour and the corresponding super-profits. Only once the rural surplus labour is exhausted do costs and prices change, and urban real wages rise. At this turning point, the economy has developed in the sense that production is labour-constrained. Following Kaldor, structuralist versions of this story emphasize the role of demand. Specifically, demand for modern sector output needs to be sufficiently strong to lead to absorption of rural surplus labour, all the while the sector's productivity increases through the Kaldor–Verdoorn channel, and the economy's average productivity increases with that and the compositional shifts.

We will say more on the role of demand in the concluding section, but for now let us consider implications for growth and distribution in the context of the data discussed here. For the sake of clarity, we abstract from primary activities. Four dynamic sectors feature consistently high-labour-productivity growth contributions – MAN, WTR, INF and FIN; and four stagnant sectors feature consistently low (if positive) or even negative contributions – TRW, EHS, AER and OTH. (RTR and PBS are borderline cases.) All sectors of the first set feature falling employment and labour shares at least in the second period under analysis; all except OTH feature rising employment shares over the same period and either rising or stable labour shares.[6] These sectoral labour shares measure *product wages* relative to labour productivity: since nominal wages grow (roughly) at the same rates, the strong relative price increases in the stagnant sectors suggest slower real product wage growth there than in progressive sectors. Despite this, labour shares rose due to very anaemic labour productivity performance.

In summary, Baumol's disease is apparent, but with crucial qualifications à la Lewis. Clearly, employment shifts towards stagnant activities, and (as has been widely documented elsewhere) the rate of labour productivity growth has slowed. Clearly, there is upward pressure in relative prices in the stagnant sectors. At the same time, this cannot be due to the pressure of dynamic sector wages rising in line with productivity growth. Specifically, labour shedding coincides (after 1979) with the opening of a significant gap between the growth rates of real consumption wages and labour productivity in progressive sectors. Structural change towards stagnant sectors has thus led to a build-up of labour reserves in jobs with relatively low *levels* of nominal wages. Accordingly, and due to institutional changes during the last several decades, bargaining power of labour remaining in progressive sectors is critically weakened. Baumol, as quoted earlier in this chapter, thus appears half-right: "[*while*] organised labour is not slow to learn of increases in its productivity, it is [*now much less able*] to adjust its wage demands accordingly".

Final remarks – an extension à la Kaldor

In a Kaldorian version of the dual economy model, Bhaduri and Skarstein (2003) derive two results that are relevant for our discussion. First, they show that, contrary to Lewis (1954), rising terms of trade for agriculture stimulate industrial production as long as agriculture does not save its proceeds but rather uses them to purchase industrial goods. Applied to our topic, technical change in the progressive sector benefits its own growth if it causes a *decline* in its relative price. This rather unexpected outcome is possible if the progressive sector's output is determined by effective demand and not by costs considerations. Intuitively, a decline in the progressive sector's relative price also means an increase in the stagnant sector's real purchasing power and therefore a rise in the stagnant sector's demand for the progressive good.

The data discussed in this chapter does not fully reflect this outcome. Terms of trade of progressive sectors are, indeed, declining, but so are their shares of employment, especially in the second period of analysis. This suggests that effective demand falls short of driving production significantly above what is warranted by productivity growth, and hence demand for labour remains below population growth. The question is, why is demand for, say, manufacturing goods, insufficient? Here are some possible mechanisms that may act individually or concomitantly: weak income and especially weak real wage growth in the so-called stagnant sectors limits overall demand in absolute terms; a high relative consumption of stagnant sectors' products, i.e. essential and non-essential services, leaves little surplus from income, and especially from wage income in the stagnant sector, to be spent on other sectors' products; potential changes in the distribution of income have an effect on aggregate demand and therefore on growth in the progressive sector. Distributive changes are apparent especially in the context of an economy that undergoes deep structural changes, as evidenced in the previous sections. Following Bhaduri and Marglin (1990), a decline in the labour share is certain to hurt economic growth in an economy with a wage-led demand regime. A decline in the labour share can, further, depress labour productivity growth if it mutes labour-saving innovations that firms would otherwise engage in to minimize the labour share of production costs (Bhaduri, 2006).

The second relevant result in Bhaduri and Skarstein (2003) is that the industrial sector's growth rate is higher, and therefore its share in real value added should increase.[7] This result rests on a crucial assumption about the sectors' import elasticities for each other's product in a set-up where trade between the two sectors must balance. In line with Engel's Law, the agricultural sector's demand elasticity for industrial goods with respect to its own purchasing power is above unity and larger than the industrial sector's import elasticity for agricultural surplus. That is certainly a reasonable assumption in the context of an economy divided into agriculture and industry. But ours is a developed economy with services and industries as the two main sectors. The magnitude of demand elasticities is likely reversed. Hence, the trade multiplier between industries and services may well be less than one, and the conclusion is that in the absence of compensating movements in the terms of trade, the services sector must grow faster than industry, an unlikely occurrence. It must then be the case that the terms of trade follow a secular decline for the progressive sectors, something that we find, indeed, for the US economy.

Last, but not least, the findings of this chapter are relevant for understanding labour share dynamics in other developed and emerging economies that are experiencing similar changes in income distribution (IMF, 2017; Karabarbounis and Neiman, 2014). Aside of structural change implications discussed earlier, the downward trend in the labour share in developed economies appears to be associated with rising globalization and declining rates of unionization (Rada and Kiefer, 2016). Outsourcing and import exposure in developed economies are especially relevant, as capital-intensive activities are said to replace labour-intensive activities such as those in manufacturing (Elsby et al., 2013). Nevertheless, outsourcing of relatively more labour-intensive activities to developing countries has not led to a rise in their labour shares either. Elsby et al. (2013) contend along neoclassical lines of thought that this unexpected result has to do with the initial level of capital intensity in these countries, i.e. labour share declines even in emerging economies if outsourcing increases their capital intensity. A more structuralist and classical take would revert to an explanation that rests on the presence of the reserve army of labour. After all, the observed dynamics in the labour share and structural changes in economies across the world fit more with a Lewisian view of the world than with a neoclassical one.

In summary, future research should investigate the character of increasing dualism in the US and other economies around the world. Of specific interest are the connections from the observed type of structural change to growth (and its apparent secular decline) and the labour share of income (and its long downward trend). Critical theories of dualism and post-Keynesian approaches to growth and distribution, very much including those by Professor Bhaduri, provide rich and fertile ground.

Notes

1 The data set covers fourteen sectors: (1) AGR: Agriculture, forestry and fishing; (2) MIN: Mining; (3) UTI: Utilities; (4) CON: Construction; (5) MAN: Manufacturing; (6) WTR: Wholesale trade; (7) RTR: Retail trade; (8) TRW: Transportation and warehousing; (9) INF: Information; (10) FIN: Finance and insurance; (11) PBS: Professional and business services; (12) EHS: Education, health and social services; (13) AER: Arts, entertainment and recreation; (14) OTH Other services. A comprehensive discussion of these sectors and the necessary SIC–NAICS crosswalk and related matters is available upon request.
2 For the wage bill, the nominal and real labour shares are the same since both the numerator and the denominator are deflated with the same price index.
3 We choose 1979 as the cutoff because it coincides (roughly) with the onset of the "conservative revolution", which marks the turning point for several critical variables, from the manufacturing labour share to the wage–productivity gap for non-supervisory workers to the income share of the bottom 50 percent. It is furthermore a business cycle peak: November 1948 and January 1980 are the relevant NBER peak months, which we compare to the latest data available (2017). The aggregate labour share from our sectoral data set saw an increase of 8.8 percent during the golden age, and a decrease of –6.6 percent during the neoliberal era.
4 These scenarios can be augmented further by assuming labour heterogeneity and thus raising the possibility of skill-biased technological change, as well as capital–skill complementarities. None of these arguments have strong empirical support. Particularly problematic is the usually required assumption that the elasticity of substitution is larger than unity. There simply is no support for this idea; see Raval (2017) for a discussion.
5 Indeed, Baumol (1967, p. 417) asserts, likely influenced by the prevailing *zeitgeist*, that "[s]ince organized labour is not slow to learn of increases in its productivity it is likely to adjust its wage demands accordingly". Note that in the original example, and if costs equal prices, the labour share is equal to unity. If other input costs are considered, this would of course not be the case.
6 Graphs provided on demand.
7 Because of changing relative prices, the change in nominal value added shares remains ambiguous. In Baumol, nominal and real value added shares remain constant while the employment share increases for the stagnant sector.

References

Ang, B. (2004). Decomposition analysis for policymaking in energy: Which is the preferred method? *Energy Policy*, 32(9): 1131–1139.

Autor, D. H., Dorn, D., and Hanson, G. H. (2013). The China syndrome: Local labor market effects of import competition in the United States. *American Economic Review*, 103(6): 2121–2168.

Baumol, W. J. (1967). Macroeconomics of unbalanced growth: The anatomy of urban crisis. *The American Economic Review*, 57(3): 415–426.

Bhaduri, A. (2006). Endogenous economic growth: A new approach. *Cambridge Journal of Economics*, 30(1): 69–83.

Bhaduri, A. and Marglin, S. (1990). Unemployment and the real wage: The economic basis for contesting political ideologies. *Cambridge Journal of Economics*, 14(4): 375–393.

Bhaduri, A. and Skarstein, R. (2003). Effective demand and the terms of trade in a dual economy: A Kaldorian perspective. *Cambridge Journal of Economics*, 27(4): 583–595.

Dietzenbacher, E. and Los, B. (1998). Structural decomposition techniques: Sense and sensitivity. *Economic Systems Research*, 10(4): 307–324.

Diewert, W. E. (2010). On the Tang and Wang decomposition of labour productivity growth into sectoral effects. In W. Diewert, editor, *Price and productivity measurement*, Volume 6, Chapter 4, pages 67–76. Trafford Press.

Dumagan, J. C. (2002). Comparing the superlative Tornqvist and Fisher ideal indexes. *Economics Letters*, 76(2): 251–258.

Elsby, M. W. L., Hobijn, B. and Sahin, A. (2013). The decline of the US labor share. *Brookings Papers on Economic Activity*, 2: 1–63.

IMF (2017). *Understanding the downward trend in labor income shares*. Technical Report, IMF.

Kaldor, N. (1978). *Further essays on economic theory*. Holmes & Meier.

Kalecki, M. (1976). *Essays on developing economies*. Humanities Press.

Karabarbounis, L. and Neiman, B. (2014). The global decline of the labor share. *The Quarterly Journal of Economics*, 129(1): 61–103.

Lewis, W. (1954). Economic development with unlimited supplies of labor. *Manchester School of Economic and Social Studies*, 22: 139–191.

Mendieta-Munoz, I., Rada, C., and von Arnim, R. (2020). *The decline of the US labor share across sectors*. Review of Income and Wealth. forthcoming.

Piketty, T. (2014). *Capital in the twenty-first century*. Harvard University Press.

Rada, C. and Kiefer, D. (2016). Distribution-utilization interactions: A race-to-the-bottom among OECD countries. *Metroeconomica*, 67(2): 477–498.

Raval, D. (2017). *What's wrong with capital in the twenty first century's model?* Harvard University Press.

Storm, S. (2017). *The new normal: Demand, secular stagnation and the vanishing middleclass*. Working Paper 55, Institute for New Economic Thinking.

Taylor, L. and Omer, Ö. *(2018). Race to the bottom: Low productivity, market power, and lagging wages*. Working Paper, Institute for New Economic Thinking.

Temin, P. (2017). *The vanishing middle class: Prejudice and power in a dual economy*. MIT Press.

15 India's growth story

A model of 'riskless capitalism'?[1]

Rohit Azad and Prasenjit Bose

Background

Methodological choice

This work belongs in the tradition of demand-driven growth models. A few words are in order on the methodological choice made here. While growth under capitalism has been the subject matter of enquiry since Adam Smith, modern growth theory came into existence arguably through Harrod (1939). It was an attempt to analyse Keynes's argument on the functioning of a capitalist economy in a dynamic set-up. Harrod (1939) had argued that under capitalism, where accumulation is driven by expectations about the market, there will be instability in this process because the market gives the capitalists perverse signals. Moreover, while the decision to invest by capitalists is individual, their decisions have a collective effect *ex post* on the extent of market available to all. His article contained two knife-edges that the growth process under capitalism throws up – one between the actual and the warranted rate of growth and the other between the warranted and the natural rate of growth.

The first knife edge also happens to be the dividing line between two mutually exclusive traditions in modern growth theory: supply-driven (Solow-Swan, Cass-Koopmans, New Growth Theory) and demand-driven (Kaleckian, Marxian). While the former does not acknowledge the existence of the first knife edge, for the latter, it is central. So, the supply-driven growth models solve just the second knife edge (by endogenising the capital-output and savings ratios), to which Harrod himself did not pay much attention in his celebrated article (of the 20-odd pages, he devoted just the last four on it). A defining characteristic of the tradition of supply-driven growth models is the presence of a production function as opposed to an investment function. The reverse holds true for demand-driven growth models.

That the investment function is critical to analyse growth in a capitalist economy can be best appreciated by looking at Sen (1970). He brings out the limitations of the supply-driven growth models by showing that introducing the role of expectations in the investment behaviour of the capitalists in a model such as Solow (1956), instead of assuming unrealistically that all savings are necessarily invested, brings back Harrodian instability *despite* assuming a neoclassical production function with perfect substitutability between labour and capital. He goes on to show that such a flexibility makes the process of accumulation even more unstable than Harrod had initially proposed. Given that all the mainstream models of growth, including the more recent endogenous growth theory, assume that *ex ante* savings are invested, Sen's critique remains valid for this entire spectrum.

As opposed to this, the tradition of demand-driven growth models takes the first knife edge as a point of departure. Kalecki (1962) presented a critique of Harrod (1939) from a different perspective. He argued that while it is true that the warranted rate of growth is unstable (Kalecki called it 'ephemeral') in that the economy slides down or explodes in either direction, there is a *stable* zero rate of growth in the absence of an exogenous stimuli. In other words, the problems of accumulation under capitalism are such that the normal state of affairs would be what Marx called a case of simple reproduction. So for there to be a positive rate of accumulation, some form of exogenous stimuli (exogenous to the process of accumulation) is required. Kalecki believed that innovations play that role from within the capitalist sector, whereas the state could also play the role from outside a pure *laissez-faire* system.

We do not present an exhaustive survey of Kaleckian or Harrodian growth models here and instead refer to authoritative accounts of the heterodox traditions presented in an edited volume by Setterfield (2010). However, a special mention of Skott (2010) from this volume needs to be made here since it draws a comparison between Kaleckian and Harrodian models of growth. Skott (2010) presents a basic Harrodian model, with inputs from Steindl (1952), as follows. If g is the rate of growth of capital stock, u is capacity utilisation (actual output O as a proportion of the technologically given full capacity output O^*) and u_0 the desired capacity utilisation of the capitalists, Harrod's argument can be interpreted as the capitalists trying to increase or decrease the rate of growth of capital stock according to whether the actual capacity utilisation is greater or less than the desired one. More formally,

$$\dot{g} = \gamma_u (u - u_0); \; \gamma_u > 0 \tag{1}$$

This system produces a steady state at the desired rate of capacity utilisation, but this steady state is unstable just as Harrod had argued. Skott (2010) then introduces elements of reserve army of labour from the Marxian tradition and income distribution from the Cambridge tradition as possible ways through which this unstable system can produce a stable equilibrium at the desired rate of capacity utilisation.

In contrast to this Harrodian tradition, which is dynamic in nature, Skott (2010) argues '[a]t a methodological level . . . the standard Kaleckian approach may have unfortunate consequences since it plays down the need to "think dynamically"' (p. 126). To substantiate this claim, he uses the versions that were presented in seminal contributions by Rowthorn (1982), Dutt (1984) and Taylor (1985) in the Kaleckian framework, where, instead of a change in the rate of growth of capital, its *level* is made a function of capacity utilisation (and/or the rate of profit),[2]

$$g = \gamma_0 + \gamma_u (u - u_0); \ \gamma_0, \gamma_u > 0 \tag{2}$$

We believe, however, that this is not the only way in which Kalecki's own work can be interpreted. In fact, Kalecki's (1962) response to Harrod's argument was presented in a *dynamic* set-up. So, much like Harrod (1939), it was the change in and *not* the level of the rate of growth which Kalecki (1962) had discussed. Specifically, Kalecki (1962) addressed the issue of whether the Harrodian instability in a capitalist system is unbounded. The concept of a ceiling provided by an upper bound to profit inflation was discussed extensively in later responses to this question but a discussion on the floor was not given as much emphasis, which was the focus of Kalecki's (1962) paper.

Kalecki argued that a precipitous fall from the Harrodian rate of growth does not make the system remain permanently unstable with a free fall in the rate of growth even below the zero rate of growth. On the contrary, the lower bound of a zero rate of growth is where the economy gravitates towards when it falls on the lower side of the Harrodian knife edge.

Patnaik (1997) presents such a version of Kalecki (1962), which produces *both* the rates of growth Kalecki was alluding to in a single function, which compares with the Harrodian function used earlier by Skott (2010), in the following form:

$$\dot{g} = \gamma_u (u - u_0) g \tag{3}$$

It is easy to see that such an investment function produces two rates of growth, one associated with a stable zero rate of growth and another, the unstable Harrodian warranted rate, with the desired rate of capacity utilisation. A diagrammatic representation of a discrete time version of this function produces the same shape of the investment function that Kalecki (1962) had presented.[3]

Addition of an exogenous component to this investment function, for, e.g., innovations, can make the comparison of this version of Kalecki (1962) with the ones used later in the Kaleckian tradition better,

$$\dot{g} = \gamma_0 + \gamma_u (u - u_0) g \tag{4}$$

This system again produces two rates of growth, but now the lower rate is positive instead of zero, just as found in Rowthorn (1982), Dutt (1984) and Taylor (1985). Seen in the light of the preceding discussion, the later representations of Kalecki can be seen as focusing *exclusively* on the lower rate of growth.

In this chapter, we improvise on this dynamic version of the investment function of Kalecki (1962) and Patnaik (1997) by bringing in interest rate and debt-related issues, some of which were also raised by Steindl (1952) and Minsky (1975). But before presenting our own argument, we analyse next how some of these issues have been dealt within the heterodox framework, beginning with the case of interest rates followed by the corporate debt and cursorily household debt.

Role of debt in heterodox models

Role of debt in growth models has been actively studied in the heterodox models since the days of Minsky's financial fragility hypothesis. While most of the initial work focused on corporate debt, the focus shifted towards household debt as a result of the economic experience of high consumption despite rising inequality since the 1980s, which posed a challenge to the stagnationist argument within the Kaleckian tradition (see Palley, 1994; Dutt, 2006; Azad, 2012; Hein, 2012). Since the focus of the present paper is on corporate debt, we leave the discussion on household debt out of this chapter.

It's easier to discuss the existing literature on the role of corporate debt and interest rates if we have a common structure to follow, which can be altered to discuss different ways in which this issue has been dealt with. What we present below is a thematic representation of existing literature and not an exhaustive one. There are broadly three endogenous variables around which most of the discussions have taken place: the growth rate g, debt-capital ratio δ and the savings ratio s, with the interest rate playing the role exogenously, through the intervention of the central bank. So, while the money/credit supply is endogenous, interest rate (r) is exogenous. This is in keeping with the Kaldorian tradition of endogenous money.

The dynamic (or even static without the dots over the variables) set-up, therefore, can be thought of along the following lines,

$$\begin{aligned} \dot{g} &= f(g, s, \delta; r) \\ \dot{s} &= h(g, s, \delta; r) \\ \dot{\delta} &= e(g, s, \delta; r) \end{aligned} \tag{5}$$

Interest rate and growth

Those dealing primarily with the relationship between the interest rates and the rate of accumulation focus on equations (5) and (6). We draw from Lavoie (1995) for this discussion since it presents a neat account, albeit in a static framework, of the role that the interest rates play across different traditions within the heterodox framework.

Lavoie compares Kaleckian, Cambridge, neo-Ricardian, post-classical and Minsky-Steindl models. The last of these is discussed under the corporate debt section. He considers their closed economy (without the government sector) versions, which is what we present here.

Kaleckian, Cambridge and Neo-Ricardian models: Savings propensity is taken as given in these models, which implies that the discussion is only on the first of the three equations presented earlier:

$$g = f(g;r) \text{ for stability: } \partial f/\partial g < 1$$

These traditions predict a negative relation between the interest rates and the growth rate since a rise in the interest rate has a dampening effect on the investment demand without any compensating effect on consumption demand (*s* is exogenously given).

The differences across these three traditions arise only in terms of which component of the profit rate, i.e. profit margin and/or capacity utilisation, makes the said adjustment in the growth rate possible. The relationship between the growth and profit rates (π) is straightforward in the form of the usual Kaleckian multiplier. And the rate of profit is given by the product of the profit share, profits as a share of output (h),[4] capacity utilisation and technologically given output capital ratio (β):

$$g = s\pi \equiv s(h \cdot u \cdot \beta)$$

In the Kaleckian tradition, the fall in the profit rate is entirely passed on to capacity utilisation (demand adjustment), whereas in the Cambridge tradition, it's entirely on the profit margin (competitive struggle). In the neo-Ricardian case, a rise in the interest rates increases the profit share as a result of the class struggle between the rentiers and the entrepreneurs. This creates a double pressure on capacity utilisation because it has to accommodate both a fall in the rate of profit (fall in investment demand) as well as rise in the profit share (fall in consumption demand).

Post-classical models: In the post-classical models, savings propensity is endogenised, so the first two of the three equations system are taken into consideration:

$$g = f(g, s; r)$$
$$s = h(g, s; r)$$

Interest rates enter not only the investment demand but also consumption since interest payments are also incomes for the rentiers, a part of which is consumed unlike retained earnings. There are, therefore, counteracting tendencies on the rate of profit, so it depends on the relative strength of the two that determines if the rate of profit rises or falls with the interest rate. However, the interest rate has an unambiguous negative impact on the growth rate, since investment is a function of the difference between the rate of profit and the interest rate and the former always increases by a lesser magnitude than the latter.

The Steindl-Minsky tradition: corporate debt and growth

This tradition of models is interested not only in the relationship between unit cost of loans (interest rate) and growth but also in the magnitude of the loan (corporate or household). So, an additional layer of argument gets added to the ones discussed so far. For this section, we start with the model presented in Lavoie (1995) before adding different ways in which debt is dealt with in this literature.

Presented here are in certain cases altered versions of the original to make the comparison across these papers easier and to locate the difference in our approach from the existing ones. So, in certain cases, the static versions have been made dynamic by making the implicit mechanism of change explicit. In other cases, the variable of interest has been suitably altered to follow the same variables across these models.

One of the earliest versions of formalising the role of credit in heterodox models was by Jarsulic (1989). Although his system is one between the rate of growth and interest rate, it can be interpreted as one between growth rate and debt-capital ratio (since the interest rate movements arise out of the process of credit creation) to suit our purpose. While the steady state is unstable, the accelerator effects (f_g) being greater than the negative effect of debt-capital (e_δ) creates a limit cycle, thereby producing a business cycle with interactive elements from the real and the financial sector. What sits with unease in this model, however, is the positive relationship between the interest rate and growth at lower rates of growth in the investment function, which becomes negative as growth rate rises, whereas logically it should be the exact opposite. This result arises from the assumption that the accelerator declines with the growth rate, which is contrary to the knife edge of investment decision as Harrod (1939) had shown, which has already been discussed in detail. Our investment function, on the other hand, has a more realistic representation, which at low rates of growth falls with rising debt-capital ratio (or with an exogenous rise in interest rates) and rises with it once a critical growth rate has been achieved.

While Lavoie (1995) discusses the dynamic movement only in the debt-capital ratio, the growth function can be made dynamic as well. His system has one steady state, the stability of which depends on whether investment rises with debt-capital ratio, which requires the negative effect of leverage on investment to be compensated by the rise in consumption as a result of redistribution of income from the firms in favour of the rentiers. (Dutt [1995] has a restricted version of a similar model.) Unlike the previous versions discussed in Lavoie (1995), interest rates affect investment *differently* from the rate of profit. So, it's possible that the direct dampening effect of interest rate on investment (which might be minor) is more than compensated for by the indirect positive effect (through a rise in consumption of the rentiers) on the profit rate. The usual negative relationship will hold if the opposite holds true. This is an interesting result, which we will reflect upon when we present our own model. The debt function is derived from the savings behaviour of the rentiers,[5] so there is no independent functional form of borrowing, and the role of the firms in determining the debt levels is passive in nature.

More recent attempts to study the effect of corporate debt and growth rate are Hein (2007) and Charles (2008a, 2008b).

Hein (2007) improvises on Lavoie (1995) by introducing two basic changes to the above system: investment $\dot{g}$ is not just a function of capacity utilisation, captured earlier in g, but also a function of the profit share (along the same lines as the celebrated model of Bhaduri and Marglin [1990]); profit margin is a non-negative function of the interest rate. In such a situation, a rise in the interest rate has two opposite effects on the investment function: lower investment due to rising leverage, while there is higher investment due to a higher profit share resulting from higher interest rate.

Charles (2008a, 2008b) uses dynamic functions which produce multiple equilibria, which come closest to our model of multiple equilibria. While Charles (2008a) focuses on the retention ratio and the debt capital ratio, Charles (2008b) focuses on the growth rate and some measure of the debt-capital ratio (he uses the macroeconomic inverse of the interest coverage ratio) to discuss the trajectory of a capitalist economy. Since Charles (2008b) is closer to our model, we focus on that. His model generates a stable equilibrium with higher growth rate and low debt burden and a saddle point with a low rate of growth and high debt burden. The multiple equilibria generated in the system is because the debt function is quadratic in nature, which in turn is generated from the fact that the central bank is targeting a sustainable debt position. The central focus of the model is on the debt function, with the investment function playing a passive role with an inherent stabilising mechanism.

We believe that a stable investment function of the following variety used across these models robs the accumulation process of its sheen, which was so central to the argument Harrod (1939) and Kalecki (1962) made. A careful look at this generic investment function used across these different traditions will help explain it:

$$\begin{aligned} g^d &= \gamma_0 - \gamma_r r + \gamma_u u \\ \dot{g} &= \left(g^d - g\right) \end{aligned} \tag{6}$$

Such a dynamic investment function is actually not much of an improvement over the earlier static versions of the Kaleckian investment function (Rowthorn, 1982; Dutt, 1984; Taylor, 1985) because it is merely making the static versions dynamically stable by *assumption*. So, this dynamic version tells us that the capitalists make a *self-correcting* adjustment to the investment process, which seems to be at odds with the unstable investment process. In fact, Harrod (1939) had the adjustment mechanism in the exact opposite direction of the $\dot{g}$ function described earlier, whereby an exuberance of investment (actual being greater than desired/expected) makes the capitalists invest more and vice versa, thereby, creating the famous knife edge.

Our model differs from the existing literature in the following ways.

First, our model addresses some of the legitimate objections raised about the financial fragility hypothesis because of the mistaken conflation of micro and macro investment processes. Critics have argued that rising investment also leads to higher profits and, hence, shifts the internal finance frontier itself, thereby, putting a question mark on the very basis of the financial instability process that Minsky was describing (Lavoie and Seccareccia 2001). Lavoie and Seccareccia (2001) also present data on the counter-cyclical nature of corporate leverage to question the Minskyan argument of its procyclicality. We agree that there is indeed a macroeconomic link missing here, but Minsky can be interpreted slightly differently so that the argument of the financial fragility holds without a macroeconomic fallacy. If there is concentration of certain sectors/corporate players in overall credit, their failure can lead to a system-wide financial stability even though at the level of the system, the debt-capital ratio might be falling. We could call it the problem of concentrated credit-driven financial fragility. We believe that such a case exists in India in terms of a few sectors in terms of demand for credit and a subset of banks, i.e. public sector banks, in terms of their share in the overall supply of credit. This point has been elaborated in the discussion on the subsection on firms' behaviour.

Second, we provide an explicit politico-economic role that the capitalist state plays in *generating* financial fragility instead of assuming the latter to arise purely endogenously through the workings of the financial side of the system. The state does so by persuading the banks under its control (public sector banks) to lend to the corporate sector and, by being an implicit guarantor, pushes the corporate sector growth through bank debt. So, the financial fragility is generated within the public sector banks and *not* necessarily the entire banking system. We believe that this is an important component of the Indian growth story. In that sense, it presents an economic basis for Minsky's financial fragility hypothesis along with the differentiated impact the process has on the balance sheets of the public as opposed to private sector banks. So, Minsky's financial fragility hypothesis is not just valid for deregulated financial systems but to regulated financial systems (like India's) as well because the regulator itself indulges in the process.

Third, the centrality of instability in the accumulation process is not given up in our model. The investment function, therefore, is defined in a way that the element of instability is inbuilt in the system. Such an investment function also has other advantages. Unlike the above traditions, the investment function used here is such that it *simultaneously* produces the opposite effects of the interest rates/debt-capital ratio on the rate of growth instead of bringing in exogenous parametric conditions as required by Lavoie (1995), Hein (2007). This will become clear if we introduce the interest rate to equation (3), which gives us:

$$\dot{g} = \gamma_0 - \gamma_r r + \gamma_u (u - u_0) g \tag{7}$$

This dynamic function generates two rates of growth, much in the same way as Kalecki (1962), the lower rate (stagnationist and stable) is *negatively* related to the interest rate whereas the higher one (exhilarationist and unstable) is *positively* related to the interest rate. At higher rates of growth (beyond a critical threshold), fulfilment of expected profits induces exuberance in the minds of the capitalists to increase investment even if there is a rise in the cost of loans ($-\gamma_r r$).[6] This is quite true of boom conditions where investment is not deterred by a rise in the interest rates, whereas in the conditions of a slump, the usual negative relation holds. Our investment function helps us capture that. It is for this reason that we leave out the complexities of the consumption demand and make a simplifying assumption where all wages are consumed and all profits saved. The argument will not change fundamentally even if we introduce different savings propensities for rentiers and capitalists. Our model produces multiple equilibria, which incorporates both the possibility of stable and unstable states in the same function, thereby producing interesting dynamics of the system transitioning between the two rates over time. We believe such a formulation throws up interesting ways in which the growth-debt trajectory of a quasi-regulated newly liberalising economy can be seen.

Recent growth in the Indian economy

The fact that the growth performance of the Indian economy in the 1990s – the first post-reform decade – was by and large similar to the 1980s, has been widely noted and commented upon. Delong (2003) suggested that the structural break in India's growth had occurred in the mid-1980s and the rather limited measures of trade liberalisation of the 1980s had a stronger growth impact compared to the more sweeping policy changes brought in 1991. Chandrasekhar and Ghosh (2002) emphasised the role played by a widening fiscal deficit (centre and states combined) in providing stimulus to growth in the 1980s and highlighted the absence of any significant increase in the average rate of economic growth, investment and savings in the 1990s, compared to the earlier decade. Ahluwalia (2002), while admitting the absence of any acceleration in the growth rate, pointed to the remarkable external stability of the 1990s growth in contrast to the unsustainable external debt build-up of the 1980s and argued that gradualist reforms of the 1990s had laid the basis for a higher growth trajectory in future.

High growth experienced in the decade of the 2000s has renewed the debate on the impact of reforms on economic growth, with some proponents of reforms arguing that liberalisation of external trade and investment has resulted in economic growth taking off dramatically which in turn has led to significant declines in poverty (Bhagwati and Panagariya, 2013). Others, while lauding the impact of reforms on economic growth as a significant achievement, have pointed out the lopsided nature of the growth process, which has led to widely different speeds at which living standards have improved for the upper-income groups and the rest of the population, as well as the continuing lag in India's human development indicators, even in comparison to poorer developing countries (Drèze and Sen, 2013). These appraisals, while contending with each other on the socio-economic impact of growth, however, converge on attributing faster economic growth to market-oriented reforms.

This chapter takes a different view regarding India's integration with the global economy by focusing on the financial aspects of the growth process. We suggest, based on the empirical analysis of Azad et al. (2016), that while trade and financial opening may have triggered faster growth almost a decade after the initiation of reforms, a crucial role was played by the state in sustaining the first boom of the 2000s and prolonging the boom beyond the 2007–08 global economic crisis. A credit bubble was generated through the public sector banking system, complemented by external debt finance, particularly in the infrastructure sector.

Stylised facts

Following are certain stylised facts based on the empirical evidence presented in Azad et al. (2016), which the theoretical model attempts to explain.

1. **Two booms:** Post-2000, there have been two phases of high growth so far in the Indian economy. The first phase saw a boom between 2003–04 and 2007–08 (five years) and a bust in 2008–09, whereas the second was a short-lived boom for two years 2009–10 and 2010–11 followed by a decline. It is noteworthy that the second year of the second boom has registered the highest ever annual growth rate in post-independent India. We present two distinct stories for these two booms.
2. **Corporate investment:** Private corporate investment grew faster than public investment during the booms, with a sharp rise in the take-off year (2003–04) which, as a percentage of GDP, increased from 6.5% to 10.3% (see Table 15.1).
3. **Flow of bank credit:** Annual flow of credit (as a percentage of GDP) from the public sector banks (PSBs) saw a structural break in 2003–04 and reached high levels during both the boom periods, with a decline in between the two booms during 2008–09. Credit flow from the private sector banks did *not* follow this trend (see Figure 15.1). This had its reflections in their respective trajectories of share of stressed loans (see Figure 15.2).

Table 15.1 Domestic savings and investment (as % of GDP)

	Savings	*Investment*	*Investment*		
			Public sector	*Corporate sector*	*Household sector*
1980s	18.6	20.4	11.1	4.3	6.7
1990s	23.0	24.3	8.8	7.0	8.0
2000–01	23.7	24.3	7.1	4.9	11.4
2001–02	24.8	24.2	7.2	5.1	12.6
2002–03	25.9	24.8	6.4	5.7	12.3
2003–04	29.0	26.8	6.6	6.5	12.1
2004–05	32.4	32.8	7.4	10.3	13.4
2005–06	33.4	34.7	7.9	13.6	11.7
2006–07	34.6	35.7	8.3	14.5	11.9
2007–08	36.8	38.1	8.9	17.3	10.8
2008–09	32.0	34.3	9.4	11.3	13.5

Source: Calculated from RBI's Database on Indian Economy (CSO data).

Note: Base Year: 2004–05.

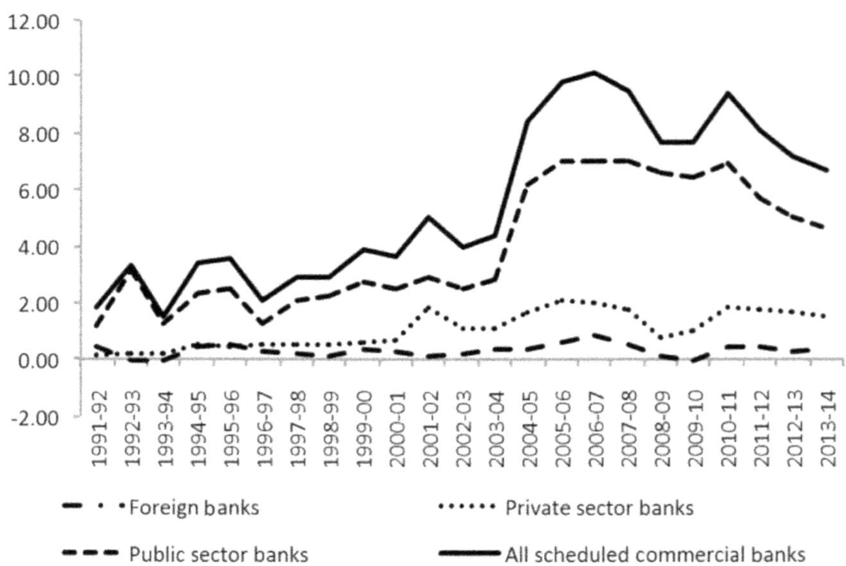

Figure 15.1 Groupwise annual credit flow of banks (% of GDP)

Source: Calculated from RBI, Basic Statistical Returns of Scheduled Commercial Banks in India.

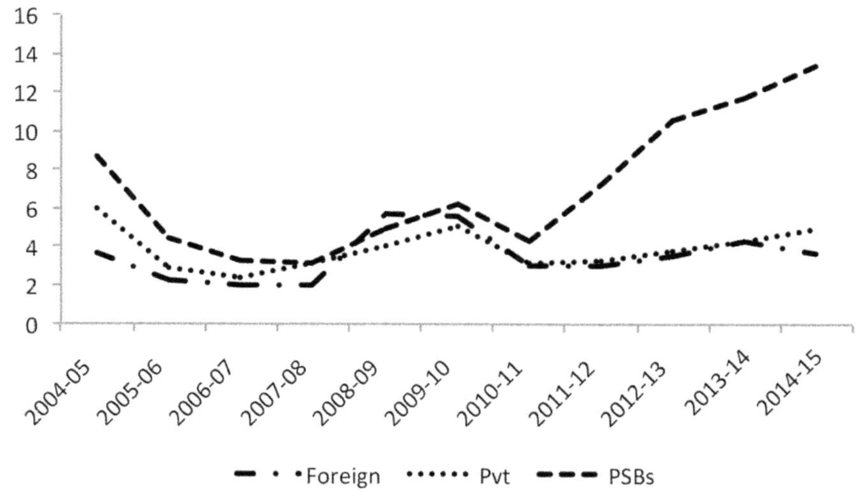

Figure 15.2 Share of stressed loans in gross advances of banks

Source: Calculated from RBI, Basic Statistical Returns of Scheduled Commercial Banks in India.

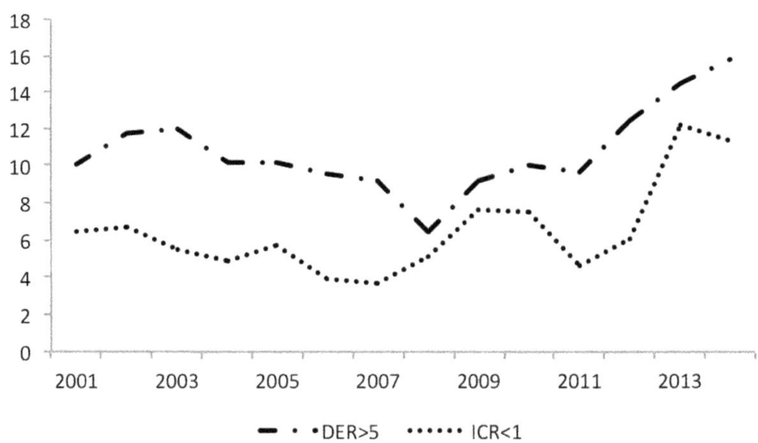

Figure 15.3 Share in total bank borrowings of firms with two financial characteristics

Source: Prowess Database, Authors' Calculations.

4. **Nature of bank credit:** There was a fundamental difference in the nature of bank credit between the two booms:

   a In the non-financial corporate sector, the share of high debt-equity ratio companies (DER > 5) in total debt fell during the first boom. Similarly, the share of bank borrowings by companies with interest coverage ratio (ICR) being less than 1 in total bank borrowings also fell during the first boom (see Figure 15.3).

b During the second boom, however, the share of DER > 5 companies' bank borrowings in total bank borrowings rose, as also the share of bank borrowings by companies with ICR < 1. This implies that by the time of the second boom, the banks were recklessly lending to already highly indebted companies (see Figure 15.3).

Since we find an opposite trend in financial characteristics of firms between the two booms, we explore a balanced sample of firms since the end of the second boom based on the Orbis data set. What we find is quite startling. As a result of the profligate lending during the second boom, in its aftermath, share of firms in total debt with the following four characteristics like negative profitability, ICR less than one, current ratio less than half and debt/equity ratio greater than five increased dramatically.

5 **Real interest rates:** One of the important developments for the first boom is that the real interest rates *fell* significantly from 12% in 2000–01 to 2.5% in 2008–09. This was also reflected in the fall of the prime lending rate of the SCBs. In contrast, for the second boom, the real rate of interest, short as well as long, *increased.*
6 **Fiscal policy:** The high fiscal deficits of the 1980s had fallen in the 1990s. Following the enactment of the Fiscal Responsibility and Budgetary Management (FRBM) legislation, fiscal deficit was reduced drastically in India during the period of the first boom. A 'pause' button was pushed on the FRBM following the global recession and the fiscal deficit expanded from 2008–09.
7 **Current account:** Prior to the first boom, there was a positive current account balance for three consecutive years starting from 2001–02 that turned into a deficit again since 2004–05. In contrast, the second boom happened despite a worsening current account deficit as a result of the global crisis. Import intensity of the Indian economy has been steadily rising in the high growth phase and continues to rise today.
8 **Gross External Financing Requirements (GEFR):** India's Gross External Financing Requirements (GEFR) – defined as the sum of the current account balance (negative) and debt servicing on external debt in that period and the short-term debt stock at the end of the previous period as a proportion of national income, which had peaked at around 7% in 1990 and 1991, the time when India experienced its first BoP crisis – fell through the 1990s, and with the current account balance turning positive between 2001 and 2004, it reached a low level around 2% in 2002 before the first boom. Prior to the second boom, in 2008, however, the GEFR/GNI had risen to 8%, a level higher than 1990–91.

A macrotheoretic model of growth

From these stylised facts, we develop a macrotheoretic model, which can be used as a framework to explain the growth trajectory of the Indian economy and analyse its fault lines.

Two constraints

Any economy functions under two constraints. With nominal commitments carried over from the past, there is an internal constraint that the rate of profit should at least be equal to the interest accrued on the debt taken in the past. At a microeconomic level, this is measured by the interest coverage ratio (ICR), which, when less than 1, means the firm does not have enough profits to even pay the interest accrued on past debt. The internal constraint of our model is the inequality that the ICR for the entire non-financial corporate sector should be greater than 1.

On the other hand, there is an external constraint set by the availability of foreign exchange. This is particularly relevant for developing economies like India with persistent current account deficits and negative net foreign assets positions. This constraint tightens when the import intensity grows with the growth rate. The external constraint in our model is the BoP condition, i.e. the GEFR should be equal to net capital inflows and change in foreign exchange reserves.

Let us look formally at these constraints, which can be seen as boundaries for the system to function well where neither the domestic financial sector comes under severe strain nor the economy is faced with a balance of payments crisis.

The internal constraint

- We make the classical assumption on savings that workers consume all their wages W while the capitalists save all their post-tax profits.[7] Taxes are levied only on profits P. GDP measured from the income side will be the sum of wages and profits, and from the expenditure side, it is the sum of consumption of workers, private corporate investment (I), government expenditure ($\bar{G}$) and net exports in domestic currency $\bar{X} - M$. This will give us a relationship between the growth rate g and the degree of capacity utilisation u, which is the ratio between actual O and technologically given output O^f.

  $$W + P = W + I + \bar{G} + \bar{X} - M$$

  $$(h + m)O = I + \bar{G} + \bar{X};\ \ h = \frac{P}{O}, M = mO$$

  Dividing by K,

  $$(h + m)\cdot\frac{O}{O^f}\cdot\frac{O^f}{K} = g + \xi + \bar{x} \tag{8}$$

  $$u = \frac{g + \xi + \bar{x}}{(h + m)\beta}$$

where,

$$g, \xi, \bar{x}, \beta = \frac{I}{K}, \frac{\bar{G}}{K}, \frac{\bar{X}}{K}, \frac{O^f}{K}$$

- The internal constraint requires corporate retained earning (profits P – tax T – dividends $[1 - \theta]$ as a proportion of post-tax P) to be more than the interest payment on accrued debt.
- Corporate sector can borrow a total of D (corporate debt) from domestic and international finance at i and i^f with shares μ and $1 - \mu$ respectively.

$$\theta(P-T) \geq i\mu D + i^f(1-\mu)D$$

$$g \geq \frac{(h+m)\left[i^f + (i - i^f)\mu\right]}{(h-t)\theta}\delta - \xi - \bar{x} \qquad (9)$$

where, $t = T/O$

$\delta = D/K$

- Upward sloping line with danger zone below it (see Figure 15.4). Corporate tax breaks, relaxation of ECB norms and appreciation of currency ease this constraint (shifts down or rotates clockwise).

The external constraint

- Being a developing country, it faces a foreign exchange constraint as well. The requirements arise, among other things, out of the current account needs as well as the international debt servicing payments accrued in the past.

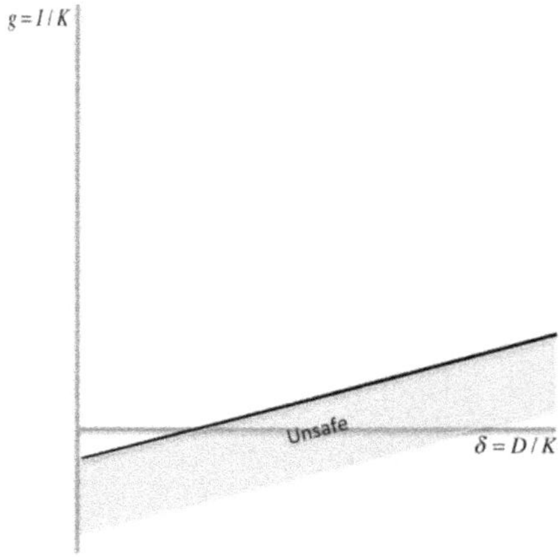

Figure 15.4 The internal constraint

- In the capital account, there are three kinds of net capital flows: F – debt, which is positively related to the difference between domestic interest rates i minus some 'country risk' ρ and international rate of interest i^f; foreign portfolio investment, FPI, which moves with the stock market and growth; and foreign direct investment, FDI, which is positively related to the difference between the rates of growth of the recipient nation and the nation of origin of finance. These, along with an autonomous component (α_0) determined by the push factors from the originating countries, result in:

$$f = \alpha_0 + \alpha_i\left(i - \rho - i^f\right) + \alpha_g\left(g - g^f\right); \qquad f = F / K; \alpha_0, \alpha_i, \alpha_g > 0$$

- External constraint can be represented as the total foreign exchange requirements from the current account (net imports) plus the interest payments on accrued foreign debt should be equal to net capital inflows and change in foreign exchange reserves. Formally, $\left(M - \bar{X}\right) + i^f\,(1 - \mu)D = F + \Delta R$ (change in reserves ΔR). Dividing this by the capital stock and substituting for f gives us:

$$i^f\,(1 - \mu)\delta = \alpha_0 + \alpha_i\left(i - \rho - i^f\right) + \alpha_g\left(g - g^f\right) + \Delta r + \bar{x} - mu\beta$$

$$i^f\,(1 - \mu)\delta = \bar{c} - \left(\frac{m}{h + m} - \alpha_g\right)g$$

$$\text{where } \bar{c} = \alpha_0 + \alpha_i\left(i - \rho - i^f\right) - \alpha_g g^f + \Delta r + \bar{x} - m\left(\frac{\xi + \bar{x}}{h + m}\right) \qquad (10)$$

$$\Delta r = \Delta R / K$$

- This is a negatively sloped line depicting the trade-off between growth and external account stability (see Figure 15.5) is ensured by the

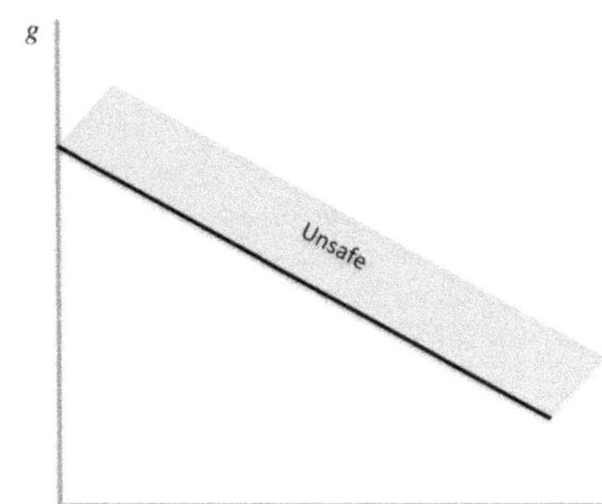

Figure 15.5 The external constraint

condition $\frac{m}{h+m} > \alpha_g$ i.e. imports rise faster than the FDI as the growth rate rises. The unsafe zone lies above this external constraint.

Behavioural functions

The model presented in this section is about investment decision-making of private firms aggregated at a macro level. There are two interdependent decisions to be made in this regard. First, how much of investment is to be undertaken? Second, how is this investment going to be financed?

For the first decision, firms have to take into account alternative forms of holding their wealth (Keynes, 1937).[8] These assets can broadly be classified into three categories: capital assets, claims over capital assets and money. For the existence of these assets, it is necessary that the net returns on all three are equal on the margin. This gives us a relationship between the expected rate of return on holding an asset, through expected profits net of risks, and claims over capital assets, through the net interest rate, which have to be equal to the liquidity premium that money commands. Since they have to be equal, the opportunity cost of directly holding a capital asset can be compared to the returns of any of the other two assets. For reasons of tractability, the first two forms are chosen for comparison. The return on holding capital assets enters the investment decision through the expectations of demand, and the return on holding a claim over an asset enters as an opportunity cost of not making the investment. This results in an investment function described later.

Having determined the size of the investment, for the second decision, firms need to make a choice between internal and external funds to finance it. Cost of the loans determines the share of investment to be financed externally.

Since the interest rate figures in this decision-making, we first present how it is determined by the lending authorities i.e. the banks.[9]

Banks' behaviour

Bank lending plays a central role in our model. Their role enters the picture through the cost of loans which is given by the sum of interest rates and lender's risk as in Kalecki (1937). Banks set a nominal interest rate i as a markup on the nominal interest rate fixed by the central bank $\bar{i}$, which is called the repo rate in the case of India. This markup represents the risk premium associated with a given debt instrument. Kalecki (1937) had argued that given the asymmetry of information about profitability between lenders and the borrowers, the lenders ask for a higher risk premium as the leverage (or debt-equity ratio) rises. Also, what matters for investment is not the nominal rate of interest but the real rate of interest, so we convert the relationship between the nominal into a real rate of interest by subtracting expected inflation from both sides,[10] which gives us the following.

$$r^d = \bar{r} + \sigma(\delta)$$

where, r = expected domestic real interest rate

$\bar{r}$ = repo rate minus expected inflation (11)

σ = risk premium

For simplicity, we assume the risk premium to be linear in debt-capital ratio. So, the risk premium consists of a constant component σ_0 representing the difference in the maturity of a particular debt instrument and treasury bonds and a variable component σ_b which increases with δ as Kalecki (1937) had argued. Accordingly, equation (11) can be written as,

$$r^d = \bar{r} + \sigma_0 + \sigma_b \delta \quad (12)$$

Both $\bar{r}$ and σ_b play a critical role in our story, the former through the central bank and the latter through the change in the risk premium demanded of the firms by the *public* sector banks. A fall in either or both will lead to a fall in the real cost of loans, which will affect investment positively as will be shown.

The reason for an emphasis on the word 'public' is because we argue that in the neoliberal period, the nature of intervention by the state changed in India from a *dirigiste* regime of direct demand management, i.e. through public investment (except in periods of economic crises) to one where it influenced the banks owned by it to facilitate corporate investment. The exact nature of this intervention, elaborated in the model below, can be briefly described as follows.

These state-owned banks were made to relax their risk function, which happened because there was an implicit guarantee on these loans provided by the state. In the process, risk-taking, the raison d'être of private investment, was passed on to the public sector banks. So, while the upside of high profits generated through successful investment projects were not shared with the lenders, the losses incurred in failed investments was passed on to the state to clean up. This is being witnessed in India today in the form of increasing corporate delinquencies and humongous write-offs of corporate NPAs by the public sector banks. This, in essence, is the process of 'riskless capitalism' the former Reserve Bank of India (RBI) governor was alluding to (Rajan, 2014):

> Faced with [an] asymmetry of power, banks are tempted to cave in and take the unfair deal the borrower offers. The banks debt becomes junior debt and the promoters equity becomes super equity. The promoter enjoys riskless capitalism even in these times of very slow growth, how many large promoters have lost their homes or have had to curb their lifestyles despite offering personal guarantees to lenders? . . .
>
> Who pays for this one way bet large promoters enjoy? Clearly, the hard working savers and taxpayers of this country! As just one measure,

the total write-offs of loans made by the commercial banks in the last five years is Rs. 1,61,018 crore, which is 1.27% of GDP.

Firms' behaviour

As noted earlier, firms make a choice between different forms of holding their wealth. We have presented the process which determines the return (interest rate) on holding an indirect claim over a capital asset. We now need to look at the expected return on directly holding a capital asset to be able to make a comparison between these alternative forms of holding wealth. The way the expected return on an investment project (holding a capital asset directly) is determined is as follows.

Assuming the life of an investment project is n time periods and the prospective stream of yields are $q_1, q_2, \ldots q_n$ corresponding to those years. The expected rate of return on this investment on the margin (marginal efficiency of investment, MEI) is that rate which, when used to discount this stream of prospective yields, gives rise to a magnitude that equals the initial cost of the investment project. Keynes (1936) postulated the MEI to be a decreasing function of the magnitude of current investment on account of decreasing returns to scale and imperfect competition (see (A) in Figure 15.6).

Kalecki (1937), however, argued that the aforementioned reasons to explain the negative slope of the MEI in Keynes (1936) are both invalid, the first one on purely logical grounds, whereas the second one contradicts the logical universe of Keynes's analysis. Diseconomies of scale may be relevant only when the capital stock is given, but the very act of investment increases the capital stock, invalidating the premise of diseconomies of scale, i.e. fixity of some 'factor of production'. Also, the case of imperfect competition, Kalecki (1937) argued, violates the competitive structure that Keynes (1936) assumed through his book (see (A) in Figure 15.6).

It is clear that the shape of the MEI schedule would be determined by both the nature of economies of scale as well as the nature of competition in an industry. With increasing returns to scale under competitive conditions, the MEI is an *increasing* function of the amount of investment (Steindl, 1945). On the other hand, if an industry is functioning strictly under conditions of *established* oligopolies, where it is near impossible to expand the market *share* of a firm through price cutting, the limit to investment of a firm is set by its expectations about the rate at which the industry itself expands (a proxy of which could be the firm's past capacity utilisation). Under such conditions, the MEI is a vertical schedule at the level corresponding to expectations about demand (see (B) in Figure 15.6). Each firm within this industry will have its own vertical MEI, the height of which is determined by the scale of operation of that firm, and the limit is determined by the share that the firm enjoys in the market (see the difference in the height as well as the position of the MEIs of firms 1 and 2 in (B) of the figure). As can be seen, for such industries, the rate of interest or the amount of credit available will have no

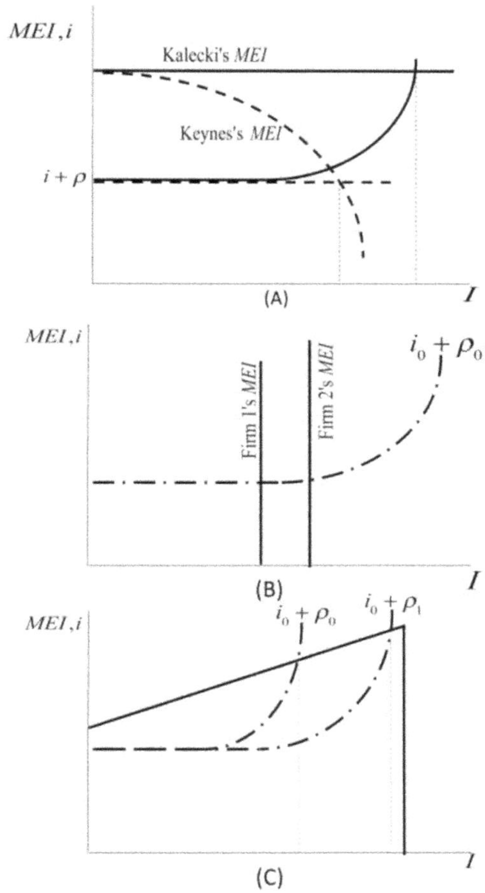

Figure 15.6 (A) Keynes's vs. Kalecki's MEI and Principle of Increasing Risk; (B) MEI in an established oligopoly; (C) MEI in a nascent oligopoly

influence on the investment level unless the firms are credit constrained and not demand constrained.[11]

But what if there are increasing returns to scale but the industries have *not yet* matured[12] into established oligopolies, i.e. industries in which large firms are still competing to establish their market shares? This would give us a kinked investment schedule. There is an upward sloping portion of the MEI showing increasing returns to scale, which is also a continuous function depicting the possibilities of expanding a firm's share at the cost of its competitors in the same industry. Since there is imperfect competition, each firm faces a limit to maximum sales set by the industry demand curve, depicted here by the vertical line at the kink in the MEI schedule (see (C) in Figure 15.6).

The process just described determines the MEI under differing stages of maturity of an industry. However, it is not just the MEI that matters while calculating the returns from an investment; another component – borrower's risk – goes into the decision-making. The rationale for borrower's risk is as follows.

As the magnitude of investment increases, it is likely that a part of that investment starts getting financed by external sources. As a result there arises a borrower's risk on account of two factors: (a) higher is the debt as a proportion of own capital, higher is the risk of a loss to own capital; (b) since capital good is illiquid, distress sale in the event of failure of expectations leads to losses, the magnitude of which rises as investment rises. This implies that the greater the proportion of borrowed funds to own funds (gearing ratio δ), the higher is the risk of losing one's own capital.

To arrive at the prospective net profit from an investment project, therefore, one needs to subtract the borrower's risk from the MEI. The higher the gearing ratio, the higher the borrower's risk and the lower the investment by firms on the upward sloping portion of the MEI, which is typically representative of new (but not necessarily financially small) entrants in industries who are in the process of getting established.

At any given point in time, there will be mature industries, where demand (vertical MEI) sets the limit to invest with no role of finance (unless there is a severe credit squeeze), as well as nascent industries, where demand (by influencing the MEI) as well as finance constraint (through borrower's risk) together set the limit to investment that the firms would like to undertake.

The Macroeconomic Investment Function: Based on the preceding discussion, we can think of an investment function for the economy as a whole, which has four components with their relative importance determined by the weightage of different categories of industries (mature or nascent) for the period under consideration.

One, there is an autonomous component of investment, γ_0, which, as Kalecki had argued, is dependent on factors such as innovations. Two, for those firms where finance matters, the cost of loan is an important factor which will affect investment negatively. The interest rate used in this function is a weighted average of the domestic and the international interest rate.[13] Three, capitalists invest based on the difference between the expected degree of capacity utilisation and their desired capacity utilisation (u_0). Four, as argued by Steindl (1952), investment decreases with a rise in the debt-capital ratio as a result of rising borrower's risk, which increases the chances of insolvency.[14]

$$\dot{g} = \gamma_0 - \gamma_r r + \gamma_u (u - u_0) g - \gamma_\delta \delta \tag{13}$$

where, $\gamma_0, \gamma_r, \gamma_u, \gamma_\delta > 0$

Substituting for u from equation (8), and r from equation (12) and endnote 13, and denoting the Keynesian multiplier by $\Gamma = 1/[(h + m)\beta]$, this gives us a parabolic function in the (δ,g) space of the following form:

$$\begin{aligned} \dot{g} &= Ag^2 - Bg - C\delta + D \\ \textit{where, } A &= \Gamma\gamma_u \\ B &= \gamma_u\left[u_0 - \Gamma(\xi + \overline{x})\right] \qquad (14) \\ C &= \gamma_\delta + \gamma_r\mu\sigma_b \\ D &= \gamma_0 - \gamma_r\left\{\mu(\overline{r} + \sigma_0) + (1-\mu)r^f\right\} \end{aligned}$$

The isocline for this function is a parabola with its axis of symmetry[15] parallel to the δ-axis.

The shape of this curve is determined by the coefficients of δ and g, with the specific shape given in Figure 15.7 derived from the fact that both these are negative. The first is negative for reasons described earlier. The coefficient of g is negative because the capacity utilisation generated exogenously from exports and government expenditure, $\Gamma(\xi + \overline{x})$, should always be less than the desired capacity utilisation u_0; otherwise the economy will be running without any aggregate demand problems due to these exogenous factors alone.

For a phase diagram analysis,[16] we take the partial derivate of this function with respect to either of the variables. A simple way of doing that would be take the derivate with respect to δ, which is negative $-\gamma_\delta$.[17] As the debt-capital ratio rises, $\dot{g}$ falls from being positive to the left of the isocline to zero on the isocline and negative to the right of the isocline. Accordingly, the arrows point in the directions as shown in Figure 15.7.

In this parabola, for every value of the debt-capital ratio, there are two growth rates possible, much like in Kalecki (1962). At lower rates of

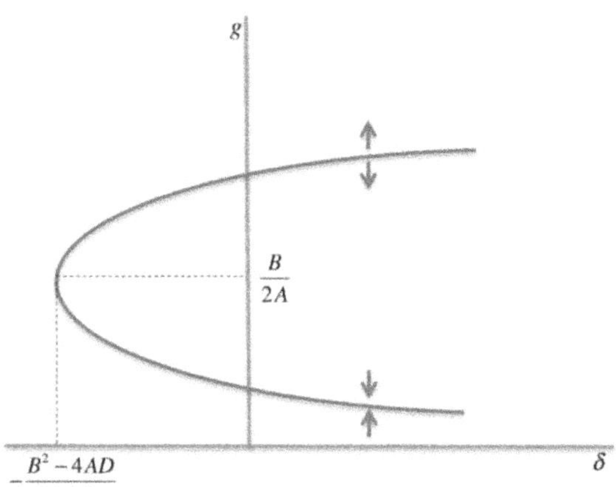

Figure 15.7 The growth isocline

growth, a decline in the gearing ratio leads to an increase in investment as there is a decline in the borrower's risk, as captured by $-\gamma_{\delta}\delta$. But after a certain point, higher growth rate itself starts dominating this risk-averse tendency of the capitalists so that even if the gearing ratio is rising, the rate of growth rises. Such an investment function generates multiple equilibria, as will be seen.

Let us consider a few stylised facts mentioned earlier to see how this curve responds to them. The discussion presented here can be considered in terms of the two symmetrical arms of the parabola, the upper arm corresponding to the 'growth begets growth' tendency whereas the lower one corresponds to the stagnationist tendency.

1 A fall in the real rate of interest due to a fall in the repo rate ($\bar{r}$), our stylised fact 5, will shift the vertex of the curve laterally to the right. Similarly, a fall in the international rate of interest (r^f) will have the same effect. For the lower arm, this means that the rate of growth would rise for a given debt-capital ratio since a fall in the interest rate pushes investment demand up.
2 There were two different *triggers* to high growth, though not responsible for its sustenance, in the two phases respectively.

   a In the first boom, it was a sudden spurt in export demand (stylised fact 7) so that export as a proportion of capital stock increased.
   b For the second, it was a policy decision in the post-global economic crisis conditions, when active injection of demand through fiscal policy was made to tide over its effects (stylised fact 6).

   Since these are both triggers and not structural changes, we present them as a sudden northward jump off the growth isocline rather than a shift in the curve itself (which would have been justified had these changes been permanent in nature). This means that the rate of growth would rise for a given debt-capital ratio since these factors push up the demand in the short run.
3. A rise in the import intensity ($m \uparrow \rightarrow \Gamma \downarrow$), our stylised fact 7, shifts the vertex to the northwest. For the lower arm, this means that the rate of growth would fall for a given debt-capital ratio since an increase in import intensity means a leakage of demand from the domestic economy, i.e. the Keynesian multiplier falls.

Financing the Investment: How is this investment financed? Firms have two options: internal funds and debt.[18] The proportion of investment financed by debt depends inversely on the rate of interest rate charged by the commercial banks. Assuming every year a constant part $a < 1$ of the debt is paid off, the debt equation can be modelled in the following manner:

$$\dot{D} = \phi(r)I - aD \tag{15}$$

Again for simplicity, we assume φ to be a linear function of the interest rate, which gives us:

$$\phi(r) = \phi_0 - \phi_r r \tag{16}$$

Using equation (12) for r and endnote 13, it gives us a differential equation for the debt-capital ratio of the following form:

$$\begin{aligned}&\dot{\delta} = \left[\phi_0 - \phi_r \left\{\mu(\bar{r} + \sigma_0) + (1-\mu)r^f\right\}\right]g - a\delta - (1 + \phi_r \mu \sigma_b) g\delta \\ &\text{where, } \phi_0 > \phi_r \left\{\mu(\bar{r} + \sigma_0) + (1-\mu)r^f\right\}\end{aligned} \tag{17}$$

The logic for the latter condition is that the weighted average of base cost of domestic debt (repo plus the term premium on a given debt instrument charged by a commercial bank) and international debt has to be lesser than the willingness of the firms to finance a part of their investment through debt. Anything contrary to that will be a non-starter as far as corporate debt is concerned because that would mean that the basic cost of debt itself is so high that the firms are in net terms just writing debt off even when there is no debt to begin with (if $\varphi(r) < 0$ at $\delta = 0$, $\dot{D} < 0 \ \forall I > 0$).

The shape of this isocline is a rectangular hyperbola in its second and fourth quadrant.[19] Partial derivative with respect to the debt-capital ratio yields the phase arrows for this isocline,

$$\begin{aligned}&\frac{\partial \dot{\delta}}{\partial \delta} = -a - (1 + \phi_r \mu \sigma_b) g \\ &\lessgtr 0 \ \ \forall g \gtrless -\frac{a}{1 + \phi_r \mu \sigma_b}\end{aligned} \tag{18}$$

Therefore, in the rectangular hyperbola, for the upper curve, $\dot{\delta}$ falls as δ rises and vice versa for the lower curve. Since the lower curve (with negative rates of growth) does not have any economic meaning, the analysis here is based on the upper curve. The phase arrows for the upper curve are accordingly drawn in Figure 15.8.

Let us look at a few stylised facts in the context of this relationship.

1 According to stylised facts 2 and 3, the increase in the growth rate was accompanied by a rise in the debt-capital ratio. This can be understood as a movement up the debt isocline.
2 Stylised facts 4(a) and 4(b) represent a clockwise *shift* of the curve, which represents a relaxation in the risk function of the banks ($\sigma_b \downarrow$). While 4(a) represents absence of Ponzi finance, 4(b) shows that a credit bubble was sought to be created in the second boom through Ponzi

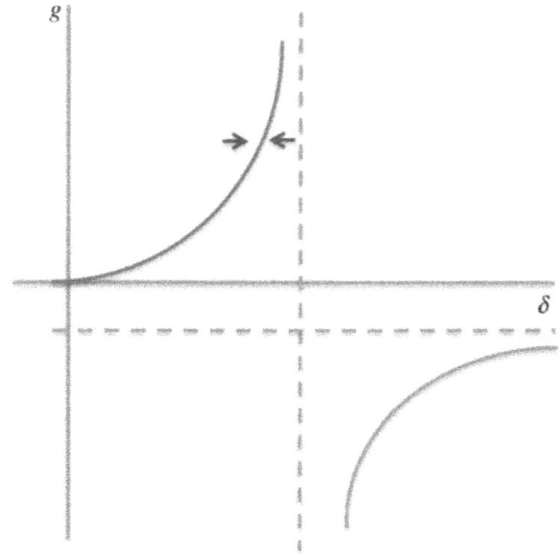

Figure 15.8 The debt isocline

finance since here, unlike the first boom, the share of debt of companies who could not even cover their interest payments was increasing.

3. Institutional reforms, such as the demise of the Development Financial Institutions (DFIs) in India and the encouragement provided to the commercial banks to expand corporate lending entails an exogenous push to bank lending. In terms of our model, it could be seen as a decline in the autonomous part of the risk function σ_0. This would move the centre of the hyperbola to the right (see endnote 15) and hence the curve would shift to the right.

Dynamics of the macro system

With the help of these two differential equations in two variables, a differential equation system can be set up of the following form:

$$\dot{g} = \Gamma\gamma_u g^2 - \gamma_u\left[u_0 - \Gamma(\xi + \overline{x})\right]\cdot g - (\gamma_\delta + \gamma_r \mu\sigma_b)\delta + \gamma_0 - \gamma_r \left\{\mu(\overline{r} + \sigma_0) + (1-\mu)r^f\right\} \quad (19)$$

$$\dot{\delta} = \left[\varphi_0 - \varphi_r(\overline{r} + \sigma_0)\right]g - a\delta - (1 + \varphi_r\mu\sigma_b)g\delta$$

Such an analytical model will help in analysing different phases of growth in a theoretical perspective while tracking the effects of certain policies under discussion regarding the future trajectory of the economy.

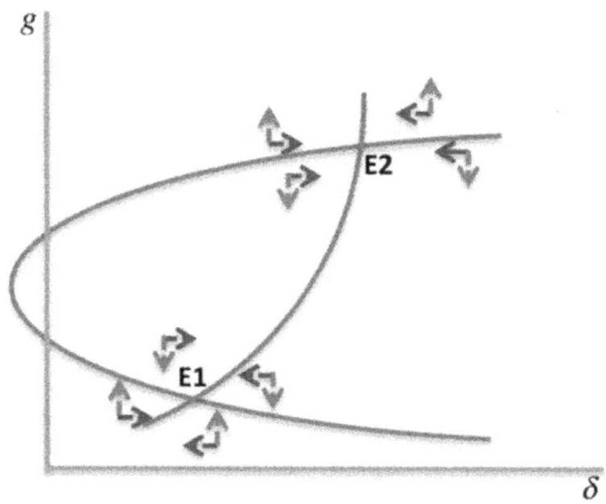

Figure 15.9 Macrodynamics of the two rates of growth in the model

This system generates two rates of growth, the lower one shown by *E*1 is a stable node and the higher one shown by *E*2 (with higher δ) is a saddle point (see Figure 15.9).

Opening up and the constraints

External constraint: The Indian economy's external constraint got relaxed with capital account liberalisation which eased the flow of finance ($\alpha_0 \uparrow$). India started attracting higher debt inflows due to the interest rate differential ($i-\rho-i^f$) as well as FPI and FDI. With the rate of growth of exports going up prior to the first boom ($\bar{x} \uparrow$), the foreign exchange problem became further relaxed. These factors pushed up the external constraint of our model, thereby, making higher growth *possible* at a given debt-capital ratio.

Internal constraint: Cheapening of credit through a fall in the nominal interest rate relaxed the internal constraint (see Figure 15.10), pushing it down. Corporate tax concessions, by increasing retained earnings and enabling the corporate sector to raise the debt-capital ratio at a given rate of growth, also relaxed the internal constraint.

Therefore, with financial liberalisation and opening up, both the constraints opened up, thereby creating *possibilities* of a wider range of growth rates than hitherto possible.

We now present a theoretical explanation of the two booms under discussion.

First boom (5 years): 2003–04 to 2007–08

The debt function: A lowering of the risk function ($\sigma_b \downarrow$) of the public sector banks partly shifts the curve to the right (as shown in the movement of the

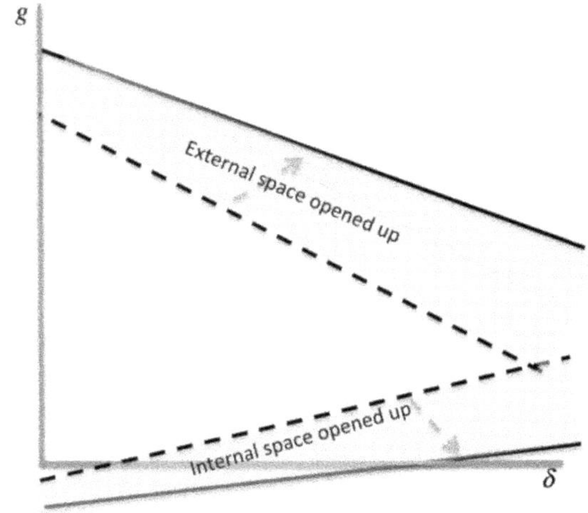

Figure 15.10 Relaxation of the two constraints

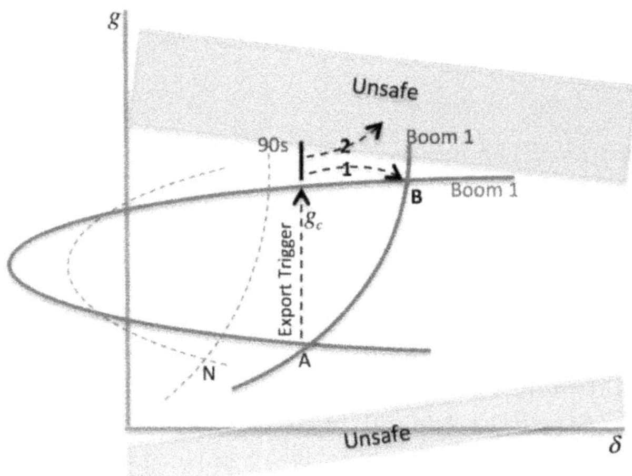

Figure 15.11 Boom of 2003–04 to 2007–08

curve from 1990s to Boom 1 in Figure 15.11). The fact that the increase in bank credit to the corporate sector had almost entirely been contributed by the public sector banks point towards an important role played by the state during this phase of economic expansion. Such a rise in the risk appetite of the banks has been facilitated through relaxation of corporate lending norms in order to promote private investments and PPPs. In terms of the diagram, a fall in the risk function shifts the centre of the hyperbola down and to the right.[20]

The other part of the rightward shift of the debt curve is because of the lowering of central bank-controlled interest rate ($\overline{r}$ ↓) as well as international interest rates (r^f ↓) during this phase, which also encouraged corporate borrowings.[21]

So there was a double-injection of corporate credit in the economy: risk function relaxation (fall in σ) as well as basic cost of credit reduction, i.e. a fall in $\overline{r}$ and r^f (domestically as well as internationally).

The growth function: Both these factors affect the growth function as well. A fall in the risk function of the banks enters the investment function through a fall in the opportunity cost of investment, which, for a given value of δ, means the lower arm of the growth curve rises whereas the higher arm falls.[22] A fall in the central bank-governed interest rate has an additional effect: the lower arm of the curve goes up further while the upper arm comes down.[23]

The overall effect on the shape and position of the parabola as a result of these two routes is shown in Figure 15.7.

Trajectory of the first boom: There are again two steady state growth rates possible: the higher one at *B*, a saddle point; and the lower one at *A*, a stable node (see these relative to point N in Figure 15.11).

Since the higher rate of growth is a saddle point, there is one path (partly depicted by 1 in Figure 15.11) which is stable whereas the rest are unstable. It is possible that the trigger of high exports witnessed before the first boom pushed the economy beyond a critical value (g_c in Figure 15.11) after which the upper arm of the growth isocline comes into play. At this point, the economy might take path 1 and *temporarily* settle at *B* (duration of the first boom). It is temporary because it is a saddle point, so that any movement away from the stable arm will be destabilising. The economy witnesses a high growth rate, but it comes along with a high debt-capital ratio.

It needs to be noted that an export trigger pushing the economy on path 1 is just as plausible as other unstable paths such as path 2 shown in Figure 15.11. But insofar as the trigger is great enough to push the economy beyond the critical value of g_c, there will be a spurt in growth and debt-capital ratio with the economy eventually hitting the external constraint.

As discussed previously, the initial trigger of high exports prior to the first boom was reversed, with the current account balance turning into a negative from 2004–05 onwards. As a result of this reversal, the economy would have slid to *A*. However, the growth in the credit financed corporate investment, which saw a structural break in 2003 (stylised fact 2, 3, 4(a)), provided the impetus to maintain the boom beyond the short period of export-induced growth.

A rising trade deficit as well as short-term foreign debt accumulation since 2003, which took the GEFR-GNI ratio to 8% in 2008, also affected the external constraint adversely. A tightening external constraint can make the higher rate of growth infeasible.

Second boom (2 years): 2009–10 to 2010–11

The debt function: With the global economic crisis setting in 2008–09, there was a drastic fall in the rate of growth of exports, which dropped the economy from *B* initially. Therefore, growth rate declined through the year 2008–09. However, the stimulus package announced by the central government, which came in the form of corporate tax concessions as well as increased government expenditure (stylised fact 6), kickstarted the second boom in 2009–10 (see the fiscal trigger in Figure 15.12).

A further increase in the risk appetite of the public sector banks ($\sigma_b \downarrow$) shifted the risk curve to the right (for reasons discussed earlier), which spurred credit-financed corporate investment,[24] similar to the first boom.

However, unlike the first boom, the domestic interest rate eventually started rising (stylised fact 5), which pushed the internal constraint up, thereby, making the debt-capital ratio associated with *C* increasingly unsustainable, which was visible in growing NPAs of the PSBs in the boom period itself. This also gradually pushed the risk curve back but not entirely towards its original position.[25]

The growth function: A fall in the risk appetite had the same effect on the growth function like in the first boom. However, unlike the first boom, here the interest rate rose subsequently. Therefore, there were counteracting effects on the growth curve too. While the focal length of the new parabola increases, for the interest rate increasing to the same magnitude as the fall in the risk function, the lower arm moves down whereas the upper arm moves up (as shown in the growth curve in Figure 15.12). The two parabolas will intersect[26] at $\delta = 1$, which is economically an unrealistic possibility, so that part of the two parabolas are not shown in the figure.

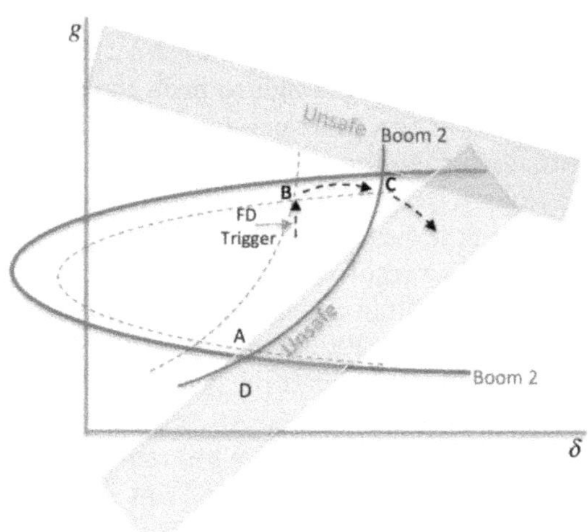

Figure 15.12 Boom of 2009–10 to 2010–11

Trajectory of the second boom: This boom was, however, short-lived both because of the unstable nature (saddle point) of this growth rate as well as a rise in the domestic real rate of interest from 2010–11 (stylised fact 5) due to RBI's efforts towards inflation targeting. The effect of this increase in the domestic interest rate was muted initially because international borrowing costs were lowered due to monetary easing in the US in the aftermath of the global economic crisis. So, r in our growth isocline increased only partially. In other words, while the cost of domestic credit increased, its international counterpart declined, causing a change in the *composition* of corporate credit in favour of higher external commercial borrowings.

With a shift in the growth isocline as a result of the increase in domestic interest rates, the growth rate fell on the unstable path of the saddle point. The economy eventually hitting the lower constraint implies debt defaults, which manifested in the large-scale accumulation of NPAs (non-performing assets) in the balance sheets of the public sector banks.

Conclusion

We have attempted in this chapter to provide a theoretical structure to the Indian growth story in the 2000s, which has been inspired by an extensive data analysis covering this period provided in Azad et al. (2016). We divided this decade in two booms: 2003–04 to 2007–08 and 2009–10 to 2010–11. The first boom was triggered by export surge prior to the boom accompanied by public sector bank lending, debt inflows and low real interest rates. The second boom, however, was a result of a more reckless lending by the public sector banks in the face of interest rate hikes by the RBI. Our argument is that such 'riskless capitalism' could not have thrived without the support, active or otherwise, of the state.

For both these booms, we showed theoretically, in a Kaleckian model, the high growth rates, though possible, are saddle points. As a result, an initial fall from the saddle path pulls the economy towards a stagnationist growth path (the lower growth rate) or hits the internal constraint with deleterious effects on the balance sheets of the public sector banks.

Notes

1 We would like to acknowledge the comments and suggestions made by Prabhat Patnaik, Robert Pollin, Gerald Epstein, Jayati Ghosh, CP Chandrasekhar, Anwar Shaikh, Mark Setterfield, Abhijit Sen, Pulin Nayak, Jyotirmoy Bhattacharya, Subhanil Chowdhury and the participants in seminars in Delhi, Amherst, New York, Colorado and Winnipeg. This study has been undertaken based partly on a project funded by the Indian Council of Social Science Research, New Delhi through the Council for Social Development, Hyderabad and partly by the Fulbright US-India fellowship. The usual disclaimer applies.

2 To draw a comparison across these traditions, we have tried to keep the form of the investment functions similar and left out the components which are dissimilar across these models. Therefore, in the Kaleckian tradition presented earlier, we

have included the desired capacity utilisation whereas the rate of profit does not find a mention.

3 See Patnaik (1997) for a discrete time version of this function.

4 If m is the profit margin, the profit share is given by $\frac{m}{1+m}$

5 That does not mean savings drives debt, because savings itself is generated as a result of investment.

6 In fact, this result will hold true even if the relative response of investment to capacity utilisation and interest rate is the *same* ($\gamma_u = \gamma_r$) unlike the Minsky-Steindl version discussed earlier.

7 This is done purely for simplifying reasons, so the results will not change even if we were to assume both that workers save and capitalists consume a part of their incomes or that the rentiers and firms have different propensities to spend as is normally assumed in the models discussed earlier. Our assumption is not altogether unrealistic, especially for a country like India, since wealth is concentrated in the hands of a few here. Moreover, data suggests that consumption didn't play as much of an important role as investment in this growth process, so discussion on the savings rate will at best be a digression without adding much to the basic story line presented here.

8 See Azad and Saratchand (2016) for a simplified interpretation of Keynes (1937) which also addresses this question of asset choice.

9 This model does not subscribe to the monetarist view of an exogenous money supply. The view taken here is in the endogenous money tradition as described in Kaldor (1986) and essays on interest rates in Kalecki (1969). Even the mainstream tradition in monetary theory, the New Keynesian economics, accepts the endogenous money argument.

10 Since our primary focus here is not on how expectations of inflation are formed, we are leaving out the dynamics of inflation from the discussion in this chapter.

11 An investment function for such an industry with the two possibilities existing (but obviously exclusive of each other) can be imagined as $g = \min\{e(\delta), f(u)\}$; $e^0, f^0 > 0$.

12 The word 'maturity' used for these industries has the same meaning as Steindl (1952) had used in the title of his seminal work.

13 $r = \mu \cdot r^d + (1 - \mu) \cdot r^f = (\mu \cdot i + (1 - \mu) \cdot i^f) - \pi$, where π is expected domestic rate of inflation.

14 Steindl's theory, taking a cue from Kalecki (1937), stands in contrast to the mainstream corporate finance theory, which argues that capital structure does not matter in investment decision-making.

15 The vertex of the parabola is given by $\left(-\frac{B^2 - 4AD}{4AC}, \frac{B}{2A}\right)$; the focus by $\left(\frac{1-(B^2 - 4AD)}{4AC}, \frac{B}{2A}\right)$; the focal length by $\frac{1}{4AC}$.

16 A formal mathematical analysis of this dynamic system has been presented in the Appendix of this chapter.

17 As is obvious, these arrows can be drawn by taking the partial derivative of this function with respect to g itself. Given that $\dot{g}$ is a quadratic function in g, it would yield a critical value of g, which is the vertex of the parabola, below which the derivate is negative and above it the derivative is positive.

18 Equity financing has not been explicitly modelled here since it does not seem to play any significant role in the Indian growth story so far. But interesting things can be done with that, especially if equity financing becomes easier when companies grow faster.

19 The centre of this hyperbola is given by $g = -\frac{a}{1+\phi_r \mu \sigma_b}$, $\delta = \frac{\phi_0 - \phi_r\left\{\mu(\bar{r}+\sigma_0)+(1-\mu)r^f\right\}}{1+\phi_r \mu \sigma_b}$.

20 See endnote 15, where, as a result of the fall of the denominators, the centre $g \downarrow$, $\delta \uparrow$.

21 The centre of the hyperbola shifts further to the right since the numerator of δ rises.

22 See equation (14), where with a fall in C, out of the two coordinates, δ decreases whereas g is unaffected both for the vertex and the focus and the focal length increases. It can be easily derived that these two parabolas intersect each other on the y-axis (not shown in the figure).

23 See equation (14), where a fall in $\bar{r}$ leads to an increase in D, which shifts the vertex and focus of the new parabola to the right with the focal length remaining the same.

24 The empirical evidence presented in Azad et al. (2016) shows that the credit injection in the second year of the boom (2010–11) marked a sharp rise over 2009–10.

25 Assuming the interest rate to have increased to the same magnitude as the fall in the risk function, i.e. , it can easily be shown, $d\bar{r} = -d\sigma_b$ by partially differentiating equation (17), for a given value of δ, the debt curve would still shift down as shown in Figure 15.12.

26 This can be derived by equating the two parabolic equations and finding the intersection point.

References

Ahluwalia, M. S. Economic reforms in India since 1991: Has gradualism worked?, *Journal of Economic Perspectives*, 16(3), 67–88, 2002.

Azad, Rohit. A Steindlian model of concentration, debt and growth. *Metroeconomica*, 63(2): 295–334, 2012.

Azad, Rohit, Prasenjit Bose, and Zico Dasgupta. *Financial Globalisation and India: Internal and External Dimensions*. MPRA Paper 63874, University Library of Munich, Germany, June 2016. URL https://ideas.repec.org/p/pra/mprapa/63874.html.

Azad, Rohit and C. Saratchand. A macrotheoretic survey of monetary policy in a closed economy. In Prabhat Patnaik, editor, *ICSSR Research Surveys and Explorations: Macroeconomics*, volume 3. Oxford University Press, 2016.

Bhaduri, Amit and Stephen A. Marglin. Unemployment and the real wage: The economic basis for contesting political ideologies. *Cambridge Journal of Economics*, 14(4): 375–93, December 1990.

Bhagwati, Jagdish and Arvind Panagariya. *Why Growth Matters: How Economic Growth in India Reduced Poverty and the Lessons for other Developing Countries*, Public Affairs, 2013.

Chandrasekhar, C. P. and Jayati Ghosh. *The Market That Failed: Neoliberal Economic Reforms in India*, Leftword, 2002.

Charles, Sébastien. Corporate debt, variable retention rate and the appearance of financial fragility. *Cambridge Journal of Economics*, 32(5): 781–795, 2008a.

Charles, Sébastien. A post-Keynesian model of accumulation with a Minskyan financial structure. *Review of Political Economy*, 20(3): 319–331, 2008b.

DeLong, J. B. India since Independence: An Analytic Growth Narrative. In *Search of Prosperity: Analytic Narratives on Economic Growth*, ed. by D. Rodrik. Princeton University Press, 2003.

Drèze, Jean and Amartya Sen. *An Uncertain Glory: India and Its Contradictions*. Princeton University Press, 2013

Dutt, Amitava Krishna. Stagnation, income distribution and monopoly power. *Cambridge Journal of Economics*, 8(1): 25–40, March 1984.

Dutt, Amitava Krishna. Internal finance and monopoly power in capitalist economies: A reformulation of Seindl's growth model. *Metroeconomica*, 46(1): 16–34, 1995.

Dutt, Amitava Krishna. Maturity, stagnation and consumer debt: A Steindlian approach. *Metroeconomica*, 57(3): 339–364, July 2006.

Harrod, Roy F. An essay in dynamic theory. *The Economic Journal*, 14–33, 1939.

Hein, Eckhard. Interest rate, debt, distribution and capital accumulation in a post-Kaleckian model. *Metroeconomica*, 58(2): 310–339, 2007. ISSN 1467-999X. URL http://doi.org/10.1111/j.1467-999X.2007.00270.x.

Hein, Eckhard. Finance-dominated capitalism, re-distribution, household debt and financial fragility in a Kaleckian distribution and growth model. *PSL Quarterly Review*, 65(260), 2012.

Jarsulic, Marc. Endogenous credit and endogenous business cycles. *Journal of Post Keynesian Economics*, 12(1): 35–48, 1989.

Kaldor, Nicholas. *The Scourge of Monetarism*. Oxford University Press, 1986.

Kalecki, Michał. The principle of increasing risk. *Economica*, 4(16): 440–447, November 1937.

Kalecki, Michał. Observations on the theory of growth. *The Economic Journal*, 72(285): 134–153, March 1962.

Kalecki, Michał. *Theory of Economic Dynamics*, volume 6 in collected works. Routledge, 2013 edition, 1969.

Keynes, J. M. *The General Theory of Employment Interest and Money*. A Harvest Book/Harcourt, Inc., 1991 edition, 1936.

Keynes, J. M. The general theory of employment. *Quarterly Journal of Economics*, 209–221, 1937.

Lavoie, Marc. Interest rates in post-Keynesian models of growth and distribution. *Metroeconomica*, 46(2): 146–177, 1995.

Lavoie, Marc and Mario Seccareccia. Minsky's financial fragility hypothesis: A missing macroeconomic link. In *Financial Fragility and Investment in the Capitalist Economy: The Economic Legacy of Hyman Minsky*, volume 2: 76–96, Edward Elgar, 2001.

Minsky, Hyman P. *John Maynard Keynes*. Columbia University Press New York, 1975.

Palley, Thomas I. Debt, aggregate demand, and the business cycle: An analysis in the spirit of Kaldor and Minsky. *Journal of Post Keynesian Economics*, 16(3): 371–390, 1994.

Patnaik, Prabhat. *Accumulation and Stability under Capitalism*. Clarendon Press, 1997.

Rajan, Raghuram. *Saving Credit* (Third Dr. Verghese Kurien Memorial Lecture at IRMA, Anand), November 2014.

Rowthorn, R. E. Demand, real wages and economic growth. *Studi Economici*, 18, 1982.

Sen, Amartya. Interest, investment and growth. In Amartya Sen, editor, *Growth Economics*. Penguin Books, 1970.

Setterfield, Mark. *Handbook of Alternative Theories of Economic Growth*. Edward Elgar Publishing, 2010.

Skott, Peter. Growth, instability and cycles: Harrodian and Kaleckian models of accumulation and income distribution. In M. Setterfield, editor, *Handbook of Alternative Theories of Economic Growth*. Edward Elgar Publishing, 2010.
Solow, R. A contribution to the theory of economic growth. *Quarterly Journal of Economics*, 70: 65–94, 1956.
Steindl, Josef. Capitalist enterprise and risk. *Oxford Economic Papers*, 7: 21–45, 1945.
Steindl, Josef. *Maturity and Stagnation in American Capitalism*. Monthly Review Press, 1976 edition, 1952.
Taylor, Lance. A stagnationist model of economic growth. *Cambridge Journal of Economics*, 9(4): 383–403, December 1985.

Appendix

A formal solution

The Jacobian Matrix

The dynamic system of our macro model is given by:

$$\begin{aligned} \dot{g} &= \Gamma\gamma_u g^2 - \gamma_u\left[u_0 - \Gamma(\xi + \bar{x})\right]\cdot g - (\gamma_\delta + \gamma_r\sigma_b)\delta + \left[\gamma_0 - \gamma_r(\bar{r} + \sigma_0)\right] \\ \dot{\delta} &= \left[\varphi_0 - \varphi_r(\bar{r} + \sigma_0)\right]g - a\delta - (1 + \varphi_r\sigma_b)g\delta \end{aligned} \qquad (20)$$

After linearising this system around the steady states (δ^*, g^*), the general form of the Jacobian matrix for this system is derived as follows:

$$J = \begin{pmatrix} 2\Gamma\gamma_u g^* - \gamma_u\left[u_0 - \Gamma(\xi + \bar{x})\right] & -\gamma\delta \\ \phi_0 - \phi_r(\bar{r} + \sigma_0) - (1 + \phi_r\sigma_b)\delta^* & -\left[a + (1 + \phi_r\sigma_b)g^*\right] \end{pmatrix}$$

Since the system is not linear, the determinant of the Jacobian matrix is dependent on the values of the variables, as seen on the main diagonal of the matrix. The nature of the two steady states would have to be evaluated separately. We look at $E1$ first.

Stability analysis for $E1$

To find about the stability of this steady state, the signs of the trace and the value of the determinant at $E1$ need to be derived. The value of g_v at the vertex of the parabola is given by

$$g_v = \frac{\gamma_u\left[u_0 - \Gamma(\xi + \bar{x})\right]}{2\Gamma\gamma_u} \qquad (21)$$

Given the fact that the steady state rate of growth at $E1$ is below g_v, the first element of the main diagonal is negative. The second element of the main diagonal is negative $\forall g \geq 0$ too. So, the trace of this matrix at $E1$,

$$trJ_{E1} = 2\Gamma\gamma_u g - \gamma_u\left[u_0 - \Gamma(\xi + \bar{x})\right] - \left[a + (1 + \varphi_r\sigma_b)g\right] < 0 \qquad (22)$$

This also tells us that the determinant of the matrix is positive since the product of elements on the non-main diagonal is negative. This steady state is a stable node as described earlier in the text.

Stability analysis for *E*2

The same exercise needs to be performed for the second steady state. Given the fact that the steady state rate of growth at *E*2 is above g_v, the first element of the main diagonal is positive whereas the second element of the main diagonal stays negative ($\forall g \geq 0$). So, from this information alone, nothing can be said about the trace of this matrix at *E*2. To determine whether there is at least one eigenvalue which is negative, we need to look at the determinant of the Jacobian at *E*2.

Since the slope of the debt isocline is greater than the growth isocline at *E*2, we get a negative value of its determinant:

$$\frac{a+(1+\phi_r\sigma_b)g}{\phi_0-\phi_r(\overline{r}+\sigma_0)-(1+\phi_r\sigma_b)\delta^*} > \frac{\gamma_\delta}{2\Gamma\gamma_u g-\gamma_u\left[u_0-\Gamma(\xi+\overline{x})\right]}$$

$$\left[\phi_0-\phi_r(\overline{r}+\sigma_0)-(1+\phi_r\sigma_b)\delta^*\right]\cdot\gamma_\delta < \left[2\Gamma\gamma_u g-\gamma_u\left\{u_0-\Gamma(\xi+\overline{x})\right\}\right]\cdot \qquad (23)$$

$$\left[a+(1+\phi_r\sigma_b)g\right]$$

$$\therefore, |J|_{E2} < 0$$

This shows that the eigenvalues of this matrix are of opposite signs, thereby establishing a stable arm for this equilibrium.

16 Supporting domestic development through coordinating the promotion of domestic value chains

P. Sai-wing Ho

For over a decade some economists have suggested that a post-Washington Consensus (WC) has taken hold. However, neoliberalism has struck back as far as the trade and direct-investment liberalization advice is concerned, thanks to the rapid emergence of the literature on global value chains (GVCs) in the last few decades. The period has seen a rapid proliferation of global division of labor manifested by the establishment and extension of these GVCs that are largely governed by developed nations' firms. The advice that is lately offered to developing nations is: instead of building industries through import substitution (IS), liberalize their trade and investment policies and allow their firms to join some GVCs. Much as how in the WC era an undue emphasis is put on external markets to the neglect of internal ones, the GVC literature similarly stresses the *global* to the neglect of the *domestic*, especially when accentuated by its anti-IS stance.

It is one of the hallmarks of the works of Professor Bhaduri to expose the deficiencies of such theories, and to emphasize the importance of generating domestic demand and tackling the joblessness problem, though he is equally critical of unthoughtful trade protection (Bhaduri 2002, 2005, 2008).[1] Using a Hirschmanian framework, the interpretation of which is informed by Smith's division of labor discussion in his *Wealth of Nations* (*WN*) (Ho 2016, 2019), this chapter explores ways to augment domestic demand and employment opportunities through putting greater emphasis on domesticating segments of otherwise GVCs and on the support of *domestic* value chains (DVCs).

What is arguably common to GVC research, Smith's division of labor analysis, and Hirschman's linkage framework is that all share an input–output dimension, although only the latter two incorporate it into their works in holistic manners. *National* development is a process that is in many ways domestic to the nation concerned. The ability to thus develop could position it to create, and receive in distribution, increasing amounts of the "opulence" that results from Smithian division of labor.[2] Smith treated development, and the associated policy issues, in rather simplified manners. Hirschman considered development as a process that would unfold through the exploitation of joint production linkages (PLs), but it needs policy support. He added demand considerations in the form of consumption linkages (CLs), which enabled him to partially endogenize the size of the domestic market by allowing for mutual interactions between PLs and CLs.

The rest of this chapter is organized as follows. The next section highlights certain features of the GVC literature and discusses its appeal to many neoliberal economists. The third section reviews Smith's discussion of division of labor and applies it to consider international distribution and development. The fourth section relates that to Hirschman's linkage analysis to show how the development process can be viewed as the unfolding of PLs, especially when reinforced by CLs. This inspires the consideration of domesticating segments of some GVCs and the promotion of DVCs, in order to localize development more, stimulate domestic demand, and generate employment. By way of conclusion, the final section considers various possible challenges that would confront such domestic development initiatives.

The GVC literature: features and policy messages[3]

A GVC refers to "the whole range of activities involved in the design, production, and marketing of a product" (Gereffi 1999: 38). Along it, "[s]pecific processes or segments . . . can be represented as boxes or nodes, linked together in networks", where each successive node "involves the acquisition and/or organization of inputs . . . labor power (and its provisioning), transportation, distribution . . . and consumption" (Gereffi et al. 1994: 2). This characterization reflects an important dimension of GVC research, namely the "input–output structure" in production where GVCs connect "boxes" or firms (Gereffi 1994: 96–97). It provides a channel to introduce two core concepts, namely "governance" of GVCs and "upgrading" by firms along them (Bamber et al. 2017: 1).

GVC research was first pioneered by sociologists. Hence, the interest in GVCs' governance or corporate-power structures is to be expected. Governance should, in principle, be heavily shaped by the pattern of (unequal) power distribution among firms along each GVC (Dallas et al. 2017). In their numerous case studies GVC researchers have indeed been keen on uncovering such structures. However, each study typically focuses on an individual GVC to describe its governance structure (lead firm, etc.). While comparisons and contrast of different GVCs' governance structures are made, there is hardly any effort to explore inter-GVC dependence, and the resulting analysis is thus not holistic.[4]

Upgrading refers to situations where, starting from a firm's initial nodal position along a GVC, it is able to improve that overtime in some sense. One could conceivably analyze the upgrading *process*. Alternatively, one could talk about upgrading *outcomes* without attaching any explanatory account. While upgrading hints at progress, the narrow focus on a standalone GVC in the typical case study prevents the revelation of systemic implications of upgrading across chains by a nation's firms. The full potential of cross-sector complementarities and their evolution are largely ignored.

While not employing the label of GVCs, neoliberal economists have during the last few decades introduced the term "production fragmentation" (Jones and Kierzkowski 1990, 2001) or "task trade" (Grossman and Rossi-Hansberg 2006). The "boxes" along GVCs are called "production blocks" in the fragmentation literature and are connected by "service links". With decreases in the cost of using such links, firms have found it beneficial to fragment production processes into more and more blocks.

In what ways does GVC research appeal to neoliberal economists? It originally emerged partly as a critique of developmentalism, where the latter is identified with trade protection in pursuit of national development. Meanwhile, early development economics (i.e. in the early postwar decades) came under severe attack by neoliberal economists as nothing but justifications for IS. There was thus a void that GVC research could possibly fill (Bair 2009: 28–29) and the framework pioneered by Gereffi gradually appealed to neoliberal economists. Most early development economists were actually in support of interweaving IS with export promotion (EP), although the misrepresentation of early development economics dies hard. Neoliberal economists have continued to portray IS as efforts by developing nations "to build a deep and wide industrial base" in imitation of the advanced nations (Baldwin 2013: 24). Similarly, GVC researchers characterize it as attempts to replicate the feat of those initial industrializers by building broad and deep industrial bases "under the watchful eye of interventionist developmental states" with *dirigiste* policies (Gereffi 2014: 17–18; Kaplinsky and Morris 2016: 633).

However, governance is not an aspect of GVC research that endears itself to the neoliberal economists, who prefer to analyze competitive situations and are quite allergic to situations of unequal power distribution in the marketplace. Fortunately, GVC researchers have downplayed the role that unequal power distribution could play in obstructing the upgrading of firms from developing nations. Thence, upgrading comes across as a spontaneous *outcome* (although what *process* enables it is left unclear).[5] This appeals to the neoliberal economists because firms are realizing their dynamic comparative advantage without state interference, and they start using GVC research as a Trojan Horse in a renewed push for neoliberalism.

As long as comparative advantage can be harnessed unimpeded, the dispersion of production blocks "increases the chances for less developed countries to participate to some extent in the industrialization process . . . even when a comparative advantage in the integrated process is still out of reach" (Jones and Kierzkowski 1990: 41). Some dub this the "new join-instead-of-build development paradigm" (Baldwin 2013: 24). Developing nations can now "join supply chains rather than having to invest decades in building their own" (ibid.: 13), which is "drastically faster and surer" than the "old" IS route (ibid.: 24).[6] This strongly rhymes with the message from GVC research that urges firms from developing nations to "participate" in GVCs and be integrated into the global economy.

It was not until relatively recently that some GVC researchers started drawing attention to the importance of social, in addition to economic, upgrading (Barrientos et al. 2011)[7], although this new concept has remained rather nebulous. Lately there are also some attempts to merge the GVC literature with that on the industrial district to possibly restore some attention to domestic development (De Marchi et al. 2017). Only time will tell if such attempts would yield substantive contributions.

Division of labor in Smith's *WN*: distribution and development

The conceptual root of the GVC literature is far from homogeneous, including a portion in world-systems (WS) theory (Bair 2009: 7–14). With reference to what certain WS theorists wrote in the 1970s, one finds some semblance with Smith's division of labor analysis.[8]

Smith describes the division of the production of various products into phases of operations, as in the pin factory (*WN*, I.i.3) where the division is organized within a workhouse, and in procuring the woolen coat (I.i.11) where the division occurs among industries. "[*S*]*o far as it can be introduced*", he (*WN*, I.i.4) argues, "[it] occasions . . . a proportionate increase of the productive powers of labour" (italics added). He optimistically suggests, "It is the great multiplication of the production of all the different arts, in consequence of the division of labour, which occasions, in a well-governed society, that universal opulence which extends itself to the lowest ranks of the people" (I.i.10). When extended to foreign trade (IV.i.31), a wider market further perfects division of labor and could further augment societal wealth. Will the "universal opulence" resulting from such global division of labor extend itself to the lowest ranks of developing nations, if only they would integrate into the global market?

There are two dimensions to consider. Given any set of final products, one is whether each final product is destined for the market internal to the nation under consideration or external to it, or both. When additionally given the division of labor that applies to each final product, the second relates to how various phases of operations are divided between indigenous and foreign producers, which pertain to the import content of what a nation exports and imports.[9] One can then conceptually distinguish between situations of purely *foreign* versus purely *domestic* division of labor, in between of which is *global* division of labor that sees foreign and indigenous producers working together. Related to any given set of final products and their associated division of operations is a certain quantum of opulence. In an approximate sense (partly because of heterogeneity considerations), the portion that is distributed to the nation under consideration is in inverse proportion of the import content of its exports and imports. To appropriate larger fractions, its firms would need to improve their capabilities,[10] domestically replicate some segments of the global production operations that are hitherto performed by foreign firms and possibly displace them.[11] Though it is tempting for producers from all nations to thus compete, one must be mindful of the systemic implications of such contests. Even for the "winning" nations, the domestic distribution of larger fractions of opulence crucially depends on the employment implications as their firms improve capabilities.

And the contest for shares of universal opulence should not be overwhelmingly preoccupied with the external market, although the options for cultivating one's internal market are restricted by balance of payments, technological, and other considerations. With regard to the production and consumption of non-tradable products by each nation, should it be possible to procure such in low import-content fashions, and should these be useful for satisfying basic types of "needs" while creating employment, then it would seem sensible to locally augment as well as appropriate the opulence associated with their production.

Thus far nothing has been said about the development of the nation concerned, although the presumed ability to replicate segments of global production operations domestically implicitly suggests so. Thanks to path-dependence considerations, its course of development would have been affected as well. At any moment, depending on what in the global division of labor a nation's firms and producers are participating in, there are varying prospects for learning and raising productivity through further division of operations. As developing nations compete to replicate nodes in the global networks of production, some replications are thus more desirable than others. In that connection and referring to an agriculture–manufacture distinction, Smith (*WN*, I.i.4, IV.ix.35) recognizes that different sectors offer different scopes for division of labor, noting that there is more room for such division and the introduction of machinery in manufactures.[12]

What process is entailed for firms to be able to domesticate nodes of the global division of production operations? This is far from spontaneous; developing nations' firms must experiment and learn before acquiring the capability to replicate. But if not spontaneous, what policy instruments are warranted? Smith's position favors non-intervention, though that is based on his belief of how manufactures could be set up in some nations through a "natural" process because of transportation cost considerations (*WN*, III. iii.20, IV.ix.20–23). He also assumed that technology acquisition could occur with ease as long as there was "extensive commerce" and thus "mutual communication of knowledge" among nations (IV.vii.c.80, IV.ix.41).

Hirschman's linkage analysis and domestic development

When Hirschman started writing about development, what are today's advanced nations had developed an extensive division of labor, with use of relatively advanced technologies. How could such extensive division be replicated[13] in the developing nations in a manner that enables them to sustain further division and progress? In analogizing the development process as the activation of linkages, many of his works, commencing with *Strategy of Economic Development* (hereafter *Strategy*), can be regarded as considering processes that could *develop* those extensive divisions.

Activating joint-PLs and division of labor

After defining backward and forward PLs in simple manners (Hirschman 1958: 100), Hirschman considers how they might spread in rich and complex fashions, and draws attention to joint-PLs:

> When industry *A* is first set up, its satellites will soon follow; but when industry *B* is subsequently established, this may help to bring into existence not only its own satellites but some firms which neither *A* nor *B* in isolation could have called forth. And with *C* coming into play some firms will follow that require the combined stimuli not only of *B* and *C* but of *A*, *B*, and *C*.
>
> (ibid.: 104)

Considered together, the joint-PLs of two industries "are likely to be larger than the sum of their individual linkage effects" when each is considered in isolation. This highlights the "cumulative character" of PLs and could be an argument "in favor of multiple development" (ibid.: 103, 104).[14]

In the course of development, "interaction . . . takes place not only between two industries, but up and down and across the whole of an economy's input–output matrix" (ibid.: 66). Hirschman ([1986] 1992: 58) cautions that the connection of PLs with input–output analysis "sometimes made for too mechanistic a concept of the linkage dynamic". The matrix-cells of a developing nation "would be empty to start with, but [should development occur over time] would progressively fill up in large part" thanks to linkage activation.[15]

While portraying that "[t]he lack of interdependence and linkage . . . [as] one of the most typical characteristics of underdeveloped economies", Hirschman believed that the "interdependence in the input–output sense is . . . largely the result of industrialization" (1958: 109, 110). He thus, initially, saw things similarly to Smith on the relative scope for division of labor in agricultural/primary versus manufacturing activities, though worded in terms of PLs. Between backward and forward PLs, he also regarded the activation of the former as more pivotal for the developing nations (ibid.: 107, 113), for it is through such activation that they could advance into the production of machines and capital equipment. But did he regard the activation as spontaneous?

By the 1960s, drawing attention to technological considerations, Hirschman (1968: 24–25) observes that "backward linkage dynamic may be held back . . . simply by 'technological strangeness'", a consideration "of particular importance for the machinery industry since machinery is usually a technological stranger to the industry in which it is utilized". He concludes that, "To identify and then to remove this sort of bottleneck, *should be a principal task of public agencies* concerned with industrial development" (italics added). Thence, he incorporated industrial/technology policy considerations into his linkage framework.[16] In *Strategy*, he (1958: 110–112) laments that "exclave export activities" and "enclave import industries" are often linkage free in situations that pit indigenous firms against transnational corporations, where the latter easily exercise their corporate power and sustain technological strangeness as a problem. Only if they are suitably nudged by certain policy measures and properly countered by state power would they help domestic firms overcome it, thereby enabling them to domestically replicate nodes on GVCs. Contrasts with the GVC literature where upgrading is regarded as spontaneous, and with Smith's belief in the ease of technology acquisition.

CL-cum-PL to endogenize market size

Hirschman had also considered trade policies. Contrary to the kind of misrepresentation made by GVC researchers and neoliberal economists, early on he emphasized the "strategic role played by exports". He was critical of excessive trade protection and premature support of infant industries. He concluded in *Strategy* that "there is no real alternative" between EP and IS. To him, imports could play important roles in "demand formation and demand reconnaissance" and could confer "awakening and inducing effects" on industrialization (1958: 123–124).[17] Those are his early demand-side considerations; otherwise, his treatment of PLs in *Strategy* focuses mostly on the supply side of the development process.

Almost 20 years after *Strategy*, he finally attempted to bring the income side into the picture (1977: 72).[18] Specifically, should "new incomes" be generated, they may be "spent initially on imports, but these imports, once grown to a sufficient volume, could eventually be substituted by domestic industries". The "'swallowing up' through industrialization of successive categories of expanding imports" he dubs CLs (1977: 72, including n. 8; see also [1986] 1992: 64).

What accounts for the generation of new incomes? Hirschman distinguished between different "impulses" of IS and argued that one circumstance under which they could arise is primary export growth (1968: 4–5). Conceivably, thanks to such growth and the income generated, imports of various consumer goods could reach a volume that makes domestic manufacture economically attractive ([1986] 1992: 65). IS policies, should they be implemented, constitute another source of new incomes (1968: 5).

Regardless of the source,[19] Hirschman sought to employ the concept of CLs to counter those critics of IS who argue that it would fail to proceed beyond the easy early phases to the higher stages of manufacture involving intermediate goods and machinery. He believed otherwise and offered two reasons. Firstly, there is "[intermediate] product convergence" – an alternative label for joint PLs – in that "some of the inputs needed for the initial import-substitution industries are likely to be identically the same (steel, paper, glass . . . as intermediate inputs . . .)", in which case total imports of certain inputs may well be large enough to jointly activate some PLs. Secondly, while "[l]arge capacity plants do characterize the technology of a few important intermediate and basic products," yet "at every stage – particularly in the machinery and equipment industries . . . small and medium-sized establishments are also to be found" (Hirschman 1968: 15). For instance, automobile assembly plants always dealt with numerous suppliers and subcontractors for needed components. These two considerations enable a mutual reinforcement between PLs and CLs and partially endogenize the expansion of the market size so that the IS linkage dynamic can better enjoy sustenance.

Expanding domestic market through catering to basic needs?

Stitching together the discussions in the previous sections, the policy initiatives considered can be grouped into a two-pronged strategy. First, through industrial, technology and trade policies, firms indigenous to developing nations are provided support to domestically replicate some nodes of operations in emulation of certain GVCs. Second, for those nations with firms that succeed, the new and/or higher incomes, in allowing CLs and additional PLs to reinforce each other to further the extent of the domestic market, can become a basis to support the promotion of DVCs to further augment domestic demand and create jobs. This subsection focuses on the latter prong.

For certain services and final products, the domestic market could be quite large even at low per capita incomes, and Hirschman (1968: 5) cites textiles as an example. The same can be said for footwear, food and food services, housing/shelter (including many simple complementary items), and transportation (including transportation equipment). In some cases locational advantages and/or non-tradability might be at play considering the weightiness of some of these products or the materials that are required as inputs, and Hirschman (ibid.: 4) offers beer and cement as examples.[20] This does not mean that what the poor can afford is adequate, nor does it suggest that the quality/safety is satisfactory. But the recognition of the presence of providers for, or producers of, those services and products is important.

Are there also domestic producers of the services and products that cater to the higher (i.e. relative to the low) end of these markets? When garments are concerned, one often finds in developing nations locally produced "brands" of such that one has never heard of in the developed nations, or they are simply brand-less. Yet at the same time there could be sub-contracting firms that produce higher-end garments destined for markets in the developed nations. In food services one similarly finds the coexistence of chains on the one hand, and many small-scale (often) roadside operations on the other. In the case of housing and shelters, there is again a wide range. Such varieties are also found in how people move around. If the number of producers catering to different segments in each of these sectors of basic needs is large enough, might there be opportunities to harness joint-PLs? Are there also joint-PLs across sectors that can be activated? At first sight there seems quite a gap between fulfilling these needs and enjoying Smith's "universal opulence", though he (*WN*, I.i.11) actually intends the latter to include the "accommodation" for many that are "simple and easy". Hence, basic as the aforementioned list might appear, it is certainly not insignificant.

The list is indeed reminiscent of what was discussed during the heydays of the basic needs approach to eliminating poverty in the 1970s. Interestingly, some proponents back then did consider complementarities and linkages. There is recognition that "there are complementarities both on the side of result and on the side of cost" (Streeten 1981: 47). There were at least implicit consideration of joint-PLs, in that "costs can often be reduced by joint supply" (ibid.; see also Streeten and Burki 1978: 412, 420). "The existence of linkages can lead to reinforcing sequences" (ibid.: 49). It thus seems sensible to pursue "a concerted attack on several fronts", with either "multisectoral integrated projects" or at least some "collaboration through links between different projects" (ibid.: 48, 154).

One daunting question that was posed then is: "How should existing productive capacities, often geared to the demand of the rich, be reoriented towards the needs of the poor?" (Streeten and Burki 1978: 416). The question that should instead be asked is: can the activities of these producers be better coordinated and organized, through exploiting joint-PLs, so that resources can be better and more fully utilized, and additional resources be mobilized, to support domestic development?[21]

Concluding thoughts

This chapter has critiqued GVC research, the latest push for trade/investment liberalization. Instead of "join-instead-of-build", it argued for a two-pronged approach to "join" *and* "build": (1) while joining some GVCs, some segments should be replicated domestically to localize development; and (2) DVCs should be promoted to extend the domestic market and increase employment.

These policy ideas must obviously be carefully refined and tailored to specific economic contexts for consideration for implementation. How might one locate joint-PLs to exploit? Are there possibilities for harnessing cross-sector joint-PLs? For relatively large nations, how could such be possibly achieved with cross-region production coordination? For the relatively small nations, are there options for building regional VCs? Who can be induced to do so? Are there obstacles of technological strangeness, and what should be done to overcome them? Are there ways to increase the use of local resources while reducing imported inputs? What are the employment implications? For any nation/region that considers them, what is the political context in which deliberation of their feasibility will occur?

The use of industrial policies to promote development has regained support in the last couple of decades, although their consideration revolves more around the first prong to the relative neglect of the second. And it is the former that could have more of a disruptive global systemic effect. One is reminded of all kinds of tension in the global marketplace that has been exacerbated by the actions and words of the Trump administration. Unfortunately, in the kind of hostile and erratic climate that that administration has created, it would be hard to imagine how interest can be generated to renegotiate certain multilateral agreements that seek to sensibly balance domestic- versus global-oriented development policies.

Notes

1 This chapter will, however, not discuss Professor Bhaduri's concern with financial liberalization.

2 Another type of division of labor, best illustrated by the tailor–farmer–shoemaker example (*WN*, IV.ii.11, 12), involves final-product specialization and exchange between parties, but does not describe how production processes are divided into phases (Ho 2016:917–918). It will not be further considered in this chapter.

3 The rapidly proliferating GVC-literature consists of a good number of articles and even a few monographs that concerns India's involvement in GVCs. See, for instance, K. Banga (2016, 2017), R. Banga (2016), Gupta (2016, 2018), Ray and Miglani (2018), and Francis (2019).

4 Hopkins and Wallerstein (1994: 17) suggest "commodity chains may be thought of as the warp and woof" of a "system of social production", although GVC researchers do not take much heed of it.

5 See, for instance, how Gereffi (1999: 56) is more than ready to generalize on the ease of upgrading from the apparel industry to automobiles, electronic products, and household appliances in the case of South Korea, and to computers, bicycles, sporting equipment, and shoes in the case of Taiwan.

6 Baldwin (ibid.: 41, 24) also argues that, with production fragmentation, what constitute "barriers to trade" have changed and agreements should be negotiated in line with the "trade–investment–services–IP nexus".

7 Pastakia (2012) can be regarded as a consideration of such in the case of India.

8 In an oft-cited passage, Hopkins and Wallerstein (1977: 128) invite the reader to "take an ultimate consumable item and trace back the set of inputs that culminated in this item", and call this linked set of processes a "commodity chain". This is a less elaborate description than Smith's woolen coat example (WN, I.i. 11).

9 Investments by transnational corporations can complicate the simple distinction here attempted, though they can be incorporated without much difficulty.

10 There are *natural* versus *acquirable* advantages. The ensuing discussion is mainly concerned with the latter.

11 Gupta (2016) and Francis (2019) represents an attempt to probe into these considerations as they relate to India.

12 There are signs that Smith (*WN*, I.xi.c.7, I.xi.c.36) is cognizant of something akin to differing income elasticity of demand across final products.

13 Hirschman did not use the term "replication", here employed to refer to replicating some important features in the pattern of division of labor that have been

attained in the advanced nations. The sequence of steps to accomplish so and the policy support to enable it would vary across nations.

14 Hirschman (op. cit.: 67) offers an alternative portrayal of the unfolding of joint-PLs that involves exploiting external economies.

15 See Hirschman (1958: 109) for a hint at relating increasing division of labor – via achieving growing structural interdependence within an economy – to rising productivity and living standard à la Smith.

16 Gupta (2018), Ray and Miglani (2018), and Francis (2019) explore such considerations in the case of India.

17 To strike a sharp contrast with the standard *infant*-industry argument for trade protection, Hirschman (op. cit.: 124, italics original) thus refers to a crucial "*pre-natal* stage", "before the infant [industry] has been born".

18 Nevertheless, he did not incorporate employment into his analysis. For instance, Hirschman (1968: 13) admits that whether "new industries are making an adequate contribution to the solution of the unemployment problem . . . cannot be adequately discussed within the limits of the present essay".

19 There is one more source of new incomes, through "the expansion of agricultural incomes [as techniques evolve, which] can be just as stimulating for overall growth as an industrial spurt" when "consumption linkages are given their due" (Hirschman [1986] 1992: 66–7). Hirschman (1968: 5) recognizes that IS could also be triggered by "cataclysmic events" like wars, economic depressions, and balance of payments difficulties.

20 See Helleiner (1973: 16) for similar considerations.

21 For a discussion of the implementation of the basic needs concept in Indian development planning through the 1970s, see Rudra (1978). For a discussion of the lessons gained from public provisioning of basic needs in that country, see Roy (1997).

References

Bair, J. (2009). "Global commodity chains: genealogy and review", in J. Bair (ed), *Frontiers of Commodity Chain Research*, pp. 1–34. Stanford: Stanford University Press.

Baldwin, R. (2013). "Global supply chains: why they emerged, why they matter, and where they are going", in D. K. Elms and P. Low (eds), *Global Value Chains in a Changing World*, pp. 13–59. Geneva: World Trade Organization.

Bamber, P., L. Brun, S. Frederick and G. Gereffi. (2017). "Global value chains and economic development", in P. Bamber, L. Brun, J. Cho, S. Frederick, G. Gereffi, and J. Lee (eds), *Korea in Global Value Chains: Pathways for Industrial Transformation*, pp. 1–16. Durham, NC: Duke University, Duke GVC Center.

Banga, K. (2016). "Impact of global value chains on employment in India", *Journal of Economic Integration* 31(3): 631–673.

Banga, K. (2017). "Global value chains and product sophistication: an empirical investigation of Indian firms", CTEI (Centre for Trade and Economic Integration, Geneva) Working Paper 2017–15.

Banga, R. (2016). "India's global value chains: integrating LDCs", *Trade Express: Strategies for Success* 4(August): 1–8.

Barrientos, S., G. Gereffi, and A. Rossi. (2011). "Economic and social upgrading in global production networks: a new paradigm for a changing world", *International Labour Review* 150(3–4): 319–340.

Bhaduri, A. (2002). "Nationalism and economic policy in the era of globalization", in D. Nayyar (ed), *Governing Globalization: Issues and Institutions*, pp. 19–48. New Delhi: Oxford University Press.

Bhaduri, A. (2005). "Toward the optimum degree of openness", in K. P. Gallagher (ed), *Putting Development First: The Importance of Policy Space in the WTO and International Financial Institutions*, pp. 69–79. London: Zed Books.

Bhaduri, A. (2008). "Some implications of economic openness with special reference to India", *Economia Politica* 25 (3): 395–404.

Dallas, M., S. Ponte and T. J. Sturgeon. (2017). "A typology of power in global value chains". Copenhagen Business School Working Paper no. 92. Frederiksberg, Denmark: Copenhagen Business School, Department of Business and Politics.

De Marchi, V., E. Di Maria and G. Gereffi. (2017). *Local Clusters in Global Value Chains: Linking Actors and Territories through Manufacturing and Innovation.* London: Routledge.

Francis, S. (2019). *Industrial Policy Challenges for India: Global Value Chains and Free Trade Agreements*. London: Routledge.

Gereffi, G. (1994). "The organization of buyer-driven global commodity chains: how US retailers shape overseas production networks", in G. Gereffi and M. Korzeniewicz (eds), *Commodity Chains and Global Capitalism*, pp. 95–122. Westport, CT: Praeger.

Gereffi, G. (1999). "International trade and industrial upgrading in the apparel commodity chain", *Journal of International Economics* 48(1): 37–70.

Gereffi, G. (2014). "Global value chains in a post-Washington Consensus world", *Review of International Political Economy* 21(1): 9–37.

Gereffi, G., M. Korzeniewicz and R. P. Korzeniewicz. (1994). "Introduction: global commodity chains", in G. Gereffi and M. Korzeniewicz (eds), *Commodity Chains and Global Capitalism*, pp. 1–14. Westport, CT: Praeger.

Grossman, G. M. and E. Rossi-Hansberg. (2006). "The rise of offshoring: it's not wine for cloth anymore", in Federal Reserve Bank of Kansas City (ed), *The New Economic Geography: Effects and Policy Implications: A Symposium*, pp. 59–102. Kansas City: Federal Reserve Bank of Kansas City.

Gupta, N. (2016). "Domestic value-added growth is vital: are Indian industries gaining by linking into value chains?", *South Asia Economic Journal* 17(2): 1–24.

Gupta, N. (2018). "Constraints to linking into global value chains: do Indian industries lack capacities and skills?", *Productivity* 58(4): 363–379.

Helleiner, G. K. (1973). "Manufacturing for export, multinational firms and economic development", *World Development* 1(7): 13–21.

Hirschman, A. O. (1958). *The Strategy of Economic Development*. New Haven: Yale University Press.

Hirschman, A. O. (1968). "The political economy of import-substituting industrialization in Latin America", *Quarterly Journal of Economics* 82 (1): 1–32.

Hirschman, A. O. (1977). "A generalized linkage approach to development, with special reference to staples", *Economic Development and Cultural Change* 25(supplement): 67–98.

Hirschman, A. O. [1986] (1992). "Linkages in economic development", in A. O. Hirschman (ed), *Rival Views of Market Society and Other Recent Essays*, pp. 56–76. Cambridge, MA: Harvard University Press.

Ho, P. S. (2016). "Linking the insights of Smith, Marx, Young and Hirschman on the division of labour: implications for economic integration and uneven development", *Cambridge Journal of Economics* 40(3): 913–939.

Ho, P. S. (2019). "Re-examining the development of Hirschman's linkage analysis with detection of Smithian flavor", *Review of Political Economy* 31(2): 247–270.

Hopkins, T. K. and I. Wallerstein. (1977). "Patterns of development of the modern world-system", *Review* 1(2): 11–145.

Hopkins, T. K. and I. Wallerstein. (1994). "Commodity chains: construct and research" and "Conclusion about commodity chains", in G. Gereffi and M. Korzeniewicz (eds), *Commodity Chains and Global Capitalism*, pp. 17–20 and 48–50. Westport, CT: Praeger.

Jones, R. W. and H. Kierzkowski. (1990). "The roles of services in production and international trade: a theoretical framework", in R. W. Jones and A. O. Krueger (eds), *The Political Economy of International Trade, Essays in Honor of Robert E. Baldwin*, pp. 31–48. Cambridge, MA: Basil Blackwell.

Jones, R. W. and H. Kierzkowski. (2001). "A framework for fragmentation", in S. W. Arndt and H. Kierzkowski (eds), *Fragmentation: New Production Patterns in the World Economy*, pp. 17–34. New York: Oxford University Press.

Kaplinsky, R. and M. Morris. (2016). "Thinning and thickening: productive sector policies in the era of global value chains", *European Journal of Development Research* 28(4): 625–645.

Pastakia, A. (2012). "Building pro-poor value chains: experiences from rural India", *Journal of Entrepreneurship* 21(2): 269–288.

Ray, S. and S. Miglani. (2018). *Global Value Chains and the Missing Links: Cases from the Indian Industry*. New Delhi: Routledge India.

Roy, S. (1997). "Public provision of basic needs: lessons from Indian experience", *Reserve Bank of India <Mumbai> Occasional Papers* 18(2): 553–582.

Rudra, A. (1978). *The Basic Needs Concept and Its Implementation in Indian Development Planning*. Bangkok: ILO-ARTEP (Asian Regional Team for Employment Promotion) Publications.

Smith, A. [1776] (1979). *An Inquiry into the Nature and Causes of the Wealth of Nations*. Liberty*Classics* reprint of the Oxford University Press edition. Indianapolis: Liberty*Classics*.

Streeten, P. (1981). *First Things First: Meeting Basic Human Needs in the Developing Countries*, with S. J. Burki, M. ul Haq, N. Hicks, and F. Stewart. Washington, DC: The World Bank.

Streeten, P. and S. J. Burki. (1978). "Basic needs: some issues", *World Development* 6(3): 411–421.

Index

For Product Safety Concerns and Information please contact our EU
representative GPSR@taylorandfrancis.com
Taylor & Francis Verlag GmbH, Kaufingerstraße 24, 80331 München, Germany

www.ingramcontent.com/pod-product-compliance
Ingram Content Group UK Ltd.
Pitfield, Milton Keynes, MK11 3LW, UK
UKHW020155200926
475702UK00016B/2711
* 9 7 8 0 3 6 7 6 3 5 5 8 9 *